The Chinese Path to Economic Dual Transformation

Economic transformation in traditional development economics refers to the transition from an agricultural society to an industrial one. Based on the practical conditions and the experience since the reform and opening up in the late 1970s, the author observes that the path China's economy takes is a dual transformation, namely, the developmental transformation from an agricultural society to an industrial economy, and institutional transformation from planned economy to market economy.

Centring on property ownership reform which is the supreme reform of the dual transformation, this book discusses land ownership approval, stock-holding system reform and maintaining ownership of private enterprises, etc. Besides, the book expounds on urbanisation in China, believing that it is not only the outcome of the dual transformation but also the booster that will help China's economy continue to develop at high speed. Independent innovation and industrial upgrading which are the keys to the enhancement of enterprises' competitiveness are also covered.

The combination or overlapping of the two types of transformations in China has had no precedent in history, and it has not been discussed in traditional development economics. Scholars and students in China's economic studies and development economics studies will be attracted by this book. In addition, this book will be a valuable reference for other developing countries which are undergoing an economic transformation.

Li Yining is a professor of Guanghua School of Management, Peking University. His research focuses on economic theories and macroeconomics.

China Perspectives

For more information, please visit www.routledge.com/series/CPH

The *China Perspectives* series focuses on translating and publishing works by leading Chinese scholars, writing about both global topics and China-related themes. It covers Humanities and Social Sciences, Education, Media and Psychology, as well as many interdisciplinary themes.

This is the first time any of these books have been published in English for international readers. The series aims to put forward a Chinese perspective, give insights into cutting-edge academic thinking in China, and inspire researchers globally.

Existing titles:

Internet Finance in China
Introduction and Practical Approaches
Ping Xie, Chuanwei Zou, Haier Liu

Regulating China's Shadow Banks
Qingmin Yan, Jianhua Li

Internationalization of the RMB
Establishment and Development of RMB Offshore Markets
International Monetary Institute of the RUC

The Road Leading to the Market
Weiying Zhang

Peer-to-Peer Lending with Chinese Characteristics
Development, Regulation and Outlook
P2P Research Group Shanghai Finance Institute

Forthcoming titles:

Experience and Theoretical Enlightenment of China's Economic Reform
Zhang Yu

Tax Reform and Policy in China
Gao Peiyong

The Chinese Path to Economic Dual Transformation

Li Yining

LONDON AND NEW YORK

Translated by Dongyan Chen and Zhen Gong

First published 2018
by Routledge

2 Park Square, Milton Park, Abingdon, Oxfordshire OX14 4RN
52 Vanderbilt Avenue, New York, NY 10017

Routledge is an imprint of the Taylor & Francis Group, an informa business

First issued in paperback 2020

British Library Cataloguing-in-Publication Data
A catalogue record for this book is available from the British Library

Library of Congress Cataloging-in-Publication Data
A catalog record for this book has been requested

ISBN: 978-1-138-80990-1 (hbk)
ISBN: 978-0-367-52919-2 (pbk)

Typeset in Times New Roman
by Apex CoVantage, LLC

Contents

Introduction

Dual transformation of the Chinese economy

Section 1 Progression of the Chinese economy to the dual transformation

Economic transformation in traditional development economics refers to the transition from an agricultural society to an industrial society, while the implementation of the planned economic system is considered to be another transition route to an industrial society. The latter is what the Soviet Union took after "the October Revolution."

Nevertheless, China's experience from the 1950s to the late 1970s suggests that it was not a success to transit into an industrial society by relying on a planned economic system. This was because while developing countries like China could set up a batch of large industrial enterprises under the planned economic system, enterprises established in this way were inefficient and costly, while various problems in the traditional agricultural society not only remained unsolved but also fossilised in new forms. Thereby, agricultural development failed, with the countryside staying backwards and farmers still living a hard life. They were barely able to make two ends meet, and their personal freedom was seriously restrained.

Since 1979, China has entered the phase of dual transformation, i.e. the combination or overlapping of institutional transformation and developmental transformation. The institutional transformation is the transition from a planned economic system to a market economic system, while developmental transformation means the transition from a traditional agricultural society to an industrial society.

The combination or overlapping of the two types of transformation has had no precedent in history, and it has not been discussed in traditional development economics. After World War II, there occurred in some newly-independent developing countries only developmental transformation, that is, the transition from an agricultural society to an industrialised society, since they had not previously implemented a planned economic system. China after 1979 was in sharp contrast. On the one hand, it needed institutional transformation by casting off the yoke of the planned economic system and replacing it with a market economic system; on the other hand, it needed developmental transformation, through transiting from a traditional agricultural society into an industrial society to enable China to grow up into a modern nation.

In summary, over more than 30 years of reform and development practice (from 1979-now), China has accumulated a wealth of experience in promoting the dual transformation. It can be generalised into eight aspects.

1 Institutional transformation as the keystone of dual transformation

The keystone of dual transformation is, namely, transiting from a planned economic system to a market economic system and simultaneously spurring developmental transformation with an institutional transformation. This is because the constraints and limitations of the planned economic system on the Chinese economy were all pervasive, involving both cities and the countryside, both industry and agriculture, both urban residents and farmers. If China did not break the bondage and restrictions of its planned economy, it would not only be impossible for China to achieve the transition from a traditional agricultural society to an industrial society but also unrealistic for it to achieve its objective of transforming into a modernised state.

2 First liberating the mind

In the preparation phase of the dual transformation, the mind must be unshackled to remove the influences from planned economics theories; otherwise, the reform and development would stumble at every step. In 1978, China's Great Debate entitled "Practice is the sole criterion for testing truth" freed people's minds, and further initiated the Reform and Opening-up to the outside world. Comrade *Deng Xiaoping's* Southern Talk in early 1992 made people think afresh and enabled China to enter the fast track of reform and development. Thus, it could be said that such enormous achievements as China made in the dual transformation within a short period of 30 years were inseparable from the initial liberation of people's minds.

3 Property ownership reform as the supreme reform

Property ownership reform must be placed at the supreme position of the dual transformation. Under the planned economic system, property ownership was fuzzy, investment entities were underspecified and rights and obligations of investors were unclear. Those were not only the major obstacles to reform but also a huge obstruction to development. Therefore, in institutional transformation, the property ownership reform was the breakthrough and the masterstroke, while in developmental transformation, defining and clarifying property ownership was the source of power. For the vast majority of farmers, rights and benefits of land ownership should be established, so was the ownership of housing property. Moreover, ownership approval should be implemented to households. This would not only protect the legitimate rights and benefits of farmers but also enable them to gain property incomes so as to raise their living standard, expand reproduction and start entrepreneurship.

4 Boosting economic growth and simultaneously improving people's livelihoods

In dual transformation, we should stimulate economic growth and at the meantime improve people's livelihoods. Improving people's livelihoods is an important means of narrowing down income gaps both between urban and rural residents and across different regions. Employment is of top priority in the macroeconomic policy. Given that transferring the agricultural labour force to cities was an urgent issue that we needed to address seriously, the issue then should not be ignored at any time of the transformation. Concurrently, as new jobs sprang up in the process of economic growth, the economy should maintain a certain growth rate. A high economic growth rate would indeed not work. Conversely, if the economic growth rate were too low, it would lead to even greater employment pressure. What's more, expanding domestic demand and improving people's livelihoods were tightly linked. Only by expanding the domestic need, could China's economic growth be steered into a virtuous cycle.

5 Necessity of continuous independent innovation and industrial upgrading

In a dual transformation, we must enhance the competitiveness of enterprises continuously, and the key to the enhancement is to encourage independent innovation. If independent innovation is insufficient, the upgrading of the industry will be slow, and enterprises lack competitiveness. In that case, China in the face of increasingly intense competition in the international market will lose its market shares or return to its past of relying on the export of resources and primary products to obtain foreign currency and the import of necessary living and production materials. Thus, it will be difficult for China to achieve the goal of modernisation. Successful independent innovation depends not only on the protection of intellectual property rights but also on the cultivation and motivation of professionals and technical personnel. We should pay more attention to policies on human resources and implement them more efficiently.

6 Necessity of steadily advancing the economic quality

Compared with countries which achieved industrialisation and modernisation at an earlier time, the environmental pressure in China seems to be more prominent. China will have to pay particular attention to the sustainability of its economic and social development. Experience since 1979 has told us that while promoting economic growth was of primary importance, it was more important to improve the quality of economic growth. One indicator of the low or high quality of economic growth is optimised structure; there is still another indicator, i.e. environmental protection, energy and emission reduction, reasonable use of resources and cleaner production. Environments are what we mutually possess with our coming generations and resources are what we share with them. It is by taking the path of sustainable development that we can have broader prospects for future development.

7 *Urbanisation as the most promising investment opportunity in the next few years*

The increase in the urbanisation rate was both the outcome of the dual transformation and also the booster that will continue to propel the realisation of dual transformation. Under the planned economic system, the progression of urbanisation was abnormally slow, and there even appeared a trend of "anti-urbanisation" in some years, when farmers were forbidden to go to cities, and a portion of urban residents was forced to move into rural areas. This situation only improved after the dual transformation process began. Improving the urbanisation rate has become the trend of the times. Urbanisation will be the most likely investment and domestic demand-expanding opportunity in the next few years, and it will ensure that the Chinese economy will continue to develop at a higher speed.

8 *Rigorous development of the private economy*

The private economy is an important component of the socialist economy. In dual transformation, rigorously developing the private economy is not only to alleviate the employment pressure but more importantly to mobilise private initiatives, which includes the motivation of the potentials of private capital. The relationship between private enterprise and state-owned enterprises revealed either in "state enterprises advance and private ones retreat" or in "state-owned enterprises retreat and private ones advance" should not be our national guideline. By contrast, the guideline should be the mutual development of both state-owned and private enterprises and between them, there exists not only cooperation but also competition, thus formulating a win-win structure. Such a guideline is the most conducive not only to economic growth but also to social stability and harmony.

The eight aspects noted above have illustrated how the Chinese path of dual transformation has proceeded step by step. Generally speaking, the experience has demonstrated that China has its unique national conditions and that transformation not based on China's national conditions will not lead to any successful experience and nor will there be "the Chinese path".

Section 2 The continuous spurring of developmental transformation with institutional transformation

Up to now, China's dual transformation has not yet been fulfilled. Reforms require to be deepened, and development needs to be continued. They both need to move to a new stage.

Then, has the relationship between reforms and development changed? No, it remains as it was 30 years ago: institutional transformation continues to spur developmental transformation. That is, reforms continue to drive development and pave ways for development. This can be elaborated in three aspects:

1 Endogenous and exogenous forces

What is an endogenous force? It refers to the function played by a system or its related mechanisms. The purpose of reforms was to remove obstacles and obstruction that emerge in a new system or in the process of establishing the new system.

What is an exogenous force? It is a certain force that the outside world exerts on the economic operation. It intervenes in economic activities or stimulates or inhibits them from the outside world. To reform is to reduce the intervention of exogenous forces to an average level, and allow no exogenous forces to intervene in or impair the automatic functions of the system and its related mechanisms.

We might as well take a man's health for example. To be able to live and work healthily, a man must have a perfect endogenous mechanism. If he is ill, his automatic mechanism can overcome difficulties and restore his health. Exogenous force is like taking medication or having an operation when necessary. Compared with exogenous force, endogenous force is the most important after all.

To date, although China's Reform and Opening-up have been carried on for more than 30 years, its endogenous forces have not been sturdy, and the economy has mainly been regulated by exogenous forces. For example, there existed in the Chinese economy a kind of "weird investment impulse circle". As has been clearly seen in recent years, local governments and various work units have each expected to increase investments, expand their projects and multiply their credits. As a result, the economy did grow with investments increased, projects enlarged and credits multiplied, but meanwhile, inflation occurred. Given the inflation, the central government relied on exogenous forces to suppress it. Local governments, nonetheless, found that they were in a hard situation, for fiscal revenues dropped, production value declined, enterprises were not plucked up and employment decreased. The central government had no other choice but to resume the regulation and control of exogenous forces to stimulate the economy and restore rapid economic growth. Then the cycle repeated itself with the economy improved for a while and tightened for another while. It shows that the endogenous mechanism has not functioned well and exogenous forces have to some extent replaced endogenous forces.

Continuing to push forward reforms is to perfect the system, so that the mechanism possessed by the system can exert its role and make the regulation and control of exogenous force supplementary.

2 Phasic achievements and the target model

Within 30 years (from 1979 to date), China has made significant achievements in its Reform and Opening-up. Nevertheless, these can only be counted as phasic achievements and cannot be proclaimed as having realised its target model. The model China has been targeting is specific as follows. From the perspective of institutional transformation, it is establishing a perfect socialistic market system.

From the viewpoint of developmental transformation, it is achieving industriali- sation and building a modernised Chinese society to enable all Chinese people to become wealthy and turn China into a harmonious society. We should deepen reforms and push development forward with determined and persistent efforts but not with relaxation. Neither reform nor development should be dropped halfway, for a halt halfway will reduce all the previous hard labour to nothing.

Be aware that many issues in the economy cannot be addressed by relying on macroeconomic regulation and control but by continuously deepening reforms. For example, there has appeared a phenomenon of "solidified social stratifica- tion" and the phenomenon was no better than the early stages of the Reform and Opening-up. At that time, channels for social mobility were unobstructed for graduates who started their university education in 1977, 1978 and 1979 (even for graduates who started their university education at various points in the 1980s). Vertical social flow and horizontal flow are two major ways to mobilise the initia- tives of the people. Nevertheless, nowadays, "the solidified social stratifications" has caused obstruction to the horizontal flow, and the vertical flow in particular. That, in turn, formed another phenomenon, namely "professional hereditary". For instance, if a father is a migrant worker, so his son will be and this may be true of his grandson. Here is the manifestation of "solidified social stratification" and "professional hereditary". The phenomenon cannot be solved by macroeconomic regulation and control but only by institutional transformation.

Moreover, up to now, the urban and rural binary system has not yet disap- peared. The planned economic system has two significant pillars. One is the state- owned enterprise system and the other the urban and rural binary system. In the past 30 years, we have mostly centred our reforms upon on the reform and devel- opment of the state-owned enterprise system. Even though many issues are still waiting to be solved, the reform has so far made significant progress. By contrast, the government has somewhat loosened the urban and rural binary system but it remains unresolved.

The urban and rural binary system is distinct from the urban and rural binary structure. The binary structure has existed since ancient times and will remain for a long time in the future. On the contrary, the binary system has been the product of the planned economic system. In 1958, the household registry was split into two types: rural household and urban household, thus segregating the rural areas from urban areas and forbidding both rural and urban households to move freely. The division left farmers secluded from cities and made the rural household and the urban household enjoy unequal rights. It significantly hindered China's economic and social development. The rural and urban binary system will absolutely not disappear by applying macroeconomic regulation and control. Instead, the cur- rent situation can only be changed by deepening reforms. To sum up, the phasic achievements are merely achievements at phases; they are not our target model.

3 Across-board consideration and panoramic arrangements

As noted earlier, there has been no precedent in the world for China's transition from a planned economic system to a socialist market economic system and the way forward needed to be explored. At that time, there was a very vivid saying – "crossing a river by feeling stones". It was right at that time, but it is far from sufficient at present. Why? Because the water in the river has become deeper, how can one cross the river without touching or seeing stones? If the stones are unevenly distributed on the river bed, what if one blindly touches the stones and comes back again? So be sure to make across-board consideration and panoramic arrangements. The leaders of the reforms should stand high, look afar, think deeply and have the vision and courage, insight and spirits of strategists. That is what many people are currently talking about: the top-layer design.

Take the system reform in collective forestry ownership for example. When the contract system was piloted in some rural areas in 1979, collective mountain forests were not mobilised, while in other areas, mountain forests were allocated and cutting down trees became a common practice. That was because the Reform and Opening-up had just begun. Many farmers lacked confidence in the Party's policy and were worried about potential changes in the policy. As a result, mountain forests trees were cut down after being contracted. The Central Government then forbid the division of the collective forestry ownership. The system reform in the collective forestry ownership was suspended for 20 years. In 2003, such reforms were piloted in several provinces like *Fujian* and *Jiangxi*, and relatively soon, on 8 June 2008, the Central Committee of the Chinese Communist Party and the State Council of China issued reform documents, resolved to promote system reforms in the collective forestry ownership nationwide.

The reform made three breakthroughs. First, deeds of forestry ownership were implemented to households, which was a great advance. It was different from what some academics proposed, i.e. deploying them to the villages, to towns or forestry cooperatives and forestry associations which were organised in top-down manners. Those proposals have been proven to be invalid. It was only by directly granting farmers their forestry ownership that their initiatives could be motivated. Second, woodland and forest trees can be mortgaged. As such, it was possible for farmers to run forest farms after they contracted woodland. Each family forest farm became a micro-enterprise. With financing activated, all things came to life. The farmers could operate the forest land, raise chickens under forest trees, plant herbs for medication and grow mushrooms and fungus. Their lives became prosperous. Third, the contract term was clarified to be 70 years and ownership would remain unchanged for that period. The wording for the term in the farmland contract was "will stay unchanged for a long time". However, how long was the duration after all? Farmers did not feel at ease about this. On the contrary, it was stipulated that the contract term for collective forest land was 70 years. It means by the end of the term the third generation of the forest farmers should have grown up. So, let Grandpa plant the trees and let the grandchildren cut them down. Initiatives involving the planting of trees were hugely motivated. It can be clearly recognised that without the resolution of the Central Committee, how dared local governments to promote the reforms? Those are the achievements of panoramic arrangements. Here, I will only touch upon institutional reforms in collective forestry ownership but will elaborate it in Section 3, Chapter 3.

Currently, many issues need across-board consideration and panoramic arrangements. They involve how to reform the allocation system of state-owned capital, the income distribution system, the financial system and the taxation system of central and local governments. They all need panoramic and strategic thinking and resolutions.

It is certain that piloting still requires future reforms. In this sense, "crossing a river by touching stones" has not been out of date yet. What is important, however, is issues should be considered in across-board manners and with strategic visions.

Section 3 Structural adjustment in the dual transformation

Structural adjustments never end. The optimised structure today only represents the present stage of structural optimisation. It does not stand for a continuation of the future economic structure due to the advancement of science and technology, people's changes in consumption habits and concepts, changes of situations at home and abroad, the enrichment in the management experience and the improved operational level of the management personnel. From this perspective, structural optimisation is forever relative, so that structural adjustments will continue.

Although structural optimisation has different standards at different developmental stages, in general, the notion of emerging industries exists in any developmental period. Structural optimisation should accord with the reality at various stages, and be interpreted as one of the standards that measure the degree of structural optimisation. At any time of the development, there are such concepts as excess production capacity and the shortage of production capacity. So the structural optimisation should be measured in the increased or decreased proportion of the production value in the aggregate domestic production value. The contraction in industries with excess production capacity, and those with a shortage of production capacity both reflect the tendency in structural optimisation; conversely, if the proportion of industries both with overcapacity and with shortage capacity has increased, this displays that structural conditions have tended to deteriorate. Therefore, discussions on the current Chinese structural adjustment must first be concerned with the development of emerging industries, the shrinkage in the proportion of industries both with excess production capacity and the shortage of production capacity, and the increase in the industries with equal production capacity.

Another issue that deserves attention in the dual transformation is that structural adjustment should follow cleaner production, a circular economy and a low carbon economy. High pollution, energy and resource-consuming industries need to make technological innovation while some even need to be eliminated. Environments can no longer be impoverished and resources excessively consumed by them. China must have resolutions in doing environmental protection; otherwise, China's economy would not be able to develop sustainably.

In the dual transformation, the optimisation of the regional economic structure is also an important part of the structural adjustment. With regards to the specific situation in China, the imbalance in regional development came into being due to natural conditions and historical and cultural factors. As a result, the gaps between the East and the West tend to expand both concerning development and residential incomes. To alleviate and gradually reverse the widening regional disparities, we must implement favourable policies in the Western regions to benefit them directly and to promote development in the West. The two most important factors in the regional economic structural adjustment are the transfer/shift of manufacturing industries to the West, and the West's previous reliance on directly exporting resources.

The industrial transfer is also affected by the cost-reducing concerns of manufacturing enterprises, particularly those labour-intensive enterprises in the out-transferring regions. For instance, with the advance of industrialisation, the costs for labour, land use, enterprise construction, logistics etc. have all shown rising trends in recent years. Thus, economically less-developed regions become the receivers of industrial transfer across regions. Those regions are mostly rich in human, land and mineral resources. They can make use of their advantages and undertake industrial transfer to speed up the development in local areas, increase the local fiscal revenues and enlarge employment. In this respect, system reform is still of primary importance. The type of system brings forth corresponding policies. Sound policies enable efficient, credibility-honouring and law-valuing government officials to be committed with vital posts. Only in this way can the less-developed areas develop quickly. At the meantime, economic structures in developed areas can better exert their advantages after being transferred to less-developed areas, making more achievements in independent innovation and industrial upgrading and continuing to take the lead in enhancing the competitiveness of local enterprises.

Similarly, new arrangements need to be made of the system and policies regarding how the West (including some less-developed regions in the developed Eastern provinces) changed its past circumstances of relying on exporting resources. For instance, the West should develop local resource-processing industries so as to increases production values and retain earnings. It should also be noted that enterprises should accelerate the cultivation of private entrepreneurs in the West and other less-developed areas in the process of industrial transfer and the resource-processing development. This is because when enterprises from developed areas migrate to the West (and other less-developed regions), their core staff along with their experienced management personnel can be brought in from developed regions. Nevertheless, their assorted production and marketing cooperative enterprises do not necessarily move in. Therefore, some cooperative enterprises are needed in the West (and other less-developed regions) to support and serve the immigrant enterprises. This depends on the efforts of local entrepreneurs. Industrial transfer and developing resources-processing enterprises provide some business opportunities, and those opportunities tend to be fleeting. If local private entrepreneurs are not able to seize them, they will be quickly taken by private entrepreneurs from outside the region.

Transferring industry to the West (and other less-developed regions) is only one phase in the local economic structural adjustment. Those areas which welcomed enterprise migration will unquestionably promote the upgrading of local industries and immigrant enterprises. The trend cannot be stopped. That is to say, the reason for enterprises in developed regions to transfer enterprises to the West (and other less-developed areas) is to take advantage of resources in these areas and to focus on the market prospects there. Once industrial immigration has been achieved, they will sooner or later begin to upgrade their industry to enhance the competitiveness of the enterprises and widen their markets, grasping more market share. This means that the structural adjustment in the West (and less-developed areas) should not be restricted to industrial transfer; rather, it should include enterprise upgrading in the future.

Structural adjustment can be a stock adjustment; it can also be an incremental adjustment. Each has its advantages and disadvantages. Generally speaking, the stock adjustment has the advantages of taking quicker and better effects, while incremental adjustment has too large an impact scope and is more difficult to control. Take a normal case for example. If we force some enterprises to close or stop some enterprises from making production or some products from being produced, then there will be negative impacts on both local fiscal revenues and local employment. That causes local governments to allow such actions as "superficially closing down but really being in operation" or "superficially stopping production but really being in production." Incremental adjustment means the structural adjustment made under circumstances when the economy steadily increases and fiscal revenues continue to rise. Its disadvantages lie in the slow effects and the prolonged production; however, this also has its advantages. First, the economy still maintains a certain growth rate, so as to provide better conditions for the adjustment of the structure and prevent more enterprises from closing down or stopping production, and more workers from losing their jobs, etc. Second, under economic growth and fiscal revenue rise, more investment expenses can be used to improve technology, so as to achieve structural adjustment in the process of industrial upgrading and economic adjustment in relatively stable environments.

In actual practice, incremental adjustment in comparison with the stock adjustment has more feasibility. It should be implemented when the economy still maintains a certain growth rate and financial revenues retain a general rising trend. In the adjustment, enterprises that cause serious pollution and consume excessive quantities of energy and resources can be picked out and forced to close or be stopped by force from producing certain products.

Section 4 Priority of fine-tuning and pre-adjustment to macroeconomic regulation and control in the dual transformation

As pointed out in our previous discussion of the relationship between endogenous and exogenous forces, reforms should be deepened to enable endogenous forces to play a prominent role and exogenous forces a supplementary role. This meets the requirements of establishing a perfect market economic system and can be achieved step by step in dual transformation.

1 The first limitation of the government

The issue lies primarily in the correct positioning of government functions. The government cannot be almighty. The role of the government in regulating the economy has limitations in all cases. There are multiple variables in the economy and their impact on the economic operation is often uncertain and hard to predict. Information that the government can collect is always limited. Also, it is impossible for the government to master all the information in a relatively short period. Even if the government has mastered a lot of information, some of it by that time may have become outdated due to the changes in the objective situation. Therefore, in short, the government is always making decisions with incomplete information. This is one of the inevitable limitations of the government in macroeconomic regulation and control.

2 The second limitation of the government

Another inevitable limitation in the government's macroeconomic regulation and control is that the opponent against whom the government is gaming is the general public, and the government is often in a passive position in the game. This is because there is only one government while there are millions of people. Millions of pairs of eyes are fixed upon the government while the government cannot fix its eyes on hundreds of millions of people. Thus, the following pattern has been formed: the government has a policy, yet the general public has countermeasures. In other words, the authority has a policy but the general public has a counter policy. The general public is in a great majority. Every person, whether s/he is an investor, a consumer, or even a saver chooses his/her counter-policy based on his/her expectations, ends up counteracting the effects of the government policy. This suggests that the government tends to be passive in the face of various public expectations and countermeasures.

3 The third limitation of the government

There is another inevitable limitation on the government's macroeconomic regulation and control. That is, the government's macroeconomic regulation and control measures tend to be over-powered or over-corrected, leading to such an outcome as "regulating with instant death and relaxing with instant chaos". This is because the government is always making decisions on incomplete information and the government's implementation of public policies is always in a passive position in gaming against the general public. The reason for "regulating with instant death" is that the government always believes its own power, so that when it tightens its regulations, it puts the economy to death and enterprises lose their vitality. The reason for "relaxing with chaos" is that when the government feels that over-tightening policies have harmed the economy, it turns to loosen its control. However, as soon as the policy is relaxed, investments become overheated, credits expand and inflation comes back again. Then, the government feels it necessary to re-tighten its economic policy. In dual transformation, the frequent re-occurrences of sometimes "being tight" and sometimes "being relaxing", occasional 'death' and occasional 'chaos' are because the market mechanism has not been complete and the functions of the government have not been appropriately located.

4 The consciousness of the limited effects of macroeconomic regulation and control as requisites for the government

A conclusion drawn from the above can only be: based on the fact that the dual transformation has achieved certain outcomes, the functions of government should be appropriately orientated. It should not be assumed, as it was in the past, that the government is omnipotent. The government should follow market rules and not disturb the normal expectations of investors, consumers and savers and macro-regulation and control should not have drastic rises and falls, or dramatic ups and downs by excessive tightening and excessive loosening. Otherwise, the regulation and control will result in a great many economic bubbles, which may even burst unexpectedly. These will damage the economy and make the general public lose their confidence in macroeconomic regulation and control.

In any economic operation, there will occur signs of abnormal operation. Even if the government information is always incomplete, signs of abnormal economic operation will still filter through. Therefore, in the future the government's macroeconomic regulation and control should focus on fine-tuning, and it should minimise overall regulation and control; instead, it should prioritise structural adjustment measures, because compared with overall regulation and control, structural adjustment measures cause less turmoil and make more prominent effects.

In future macroeconomic regulation and control, apart from emphasising fine-tuning the government should also take pre-set measures. It is very important to choose the initial timing for macroeconomic regulation and control. In the past, the starting time for macroeconomic regulation and control often lagged behind and it was more likely that the ending time dragged behind. Both types of lagging behind caused losses to the national economy and added difficulties to ensuing economic operation for a long period.

In macroeconomic operation, government regulation and control used to target adjusting aggregate demand and were mainly applied to short-term adjustments to unemployment and inflation. In the 1970s, the US economy was caught in stagflation. Simply adjusting demand could not solve the problem and only focusing on short-term adjustment was not sufficient either. So initiated by the United States, and then followed by other countries, macroeconomic regulation and control changed from simply adjusting aggregate demand to equally adjusting supply and demand, from making short-term adjustments to equally weighing short-term and mid-term adjustments, and from making the overall regulation and control to equally valuing overall regulation and control and structural regulation and control. These have become in the many developed Western market economies the most conventional means of regulation and control and can be used as a reference in China's dual transformation.

In China, the major reason that led to the lagging behind of macroeconomic regulation and control was not only that the government was getting access to incomplete information, but more importantly that the government did not rigorously filter the information that was in its control. Thereby, the government was inclined to be deluded by reports from different regions and departments, as they only disclosed good news but not bad news. Many real cases in economic operation were not necessarily mastered by the government, and thus, the timing for macroeconomic regulation lagged behind. In future macroeconomic regulation and control, the government should learn from the past, doing its utmost to hold in hand the real situations in the economic operation, placing pre-setting in an important position and managing to equally value pre-setting and fine-tuning.

5 Right attitudes towards price adjustment

Finally, we need to talk about the issue of the price fixing policy in the macroeconomic regulation and control. Since we need to continue institutional transformation, we need to understand the limitations of price fixing policy, because it is a means that destroys the market mechanism and prevents it from playing its role. Also, in the economic life, the price of commodities always has impacted over each other with one being the cost of the other. In macroeconomic regulation and control, price fixing is applied to constrain the price of a certain commodity from rising. Experience has shown that price fixing policy is only effective in the short term, and that its damage to the economy cannot be underestimated because the price fixing policy leads to more prominent and serious structural imbalances. The imbalance was because it was impossible to regulate the price of all commodities; rather, what can be done to fix the price of certain commodities. In this way, under the conditions of commodities bearing the cost of each other, the prices of certain commodities were frozen when the prices of other relevant commodities were allowed to fluctuate, resulting in the reduced supply of the commodity with a frozen price and the breaking-down of industrial chains, which made the structure even more inharmonious and led to a series of aftermaths.

The outcomes from control over resource price are the same. Whether the resources are land, water, mineral or human etc., it is impossible for them to have an unlimited supply. While China has comparatively sufficient human resources, the supply is still limited when they are categorised by age, types of technical work, professional levels and residential areas. Therefore, the principles for the use and allocation of land, water and mineral resources cannot be made completely on market needs and, the government can implement quotas when necessary. However, both advantages and disadvantages exist with quota management. It cannot be used randomly, or it will harm the economic operation. The weakness of quota management also includes the prevalence of "rent-seeking" activities. That is, the departments and officials in charge of the quota distribution exploit their power, seek dishonest gains and profit by illegal means like bribery or other inappropriate means to transfer quotas to make profits. Quotas may not necessarily be implemented under openness, fairness and justice. This will greatly lower the government's credibility, and seriously affect the enthusiasm of many enterprises.

It is natural that prices for resource products have their particularity. Therefore, the reality that the supply of resources is limited should be taken into consideration. The quota can play a certain role under such conditions. However, when we put the three principles of "fairness, justice and openness" into practice, we should take notice of the long-term effects of quota management. That is, a quota system can lead to the existence of a double-track price system in the long run and even induces the break-down of normal industrial chains, distorting the structural reality and resulting in more severe structural disorder. Regarding unreasonable prices for resource products, the most effective countermeasure is to promote the reform in the resource pricing system. It is only through reforms that the fixing of resource products turns to be reasonable and avoids adverse consequences due to unreasonable pricing. It once again confirms the principal role of institutional transformation in the process of dual transformation.

Furthermore, it should be emphasised that in the dual transformation, the government should make effective management and market operation its objectives. An effective government is one that does what it is supposed to do while an effective market means one that functions as it is intended to do. Whatever the market is unable to do or cannot do well should be done by the government. In this way, the relationship between the government and the market can be coordinated. Problems touched upon in this introduction will be elaborated in ensuing chapters.

1 Significance of defining land ownership

Section 1 Economic disequilibrium and the establishment of market entities

1 The proposal of two types of economic disequilibrium

I have always considered *Chinese Economy in Disequilibrium* as my representative work on socialist economics theories. Its manuscript was written between 1987 and 1989. The full script was handed over to Economics Daily Press in December 1989, and the first edition came out in August 1990.

In the book, I categorised economic disequilibrium in Section 4 (*Market Self-regulation in Resource Allocation*) and in Chapter 2 (*Market Regulation and Resource Allocation*). My basic views are as follows:

Under equilibrium conditions, the market is fully developed with flexible pricing, and resource investment of microeconomic units is governed by self-benefits. Resource allocation is constrained by market prices, and resources flow out of inefficient sectors, regions and enterprises and are invested into efficient ones. Nonetheless, economic equilibrium is merely a hypothesis, as real world practice is in disequilibrium. Otherwise, why have so many Western economists been discussing disequilibrium for ages? According to the analysis of Western economists, reasons for disequilibrium roughly reside in the imperfectness of the market due to the existence of monopolies, inflexibility in making pricing adjustments due to unexpected factors or asymmetric information. Additionally, bidding for a price or outcry auctions only exist in a few commodities in economic life when it is only by out-crying like auctioneers that supply and demand can be balanced. Therefore, fundamental measures against economic disequilibrium are simply increasing the extent of government intervention (use government regulations to make up market deficiencies), or fully developing market mechanism, so that prices will be in a more flexible state, and commodity pricing may play a greater role in commodity trades. With regards to China's train of thoughts on reforms in the 1980s, the school that advocated liberalisation of prices might be influenced by Western economists who favoured the price liberalisation policy and promotion of a fully developed market mechanism.

I proposed, at the beginning of the 1980s, the necessity of categorising a disequilibrium economic state into Type I and Type II economic disequilibrium. Type I economic disequilibrium refers to the state where the market is underdeveloped with inflexible pricing, coexistence of excess demand and supply, and the co-occurrence of constraints on demand and supply. Under this type of disequilibrium, microeconomic units in market activities are commodity producers who operate independently and assume full responsibilities in case of profits or losses. Thus, they are market entities in a standard market sense, having investment opportunities and rights to select self-operation methods, and automatically bearing investment and operational risks.

Type II economic disequilibrium refers to the state where the market is underdeveloped with inflexible pricing, coexistence of excess demand and supply, and the co-occurrence of demand and supply constraints. Under such disequilibrium, microeconomic units involved in market activities are not commodity producers which operate independently and assume full responsibilities in case of profits or losses. Hence, they are not market entities in a standard sense, for they don't have investment opportunities or rights to automatically select operation modes; neither do they automatically take investment or operational risks or fully take those risks.

Economic disequilibrium in developed Western countries' market economy belongs to Type I disequilibrium, while the disequilibrium in China in the 1980s belonged to Type II disequilibrium. Consequently, I draw two important conclusions as follows.

First, it is right because China's economy belonged to Type II disequilibrium, i.e. being in a state where the market is imperfect and also lacks true market entity status, Chinese economic reforms should not take releasing prices but take reforming property ownership (clarifying and defining property ownership and fostering independent market entities) as the masterstroke. The best solution to the reform of property ownership is transforming enterprises' stock-holding system.

Second, China must take two steps in economic reforms. The first step is to enable China's economy to change from Type II economic disequilibrium to Type I disequilibrium through property ownership reforms. The second step is to gradually enable China's economy to move from Type I economic disequilibrium closer to economic equilibrium through market-perfecting measures.

The above are my basic thoughts about China's economic reforms.

2 Up-to-date achievements from property ownership reform

For the last 30 plus years (the 1980s-2012), China has made significant achievements in its property ownership reform. The achievements can be roughly summarised into five aspects:

(1) Most state-owned enterprises have been reorganised into joint-stock companies, among which some have become listed companies.

The aforementioned is a remarkable achievement. Note that in the reform of state-owned enterprises, China used to take such measures as "granting power and allowing a bigger share of profits", "the substitution of tax payment for profit delivery" and "enterprise contract system" etc. Nevertheless, none of the measures brought about prominent outcomes, particularly the contract-based learning exemplar of Capital Iron and Steel Company (CISC), which was openly advocated by the government. Practice has proved the disadvantages of the advocacy outweighed advantages and that CISC was a typical exemplar, which was "unlikely to be followed". It came late to other enterprises that "Capital Iron and Steel Company was a product of a special policy". Without special government policies, no other companies could emulate it. So why should disadvantages outweigh advantages? That is because the enterprise contract system urged enterprise contractors to care for short-term interests and lacked long-term considerations, which brought about competition in using large equipment and ended up exhausting it. Future development strategies and visions of the contract-implementing enterprises were not taken into account. In addition, the enterprise contract system always lay the property ownership issue aside, neither clarifying nor defining it. As a result, enterprises' property ownership remained fuzzy.

After Comrade *Deng Xiaoping's* Southern Talk, the business world began to consider programmes in relation to the stock-holding system reform. Particularly after the 15th National Congress of the Communist Party of China, large state enterprises and big banks started to rank stock-holding system reforms as key projects and even did some research on listing state enterprises in the market. Thus, the reform of state-owned enterprises went into the fast lane.

(2) Since the1990s, private enterprises started to develop on a large scale and great changes took place in the economic life with private enterprises gradually recognised as important components of the Chinese national economy.

Private Chinese enterprises, which gradually matured during the period, have become new economic factors after the Reform and Opening-up. They were distinctive not only from private sectors run by the national bourgeoisie before the founding of New China but also from those on the early days of New China (until the transformation of private industry and commerce in 1956). After the Reform and Opening-up, one group of private entrepreneurs after another growing up in various areas devoted themselves to the socialist cause in response to the call of the Central Committee of Communist Party of China and became builders of socialism. Of them, the vast majority were born after the founding of the People's Republic of China and received education in New China. Some even pursued higher education after the entrance examination to colleges was resumed in 1977, among whom many once went to the countryside or mountainous areas and received labour training in rural areas. They committed themselves to the Reform and Opening-up cause in accordance with the Party's call and directly participated in private enterprises' entrepreneurial process. Some of them even switched from being "inside the system"[1] to staying "outside the system".

Thus, it is reasonable to say that a great majority of private entrepreneurs knew in practice the supreme significance of clarifying and defining land ownership to the development of private enterprises. Without clarified property ownership, what can we say about maintaining and securing private enterprises' property ownership? Hence, private entrepreneurs were both beneficiaries of the property ownership reform, and its promoters and facilitators.

(3)   Almost all collectively owned enterprises were reorganised after the 1990s and became enterprises under the clarified stock-holding system, enterprises under the cooperative stock system or enterprises operated with private capital.

When socialist transformation was conducted in industry, commerce and handicraft in 1956, there emerged a group of collectively owned enterprises in cities. Their ownership was still vague. Who were their investors? It was always a mystery, because without identifying a specific investor, "collective ownership" was an empty concept. The situation lasted until the Reform and Opening-up started. In rural areas, there also emerged the collectively owned enterprises which were generally called "commune and brigade enterprises", but it was always unclear who was the investor of "commune and brigade-owned enterprises".

However, after the household contract system was implemented in agriculture, labour productivity was greatly improved and there appeared rural surplus labour. So small township enterprises were actively run in rural areas. These newly established township enterprises were usually formed by farmers with funds pooled in the form of stock-holding or stock cooperative systems. Although property ownership of previous "commune and brigade enterprises" was unclear, they were renamed township enterprises. Thus, newly-formed township enterprises and previous "commune and brigade enterprises" were generally called township enterprises, and both were incorporated in the collectively owned enterprise system. In addition, in the 1980s, there was another type of collectively owned enterprises in both urban and rural areas. They were actually privately-invested and privately owned, but under the then-circumstances and by convention, they were "affiliated" to collective organisations and regularly paid a certain amount of administration fees to the organisers so as to be known as "township enterprises" or "collective enterprises".

Mainly after the 1990s, all types of collectively owned enterprises underwent a property ownership-defining process. Although some were still called collective enterprises, their investors were specified, that is, which shareholders were exactly involved. Business forms were also converted into a stock-holding system or a stock cooperative system. "Collective enterprises", previously affiliated to a certain collective organisation successively broke away from the "affiliated" relationship, and resumed their nature, i.e. whether they are privately owned, privately-cooperated or enterprises under the private stock-holding system. Ownership was crystal clear. That was the achievement of property ownership reforms.

(4)   After the 1990s, especially after entering the 21st century, there have appeared more and more enterprises with mixed ownership.

Among the mixed-ownership enterprises, some are coalitions of state-owned and private capital, some coalitions of state-owned and foreign capital and others coalitions of state, private and foreign capital.

As a matter of fact, after an enterprise, whether it was state-owned or privately owned became a listed company, an investor in the stock market became one of its shareholders. Thus, the listed company became a mixed-ownership enterprise. If its employees held shares, even though the company was not listed, the enterprise became mixed-owned. Absolute or relative shareholding varied on the basis of the specific circumstances of the enterprise.

The establishment and development of mixed-ownership enterprises were preconditioned on defining property ownership. That is to say, if property ownership remained empty and property ownership failed to be implemented to a specific investor, such an enterprise would be unable to be sustained for long, not to mention further expansion.

(5) Likewise, cooperatives worthy of their names were an achievement after the Reform and Opening-up. Every cooperative must have been established, operated and administered by law.

A typical example in this respect is farmers' specialised cooperatives, which have developed greatly in recent years on mainland China.

As will be mentioned in the next section, property ownership reforms in rural areas have been carried out relatively slowly. From 1979 onwards, implementing the household contract system was undoubtedly a significant reform measure with profound meaning in developing agricultural production, but that was not a property ownership reform in its real sense; rather, it was only an agricultural operation reform. The real launch of rural property ownership reform was the collective forest tree ownership reform promoted nationwide in 2008. The forest farmers contracted collective forest land. They did not only have defined property ownership, which was eligible for mortgage, but also were issued forest deeds, which were implemented to households.

In spite of that, it has to be pointed out that under the agricultural contracting operation mode, farmers' specialised cooperatives have been set up one after another, which has been a new phenomenon in the last 10 years. To date, though much of farmers' contracted land has not been defined, it has already become a consensus among farmers that land can be shares. It is more common to have cash rather than land as shares, though. In fact, that was exactly the pilot reform of rural property ownership, as farmers' specialised cooperatives have already become market entities. Thus, defining and clarifying property ownership must be an essential prerequisite.

Compared to processes of defining rural land ownership and farmers' gaining three rights, namely contracted land and homestead use rights and property ownership, property ownership reform of farmers' specialised cooperatives have moved undoubtedly a step ahead.

3 Issues to be pushed forward in property ownership reforms

It should be acknowledged that in the past 30 years of the Reform and Opening-up, progress in China's property ownership reform has been quite remarkable.

Results from state enterprises' stock-holding system reform are that many large state-owned enterprises and commercial banks have become listed companies and independent market entities in the construction of a modern enterprise system. Undeniably, even with those achievements, we should be clear-minded that large state-owned enterprises, especially those listed companies still have some distance before they eventually complete property ownership reforms. For instance, it still needs to make large-scale state-owned enterprises and commercial banks real market entities, corporate governance structure complete, the Shareholders' Meeting, the Board of Directors and the Board of Supervisors play their due role, the behaviour of the listed enterprise open and transparent and shareholders assured.

Stocking-holding system or stock cooperative system of private enterprises, including micro, small, medium, large enterprises or stock cooperatives has also made remarkable achievements. Normally, private enterprises' selection of a stock-holding system or a stock cooperative system accords with their development trends. It is also private investors' option among the two forms, i.e. stock-holding system or stock cooperative system on a voluntary basis. But many private investors still have concerns over property ownership. They are generally worried about the security of property ownership, often withdrawing their businesses or transferring their businesses abroad after making some profits. Why is it so? The primary cause is that they still have doubts over domestic investment environments in China and lack confidence. As long as a private enterprise has a big business, the private investor's sense of distrust intensifies. They expect the government and society to be more concerned about the security of private capital, anticipating that they are not discriminated against but treated equally in legislation and judiciary. That actually indicates that there is still much work to be done to protect property ownership of private enterprises. If private investments are not treated equally, private investors will never feel at ease.

Compared with state-owned and private enterprises' progress in property ownership reform and entity status of the market, there are still a considerable number of limitations in farmers' status as a market entity. That is because, since the Reform and Opening-up, the focus of property ownership reforms has been laid on the reform of enterprises without realising that the property ownership reform in rural areas should receive equal attention. That is primarily an issue of theoretical understanding.

For a long time, experts engaged in research on reform theories believed that the most important property in rural areas was land, and that it had been clearly defined in China's Constitution that land was collectively owned, and that the rural contracting system, applicable to China at the current phase was just established collectively owned land. Thus, property ownership reforms in rural areas were considered to have been rudimentarily completed with the implementation and popularisation of the household contract responsibility system since the early 1980s, and pending reform tasks were simply to continuously develop and boost the collective economy.

The inadequate knowledge of rural property ownership reform seriously hindered deepening of rural property ownership reform. For many years since the mid-1980s, why were the majority of contracted households still so poor? Many people attribute it to three reasons. First, farmers only know how to grow crops. Yet, how much could they earn by growing crops? How could they avoid poverty? Second, farmers did not know how to run township enterprises and in some villages, no-one volunteered to organise enterprises. In that case, it was impossible for them not to continuously live in poverty. Third, the rural household contractors had no relatives, friends or hometown fellows in the town and had no idea where to find a job or set up small businesses. They depended completely on luck when they left their hometown. Some found work in the outside world and others lost valuable time, failed to earn money and had no other choice but to pack for their hometown. Some researchers did not understand that the reason for contracted farmers' continued poverty was strongly related to the prolonged decision on reforming rural property ownership. Farmers did not have property ownership, thus gaining no property income. Apart from planting some crops, raising livestock and poultry, what other ways could they have to improve their wealth? Far from that, as contracted households did not have property ownership, their own homestead, as well as houses built on farmers' own homestead were demolished at a very short notice and farmers' contracted land, and their own homestead were enclosed in the same manners. Farmers were likely to receive land compensation and house demolition fees, but the amount was too small. How could farmers not be poor? How could landless farmers not appeal and make their complaints?

Those are issues resulting from defining property ownership. Among the experts who study the rural area, agriculture and farmers, some realised in the 1980s and 1990s the crucial significance of defining property ownership, but their voices were not loud enough to draw more attention from the society to the issue of rural property ownership reform. With the entry into the 21st century, defining rural land ownership drew more attention from people who cared about three *nong* [rural] issues, issues related to rural areas, agriculture and farmers. How to gradually push on a new round of rural reforms came to be people's concern and be more widely discussed. At the beginning of the 21st century, people who cared about continuously deepening property ownership reform observed two new situations, which greatly motivated their enthusiasm for accelerating property ownership reform in the countryside.

The first new situation was that, just as has been pointed out in the introduction chapter of the book, the collective forest ownership system reform, which could be belated for many years, finally began to be piloted in 2003. Pilot sites were in *Fujian, Jiangxi* and several other provinces. Very soon, the State Council of the Central Committee of the Communist Party of China issued a decision on carrying out a collective forest ownership system reform nationwide. While collective forestry ownership reform appeared to be later than agricultural household contract system reform, it was one step ahead in terms of defining land ownership. That is, after areas of forest land was measured, forestry ownership was implemented to households, forest contracting households received forest deeds and forest land could be mortgaged. The new situation not only encouraged forestry contracting households, but also inspired rural contracting households. They thought that only by defining land ownership could farmers be assured and freed from worries that the land (including the contracted land and homestead) and houses on the homestead would not be seized and demolished by force. The collective forestry ownership system reform was solidly carried out in rural areas and was greatly welcomed by farmers. They called for quick approvals of land ownership and early awarding of deeds in rural areas.

The second situation is after the entry into the 21st century, the rural land circulation has greatly increased. Subcontracting, leasing, and buying rural land shares have been increasingly promoted in the rural area. People ready to subcontract or to lease their contracted land to others hope to benefit from subcontract fees and land rent so as to facilitate their migrant work, and set up shops or workshops. Those ready to rent land or subcontract land under their names wish to conduct scale management, expand cultivatable land areas in agricultural production, improve efficiency, raise production and become large planation families. Farmers who became shareholders of their contracted land in specialised cooperatives usually acted on the following three reasons: first, they were planning to go to the town to work and to set up stores or manual workshops to earn more income. As there would be no labourer to farm the land, there was no better way than making the land into shares, which would enable more gains (shares and bonuses) and stop the land from lying fallow. Second, being a shareholder in the farmers' specialised cooperatives would be more reliable than leasing or subcontracting the land to other farmers. They believed that the leaders and managers would make good use of the land and would not trap them into losses. Third, in case that migrant work or business-running was not smooth, as the land became the shares in farmers' specialised cooperatives, they could still find a job within the cooperatives when they returned to their hometown. By contrast, if the land was subcontracted or leased to other farmers, it was inconvenient for them to take it back prior to the expiry of the lease or subcontract term to manage it themselves. Thus, defining land ownership has become increasingly important for farmers and had more practical meaning. That is because, with land circulation speeding up, farmers were worried whether after their contracted land was subcontracted, leased or became shares, their own property ownership would change in land circulation, for example being seized or replaced, subcontracted by others or even rented to a third party, resulting in future property disputes. Their greatest concern was whether they would lose their property ownership in land circulation in the long run due to the lack of approval of property ownership. They felt that they would rather have the contracted land extensively operated by those at home, i.e. the sick and the elderly, the weak and the disabled, than have it circulated out without its ownership established. To them, it seemed safer.

Seen in this light, a new round of rural contracted land property ownership reform is to define ownership of farmers' contracted land, homestead and houses on homestead. At present, the huge project is being implemented step by step. It is the beginning of new changes in the countryside.

4 The current state of Chinese economic disequilibrium

According to what has already been stated, features of type II economic disequilibrium involve incomplete market and lack of market entities in a real sense, while type I is merely characterised by an imperfect market. Therefore, the key to transforming from type II economic disequilibrium into the first is to establish land ownership, clarify property ownership and cultivate the real market entities.

After 30 years' reform, China's property ownership reform has so far made many achievements: the market entity status of state-owned enterprises has basically been established. The most important issue at the moment is to remove business monopolies, realise fair competition among enterprises of different ownerships and continue to improve corporate governance structure and so on. The market entity status of private enterprises has also been established. At present, one important issue is to bring ownership protection over private investors into effect by legal means, achieve fair play between private and state-owned enterprises, and eliminate ownership discrimination. Currently, land ownership reform to be urgently pushed forward is mainly in rural areas. Defining land ownership has been postponed again and again, so that the launch has been delayed for a long time, and experiments have just started. Only by putting reforms into practice can farmers appear in the Chinese economy as market entities.

So, if asked: "At what kind of economic disequilibrium state do you think China currently is?", I will make the following reply: "Economic disequilibrium in current China still belongs to type II disequilibrium, because there is still a distance before China can define and clarify its property ownership. Furthermore, the status of market entities has not been fully established. For instance, property ownership of several hundred millions of farmers has not yet been defined, so they can't become real market entities. Further property ownership reform should be conducted".

Such an answer is based on the current and actual conditions of the Chinese economy. Although certain progress has been made in more than 30 years' property ownership reform, defining rural land ownership has just started, as the rural property ownership reform has been valued for a long time and neither has it been taken seriously. It is only when defining land ownership is implemented into farming households, and agricultural subcontractors become family planters with clearly defined ownership, or market entities with independent or cooperative operation, that China can be recognised as having stepped across type II economic disequilibrium into type I disequilibrium. And then, by further perfecting the market, China's economy will also move from type I of economic disequilibrium closer to equilibrium.

Economic equilibrium is, after all, a kind of theoretical assumption, which is more likely not to be fully achieved. That is because there objectively exist information symmetricity, incomplete competition, limits in resource supply and individual economic operation not necessarily based on the principle of maximum interests. Those phenomena will not completely die out. Nevertheless, it is expected that type I economic disequilibrium should draw closer to economic equilibrium. That is to say, an increasingly perfected market is still an achievable objective. That's enough.

Session 2 Defining land ownership: the launch of a new round of rural reform

1 Significance of defining land ownership

Defining land ownership is the beginning of a new round rural reform in China. To illustrate profound significance of the reform, we start with the urban and rural binary system in China.

The planned economic system differs from the urban and rural binary structure, which has existed since ancient times. Take, for example, the alternating period between the Northern *Song* Dynasty and the Southern *Song* Dynasty. At that time, as North China was captured by *Jin* soldiers, inhabitants of the Yellow River basin moved to the South. The move was free. There was no restriction that urban citizens were only allowed to move to cities in the South and rural residents to rural areas in the South. Again, after the mid-*Qing* Dynasty, a ban was lifted in the Northeast of China, so that people in *Shandong* were allowed to move to the Northeast. Rural residents in *Shandong* could be apprentices and staff, and migrant workers, set up shops or manual workshops, purchase or build houses in Northeastern towns. Urban residents in *Shandong* could lease, farm or buy land, buy or build houses. People could move freely between the Northeast urban and rural areas without residence restrictions. The situation lasted until the early 1950s. However, since the late 1950s, due to the establishment of the planned economic system, household registration was divided into urban and rural household registries and the dual system came into being with urban and rural areas separated from each other. Since then, urban and rural areas have become closed units and the flow of production components was greatly restricted. Under the urban and rural dual system, urban residents and farmers did not have equal rights; nor did they have equal opportunities. In a sense, farmers had the status of "second-class citizens".

The establishment of the urban and rural binary system has played an important role for the existence and continuity of the planned economic system. Briefly, the planned economic system actually has two pillars: one is the state-owned enterprise system with an undivided role between the government and enterprises and unclearly-defined property ownership; the other is a dual system with urban and rural segmentation and restrictions on the flow of production components between urban and rural areas. Two pillars supported the overall running of the planned economic system. In other words, limiting the flow of production components between urban and rural areas means binding broad masses of farmers to farmland and to their residences. Only in this way could the planned economic system be consolidated and operated.

Chinese economic system reform started with the implementation of the rural household contract system. The system mobilised the farmers' production enthusiasm, and created conditions for the rise of township enterprises and for agricultural labour force's becoming migrant workers. It then played an inestimable role in promoting Chinese economic system reform. However, the implementation of the rural family contract system just rejected an extreme form of organisation (the People's Commune System) in the urban and rural binary system but did not change the fact that the urban and rural binary system continued to exist. Urban and rural areas were still isolated and the two kinds of household registration system still existed. After the Third Plenary Session of the Twelfth Chinese Communist Party Congress in 1984, the focus of reform shifted from the countryside to the city, and institutional reform of the state-owned enterprises became a popular "hot topic". That was obviously a very important reform plan; nevertheless, comparatively speaking, rural reforms were neglected. When did greater concerns over rural reform start? When did a new round of reform of the "never-touched-upon" urban and rural binary system come into being? It should be said to be after the 21st century. It has repeatedly been stressed above that the collective forestry right system reform has played an important exemplar role in this aspect. The collective forest ownership system reform, that is, the implementation of collective forest ownership to households, used to be called "the first spring thunder in the new century". That was no exaggeration in comparing forestry ownership reform to "the first spring thunder in a new century", because it corresponded with the actual situation of Chinese economic system reform.[2]

Implementing collective forest ownership to household and issuing forest ownership deeds to forest farmers was "defining land ownership". From then on, forest farmers had property ownership and also property income. Forestry ownership can be mortgaged and the economy in the forest areas was activated and collective forest land took on a new look. It is the power source of the reform and development. Practice brought up a topic to the theoretical circle: if collective forest land can be reformed in this way, why can't collective farms be reformed similarly? In the countryside, forest farmers are the minority while the great majority of people are farmland cultivators and production operators. After defining ownership, couldn't enthusiasm bust out of farmers? The real change to the outlook of the countryside cannot only rely on forest farmers; rather, it must rely on the contractors of the farmland. Only after contractors' farmland ownership has all been defined, can they become market entities and can China be a rich and powerful state with the socialist market economy.

2 Defining land ownership and safeguarding farmers' rights and benefits

According to survey data collected in *Zhejiang, Chongqing, Henan, Shandong, Sichuan* and other cities and provinces by a research group of CPPCC's[3] Economic Committee, the reason for farmers to warmly support defining land ownership was primarily because they believed that after the land approval, their property ownership and benefits would be genuinely protected. Note that in the name of the collective land ownership, contracted land, farmers' homesteads or houses, whether they were inherited old houses or newly built or expanded houses with farmers' own earnings in recent years, were not recognised as privately owned, not to mention the increasingly fertile contracted land after years of cultivation. If the government and big enterprises decided to occupy the land and get houses on it demolished, farmland contractors had no other choice but to follow the arrangement, giving up contracted land and homestead, and looking on helplessly as both old and new houses on the homestead were being demolished. The compensation fee that farmers could receive fell far below market price. There were incidents, almost everywhere, of farmers' resisting land grabbing or enclosure or enforced folk houses' demolishing. Farmers' rights and benefits were not respected, let alone being reasonably or adequately compensated. Be aware that to farmers, loss of land and houses did not only mean losing means of subsistence, but also means losing production materials that they relied on for earnings, and means of making a living. They could not get full compensation, but only a sufficient amount for their current living. What should they do in the near future? They dared not even think about it. That farmers lost their land and houses was just the origin of social turmoil most concerned by authorities and rulers of all dynasties and negations, when such situations, however, could have been avoided. From this perspective, the significance of approving land ownership in guaranteeing farmers' rights and benefits cannot be overstated enough.

Naturally, land is distinct from other production material (such as machinery and equipment, tools, livestock, transport vehicles etc.); the other material could be sold at their free will by the owners to people with a need for those means of production, but land may not be allowed to be sold in this way. It is mainly because in some countries and regions, land supply is limited and there are restricted land use conditions by the law. There are strict rules on what kind of land can be transferred to what kind of buyers, and how the purchased land is used. The rules cannot be violated but must be complied with in land deals. With regards to this, we made an investigation when we inspected Japan, finding detailed stipulations on land trade in that country. Urban dwellers and business entities could lease land from farmers, but could not buy land in rural areas, and there should be no change in the use of the leased land. For instance, it could be laid fallow; neither could houses or factories be built on it etc. If the leased land used to be farmland, only crops were allowed to be planted on it. Legal responsibilities of violators would be investigated, which was an illustration of specified restrictions. To Japanese experts, those stipulations were what everyone should abide by. Why was this? Such stipulations were essential for the maintenance of socioeconomic stability, as there were a dense population and less land in Japan.

China's progressive land ownership approval also takes no change of land uses as a norm, so as not to let the limited arable and construction land be switched for other purposes. Therefore, what is most important for Chinese farmers in defining rural land ownership is: under the premise of no change in the agricultural land use (arable and construction land), farmers' property ownership and interests were guaranteed, so that rural land would not be seized with a low-offered price or farmers' houses demolished with reasonable compensation by government or enterprises with the government's permission. After the land ownership was approved, farmers would have three rights and three deeds. Farmers' three rights are contracted land management right, homestead use right and property rights of building houses on their own homestead. Their three deeds are land use deed, homestead use deed and the deed of building houses on their own homestead. In all, farmers' three rights and three deeds were protected by law.

Why did farmers become "landless farmers"? Why could farmers become "jobless"? Why did farmers become homeless or dependant on other people for a living? Those were because farmers' property ownership and interests were not effectively protected by the law. After establishing ownership, farmers' three rights and deeds were guaranteed. No person or unit was allowed to invade farmers' contracted land, homestead or houses built on homestead at their free will. If farmers' land needed to be commandeered and farmers' houses demolished, legal procedures and contracts should be acted upon strictly, which required farmers as one party and the government or an enterprise or a public institution as the other to reach a deal based on a price upon which both parties agreed. Thus, the farmers felt assured, because their rights and interests were protected.

3 Land ownership approval and land circulation

In recent years, land circulation has been gradually promoted in China's vast rural areas through subcontracting, leasing or entrusted businesses, or converting land into shares and joining farmers' specialised cooperatives, agricultural, industrial and commercial enterprises and so on. Rural residents conducting business activities like doing migrant work, setting up shops, opening mills etc. think that they would rather circulate their contracted land so as to gain a higher income than leave it idle or let the elderly farm, harvest and sell with low efficiency.

But our research in several provinces, *Hubei, Jiangsu, Shandong* etc. discovered that farmers engaged in the land circulation had a common concern: i.e. feeling unassured, namely whether the contracted land still belonged to them after being circulated over time. They are wondering whether the land rented out, or turned shares can be taken back again to be self-operated; what would happen if the other party was not willing to return the land; what should be done when the other party was unwilling to return the land, or wanted to return another plot with the same area but lower quality? Questions such as those made farmers engaged in land circulation feel ill at ease.

After land ownership was approved, farmers were awarded management deeds of the contracted land, thus gaining baselines for potential disputes over land subcontracts, leases and purchase or withdrawal of shares. That is, farmers, holding that established land ownership asserted their own rights and interests, were willing to circulate land by subcontracting, leasing or buying shares. The key issue lay in the following: first, there was no need for farmers to worry about losing their own property ownership after subcontracting, leasing and buying shares. Second, there was no need for farmers to worry about not receiving the due benefits, like subcontract income, rentals or share bonuses etc. It, then, formed a virtuous circle.

That is, farmers were confident of land circulation after the approval of property ownership. It resulted in many farmers' willingness to get their contracted land subcontracted, leased or converted to shares so as to gain the agreed-upon income, enabling more and more farmers to join land circulation and further expanding the scale of agricultural operation.

When doing research in some cities and provinces, we also found that while land ownership approval created safe and assured conditions for rural contactors engaged in the circulation, an important issue still remained to be solved. That is, it still needed a perfect accompanying land circulation market. In many places, there was only an office, an information centre or a hall that provided land circulation information services for both trading parties. It was much better to have such an office, an information centre or a hall than no such facilities. However, it must be admitted that such facilities were far from sufficient. Note that a land circulation market is what is more urgently needed in land circulation for both supply and demand parties. The market could provide not only supply and demand information, but also trading opportunities and increasingly rational trading prices in market competition (or actual benefits in land circulation) for both parties. Each party (whether the supply party or the demand party) had opportunities to make choices and decisions. On the one hand, that could promote standardised land circulation behaviour like subcontracting, leasing or purchasing shares and minimalizing information asymmetry between the supply party and the demand party; on the other hand, it could enable more and more potential supply and demand parties to dismiss their "looking–on" state and be involved in land circulation. From the perspective of reducing information asymmetry in land circulation, that was a practice which combined efficiency and fairness.

In the near future, when we gradually expand the pilot scope of the land ownership approval and promote the land circulation, it is necessary to cultivate intermediary services in land circulation market to actively guide orderly and standardised circulation operation. Be aware that it is of great significance for perfecting land circulation market. A sound and perfect intermediary service system can prevent changes in land use and keep contractors from transferring contracted land to non-agricultural personnel to be engaged in non-agricultural activities. At the same time, perfecting intermediary services and standardising their operation also help to reduce supply and demand disputes in land circulation, and prevent suppliers (rural contractors) from losing land, being landless or receiving due income after land circulation. In addition, it should be mentioned that a rural land assessment system should be constructed to accompany land circulation. Fostering a batch of asset assessment professionals, both familiar with rural reality and mastering assets assessment, will help guarantee farmers' benefits and also strengthen their confidence in further promoting land circulation.

4 Arable land increase after re-measurements

After land ownership approval was completed in some pilot counties and cities, we did a survey, finding reports of increase in arable land areas in almost all places that had completed land ownership approval. It is said in the report from the city of *Jiaxing, Zhejiang* Province that land areas increased by about 20% after being re-measured. It is similar to the report from the city of *Huzhou* and the city of *Hangzhou, Zhejiang* Province where arable areas also increased by about 20%. How could the phenomenon occur? We generalised after informal conversations with the grassroots cadres and farmers in *Yaobang* Village and the Towns of *Xindai* and *Pinghu* of *Jiaxing* City that the increase was roughly due to the following four reasons.

First, more than 30 years ago when the land started to be contracted, land quality was uneven with both "good" and "bad" land. Therefore, the contracted land area was calculated in this way: one "good" *mu*[4] was a *mu*; two "bad" *mus* were converted into one *mu*. Farmers agreed upon this. After more than 30 years, farmers with contracted land carefully safeguarded their contracted land. Additionally, with the improved water conservancy irrigation facilities, disparity between "good" and "bad" land decreased. Now when the land was re-measured, famers had no objection to having one *mu* counted as a *mu* and then arable land increased.

Second, according to the recollection of elderly farmers, when the contracted land was initially measured, the land was composed of plots with ridges running across the land and occupying a lot of land. When the measurement took place, the field ridges were removed. Moreover, the zones where sunshine was blocked on both sides of the ridges were not included in the counting of arable land. Farmers thought at that time that that kind of removal was reasonable. Thirty years passed after the land contract and changes took place in rural areas. Farmers generally used tractors to farm the land and some even used seedling planting machine to plant rice shoots; ridges were demolished and plots of land were joined into large pieces. When the land was re-measured, arable land increased as it should be.

Third, previously, moors and low-lying lands with aquatic plants at the edges of fields were not used. Thirty years later, land at all edges was used. Thus, when farmland was re-measured, arable land area increased.

Fourth, originally, farmers needed to pay agricultural taxes, so when farmers reported their arable land areas to the relevant authority, they reported as few areas as they could, which was the case for almost every household. When the area was obviously one *mu* and three *fen*[5] of land, only one *mu* was reported. Everybody had a tacit understanding of the practice but none disclosed the behaviour of the others. Now, the agricultural tax was cancelled, and the land was just re-measured, so every household reported the real figure. Additionally, the land could be converted into shares, subcontracted and leased. Reporting fewer areas could only cause one loss. "Only a fool reports fewer [areas]!", said farmers. Truly, the remark mirrored the local situation.

After our survey on land ownership approval in *Zhejiang*, we attended the National, Provincial, (Municipal and Regional) Economic Committee and Agriculture Commission Directors' Meeting in the city of *Qingyuan, Guangdong* Province. The meeting was convened by the Economic Committee of the CPPCC. At the meeting, we talked about the increase in arable land area in *Zhejiang* Province after land ownership approval with superintendents of Economic Committee and

Agriculture Commission of CPPCC in the Midwest of China. They responded: "If arable land is re-measured for land ownership approval in our regions [Midwest], there will be a lot more increase in arable areas, as initially, there were cases where three *mu* of "bad" land was converted into one *mu*. Besides, we have a lot more of moorland and in recent years, edges of fields have been put into use." If it is really the case, the area of the arable land nationwide after re-measurement will not be 1.8 billion *mu* but more than 2.1 billion *mu*.

5 Land approval and farmers' income growth

Farmers' income growth was the most remarkable achievement after land ownership approval. As reflected by farmers in *Hangzhou, Jiaxing* and *Huzhou* of *Zhejiang* Province, farmers' current income was much higher than it used to be. A set of preliminary data in *Jiaxing*'s report displays that before the land ownership approval, *Jiaxing's* urban and rural income per capita was 3.1:1, afterwards, the urban and rural income per capita became 1.9:1. The obvious reduction in the income gap between urban and rural areas does not suggest an obvious reduction in urban income per capita but a significant increase in rural income per capita.

The preliminary analysis of our survey in *Pinghu*, a city affiliated to *Jiaxing* City, suggested five reasons for rural income growth per capita.

First, after property ownership approval, farmers' ownership and interests of contracted land, homestead and self-built houses on homestead were guaranteed, their confidence in production operation boomed, motives energised, enthusiasm fully mobilised, and potentials exerted. Land ownership approval could be regarded as the source of farmers' wealth.

Second, with property ownership, farmers had corresponding property income. Their property can be categorised into two types: first, land, composed of contracted land and homestead; second, houses, mainly self-built houses on the homestead. Property income, brought about by contracted land includes fees from land subcontract fees, lease fees, land share bonus and land transfer payment etc. Property income, brought about by famers' self-built houses on homestead includes house-renting earning and house transfer payment. If farmers do migrant work or businesses, set up stores or manual workshops, in addition to wages and profits, farmers can also get subcontract fees, rents and share bonuses owing to subcontracting and leasing contracted land and buying land shares, and rent from renting family houses. On the outskirts of *Jiaxing City, Zhejiang* Province, we saw that old houses on farmers' house sites had been pulled down and rows of four-floored new residences had been built. Some were inhabited by farmers per se; one half of other houses were inhabited by farmers and the other half by urban residents and the other half leased to business people from other places; still others were totally rented to urban residents, businessmen from other places and migrant workers. Farmers had a great deal of rental earnings.

Third, after land ownership approval, farmers, through land circulation, subcontracted or leased land from other farmers in the same villages, who did go away to be migrant workers or do other businesses. Some were used for expanding farming scale, some for expanding breeding scale and still others for developing vegetables, fruits or horticulture. Their income increased.

Fourth, another portion of farmers subcontracted their contracted land, leased it to others or turned their land into shares in farmers' specialised cooperatives. Thereafter, some worked in cities, opening stores and workshops, or setting up micro-enterprises. Their businesses were prosperous and their income was abundant. They then moved their families to cities and towns. Their rural houses were either kept as temporary accommodation for their return to the countryside or rented out for rental income.

Fifth, farmers' specialised cooperatives had made great progress. The major reason was farmers' property ownership approval. Farmers had sufficient motives to run the specialised cooperatives, and economic power of professional cooperatives was strengthened by improving operation and management. The cooperatives grew up on the path of standardisation. They also increased the income of cooperative members.

Given the above, land ownership approval has played a prominent role which cannot be neglected in promoting farmers' income and narrowing down income gaps between urban and rural areas.

6 Four pending research questions in furthering land circulation

At present, rural land circulation after ownership approval is still at an experimental stage. In view of land circulation issues emerging from counties, which have made great pilot progress, the following aspects need to be further discussed and appropriate solutions should be figured out. There are roughly four questions:

(1) The "non-food" tendency

It is encouraging that after the land approval, land circulation in various forms has speeded up. But at the same time, the "non-food" use of land has increasingly aroused people's attention. "Non-food" here refers to the process where grain crops were grown on the contracted land by the contractors prior to the subcontracts or leases; however, after the contracts or leases, other crops, such as vegetables, strawberries, fruit trees, fertilisers (for breeding) and the like were grown on the land. "Non-food" as a tendency will become more serious in the near future and the tendency is determined by the gaps in market price. After land was circulated, a compulsory stipulation that land previously cultivated for grain crops should only be allowed after circulation to plant grain crops, would not be appealing to contractors and subcontractors, for the income from planting grain crops was too mean and it was hard to attain profits. That is equivalent to the previous practice that bound the original rural contractors to the original contracted land and farmers could only allow the elderly, the weak, women and the young to be engaged low-efficiently with grain production activities. Thus, it became a difficult issue. Furthermore, a compulsory stipulation that land previously cultivated for grain crops should only be allowed after circulation to plant grain crops might not bear fruit, because the cost for surveillance was high and who would come to supervise regularly was a question, particularly after improved vegetables and newly-planted fruit trees already became sources of income for new contractors. Should vegetables and trees be evicted and grain crops replanted? Who is to implement the task? That will surely lead to disputes. What should we do?

At present, it is impossible to take rigid and compulsory measures like collecting fines or eradicating non-food crops and tree seedlings. Otherwise, those measures would not only cause high supervision costs and incur a heavy workload but also hinder land circulation and intensify discrepancies between farmers and the government and place the government and rural organisations at the grassroots level on the opposite side of farmers. Village officials also oppose this kind of practice, because they do not want to offend suppliers and buyers in land circulation and provoke criticisms from villagers. It seems that the fundamental solution to the problem is to give subsidies or rewards to new contractors who continue to grow grain crops after land circulation and gradually raise the price of grain crops. These measures will not completely restrain the non-food tendency. Therefore, we should not relax our work in educating, enlightening and persuading, at a great length, both demand and supply parties in land circulation.

In the process of land circulation, apart from a "non-food", there is also a "non-agricultural" tendency, namely the tendency of transferring contracted land flowing out from farmers for uses beyond agriculture (such as building factories or commercial housing etc.). While such a problem is more serious than "non-food", it is easier with which to deal. That is, it can be constrained according to the law, regulations and land management bylaws. The key lies in the implementation of the following principles: the law must be observed and strictly enforced; lawbreakers must be prosecuted.

(2) Qualification review system and industrial and commercial enterprises' access to rural areas

Qualification review is another issue that needs to be resolved in current land circulation. After the land ownership approval, a growing number of young adults among the farmers would like to satisfy their desire of going to towns and cities to do migrant work or businesses, therefore willing to subcontract or lease their contracted land to others. Meanwhile, in some places, there were not many farming households who wanted to take in leased or subcontracted land. It induced the readiness of commercial and industrial enterprises to subcontract and lease the contracted land of farming households and perform production activities. In other places, farmers and commercial and industrial enterprises, along with farmers were all demand parties. Compared with farmers, however, the commercial and industrial enterprises were in a more advantageous position owing to their outcry for a higher price for subcontract fees or rents. Why should this phenomenon occur? On the basis of our survey in some areas, it might be due to three reasons. First, commercial and industrial enterprises have large-scale businesses and sufficient funding. They could expect a high profit rate after the land was circulated to them. Thus, they are ready to offer higher prices as subcontract fees or lease. Second, some commercial and industrial enterprises used subcontracted or leased land as raw material bases (for instance, some food industry enterprises need to have their own raw material bases). What they were more satisfied with was that they could have a continuous supply of raw material in the future, not that they could just sell products from the land to the outside world. So these enterprises did not pay great attention to cost accounting of the whole production process, the sum of subcontract fees or rents, but to the belief that as long as the supply of raw material was guaranteed, it would be satisfactory. Third, other commercial and industrial enterprises subcontracted or leased the land as their reserves. At the moment, they would retain the original farming conditions and when opportunities came, they would transfer the land for other uses (for instance, building factories, warehouses and staff quarters etc.). So, in order to ensure that enterprises had reserved land, they considered it cost-efficient to pay more than farmers for the subcontract fees or lease, because land was a rare resource and hoarding land had more advantages to the enterprises than hoarding money.

Therefore, there are different opinions on whether industrial and commercial enterprises should be prohibited from entering land circulation process after land property approval. Some held that business enterprises should be allowed to be demand party of land circulation. They reasoned why was it impossible, as long as people were interested in investing in agriculture, bringing capital and technology to the countryside and doing good to agricultural production without violating land use directions? Others disagreed, holding that industrial and commercial enterprises should be banned from subcontracting and leasing land. They reasoned enterprises will squeeze out farming experts and big planters among the farmers who are willing to expand their farming scale. Moreover, the background of those enterprises is complicated with a wide business scope. Once they suffer operating losses in other areas, they will subcontract or lease land to others, which will be adverse to rural socioeconomic stability. There is a third opinion that industrial and commercial enterprises should not be unconditionally allowed in the land circulation process, nor should they be absolutely forbidden from investing in agriculture. Rather, a system should be set up to review entry qualifications of industrial and commercial enterprises in the land circulation process. Decisions should be made after qualification review, i.e. the review of the applicants' past investment experience, capital conditions, stock conditions, achievements and strengths in agricultural techniques.

After our analysis of the above three opinions, our conclusions were: the first and the second opinion are not conducive to the development of agriculture, while the third is feasible. However, the issue is what the qualification review criteria are.

What kind of qualification can be considered as valid? What kind of deficiency is seen as invalid? The following three criteria can be accepted by most people:

> First, have certain agriculture-related experiences, have some good performances and be recognised as agricultural enterprises in the agricultural industry;
> Second, have good social reputations, sufficient strength in management and professional skills and the ability of undertaking agricultural development.
> Third, have well-justified and scientific development plans on how to develop and use the contracted land, which is obtained after the land circulation.

(3) Can contracted land, homestead and self-built houses on the homestead be mortgaged after the land ownership approval? Can contracted land, homestead and self-built house on homestead, which have been used for mortgage, be further subcontracted and leased to others?

With land ownership approval, contracted land use rights, homestead use rights and property rights of self-built houses on homestead have all been defined, and farmers have got relevant deeds of rights. All these satisfy financial institutions' mortgage terms, so that farmers can use their deeds to get loans. There should be no additional terms on top of those conditions. Note that farmers had always felt that it was difficult to receive loans. That is because, on the one hand, there were fewer financial institutions at the grassroots level; on the other, farmers as loan applicants lacked mortgages. Before the approval of land ownership, it was impossible for farmers to get mortgaged loan by making use of contracted land. Changes only took place after land ownership approval. That is, after farmers registered their contracted land management rights, homestead use rights and property ownership of self-built houses on the homestead registered, and got corresponding deeds granted, they could get loans through mortgages. The remaining issue was to establish financial institutions at the grassroots level. When doing surveys after the land ownership approval in rural areas of *Hangzhou, Jiaxing* and *Huzhou, Zhejiang* province, I found that there had been good conditions for rural mortgaged loans in the rural areas of those three cities and that mortgaged loan work was proceeding smoothly without any sign of loan risks and that both residents applying for loans and financial institutions were fairly satisfied.

An issue that needs further discussion is whether after land ownership approval farmers can further subcontract or lease mortgaged contracted land, homestead or houses to others in land circulation process. For example, to be migrant workers and do businesses or open workshops in cities, farmers first obtain bank loans as their initial business capital by mortgaging their land and houses, and then they rented their land and houses to others and moved to cities with their wives and children. Such a phenomenon was quite common. To avoid potential disputes between supply and demand parties in land circulation, it should be made clear that the land had been mortgaged to banks when the two parties signed land circulation contracts. The fact should not be concealed from the demand party. The mortgage holdings apparently belong to the party that holds the property ownership deed and the repayment of mortgaged loans should be sole responsibilities of the property ownership holder.

(4) Should the establishment of contracted land property ownership and land circulation respect history? If we respect history, what should be the starting point? Should it be1980 or should we trace it before that?

In our survey of some cities and provinces which had carried out the work of establishing land property ownership and practising land circulation, we found that rather than remove historical facts and start from the scratch, we must respect history. But who on earth should be the starting point? The great majority of interviewees believed that the point should be around 1980 when the family household contracted management system started to be promoted and that it should not be traced further back.

The reason is: it has been a long time since the land reform in the early 1950s. Many original records of the land reform do not exist anymore. Over the years, the majority of witnesses who experienced the reform have died. Although some of them are still alive, they are advanced in age and cannot give good accounts of the then circumstances because their memories have faded; even if some are still alive, they are advanced in age with faded memories and they could not tell clearly what had happened. It is aside from the fact that they have experienced institutional changes from agricultural cooperation, established people's communes to "three-tier ownership with brigade as the core" to replacing communes and establishing towns to household contracting etc. It was therefore unrealistic to look before agricultural cooperation or before land reform; it could only disrupt land ownership establishment work and fail to facilitate its development.

In this respect, there must be a clear resolution: all work without exception should start with the rural household contract system; otherwise, people will be stuck in endless disputes family-vs.-family, village-vs.-village, and county-vs.-county disputes. Surely, we also need to solve historical issues from the last 30 years, that is, after the implementation of rural family contract system. For instance, a family had no son but several daughters. When daughters got married one after another and all left home, their contracted land remained at home, not a *fen* of the land was reduced. Another family had no daughters but sons. The sons all grew up and married, but there was nothing added to the contracted land. The latter household voiced complaints. How to solve the problem? If we add contracted land to the latter, where does the land come from? If there are a number of households like the latter and they also require more land, what should we do? Those are practical issues that we will face in the establishment of land rights. There cannot be a unified solution. We can only make an adjustment scheme according to the situation of each particular village. If two parties fail to reach an understanding, the issue can only be laid aside. Originally, there was a policy in some places regarding the contracted land distribution, i.e. "no more land for the increasing population and no less land for the reduced population". That was practised for many years. When there is no new policy, we can only implement the existing one and leave the issue for the future. It is also "respecting history".

We only believe that "the next generation will be wiser than us" and that they will do coordination with great wisdom.

Section 3 Review of Chinese stock-holding system reform and the development of capital market

1 Reconstructing microeconomic foundation as the most prominent issue in China's dual transformation

In the process of transforming from an agricultural to an industrial society, large industrial enterprises were gradually established; however, under the planned economic system all those established were state-owned enterprises. Thus we think, in the process of transforming from a planned to a market economic system, the greatest feature of the Chinese economy is lack of real market entity. Existing and newly built industrial enterprises are all state-owned, being no more than affiliations of the government for having to produce according to government instructions and having no autonomy in business operations.

After the Reform and Opening-up, China must carry out dual transformation, i.e. transforming on the one hand from an agricultural to an industrial society and on the other, from a planned to a market economic system. Two types of transformation overlap. At that time, there were basically two different strains of thought in China. The mainstream held loosening the price should be the focus of the reform, while the other insisted on ownership-prioritised reform. Not enough attention was given to the latter and it was once thought to be a heresy. There was fierce competition between two sides.

The views of the school in favour of ownership-prioritised reform are: in order to realise industrialisation and be transferred into the market economic system, the most important issue is to reconstruct microeconomic foundations of socialism. The only way towards reconstruction is to separate government functions from enterprise management, separate government's public management function from being state enterprises' investors, establish clear land ownership, clarify investment entities; diversify investment entities, transform state-owned and collective enterprises into enterprises with clarified property ownership or property ownership specified to investment entities.

China's stock-holding system reform was finally launched in the late 1980s, but it was launched under academic debate. At that time, main arguments focused on the following five aspects:

(1) The biggest debate was: wasn't the stock-holding system reform privatisation? Those advocating pushing forward the system held that China's stock-holding system reform, whether it was reform of state-owned enterprises, or of collectively owned enterprises, was not simply a behaviour of selling

enterprises to private individuals; rather, it is a behaviour of treating stock and increment separately. State-owned asset stock was first converted into shares but not circulated, while state – owned asset increment, namely, newly issued shares could flow. Then the stock-holding system reform could be launched. In this way, the stock remained still, but the increments preceded. State-owned enterprises were transformed into state-controlled holding (including absolute and relative holding) enterprises. How could that be privatisation?

(2) The debate also lay in whether deficit state-owned enterprises, small state-owned enterprises, the non-key sectors of state-owned enterprises in the national economy could be sold. Advocates of promoting the stock-holding system believed that it was feasible to sell some state-owned enterprises, because the sale was nothing but changes in the form of state assets, namely, changing state-owned assets' physical form into their monetary form while the monetary form could be used for new investments. This did not equal loss of state-owned assets.

(3) Another argument resided in that: it was not appropriate to implement stock-holding system reform in state-owned enterprises with good efficiency; instead, the reform should be first carried out in enterprises with low efficiency. This was the popular saying "A pretty girl shouldn't be married first" at that time. Those advocating stock-holding system reform held that state-owned enterprises, regardless of being operated with good or low efficiency, should both be transferred into the stock-holding system. If we did not allow reform in enterprises with good efficiency, might we ask how long they could sustain themselves in the face of fierce competition? Should we wait until they could sustain themselves anymore and then carry out reforms?

(4) There was still another argument. That is, social burdens of state-owned enterprises were too heavy. The practice that "enterprises ran the society" had been implemented for many years. Once transformed into stock-holding enterprises, state-owned enterprises had to peel off non-operation assets, which might cause social unrest. Those proposing pushing forward the stock-holding system reform thought that the situation, i.e. "enterprises run the society" was a matter that had to be resolved sooner or later. The longer this was postponed, the heavier the weight on the state enterprises' shoulder would become and the more difficulties the enterprises would face when they tried to solve them. It might just as well solve the issue by means of the stock-holding system reform, so that enterprises, instead, would be able to "go to the battle with light packs".[6] Peeling off non-operation assets should be resolved jointly by the government and enterprises, because when state enterprises performed the role of running the society, they assumed responsibilities that should have been fulfilled by the government and profits were over to the government. The government then should not avoid the issue.

(5) Finally, it is worth noting that some people claimed that the biggest issue facing China's state-owned enterprises at that time was that management was not in the right place and its efficiency was low. Then, emphases should be laid on improving management and with such improvement, a great majority of

issues of Chinese enterprises could be solved. On the contrary, people taking their stand on the stock-holding system reform insisted that it should be impor-tant to improve management; nonetheless, advancing management should not replace property ownership reform, as management was an everlasting job and should be emphasised at any time. Property ownership reform and corpo-rate governance structure of enterprises established under the stock-holding system are the premises for improving management level. Furthermore, the biggest barrier that hinders enterprises from raising their management level was the existence of a system where the government and enterprises' obliga-tions were not clearly differentiated, while stock-holding system reform was the right method to push forward the division of obligations. Under heated debate, China's stock-holding system reform evidentially kicked off.

2   Equity division reform: the second revolution in Chinese stock-holding system reform

When the Chinese stock-holding system reform was launched, what was imple-mented was a double-track system, namely separate calculation of stock and the increment. Stock is non- tradable share, while increment is tradable share. Stock reform proceeded, followed by increment reform. Those were obviously temporary measures in accordance with China's situation in dual transformation phase. They greatly reduced difficulties when stock-holding system reform was launched. China finally took the first step on stock-holding system reform, though the practice was not considered to conform to international convention. Neverthe-less, Chinese designers of the stock-holding system reform should not be blamed, for if we wanted to reach our destination in one step and put all our shares in full circulation, the reform would have long stayed at the stage of discussion.

Experience is accumulated at a slow pace; talents are gradually trained and introduced. With experience and talents, there comes the possibility to further reform the stock-holding system.

Approximately 10 years after the launch of stock-holding system reform, the number of stock-holding enterprises (including listed companies) increased, and there was more financing, but no great changes took place in enterprises' opera-tion mechanism mainly due to irrational share structure. Because the state-owned enterprises were restructured into stock-holding enterprises, capital stocking remained static as non-tradable shares, and the proportion of non-tradable shares was generally as large as 70% and above. In some state-owned enterprises, up to 80% or 90% of their total shares were non-tradable. As such, the General Meet-ing of Shareholders could not be held, and small shareholders never attended it. Directors in the Board were unanimously assigned by state-owned enterprises. They did not play any practical role. Therefore, starting from the 21st century, the business, security and academic circles all called for the second stock-hold-ing system reform dealing with the division of tradable and non-tradable shares, namely, unifying the double-track of stock-holding system into a monorail one.

Regarding the equity division reform, one issue has incurred a lot of debate. That is: should the current holder of a certain share be given a certain amount of compensation when it is changed from a non-tradable into a tradable share? Those who insisted on no claim for compensation believed that there was no ground for the compensation and that granting it meant loss of state-owned assets, which would cause damage to China's state interests. Those who insisted on compensation believed that a certain amount of compensation should be given to stock-holders of such a share. The reason was that when this type of stock was listed, enterprises issued a prospectus, where it was clearly written that state-owned shares (non-tradable shares) would not be listed for the time being. It was just with this specification that the premium price soared so high; otherwise, investors would not rush to buy newly-issued shares. At the present, equity division reform started and state-owned (non-tradable) shares were about to be listed, so wouldn't the practice violate commitments on the prospectus? As stipulated in the *Contract Law of the People's Republic of China*, any party who breaches the contract, thereby causing loss to another party, shall be appropriately compensated, or paid to make up the loss. Therefore, compensating a tradable shareholder is well-grounded. As to how much after all the shareholder should be compensated, this should be determined by market, that is, deciding to give "four out of ten", "three out of ten" or "two out of ten" away by negation. Chinese equity division reform was finally promoted smoothly and properly. Non-tradable shares of state-owned enterprises became tradable ones batch by batch at different times.

In the review of the reform process of Chinese stock-holding system, what in particular needs to be mentioned are the 14th National Congress of the Communist Party of China, held in 1992, and the 15th National Congress of the Communist Party of China, held in 1997. At the 1992 congress, it was confirmed that establishing the socialist market economic system would be the orientation of reform, which provided a premise for the advancement of property ownership and stock-holding system reform. At the 1997 congress, it was confirmed that the stock-holding system was a kind of form used for organising modern enterprises' capital, conducive to division of ownership and management power and promotion of enterprises and capital's operational efficiencies. It was also pointed out at the congress that capitalism could use stock-holding system, as could socialism and that it was too rough to say that a stock-holding system was state-owned or privately owned; rather, the key issue was in whose hands shares lay.

As a result, China's stock-holding system reform has progressed quickly since 1997.Large state-owned enterprises, including state-owned commercial banks, have been successively on the way to stock-holding system reform. The second stock-holding system reform in China, i.e. equity division reform was carried out at the beginning of the 21st century.

3 Mobilised initiatives of private capital: preliminary signs of a functional capital market

After China's Reform and Opening-up, the stock-holding system as the basic form of capital organisation was first adopted by township enterprises. In the early 1980s, a batch of stock-holding township and urban collective ownership enterprises were set up in some Chinese cities and provinces by means of folks' buying shares or pooling wealth. The characteristics of stocks were that stocks were transferrable but not withdrawable. However, stock transfer needed to have a venue, a circulation channel and a trading platform. At that time, there were no available venues where investors transferred their holding township enterprise stocks. So such stocks were bought and sold at some farmers' market stalls. There were also people who set up street stalls to buy and sell stocks of township enterprises. Although there was no law for such a trade to abide by, they indeed lasted for a period of time as temporary measures.

Because there were all kinds of issues with non-standard securities, especially that they could lead to such phenomena as fraud and illegal fund-raising, rights and interests of investors could not be protected, so later they were banned step by step. However, this process history illustrates the enthusiasm of those at the grassroots level in stock enterprises and initiatives of investors in buying and selling stocks.

This contributed to the drafting and issuing of the "Securities Law". The Law was initially drafted in 1992 and approved in a high rate in 1998 by the Standing Committee of the National People's Congress (NPC). Since then, China's stock and securities markets were on the track, i.e. having laws by which to abide.

By the beginning of the 21st century, although equity division reform was successively promoted and there has been significant progress, it has just started to mobilise the enthusiasm of private capital. Further development of private enterprises still faces many restrictions. The biggest barrier to hindering folk capital in all walks of life is still the industry access issue. That is, the field access threshold is very high, making the folk capital prohibitive. One after another, "*36 Non-state Economy Articles*" and "*New 36 Non-state Economy Articles*" have been issued, but they did not inspire enthusiasm of private capital as much as they had been originally thought, because such phenomena as "glass door" and "swing door" did not disappear. Instead, various kinds of admitted access thresholds existed in disguised forms; of which some were even raised. On the one hand, high access thresholds are due to industry monopoly and stockholders' unwillingness to give up their privileges and existing benefits. On the other hand, the thresholds might be related to the long-delayed implementing bylaws of "*New 36 Non-state Articles*" and lack of detailing, like some missing details or no detailed regulations in bylaws.

The earlier-noted issues still need to be improved. The incomplete places in bylaws need to be discussed, supplemented and revised to make it complete. At the same time, the role of capital market in mobilising private capital's enthusiasm needed to be further exerted.

In the 20 years following *Deng Xiaoping's* Southern Talk, with the development of China's stock-holding system reform and the development of capital market, capital market's role in promoting structural optimisation has been preliminarily revealed. We can also give some explanations in the following three aspects.

The first effect of the capital market in structural optimisation has been reflected on increment adjustment in recent years. Increment adjustment refers to the process of encouraging emerging eligible industrial enterprises to be listed, or encouraging eligible enterprises with insufficient capacity industry to be listed, or making the two types of enterprises already listed expand their shares and increase their capital.

The second effect is reflected in stock adjustment. Stock adjustment means transforming enterprises with insufficient capacity by merging and reconstruction, and supporting those with great market potentials through technological innovation to be listed in market or merging with enterprises already listed in the same industry.

The third effect is reflected in exerting the function of a delisting mechanism. For instance, some backward enterprises already listed or listed enterprises with severe overcapacity should be forced to exit the market, thus urging those listed enterprises still promising in devoting themselves to independent innovation and industrial upgrading within a relatively short period of time to improve their operation and management. The aforementioned effects in optimising capital market structure are obvious and have been testified in the practice of the Chinese capital market.

However, we cannot deny that capital market so far has failed to play a full role in the structure optimisation. What is the primary cause? We should make a rigorous summary. Generally, there are mainly four reasons, as follows:

(1) China needs a complete capital market system, which normally includes a main board, a small and medium-sized enterprise board, the growth enterprise board[7] and the third board etc. Through efforts in recent years, the main board market has become comparatively comprehensive; the small and medium-sized enterprise board and the growth enterprise board markets are still at a pioneering stage, while the third board market is still in active preparation and some pilot projects have just started and still have not adapted to the development demand of the capital market. There is still a long way before the capital market can play a full role in the aspect of structural optimisation.

(2) For any board in the capital market system, there is a common issue, namely, how to increase information disclosure, how to urge listed companies to be publicised and transparent. That is closely related to investors' increased degree of confidence with the capital market.

(3) The work of security-regulating sectors needs to be in place. Listing standards must be strictly controlled rather than be ignored in approving listings (irrespective of which board). Otherwise, not only will investors be disappointed, but also it will spoil the reputation of the Chinese capital market.

(4) Although speculation is hard to avoid in the capital market, excessive speculation in some boards of the Chinese capital market in the last phase has caused great rises and falls in stock prices and reduced average investors' confidence.

Reasons for the emergence of asset bubbles in the capital market are lack of information disclosure and transparency from listed companies, and securities regulation work out of place. Apart from those, it was also due to, to some extent, the existence of monopolies, the pouring of private capital into the stock market caused by outlet shortage for private capital and excessively high access thresholds without outlets. In this case, speculation behaviour in the capital market should be reduced, and it is necessary to let the private capital have wider outlets, for instance, by lowering the threshold for field access and reducing government's examinations and approvals, including simplifying access level. It is possible to squeeze out part of asset bubbles by allowing more and more private capital to fulfil the potential of investing in the real economy.

4 China's technological breakthroughs and the further role of capital market

What is a new economy? A new economy is technological innovation plus capital market, which are linked to each other, inseparable.

However, as has already been pointed out earlier that at current stage, to make capital market further exert its function, an important issue is to restore a great many investors' in the Chinese capital market. If they lack confidence, not to mention their loss of confidence in Chinese capital market, this will make them successively withdraw their capital from the capital market. What makes us most worried is that when private capital then becomes idle, it will be transferred abroad.

As noted earlier, one of the reasons for investors' lack of confidence is the imperfect capital market itself, and financial supervision's not being in position. Therefore, with respect to this, necessary measures should be taken to make the capital market standardised and legalised. Another reason is that macroeconomic regulation and control should by all means avoid being greatly tight or greatly loose, causing the economy to rise and fall sharply and making investors view the capital market as a fearful path. Note that economic operation is inertial; so is the system, which is called "path dependency" in institutional economics. It means that people are inclined to having dependent psychologies like "following the majority", "following superiors", "following convention", so once a trend has come into being, it is very difficult to reverse it.

What the common saying "to brake is easier than to start" reflects is that as long as the government has implemented a tight policy, and once it is excessively tight, it is not easy to make the economy resume its normal operation. Why do we say that it is easy to "brake"? That is because the initiative of "braking" is under the control of the government. If the government turns to being tight, fiscal floodgates will be closed and so will credit floodgates, and the government's tight policy quickly takes effect, just as a car is braked in action. Why do we say it is difficult to "start"? It is because the initiative of launching the market is not under the control of the government, but under the private consumers and investors' control. No matter how hard the government steps on the accelerator, the car of the market won't start. In other words, as long as consumers do not buy, what effective countermeasures can the government have? As long as investors don't invest, what effective countermeasures can the government have? To put it simply, the government will have to wait. It is only until general customers have restored their market confidence that consumption will gradually recover and it is only until the general investors have restored their confidence in investment prospects that investment will gradually recover. Given this, to restore people's confidence in the Chinese capital market, we not only need the capital market itself to be robust and perfect, but we also need the government to lay more emphasis on fine-tuning and pre-setting its macroeconomic regulation and control. The government should have a sense of propriety and elasticity in regulation and control. A greatly tight or a greatly loose policy should be avoided unless in an emergency; otherwise, do not cause great turmoil or large fluctuations in the capital market, so that the general investors can restore their confidence and faith in the capital market.

At the micro level, the quality of listed enterprises in fact also involves people's confidence and trust in the Chinese capital market. Listed enterprises are public companies. If performances of those enterprises are transparent and strongly competitive, they can gain the public's trust. If the quality of listed companies declines, no matter what measures the government takes, they will not be useful, because enterprises' listing quality is the foundation on which the capital market can survive and prosper.

As can be seen from here, people's confidence and trust in the capital market in terms of quality of listed enterprises is based on overall quality of enterprises. If the quality of most listed companies declines, though it is definitely not good news to investors, as long as it is frankly disclosed to investors, it will not bring about great disturbance. By contrast, if truth is concealed from the public, it will lead to upheaval in the capital market. Moreover, it is easier to let the public lose faith in the capital market and listed enterprise, but much more difficult to rebuild public confidence and trust, which are accumulated over a long period of time.

Next, I will make some supplementary remarks on such issues as how to further exert the role of structural optimisation, improve resource allocation efficiency and make technological innovation etc. To exert the aforementioned role of the capital market, another point, apart from earlier-mentioned content, should be added. That is, general investors, securities practitioners, securities regulators and government staff should rediscover the power of the capital market. Economists, financial and managerial experts are no exceptions. Even experts who have been involved in the establishment and development of the capital market since the Reform and Opening-up also need at present to rediscover the power of the capital market, because great changes in this field have taken place in the last decade. Those who used to be familiar with the capital market are almost shocked at such rapid changes.

That is, renewal of concepts, and conceptual renewal is the companion of financial innovation. Twenty years ago, who could predict the emergence of so many new financial products with such great impact? Practice cannot keep up with conceptual changes; even theorists fail to keep pace with changes in an objective economic situation. Everyone exclaims at this, feeling stressful. What kind of pressure? The pressure of not being able to keep up with the situation.

The power of the capital market is mainly reflected in mobilising and pooling originally idle private capital in all parts of the country into the capital market and using it as investment. Rosy prospects of emerging industries, tremendous power of technological innovation and flexibility in money raising, funding and financing and profit prospects constantly attract private capital investment. These are all unprecedented.

We may as well give several examples.

One is the rapid development of the investment banking business. Investment banks in the world used to be engaged in investment, but later developed and did large-scale acquisitions and mergers. Capital used in investment banks' acquisition and merge relies on bond-issuing. In recent years, investment banks have started to break away from the real economy, specialising in financial services, where investment banks promote a certain kind of financial service programme in response to customer demand so as to satisfy customers' needs. However, the bigger volume of business investment banks have, the greater the risk will be, so that they suffer greater liabilities and losses in international financial environments. Nevertheless, this kind of "speculating in money with money" also illustrates great strengths of the capital market. A success is an investment bank and a failure is also an investment bank. In recent years, Chinese investment banks have developed very quickly and the path is to learn from foreign investment banks and imitate them. Generally speaking, investment banks in China have no more than three major businesses: first, being involved in acquisition, merger and reorganisation; second, helping enterprises to seek financing abroad; third, being enterprise's strategic investors and helping them to make further technological innovation and expand their market. However, they have shared increasing similarities with overseas counterparts (that is, gradually getting away from the real economy) and risks increasingly intensify. If this situation continues, they will be likely to have more serious issues and once there is a big issue, it will do great harm to the Chinese society, for which we must be alert.

The second example is that venture investment rapidly goes toward specialisation. Similarly, venture investment originally prevailed in foreign countries and was introduced from abroad to China. Venture investment was promoted worldwide with the development of high-tech innovation. It is even said that without the development of high-tech innovation, there would be no venture investment, and with venture investment, high-tech innovation has sped up and increased in numbers. Today, many enterprises have developed into high-tech companies on a huge scale. Initially, they were all involved in venture investment and the involvement of venture capital significantly accelerated the development of the high-tech enterprises. China's venture investment began with *Deng Xiaoping's* Southern Talk. Up to now, it has been about 20 years. Although it started late, it has developed rapidly. This mainly depends on three points: first, there were many venture investment opportunities in China; second, people who engaged in the venture investment industry were good at learning from overseas venture investment industry, as they constantly summarised and drew experience and lessons from their overseas counterparts; third, China's venture investors became specialised at a fairly early stage of the venture investment. Specialisation was important. A venture investor who is planning to be engaged in the investment to a certain industry must be an expert in the industry or an expert who is familiar with the industry and he must also have some knowledge of the past, present and future of a certain enterprise which is in operation in the industry, thus being familiar with profit outlook, market extension prospects of this industry and this enterprise and the internal situation of the enterprise. So it is generally held that what venture investment takes a fancy to is not the rate of return at this stage but the rate of return in the long run, not the scale of an industry and enterprises at present but the scale of an industry and enterprises many years from now on.

But whether it is in China or elsewhere, the profit of venture investment always goes hand in hand with investment risks, and such a relationship persists between the two: the higher the profit is, the greater the risk becomes; the smaller the risk is, the less the profit tends to be. What is special, however, about the venture investment industry is: some investment may not bring in any money at all; rather, it will lose heavily. The reasons were: a wrong choice was made on the investing target; there were are too many investors involved in the venture capital investment, or the timing of the involvement was inappropriate, i.e. either being too early or being too late. Another factor was the changes in policies. It is a factor of prime importance to the success or the failure of venture investment. For example, a certain new product was originally thought highly of, but later for various reasons, the policy changed to be unfavourable to the product and the industry. For instance, the government changed from initially supporting the production of a certain product in a certain industry to constraining it from developing and increasing production and so on. Therefore, people engaged in venture capital should be psychologically prepared for this.

5 China's urgent need for new entrepreneurs

From the late 19th to the early 20th century, there emerged a group of Chinese entrepreneurs who were pioneers of modern industry and commerce, composed of officials with new thoughts and concepts, and some private entrepreneurs who aimed at the revitalisation of enterprises. After the founding of the People's Republic of China, China quickly changed into a planned socialist economic system, and there was no mention about entrepreneurs of the planned economy era. Since enterprises were all state-owned, they were all appendages of government departments, and all obeyed the government's instructions. They had no autonomy in business operations. Hence, there were only enterprise officials but not entrepreneurs in the real sense.

Changes took place after the Reform and Opening-up in 1979. Entrepreneurs in New China came into being from then on, but at that moment, they all came from outside the system. They were mainly made up of youths coming back to cities from the countryside, production and construction corps or agricultural reclamation farms, talented people or skilful workmen, and those released and rehabilitated after rededication of wrong accusations. They came across the great Reform and Opening-up opportunity, and some made a fortune.

Since *Deng Xiaoping's* delivery of the Southern talk in 1992, a major turning point has occurred to the Chinese economy, and changed the course of contemporary Chinese history. There have surged great market economy-oriented reform tides with private entrepreneurship enthusiasm mobilised. In China, a batch of new entrepreneurs appeared, who were later called the "Ninety-two Party".

The "Ninety-two Party" were a group of entrepreneurs who grew up under the inspiration of *Deng Xiaoping*'s Southern Talk. Many of them, then very young, had professional knowledge, broad horizons, new management concepts and operation thinking, a world vision, a sound understanding of the significance of a stock-holding system reform and some knowledge of strengths and functions of capital market in the modern economy. Crucially, they were dedicated to institutional, technological and managerial innovation not simply for individual career achievements but more for passion of revitalisation of China and aspiration of getting Chinese economy ranked among the best in the world. The biggest difference between "Ninety-two party" entrepreneurs and those rising after the Reform and Opening-up in the early 1980s was that the "Ninety-two party" were not formed outside of the system, but first grew up within the system and then switched to the outside of the system.

"System" mentioned here refers to the original planned economic system. To be more exact, it refers to the loosened planned economic system. That is because within the rigid planned economic system, people were not allowed to switch from within the system to the outside of the system. After 1992, nonetheless, the socialist market economic system came into being. So those who moved out of the planned economy system switched into the emerging socialist market economic system. The 'inside" or "outside the system' was just approached from this perspective. Note that it is impossible for anybody, as part of a society, to break away from any system and enter a non-system state, unless he was Robinson Crusoe on an isolated island.

The "Nighty-two Party" entrepreneurs are an important group that could reflect China's reform process. They first grew mature within the system and then shifted to the outside of the system. As a result, they knew both the real practice of the economic operation within the system and understood all the sweetness and bitterness of being outside the system. They were good at learning from developed countries' mature experience, and introduced them into blank areas of China's market, becoming pioneers or outstanding figures in the new and high technology industries. All those were achieved in the old-new institutional transition period, and in grey areas of market operation. Thus, they deserved being called "new entrepreneurs". Undoubtedly,

"Ninety-two party" entrepreneurs played an irreplaceable role in the 20 years following *Deng Xiaoping*'s Southern Talk.

Now, the majority of the "Ninety-two party" are about 50 years old. During the past 20 years, they contributed much energy and wisdom and are still struggling in the market and will continue to play a role. However, following them came, much younger entrepreneurs, to be more accurate, one group of future entrepreneurs after another, dedicated to testing waters or finding paths in China's reform and technological innovation. In early 2013, *Qi Bin*, director of the China Securities Regulatory Commission delivered an academic talk entitled *Future Ten Years:*

Transformation and Breakthroughs in the Chinese Economy in a lecture series on China's Capital Market Practice of *Guanghua* School, *Beijing* University. He made the following remarks in his presentation:

On 27 September, 2011, the American *Washington Post* published an article with a very eye-catching title "*What Should Americans Really Fear about China?*" It was said in the article that the real advantages of China lay in her next generation. They just graduated from China's top universities, stepping out of universities into the market to start entrepreneurship. They have become or are about to become entrepreneurs.

Qi Bin quoted a paragraph from the article in the *Washington Post*: a reporter from the *Washington Post* visited a cafe next to *Haidian* Street in *Beijing Zhongguancun* Science Park. In it, there were tens of tables, and around each table were a few young people chatting about entrepreneurship, because innovation has become convenient now with many people working through the internet. The reporter found that 30 years ago in the United States, young Bill Gates and Steve Jobs, like those young people in current China, had just stepped out of the campus into the market and started to set up businesses. In today's China, many grass-roots entrepreneurs will become an important force that propels China's economic transformation.

Isn't there far more than one café in *Haidian, Beijing* which gathers young Chinese entrepreneurs and pioneers? Isn't there only one Science and Technology Park like *Beijing's Zhongguancun* in China? Capital market supports these young innovators and entrepreneurs to grow up to be strong and sturdy. They are the hope of China.

Notes

1 The planned economic system. [Trans.]
2 Refer to Section 3, Chapter 3 for forest ownership system reform. [Trans.]
3 CPPCC stands for "Chinese People's Political Consultative Conference". [Trans.]
4 *Mu* is a Chinese area-measuring unit. One *mu* equals approximately 0.16 acres. In Chinese, *mu* can be used with numerals but conventionally, it becomes unaccountable in English. To solve the clashes here, *mu* is used in plural forms in the translation. [Trans.]
5 *Fen* is also a Chinese area-measuring unit. One *fen* equals 1/10 of a *mu*. [Trans.]
6 Chinese idiom, meaning doing something with less burden. [Trans.]
7 A growth enterprise board market is also called the second board. [Trans.]

2 Coordinated development of state and private enterprises

Section 1 Reform of state capital system

1 The reforms of the state capital allocation system and the state enterprise management system

The state-owned (alternatively state) capital system is divided into two tiers: state capital allocation system at the first tier and state enterprise management system at the second tier. Systems and reforms at different tiers should not be lumped together, making matters confusing.

For many years since the Reform and Opening-up, the reform of state capital system in which we have been engaged essentially focused on the reform of state enterprise management system, i.e. reforms at the second tier, while the reform of state capital allocation system, i.e. the reform at the first tier, has not actually been carried out. Major tasks of the State Assets Administration Committee (CAAC) reside in the supervision and administration of state enterprises. It can even be thought that the reform of the state capital allocation system has been ignored.

Therefore, China's state capital system reform at this phase must be carried out simultaneously at two tiers and the emphasis should be laid on the first tier of the reform (the reform of state capital allocation system). It should not be denied that over the years, great achievements have been made in the reform at the second tier, i.e. the reform of the state enterprise management system. To sum up, we should recognise three achievements.

First, state enterprises have been restructured on the whole into stock-holding enterprises, of which many have also become listed companies. Those enterprises have been involved to various extents in market competitions, adapting themselves to market environments and being tested in market competition.

Second, in recent years, state enterprises, by means of merging, reconstructing and reorganisation of production components and withdrawing from some areas, have eventually achieved initial adjustment in industrial structure, and made more contributions to the socioeconomic development with increased efficiency and rising output values.

Third, in areas pertinent to significant issues of the national economy, state enterprises as the backbone of industries have played an important role in guaranteeing the stability of economic development and ensuring self-governing and independence of the Chinese economy. This was fully reflected in China's state enterprises' overall performances during the Asian Financial Crisis in the late 1990s, the American Subprime Mortgage Crisis and the European Debt Crisis at the end of the first decade of the 21st century.

At the same time, however, we should not ignore that to date, reforms still need to be deepened in many areas of state enterprises' management system. Malpractice or issues in the current state enterprise management system can be summarised into the following points:

(1) Government intervention has been excessive. Up to now, state enterprises have not become a market operation entity in its real sense. Rather, they can be considered "an incomplete market operation entity" at the most.
(2) The management mechanism has been inflexible. This is the outcome of excessive government intervention. Upon initial signs of market fluctuation, state enterprises cannot adapt themselves to changing situation. On the contrary, they have to go through complicated application procedures and wait a long time for high authority's approval. When the approval is granted, situations have already changed with the result that the enterprises end up missing the best opportunity.
(3) Corporate governance structure is incomplete. On the one hand, it was because state stock-holding enterprises hold a high ratio of stock, the Shareholders' Meeting could not be held or even if it was held, the Board of Directors did not function; nor did the independent directors. On the other hand, as it was likely that the management system still followed conventional practice, some secretaries of the Communist Party of China as the first in command played the role of a dictator. Accordingly, the Board of Supervisors could not perform their due role.
(4) State enterprises' drive for innovation was not sufficient and their innovation capability was weak. The most important reason for the phenomena was that due to system and mechanism constraints, state enterprises were reluctant to decide on their own whether to carry out larger technological innovation activities; nor do they have the authority of their own to carry out institutional innovation and managerial innovation experiments. Some senior executives believed that there were risks in carrying out innovation, whether it was technical innovation, institutional innovation or managerial innovation. Therefore, they were afraid of shouldering responsibilities and the general symmetricity between profits and responsibilities. This differentiates state enterprises from non-state enterprises run by private investors. Another important reason was that as state enterprises believed a trade monopoly still existed, there was no rush into innovation.

Give this, if state capital system reform merely stayed at the second tier and had not carried out rigorous reforms at the first tier, i.e. the reform of the state capital allocation system, it would be difficult to make breakthroughs in state enterprise system reforms and existing malpractice or problems in the system would be persistent.

2 Urgency in reforming the state capital allocation system

Why should the state capital and its investment areas be preserved in the socialist market economy with Chinese characteristics? A fundamental reason is that the state capital along with its investment can play a more significant role than private capital and its investment and correspondingly, it also shoulder greater social responsibilities.

One significant difference between state capital and private capital or non-governmental capital is that: to achieve national development strategies, a state should make certain policies to attract private capital to invest in pertinent areas, while private capital has options in making decisions on benefits brought about by the policies. Nonetheless, the priority of state capital is not how beneficial the policies are but its social responsibilities. Even when it faces long rewarding periods and a low return rate, state capital should still invest in accordance with the needs of the country. At the same time, there are investment opportunities which meet the requirements of national investment strategies and can potentially bring high social investment profits but low benefits to the investors. Under such a circumstance, the private investors will make investment decisions after taking a lot of factors into consideration, while state capital shall undertake investment tasks in accordance with the overall interests of the state and its social responsibilities. This is the biggest difference between state capital and private capital.

The special nature of the state capital has determined the direction and actual practice of the state capital allocation system reform. These can be discussed in four aspects.

First, the focus of the reform is on improving the allocation efficiency. The focus of economics has long been on the changes in production efficiency, which is analysed by the ratio of input to output. On the premise of a given ratio of input to output, more input surely brings about more output and less input leads to less output. If input remains the same, the increase in output suggests that production efficiency has been raised. Alternatively, if output does not change, decrease in input also suggests growing production efficiency. In view of this, it is important for any type of investors to pay close attention to production efficiency.

Resource allocation efficiency is efficiency in another sense. Assuming that the investment is given, there may be several ways of allocating resources. If mode A is used to allocate resources, output can be N at a given technical level; if mode B is used to allocate resources, the output is N + 1 at the given technical level. Then Mode B indicates raised resource allocation efficiency. Conversely, if mode C is adopted to allocate resources, there could be N − 1 output at the given technical level, suggesting decreased resources. In light of this, resource allocation efficiency and production efficiency are of equal weight. Therefore, attention paid only to the changes in production efficiency but not to those in resource allocation efficiency does not correspond to the principles of capital use.

The significance of conducting state capital allocation system reform should be crystal clear. However, as time and energy used to be devoted mainly to the reform of the state enterprise management system in the previous phase, no consideration or no substantial consideration has been given to the reform of the state capital allocation system. This has greatly affected the enhancement of state capital allocation efficiency.

Second, the reform can easily mobilise the enthusiasm of state enterprises. Our previous discussion has pointed out the existing malpractice and issues in the state enterprise management system, of which the most prominent are excessive intervention from the government in the economic activities and state enterprises' not becoming the real operation entity of the market. This is to a large extent because key emphases of SAAC were not on raising the efficiency of state capital allocation system; rather, the Committee took over things that state enterprises could do as a market operation entity and made collective decisions through complicated application and approval procedures. The practice did not only make state enterprises easily miss good opportunities but also set back their initiatives. On some occasions, it can also make some enterprises fall into the habit of relying on SAAC for everything. Supposing that the state capital allocation system reform is directly managed by SAAC through the reform of state capital system, state enterprises will become real market management entities and their initiatives and enthusiasm are motivated.

Third, state enterprises will subsequently be committed to the improvement of corporate governance structure. Since state enterprises have become market management entities, a sound enterprise management system should be set up, which involves Shareholders' Meeting, Board of Directors, General Manager and Board of Supervisors. Thus, the state shares do not necessarily hold an absolute majority; however, in the case of dispersive non-state stock-holding, state shares can take a great majority. This actually is to use fewer state shares to obtain the control of enterprises. When there is equity participation in a certain state enterprise from more than one state investment unit investing, several relatively big shareholders may come into being. This can also help to change the structure of the Board of Directors and make it easier for directors to reach rational and democratic decisions.

Fourth, with the establishment of state enterprises as market operation entity of mobilised initiatives of state enterprises and optimisation of cooperate governance structure, changes will also occur to another malpractice or issue of state enterprises, i.e. insufficient drives for innovation and weak innovative capacity. There were mainly three obstacles that stopped state enterprises from innovation. First, the government intervened excessively, which made enterprises lose initiatives and enthusiasm; second, enterprises were concerned that hard work could only bring forth few gains and high risk responsibilities due to asymmetry between responsibilities and benefits; and third, some enterprises relied on trade monopoly in actual life, holding that there was no need for innovation, as they could still make great profits under the protection of trade monopoly. Changes will take place by reforming the state capital system at both tiers. The aforementioned three obstacles unfavourable to the independent innovation will gradually die out, thus leading to tides of future independent innovation, technical breakthroughs and industrial upgrading of state enterprises.

3 Assumptions for the state capital allocation system reform

The objective of the state capital allocation system reform is to strengthen SAAC's power in allocating state capital and remove its power in superintending each individual state enterprise. The preliminary assumptions are as follows:

(1) SAAC will be only responsible for allocating state capital, and maintaining and increasing capitalist value, namely being in charge of increasing the allocation efficiency of state capital.

Specifically speaking, SAAC can set up several national investment funding enterprises based on one trade or several trades, allocate the current state shares to be held by an certain state investment funding enterprise as the state capital that the enterprise has invested into the enterprises, and assign members to the Board of Directors according to the share structure of the state enterprise. If a state enterprise is made up of more than one state investment entity, the investment funding enterprises can assign, according to the share structure, their respective members to the Board of Directors. Then there can be the following system: State Asset Administration Committee – -State Investment Funding Enterprises – State Enterprises.

Under this new system, SAAC will be the superintendent of the State Investment Funding Enterprise (SIFES), while SIFES is the fund-sponsor of state enterprises. State enterprises along with other stock enterprises are the market management entities and the relationships between them are fair competition and partnership. There will be no more prejudice due to system or identity among enterprises.

(2) While in-drawing state shares from state enterprises to their total capital, different SIFESs under the name of SAAC will clean up and appraise debts of the capital of a state enterprise and its operation performances. After some time, they will switch to appraise its capital operation. The appraisals should be regular and their focus should be on the production efficiency and resource allocation efficiency of the particular state enterprise.

It is likely that three options will follow the appraisals: first, maintaining the current status of corporate equity structure; second, gradual withdrawal of part of or all state capital; third, increasing the state capital investment. Operation details involved in the second and the third options will be discussed by the SIFE and the Board of Directors of the particular state enterprise. The reason for the second option is that the state enterprise was in a poor operation condition, its state capital will have to be transferred to other state enterprises to raise resource allocation efficiency or used as capital of newly built enterprises. The reason for the third operation is that state enterprise still has developmental potentials or space and needs new investment shares to raise the state capital allocation efficiency or new capital investment to build a new branch etc.

Withdrawing state capital from a particular state enterprise or adding investment to a particular state enterprise is approached from the perspective of improving the overall efficiency of the resource allocation. It also has the following two effects:

First, generally speaking, the major reasons for mal-operations of a state enterprise rest upon management chaos, low efficiency and insufficient use of equipment. Thus, SIFE's withdrawal of capital can lead to warning effects. That is, if an enterprise does not make any change within a certain time limit and the mal-operation remains the same, the ruling of withdrawal will be honoured.

Second, from the perspective of structural adjustment, the SIFEs can invest their state capital to some underdeveloped or under-expanded areas. For this, some state capital should be withdrawn from some investment areas and private capital should be let in. Alternatively, some enterprises with production capacity shortage need urgent extra investment. From the perspective of structural adjustment, SIFEs can withdraw their state investment capital from some industries and invest it into the areas where it is most needed.

Whether it is the first or the second option, they both meet the objective of SIFEs, i.e. enabling the state capital a higher allocation efficiency and allowing the state capital to play a significant role.

(3) When necessary, SIFEs, by following certain procedures and with the approval of upper authorities, can issue enterprise bonds. This will be funds that SIFEs raise when they need new state capital to promote higher state capital allocation efficiency. The debt services will be under the charge of the state capital investment enterprise which issues the bonds.

When a particular state enterprise needs fund raising, it can also issue its own bonds but these bonds are different from those issued by the State Capital Funding Enterprise. The purposes and debt services of the bonds are under the charge of the enterprise which issues the bonds. There is no difference between these bonds and those issued by an ordinary enterprise.

(4) Why does increasing the state capital allocation efficiency need to carry out the earlier-noted reforms in the state capital allocation system while improving private capital, and folk capital efficiency does not need such a particularly formed institution?

This is because the ownership of state, private and folk capital is different. State capital belongs to the state; private and folk capital belongs to private investors. State capital in the state enterprises does not come from state capital per se. After the state capital allocation system reform, the state capital has been embodied in the quotients of the state shares. They come from the holding of the state shares by State Capital Investment Enterprises. The increased or decreased holding of the state shares, or the withdrawal or investments by state enterprises does not depend on enterprises per se but on different investors with enterprise equity, including one particular or several particular state stock-holding SIFEs, and also investors in other aspects. As a result, the decision-making power on decreased holding, withdrawal, increased holding or new investment lies in investors of state capital, not in state enterprises per se.

Investors of private and folk capital are individuals, or non-governmental investors. They don't need such a complicated set of procedures for decreased holding, withdrawal, increased holding or new investment. Since state enterprises have been share-issuing enterprises or listed companies, they can completely rely on the bond market to realise their own investment intentions. Through trades in bond markets, they can achieve the goal of self-regulating investment structure. They themselves are the decision-makers who can improve their own resource allocation efficiency. So, as long as there is an improved and sound stock market, there will be no need to set up another institute to improve their own resource allocation efficiency.

4 Respective social responsibilities of a two-tier state capital system

After the reform of the two-tier state capital system, the objectives and social responsibilities of SIFEs have been clarified. The objective of SIFEs is to play a bigger and better role in the development of national economy by managing the allocation of state capital, raising resource allocation efficiency, maintaining or increasing state capital value. What SIFEs are most concerned about is state capital allocation efficiency, which is also the rationalisation of economic structure. The rationalisation of economic structure never ends, nor does the improvement of state capital allocation efficiency. Therefore, the working priorities of SIFEs should always be maintaining and increasing state capital value and improving state allocation efficiency.

The primary social responsibilities for an average state enterprise, like those of various other types of enterprises, are providing societies with high quality products and services, qualified personnel and experience. These are also the biggest contributions that it can make to the society. In brief, by providing high quality products and services, the enterprise can increase the market competitiveness of the products and services, continuously expand the market, increase profits and satisfy customers at the same time. If enterprises can improve the quality of employees, their technical level, management and marketing abilities included, the enterprises' further development will be secured. If an enterprise can provide experience applicable to other enterprises, thereby enabling different enterprises to develop together, this will be also a great contribution to the society.

So, do state enterprises (including absolutely or relatively state stock-holding enterprises) differ from other enterprises (non-state enterprises) in performing social responsibilities? The issue can be analysed from two perspectives.

On the one hand, state enterprises as market management entities should be responsible for all investors under the conditions of sound corporate governance structure. It is against the principle of the stock-holding enterprises for state enterprises to consider only the interests of state shareholders and ignore those of other investors. From this perspective, state enterprises must follow resolutions of Shareholders' Meeting and the Board of Directors; otherwise, internal instability will occur. Therefore, the state shareholders and other investors can reach a full agreement on performing corporate social responsibilities, i.e. providing products and services with high quality, increasing competitiveness of enterprises, promoting more talents and supplying experience. In the same vein, increasing enterprise profits, along with performing corporate social responsibilities, is the shared aspiration of all investors and achievable for the enterprises.

On the other hand, if state shares of an enterprise have an absolute or relative holding status, it should take more initiatives in undertaking missions that conform to the national development strategies, even if those missions involve less short-term interest but more long-term interests, less enterprise interest than social interests. As mentioned earlier, if it were not the case, why should there be enterprises with state holding capital? However, even if state enterprises make the investment decision, they should still need to follow certain procedures, illustrating the significance of the engagement and its long-term deployment so as to take advice from investors in all walks of life. Stock-holding enterprises, after all, have a set of procedures. Practice not conforming to the decision-making rules will sooner or later cause internal discord, definitely incurring a negative impact on the future development of enterprises. To achieve national development strategies, state enterprises should comply with market economic rules, fulfilling contracts, and even long-term contracts. Surely, the contracts, even the long-term contracts, should be signed on the condition of fair competition.

In a word, through the establishment of SIFEs and exerting their role, state shareholders of state enterprises are no longer state enterprises per se but SIFEs. Thus, state enterprises as stock-holding enterprises and listed companies are the same as other stock-holding enterprises and listed companies in the operating process. A fair competition pattern between enterprises will come into being.

When we talk about the respective social responsibilities of the two tiers of the state capital system, one point is shared by both SIFEs and state enterprises, namely, paying attention to the environmental security. That is, we have to stress the quality of economic growth.

Today, China, along with many other countries and regions in the world, has noticed that the quality of economic growth is of great significance and that the most important thing in improving quality of economic growth is to decrease resource consumption rate and improve environmental quality. Be aware that indiscriminate exploitation, deforestation and abuse of resources will throw the coming generations into the plight of resources depletion and make even our generation unable to have a normal life due to excessive resources consumption. By the same token, if this generation causes serious damage to environments in the course of industrialisation and urbanisation by letting wastewater flow into the rivers, lakes and bays, so that water becomes polluted, waste gas make the air foul, or waste residues stacked everywhere. . . . People will suffer from incurable diseases and have difficulties in enjoying a healthy life. In this way, the faster the economy grows, the more severely people's living environments will be damaged. Not only is it difficult for future generations to survive, even this generation will face an endangered situation. What is the point of rapid economic development in such an environment?

Therefore, no matter whether state capital system reform is at the first tier or at the second tier, the economical use of resources and cleanness and governance of environments must be considered as important social responsibilities, in which enterprises should not have the slightest relaxation. However, there are differences in whether the earlier-noted social responsibilities are performed at the state capital allocation tier or at the state enterprise tier.

Since the missions of SIFEs are to improve state capital allocation efficiency, and make the established state capital more reasonably allocated so as to achieve the optimised investment structure, they should view the situation globally and implement the tasks of optimising structure so as to both ensure the development of new industries and improve the quality of economic growth, namely, saving resources and control environments, so as to achieve sustainable economic and social development. However, taking merely improving the earning rate of the state capital investment as the primary task of state capital allocation does not conform to the original intention of the state capital allocation system reform.

State enterprises established in the state capital system reform have the same fair competition status as ordinary enterprises. They should all observe state environmental protection and governance regulations and laws. State enterprises as the state stock-holding market economy entity should also take the lead in observing those regulations, performing their due social responsibilities. Other enterprises in the same industry usually set their eyes on state enterprises, believing that the state enterprise should play an exemplary role in complying with regulations regarding energy saving, emission reduction and elimination of environmental pollution. This is a spur to state enterprises and also a kind of expectation. It is hoped that state enterprises will not make many other enterprises disappointed in performing their social responsibilities.

5   Broad cooperative prospects between state and private enterprises after the capital system reform

In recent years, there has been a popular saying in society "State enterprises advance and private enterprises retreat". This mainly refers to conditions during the 2008 American Subprime Mortgage Crisis and the subsequent European Debt Crisis, when many private enterprises whose main businesses were exporting to Europe and the United States stopped production or were closed down. When they were in financial difficulties, the monetary policy tended to be tighter and it became very difficult for them to get loans from banks. By contrast, state enterprises have better financing opportunities, for banks came to their doors one after another, willing to render loans. This is the truth about the saying "State enterprises advance while private enterprises retreat". In the past few years when doing surveys in large and medium-sized cities of *Guangdong, Zhejiang* and *Jiangsu* Provinces, we felt that the saying was evidential and could not be denied.

In addition, we also found a fact in our survey of these years that private enterprises were often excluded from project biddings either because the passage of information was obstructed, thus making the message unable to reach non-insiders or because state enterprises were unfairly treating each participant from private enterprises, therefore making them feel quite grieved. This is one of the points for the popular saying "State enterprises advance while private enterprises retreat".

While the above saying has been popular in society in recent years and there have been frequent cases where private enterprises had not been treated fairly, it should be pointed out that neither "state enterprises advance while private enterprises retreat" nor "state enterprises retreat while private sectors advance"[1] were objectives of government policies. Under the socialist market economic system with Chinese characteristics, both state enterprises and private enterprises should be supported by government policies, competing fairly and developing collaboratively. There should be competition and cooperation between state and private enterprises. Competition is actually a race. Whoever gets ahead in independent innovation, technological breakthroughs or industrial upgrading will expand market shares and become winners. There will be losers in competitions or races and some enterprises will even be eliminated, but as long as they are the outcomes of fair competitions, they cannot but be taken as normal phenomena in the market economy. The bankruptcy of enterprises is also normal. What's more, the enterprise bankruptcy is nothing but the beginning of the reorganisation of production factors. The market economy develops right in the process of continuous reorganisation of production factors.

"Win-win" or "all-win" is the common goal of state and private enterprises. A market place is a battlefield. There is some truth in this remark, for both sides rely on strength, wisdom and even luck. Meanwhile, a market place is not equal to a battlefield, which counts victory as one party being beaten by another; even if one party has surrendered, he will still be eaten up, though by peaceful means. Market places are not like that. Both parties do not necessarily have to strike the opposite party down or eat it up to end a competition; rather, what is more common is the phenomenon of win-win or all-win. It is the same with state enterprises or private enterprises in the market competition, whose goal is also win-win or all-win.

Through the state capital system reform, state enterprises as market entities share an equal status to non-state enterprises. Discrimination against ownership no longer exists. All enterprises are equal before the law. Whether they are state or privately owned, enterprises that go abroad are all Chinese enterprises; whether they are created by state or private enterprises, some brands are all national brands. Each enterprise has done its outmost for the economic development of China and contributed its intelligence and wisdom to the prosperity and progress of China. Therefore, discrimination against ownership is groundless. Assuming this is a habit in the society and it has been formed over years, then it should be clearly pointed out that the outdated opinion or view was due to the legacy that "an official business is greater than a private business" in the feudal society or the view that "state business is superior in the planned economic system". Now, if SIFEs, through the reform of the state capital system at two tiers, are set up at the first tier, they will take charge of the allocation and re-allocation of state capital, increase, on the premise of maintaining value or increasing value, allocation efficiency of the state capital as the objective, adjust the ratio of state shares in a certain state enterprise to total enterprise shares by either increasing holding or reducing holding, or withdrawing holding completely or building up new enterprises. In this way, state enterprises at the second tier (including absolute or relative stock-holding enterprises) become real market operation entities. They enjoy the same status as the other enterprises with both competitions and cooperation between them.

Competition between state and private enterprises has been long-standing, conforming to the law of the market economy. Without competition, there would be neither innovation nor new market shares. Likewise, cooperation between state and private enterprises is long-lasting. This also conforms to the law of the market economy. Private enterprises in many aspects are cooperative partners or units supplying accessories or parts for state enterprises. One industrial chain has many links, which involve a good number of suppliers and processing units, among which there are both state and private enterprises. State enterprises are inseparable from their collaborators, the private enterprises and vice versa.

Ultimately, the greatest outcome of state enterprises through the state capital system reform at two tiers will be that they have become real entities of market operations. Like other stock-holding enterprises and listed companies, state enterprises will set up a perfect and sound cooperative governance structure and perform their functions through Shareholders' Meetings and Boards of Directors. They will make their own decisions and the government sectors will no longer directly intervene. The state enterprises have more independent participations in market activities with extensive cooperation with private enterprises included. This is a predictable prospect.

Section 2 Property ownership protection and institutional transformation of private enterprises

1 Current difficulties encountered by private enterprises

In recent years, Chinese private enterprises have encountered many difficulties. They can roughly be summarised into eight aspects according to surveys done by the Economic Committee of the 11th CPPCC in several eastern, central and western provinces, municipalities and autonomous regions.

First, costs have risen with a rise in the labour cost in particular. This is mainly because the growing living costs pushed up wages. At the same time, there even occurred difficulties with recruitment in some places. Why did enterprises find it difficult to recruit employees? According to surveys, farmers in several southwestern provinces of China believed that wages for migrant work did not rise substantially in coastal provinces in comparison to wages in the last few years, and that the travel distance was too far and that commodity prices were much higher. Therefore, it would be better to live nearby and employment would make their livelihoods much easier then migrating to the coastal provinces. While wages in some places rose, the housing prices, living costs and the fees for raising their children and costs for education fees would rise at a faster speed than before and the costs of return journeys to visit their parents and family would be rising as well. Private enterprises generally felt that it was easy to manage their businesses under the pressure of rising labour costs and recruitment.

Second, due to international economic turmoil, private enterprises who were operating export businesses generally felt that the orders dropped substantially and that it was increasingly difficult to carry on their businesses. Moreover, the sovereign debt crisis in some Western European countries continues to spread and its negative impact on Chinese exports still exists, so it will be difficult for private enterprises in export businesses to recover soon.

Third, the speed of appreciation of the RMB exchange rate continued. It was another blow to the export businesses of private enterprises and it has increased private enterprises' difficulties.

Fourth, the financing issue has so far failed to be mitigated. Private enterprises reported one after another that getting loans from financial institutions was as difficult as it used to be and they had to turn to unofficial private loans. Moreover, the more difficult it is to borrow money from financial institutions, the higher the private loan interest rates will be. However, even though the private loan rates are very high, private enterprises have no other choices but to bear them.

Fifth, the expenses of taxation are still heavy. For example, value-added taxes are high; so are sales taxes, but fees are even higher. The so-called saying that "taxes have shores, while fees are endless" has been the consensus among enterprises. It is in this case that the private enterprises reflected that if this situation proceeded like this, they simply could not carry on.

Sixth, mutual arrears are destructive to the normal market order. There are numerous ramifications between the businesses of private enterprises. However, as long as the capital chains and industrial chains are still smooth, the market order will not be in great turmoil and enterprises are still able to conduct their businesses even if the enterprises have come across some operation difficulties. On the contrary, when financing is difficult and the financing costs are exceedingly high, some private enterprises were caught in the capital chain rupture, which will lead to industrial rupture sooner or later. As a result, issues like mutual arrears, various service fees and project payments turn up and the normal market order is damaged. The areas of inflection will be enlarged and they will be difficult to put back to order. Some enterprises have no other choice but turn to folk debit and credit sides. However, this will not ease the situation. With the burdens of interests becoming heavier and heavier, they will finally crush the enterprises. Some owners of private enterprises "tread the ground", or hide themselves, or go abroad to avoid their debtors, which will make the arrears even more difficult.

Seventh, to date, although "36 Non-state Economy Articles" have been publicised for eight years, the principle of fair treatment of private enterprises has not been implemented. For instance, access restrictions have persevered either covertly or overtly. "No restriction means permission" is simply an empty remark. Furthermore, private enterprises are still being discriminated against in the government's purchase bidding etc. The unfair treatment of the private enterprises reduced not only private enterprises' operation enthusiasm but also the investment enthusiasm of private capital holders, which further hinders the normal operation and development of private enterprises.

Eight, the examination and approval of extension projects and new construction have become even more cumbersome and stricter and more stamps need to be affixed than several years ago. These are the actual situations reported in many places. The practice which is called excessive administrative intervention and choking restrictions in relation to private enterprises has made some private enterprises lose their confidence in business prospects.

The difficulties in the above analysis have resulted in a serious consequence, that is, the gradual withdrawal of private capital from the real economy, because the private owners are concerned that if they continue to stay in the real economy, they will end up in the trap that "the more one produces, the more losses he will suffer". In that case, they will not be able to pull themselves out of it, even if they want. But after they withdraw from the real economy, where will they invest their capital? There are only three possible directions.

First, move their businesses abroad, including Southeast Asian countries which have comparatively lower labour costs, so that they can set up their plants or merge local business, or move to the United States, Canada or Australia and wait for opportunities to restart their businesses.

Second, move to the virtual economy and undertake speculation and speculate on whatever is popular.

Third, decide when is the best time to withdraw from the market and give out loans or rent out property, so that the capital does not become idle.

All these are not conducive to the development of the Chinese economy, nor to the private economy itself.

2 *Private enterprises' difficulties in relation to property ownership protection*

The analysis above is about various difficulties encountered by private enterprises in business operation. Next, I will talk about their difficulties from the perspective of property protection.

According to surveys done in some places, there are roughly four types of difficulties.

(1) Some local government sectors did not honour their own credibility and failed to fulfil their commitments when they dealt with the investment and production of private enterprises, which made private enterprises suffer great losses. For instance, when attracting private capital from other localities to make initial local investment, some local government sectors made many

commitments. Nonetheless, once the private capital flew in, the project construction was started or the construction was completed and put into operation, the superintendents of the government sectors were posted away and the new superintendents refused to recognise commitments or contracts made or signed by their former counterparts. Everything had to start from scratch. The private enterprises had no say in this matter and it was too late to withdraw their capital. The poor behaviour of local government sectors and their superintendents made the investors of private enterprises complain bitterly.

(2) Government sectors asked private enterprises to provide charitable help in the name of public service facility construction, public utility works development and cultural, educational and public health facility construction and some of them were unalterable quotas. Otherwise, the government sectors would create difficulties for private enterprises in various names, even summoning private enterprise owners for interrogation, arresting them or confiscating their personal properties, which were blackmails and extortions in disguised forms, disregarding the law. Under such conditions, private enterprises had no other choice but to "donate".

(3) On the pretext of some illegitimate procedures, incomplete formalities or insufficient documents in private enterprises' preparation and organisation processes several years ago, the government sectors opened the old accounts, liquidated them and issued their solutions, though there were then regulations and conventions. As a result, private enterprises were accused of seizing state or collective property and their properties were completely or partially confiscated.

(4) Local government sectors sometimes first intimidated private entrepreneurs with such accusations as "being involved in underworld", "colluding with the leader of the underworld", or bribery, and if entrepreneurs did not give in, they would arrest them on the above-mentioned charges and confiscated their personal properties. Once this occurred, it was useless to make an appeal.

These four type of difficulties occurred in some places in China. It is unclear how many times more harm has been done to private enterprises and the entrepreneurs per se than various kinds of losses that they suffered in the business operation processes.

3 How to mitigate difficulties encountered by private enterprises

(1) The issue of property ownership protection

Mitigating the aforementioned difficulties encountered by private enterprises should not rest solely upon private enterprises per se; the government should also envisage its own responsibilities and make relevant and pertinent countermeasures. The government should act on laws and regulations particularly in relation to the protection of property rights and rectify its position in the market economy. The government should not be above the laws and regulations. Nor should it disregard them. This is the most important measure for the development of the private economy and the strengthening of entrepreneurs and private capital holders' investment and operation confidence.

Laws must be observed and lawbreakers prosecuted. The government must manage state affairs according to the laws. Officials, regardless of their ranks, must obey laws and regulations. Personal views shall not be put above laws. Neither should the power of an individual. There should be no such case as is in the saying "Power is superior to laws". This guarantees that the enthusiasm of private enterprises and private entrepreneurs can be motivated.

Everybody should honour credibility, to which government at all levels is no exception; nor are officials at different ranks. It is groundless for a new superintendent of a local government to scrap a contract signed by his former counterparts and private enterprises, as the contract is under legal assurance. If the new superintendent thinks that there are indeed unseemly clauses in the signed contract causing damage to state interests, or even involving bribery, he should go through certain procedures and resolve the issues via the court. It is not the new superintendent who has the final say. Justice should be fair. It is only judicial fairness that brings obedience of the general public.

Handling delimitation of property ownership and property ownership disputes should be based on the pertinent fair and reasonable regulations and conventions of that time. They should not be dealt with by seizing state and collective property using false pretexts. Everything should be based on facts. If the initial practice was not reasonable, they should not be exaggerated; nor should they be compressed. Wherever additional payment is required, request the payment and receive it; wherever fines are demanded, collect them; wherever compensation is necessary, get it; whatever belongs to enterprises, give it to them. Only in this way, can the prestige of the local governments be established and the issues left over by history be properly addressed.

To sum up, the protection of property ownership should be treated as a primary issue that is related to the future healthy development of private enterprises. If deprivation of private enterprises' property ownership which occurs at somebody's free will is not handled according to the law, damages will not be trivial. This will force private enterprises to know when the best time is to close down. That is, they will no longer trust the government; instead they will withdraw their capital once occasions serve, move abroad, idle their capital or turn themselves from capital holders to rentiers.

(2) The transformation of government functions

Many difficulties encountered by private enterprises in the economic operation are related to the government's persistence on its past practice. As it stands, the function of the government under the socialist market economic system lies in the government minding its own businesses, i.e. minding issues that the market cannot do or is not able to do, for instance maintaining market order or upholding the principle of fair competition. However, in reality, the government "the visible hand" is marked as "being hands that never idle". Interventions from the government are comprehensive. There are many things that do not need the government intervention; nevertheless, the government will never leave them alone. Too many examinations and approvals result in the government's choking management. For instance, if a private enterprises wants to get access to a certain field and make an investment, or is prepared to enlarge production scales or start a new project, the examination and approval procedures are very complicated. Applications need to be reported to one department after another. Some private entrepreneurs complained at one symposium: "One more procedure comes with one more stamp and one more stamp will bring in a "reward." The "reward" is the benefits of the administrative body and its staff. So cancelling or simplifying examinations and approvals was what the enterprises called for at the symposium. If the government does what it is supposed to do, private entrepreneurs will surely applaud and shout "Bravo".

(3) On trade monopoly

Since the issue of "36 Non-State Economy Articles", the phenomenon of trade monopoly has caught people's attention, voices of criticism like "glass door" and "swing door" have been lingering, which suggests that trade monopoly has by no means disappeared. Where lies the key point that stops the issue from being solved? When conducting surveys, we heard three different accounts:

First, bylaws have not come into being. Shortly after the publication of "New 36 Non-State Economy Articles", private enterprises called on the issue of the bylaws at the first opportunities. Although some bye-laws had been publicised, private entrepreneurs in pertinent fields argued that those bylaws were too general and vague to solve any issue concerning admitted access to certain areas.

Second, it is held that the difficulties in solving admitted access to certain areas is mainly related to regional protectionism. Specifically speaking, to protect local enterprises, notably state enterprises, local governments of some places did not admit private entrepreneurs in other localities to set up new factories in the local areas due to concerns that local enterprises would be defeated by private enterprises that had newly joined the trade and were very competitive. This kind of regional protectionism tendency basically neglected "36 Non-state Economy Articles" or "New 36 Non-state Economy Articles". The local government acted upon their own will and closed their doors to private enterprises.

Third, trade monopoly under the pretext of raising admittance threshold generally proclaims to outsiders that a certain trade has never limited the access of qualified private enterprises and that it is only because they are not qualified that access is not admitted. Therefore, no permitted access is because "lowering qualification examination standards" does not serve state interests. Sectors which oppose the access of private enterprises even propose that trade monopoly does not actually exist and what exists is a trade qualification examination. Private enterprises applying for admittance will be granted access as long as they wait until they have passed the qualification examination.

These three accounts all sound plausible. As a result, they have all become the shield of those who avoid "trade monopoly". In fact, up to now, the phenomenon of "trade monopoly" has continued in China. All the accounts which pretentiously avoid the existence of trade monopoly have suppressed the truth. How should we resolve the difficult issue? The key still lies in government's reform resolutions and measures. We need to select areas for good breakthroughs and the breakthroughs should be in key areas like energy, railway, finance etc. Private enterprises should have faith in this.

(4) Tax cuts

One of the difficulties for private enterprises in business operation is that taxes and fees are overcharged. The solution to this issue similarly lies in the government's resolutions in tax system reform and reform measures.

When discussing informally with private entrepreneurs, we asked: "Within the two difficulties, overloaded taxes and fees, and financing, which do you think should be tackled first?" Nearly all of them responded at once: "Taxes and fees should be tackled first." And they explained: "Financing is surely difficult but deficit and loss in the business operation cannot be solved by simply relying on the single measure of convenient financing. If taxes and fees are still so heavy, what is the point of financing? Taxes are heavy and so are fees. Fees on the top of taxes are like frost topped on snow. We will sooner or later close down." Those remarks reflected what reality was like and also how disappointed they were.

According to a survey, the security of property rights was ranked first in the sequence of urgency, which was thought by private entrepreneurs to be the most important issue. To them, if property rights were not delimited or even protected, properties could even be seized overnight. Would there not be any other issue that needed to be solved more urgently than this? In the sequence, reducing the loads of taxes and fees ranked second. Private entrepreneurs held that as the taxes and fees were so heavy that they could not make profits, as they were even running at a loss. The more they produced, the more they lost. If things continue this way, what can we say about enthusiasm? Then next in the sequence were financing, rising costs for production component, excessive and choking management of the government and the issue of admitted access to some areas. Note that the sequence was found in not only one city. It is likely that those are comparatively prevailing issues.

(5) Financing difficulties

Difficulty in financing has been long-standing. Entrepreneurs, academia and grassroots government sectors have appealed for solutions to private enterprises, medium-sized, small and micro-enterprises' financing difficulties for many years. Nevertheless, even up to now, the issue has not been effectively resolved. A careful analysis reveals that the difficulty is related to issues of the enterprises per se (for instance, an overspread stall, low efficiency in capital use, imperfect operation and management and lack of appropriate deposits etc.) and also to those of financial institutions (for instance, the upward movement of financial business gravity and the lack of major financial institutions at the grassroots level; high loan costs for small enterprises, concerns that when mortgaged loan cannot be repaid, financial organisations will have no way of handling mortgages like housing and land, and attending to human relations and taking in gifts or cash from the part of the staff of the financial institutes, who are responsible for the loans etc.). In whatever sense, the government should also undertake certain responsibilities. Those difficulties mainly reflect the fact that although the relevant government sectors have discussed the issue and have not resolved them due to the lack of solid financial reform measures, the issue of financing difficulties, which have been appealed to by entrepreneurs and academia for many years, remain unsolved through financial reforms. Private enterprises reflected that as long as the government was greatly determined, the issue of private enterprises' financing difficulties should be solvable. Then, why did the authorities fail to come up with financial reform schemes satisfactory to both private enterprises and financial institutions? This question is quite complicated and indeed needs to be carefully planned in an overall manner and should not be approached by attending to one side and ignoring the others. The reform measures should not cause credit inflation, which leads to macroeconomic imbalance; nor should they cause the rise of bad debt rate, affecting financial security.

Ultimately, the fundamental cause is still the lack of top-level design, which makes it impossible for financial reform plans perfecting the mature market economic system to be introduced on an earlier date. Similarly, protecting property ownership, shattering trade monopoly and reducing enterprise taxes all need top-level designs. No temporary remedies will be able to solve fundamental issues.

4 Private enterprises' institutional transformation

The previous section has mainly discussed how government should help private enterprises to overcome some current issues. We believe that as long as the government is determined to follow the top-tier arrangements and implement them step by step, private enterprises will not only overcome current difficulties but also greatly enhance their confidence and create good conditions for their future development.

Then, how should private enterprises from their own perspective make self-adjustment and self-improvement to adapt to changes in the new situation? Will private enterprises be able to adapt to new situations by stagnating and still following previous developmental patterns? This is definitely infeasible. As a result, the system for private enterprises' transformation will naturally turn up.

While the transformation of the private enterprise system has become urgent, many private enterprises, as has been known, have not come to realise the necessity. In a nutshell, private enterprises are in urgent need of institutional transformation. That is, the private enterprises are in great need of transforming their mode of development. Enterprises, whether they are state or private enterprises; whether they are listed companies in the motherboard market, small and medium-sized enterprise board market, or the growth board market, or family enterprises that still preserve traditional forms, all need to transform their mode of development to achieve institutional transformation.

The change in the enterprise development mode is in line with that in macro-economic development and they are integrated with each other. From the mac-roeconomic tier, the pursuit for the quantity of GDP should be changed to the pursuit for the quality of GDP, namely quality of economic growth or changing quantitative growth into efficiency growth, changing the structural imbalanced state into optimised structure. This has been the law of macroeconomic develop-ment. Enterprises must change their development mode correspondingly. If enter-prises still maintain their previous mode of development which attached more importance to output value and the expanse of operation scales rather than to the pursuit of quality, valuing the ratio of costs to profits, emphasis on ecological protection and environmental governance and achievements in self-innovation and enterprise upgrading, difficulties will amass and enterprises will be eventu-ally excluded from the market. As the market is merciless, what is the point of financing if enterprises are not devoted to changing their development mode? And what is the point in gaining freer access to the field? The fate that awaits those enterprises which insist on the traditional development mode can only be stopping production, bankruptcy, being merged or being reconstructed. Be aware that the prerequisite for all these should be the transformation of the private enterprise system, i.e. the transformation of the mode of development. If private enterprises can successfully transform themselves, richer and easier financing conducive to the enterprise development will come about. In the same vein, it is self-evident that if the mode of development of private enterprises is transformed smoothly, admitted access will be broadened and this will speed up enterprise development.

Why dos the private enterprises' change in the mode of development mean the transformation in system? This can be analysed from two perspectives.

On the one hand, changing enterprises' mode of development and the great development after the mode change are both directly related to the clearly-estab-lished property ownership and the explicit delimitation of the ownership. Property ownership disputes and infringement are inevitably attributed to the responsibili-ties of the government (for instance, the government tears up original contracts or new administrators of the government sectors refuse to acknowledge previous commitments etc.). However, they also have something to do with enterprises per se. For instance, from the time that private enterprises were established, prop-erty ownership was unclear. Nobody knows for sure whether it was ever clearly defined. Even after they became listed companies, old problems were not clari-fied. Thus, various kinds of property right disputes occurred. These are what hin-der the future development of private enterprises. They may even drag private enterprises into the "property ownership trap", making them unable to pull out for a long period of time.

Therefore, one important task in private enterprises' institutional transforma-tion is to establish the property ownership, namely making clear the property ownership and the investment entity. The listed companies should comply with the listed standards and the structure of the share rights should be open and trans-parent. The unlisted companies should also have clear property rights in order not to let the unclarified ownership cause obstacles in the future development. The vague property rights of some family enterprises may not have disputes or conflicts today. However, who can guarantee that there will not be any trouble forever? The earlier and the clearer the property ownership is, the better things will be. This has been proved by many facts,

On the other hand, changing enterprises' mode of development and the ensuing great development after the change are also closely related to the democratisation and scientification in the enterprises' decision-making. The listed companies among the private enterprises must establish perfect corporate governance structure and standardised decision-making procedures to help with their decision-making on significant events. If corporate governance structure is not perfect but practically performs no function, they must be reformed and this is institutional transformation. If family enterprises or private enterprises have not been reformulated into listed companies or are still controlled by "parents", this kind of decision-making is traditional. Even if "parents" are people with ability and experience, their experience may be wealth or may also be a burden which causes enterprises a lot of difficulties. So family enterprises should follow the route of democratic and scientific decision-making. In addition, the equity and management rights are not born into a natural unity, they can be separated or unified and the separation is a norm. The unity of equity and management is conditional. This applies to family members. Entering the administration and supervision authorities is conditional for everyone. The entry should be in accordance with rules of procedures; otherwise, there will be disruption in the future administration and operation of the enterprises, which may lead to the split of family enterprises. The manager system has been adopted by more and more family enterprises, where managers are employed from outside the family or from within the family members. Generating managers within the families should also follow the rules of procedures.

The earlier-noted two perspectives tell us that the change in the mode of development in private enterprises includes establishing property ownership, explicitly delimiting the property rights and also the democratisation and scientification of decision-making of the enterprises. Only in this way can an enterprise meet with the requirements of a modern enterprise. Fortunately, many family enterprises have recognised this view. They are willing to retain the form of family enterprises; or be changed into family-controlled listed family; or not be listed for the moment but get property rights more clarified; and get business decisions of the enterprises more democratic and scientific.

All these have become the consensus of the enterprises.

5 *From small proprietors' consciousness to modern entrepreneurs' philosophy*

Since China's Reform and Opening-up, there have emerged a large number of entrepreneurs, who are usually called "grassroots entrepreneurs". "Grassroots" means ordinary people at the bottom layer of the society.

These "grassroots entrepreneurs" are in general conceptually renovated twice. Initially, they had strong small farmer consciousness', which is featured as having a narrow vision, only targeting sufficient food and clothing, conservative behaviour, and adherence to the belief that no rich water should flow into outsiders' field. Even if they have set up their small businesses, they are easily contented, feeling that life could be stopped here. This is a common phenomenon at the beginning of the reform.

Market is the place where people can be educated and nurtured. Those "grass-roots entrepreneurs" who initially bore strong small farmer consciousness grew up out of the market struggles, had market concepts and were equipped with businessman consciousness and proprietor consciousness. This is the first renovation in concept, namely going from small farmer consciousness to businessman consciousness and proprietor consciousness. The major difference between the two types of consciousness is that the businessman consciousness and proprietor consciousness have a deeper and wider understanding of the market. The farmers have a strong view of predestination. That is, they strongly believe that their fate is held in the hand of Heaven and that they can only depend on Heaven for food and live by obeying their predestined fate, so that they are contented with small fortunes, reluctant to leave their homeland and life will be enough as long they can be self-sufficient. Unlike farmers, one most prominent change after the "root entrepreneurs" have had small businessman and small proprietor consciousness is that they know that it is possible to change their fate if they struggle in the market and that market is the place where they can change their fate. It is right because of this that "root entrepreneurs" are confident of the future prospect. In adversity, they know that as long as they rely on their hard work and learn from their counterparts and seize opportunities with the help of friends, they will build up their business step by step and achieve their career success. Thus, the "root entrepreneurs" from the bottom layer of the society all grow wealthy by relying on their own or their family members' hard work. They are not satisfied with the primary accumulation; rather, they always want to enlarge their production scale, leave their home and expand their business in a broader market.

Nonetheless, there is still a big gap between the small businessman consciousness, small proprietor consciousness and the ideas of modern entrepreneurs. Not a small number of "root entrepreneurs" will stay on this phase after they travel a distance on the road. Although to them, they were no longer what they used to be, they started to feel puzzled, not knowing what the next step should be. Then they had the idea of "stopping as it is enough". They started to lower their initial entrepreneurial ambitions after several market turmoils, or had the idea of "leaving off" at the best time after they experienced several setbacks themselves, or witnessed their colleagues suffering from one setback after another.

By contrast, some "root entrepreneurs" continued their struggles in the market and marched forward to achieve their goal of being new entrepreneurs. They experienced a second conceptual renovation. That is, they were changing their small business and small proprietor consciousness into the concepts of modern entrepreneurs.

What are the concepts of modern entrepreneurs? The concepts can be summarised into four characteristics, which deeply distinguish the concepts of modern entrepreneurs from small businessman consciousness and small proprietor consciousness.

(1) Consciousness of property ownership

It is not right to say that small farmers, small businessmen and small proprie-tors have no consciousness of property ownership. "Grassroots entrepreneurs" did not lack property right consciousness when they experienced changes from small farmer consciousness to small business consciousness and small proprie-tor consciousness. They knew which properties were theirs and which were not. If their properties were invaded and seized by others, they would strive to safe-guard them. Yet, they usually looked at this from a traditional concept of property. They lacked the property ownership consciousness in the operation of modern enterprises. For example, the merger of enterprises and capital reformulation are the beginning of the reformulation of production components, which cannot be treated simplistically as the loss of property. If there is loss in the property rights, the loss has existed before the merger and reformulation. Nevertheless, the refor-mulation of production components is just the beginning of the refunctioning of the property rights. In addition, the bankruptcy of enterprises is undoubtedly the loss of property rights but it is only through the bankruptcy of enterprises that the further loss of property rights may be avoided. Furthermore, it is easy to establish current property ownership after the enterprises have been changed into listed companies, so that it is easier to define the current property rights, further expand property values and prepare conditions that can bring in more production value and property rights. Therefore, in the operations of modern enterprises, a new understanding of the role of property ownership will contribute to the growth and development of the enterprises.

(2) Risk awareness

Modern entrepreneurs should be good at estimating investment and operation risks but more importantly, they should be good at taking ventures and initiating new businesses, because it is always hard for any investment or business to evade risks. Dare not the entrepreneurs take risks whenever they encounter risky invest-ment projects? Do they shrink back from them? Do you stop stepping forward? If yes in those cases, nothing can be accomplished. Modern entrepreneurs should have the courage to invest and dare to innovate – that is, dare to take ventures. It is certain that risks should be carefully assessed but assessments do not always con-form to the reality. Moreover, it is only afterwards that people know how much the innovation profits are. This is because innovation occurs where no predecessors ventured. An entrepreneur without risk awareness is unlikely to become a modern entrepreneur.

(3) Consciousness of innovation

Entrepreneurs and innovators are synonyms in economics. Innovation enables potential profits. The person who is innovative must have the vision to spot where the potential profits are, have courage and dare to take ventures and possess the organising capacity to combine production factors and generate high efficiency. These are prerequisites for becoming entrepreneurs. The differences between modern entrepreneurs, and small businessmen and proprietors lie in this: modern entrepreneurs must understand both the necessity and urgency of innovation, be engaged in innovation, have the courage to make innovation, establish their business and brands by relying on innovation and expand the market shares by constant innovations.

(4) Consciousness of teamwork

A team is collective in two aspects. One is the enterprise team, which consists of science and technology research and development personnel, administration personnel, operation personnel and the broad masses of workers. The other is the team which consists of other enterprises in the same trade. If they are "going-abroad" enterprises, they constitute a Chinese enterprise team, where state and private enterprises are not differentiated. A team depends on the sense of identification with which comes cohesive force, and owing to cohesive force, there forms team competitive capacity. Teams or team consciousness in whatever sense is necessary. In this sense, a successful modern entrepreneur is never struggling alone. No matter how intelligent, capable and hardworking the entrepreneur can be, he can't achieve anything great alone; rather, he must rely on his team, knowing how to form teams and make their teams play an efficient role.

As the saying goes "small fortunes are obtained by diligence, moderate fortunes by opportunities but great fortunes by wisdom". This does not mean that hard work and opportunities are not important for great wealth; it just means that great wealth surely needs hard work and opportunities, but more importantly, it relies on wisdom, great wisdom. Where is great wisdom embodied? It is embodied in the entrepreneurs' essential consciousness of the property rights, risks, innovation and teamwork.

Section 3 Deepening financial reforms

It has been more than three decades since China launched the Reform and Opening-up in 1979. Through the Reform and Opening-up, great achievements have been made in the transformation from the socialist planned economic system to the socialist market economic system, and the market mechanism has taken primary shape. Nevertheless, the self-adjustment mechanism under the market system is still not perfect; rather, it relies on excessive administrative intervention and macroeconomic regulation and control to take effect.

Finance is an obvious example. For instance, during the transitional period, it is right because of the imperfect economic operation mechanism under the market system that the economy always fluctuates violently. Thus, there has been a long-standing phenomenon – the "impulsive investment circle", where investment and credit volumes are expanded blindly, resulting in an excessive amount of currency in circulation, and leading to investment-pulled inflation where commodity prices keep rising. With regards to this, the Central Government has to switch to tight measures, reducing investment and loans and cutting the currency amount in the circulation. With the decline of the amount of currency in circulation, the price-rising tendency is finally suppressed. As such, there appears another phenomenon, i.e. decrease in the economic growth rate and increase in unemployment rate (even though China has only a registered urban unemployment rate at present. This is because farmers with contracted land are assumed to be in full employment; thus, the registered urban unemployment rate does not include migrant farmers who have left or lost their land or migrant farmers who have already moved into cities and towns but are under unemployment and no-employment conditions). With a decrease in central and local fiscal revenues, the central government has to loosen the monetary policy again to stimulate economy, increase credit loans and the amount of currency in circulation. Then the situation resumes the loose condition before the tightening, predicting that another inflation will come again. Then this circulates with big rises and great falls. The "impulsive investment circle" phenomenon has never disappeared. This indicates that the endogenous mechanism cannot really perform its adjustment functions due to its incompleteness during the period of China's institutional transformation. It is only through administrative intervention and macroeconomic regulations and control that the economic operation is maintained.

The above are the essential understanding of the necessities of deepening financial reforms in China.

1 Objectives of financial reforms

Following the earlier discussion on the necessities of deepening financial reforms, we should be clear: what is the objective of financial reforms in China? How can we gradually achieve the objective? What are the major obstacles to the objective?

With respect to China's financial reality and financial institutions' role under the socialist market economic system, the objective of deepening financial reforms should be defined in terms of an overall objective, a financial institutional objective and a financial structural objective. This is because the three objectives are respectively the macro, micro and structural objectives. They form a perfect system and specify the reform tasks. The combination of the three can reflect a panoramic picture of China's financial future and its general trend.

The macro objective can be roughly summarised as this: China's financial system should be a system that accepts market adjustment as the first adjustment, that is, the basic adjustment system and market adjustment should cover the whole society. Meanwhile, it should be a system which takes government regulation as the second adjustment, that is, an adjustment system at high level and government adjustment should cover the whole society. The relationship between the market's basic adjustment and government's regulation at high level has been elaborated in *Chinese Economy in Disequilibrium* and here we only recapture some key points. The relationship between the market's basic adjustment and the government's high level regulation under the socialist market economic system is: let the market do whatever the market can do and let the government do only what the market cannot do or cannot do well. In other words, the government's high level regulations should also cover the whole society; however, if there are things that the market can do, let the market do it. To be more specific, the government should only do such things as enacting financial laws and regulations, supervising finance, enacting and implementing monetary policies, issuing currency, managing foreign exchanges, maintaining financial market order, planning the overall pertinent finance and establishing policy banks and their operating principles. Those things can only be managed by the government, because they are beyond the market's power.

The micro objective is mainly to define objectives and tasks of different commercial financial institutions, whose overall aim is to achieve the best benefits. Benefits are divided into two categories: first, enterprise benefits that enable investors to gain as much profits as possible and promote their development and expansion and second, social benefits which include providing quality financial services and new financial products for the stability and growth of the national economy. In addition, the social benefits of financial institutions also include helping the poverty-struck areas and people to cast off poverty and become better off. There may be some conflicts between enterprise and social benefits. Commercial financial institutions must be good at coordinating and managing to achieve both. Take for example commercial banks' loans to micro, small and medium-sized enterprises and farming households. Such loans often have high costs and bring in less enterprise benefits. However, this should be one of the best performances of the enterprises because the loans help micro, small and medium-sized enterprises and farmers to survive and develop, thus harvesting very good social benefits. If they can work to reduce costs and expand service areas, commercial financial institutions can attend to both enterprise and social benefits.

In regard to structural objective, the major issue is that structural incoordination is prominent to the financial system. Take the banking industry for example. Big commercial banks with state-controlled shares are powerful, and policy banks and medium-sized stock-holding commercial banks are comparatively weak, while at the grassroots level there are hardly any small-sized commercial banks which can conduct businesses in small towns and the countryside. The further we look into the grassroots, the fewer banks there are and even in the existing banks, many services were not provided, so that banks offer little support to the development of grassroots economy. Take banks' categorisation of service clients for another example. Banks do not give sufficient attention to enterprises in the field of the real economy. On the contrary, far more attention is given to enterprises in the virtual economy, so that credit loans flow to virtual economic areas in large volume. The issue of insufficient funds in the real economy, particularly in the manufacturing industry has remained unsolved. For one more example, currently, there is a noteworthy phenomenon in the Chinese economy. That is, there is abundant private capital but we lack a normal channel to transfer it from underground finance into formal finance. If it can be transferred into formal finance, underground finance will surely benefit China's economic development, but the change has not been achieved yet. Those are financial structural issues that need to be solved urgently.

Further analyses reveal that many other issues remain to be discussed and solved in financial structural reforms and adjustment. Again, take the banking sectors for example. The relevant items to be discussed and solved are listed as follows

For instance, is the current banking system adapted to the requirements of dual transformation? Shouldn't it be reconstructed, i.e. shouldn't the existing financial institutions be merged or split by means of combining corporate restructuring and structural adjustment? But this kind of restructuring by merging or splitting needs enterprises' voluntary engagement. Enterprises must have the power to make free choices or decisions. The reconstruction should not be planned or presided over by the government; nor can it be enforced by the government. There have been lessons from the evil fruits of "matching by force" and such errors should not be committed again.

Next, how should we define the status of the rural commercial and village banks as well their scope of services? This is also an issue of division of labour among financial institutions in expanding rural credits, supporting family farms and further developing farmers' specialised cooperatives. One suggestion is that: the two tasks can overlap and it will be better if there is competition among them, but in general, the village banks should prioritise small loans.

Moreover, is it necessary to establish township construction banks with policy purposes in the process of urbanisation? Establishing such banks is to achieve particular urbanisation goals, provide medium-and long-term credit for some towns and offer financing for the public service facilities in the urbanisation process and push the completion of projects like low-rent housing construction and environmental governance. This is not contradictory to commercial loans in urbanisation. A township construction bank is a policy bank. Its nature is the same as other banks. Establishing such new banks is an important measure in financial construction reforms.

2 Marketisation of interest rate

As noted earlier, Chinese financial reform should move along the path of treating the market adjustment as the basic regulation and the government regulation as the high level regulation. So the marketisation of interest rates will become the trend of the times.

Marketisation of interest rates is not the same as liberalising interest rates or giving interest rates free swing. Rather, restrictions on interest rates should be removed. Nonetheless, this does mean paying no attention to the fluctuation of interest rates or letting it alone. Marketisation of interest rates has both its advantages and disadvantages. It should be pushed forward steadily in the process. Instead, victories cannot be achieved quickly or even at one shot. It should be achieved by looking across the board, or by overall consideration and arrangement. The vibration in Chinese banking sectors and its ensuing near future or medium and long-term advantages and disadvantages due to the marketisation of interest rates is still subject to explorations and trade-offs, and detailed countermeasures against vibration are needed.

In the near future, the marketisation of interest rates will be helpful in arousing initiatives of private capital to access financial market so as to expand the scale of the financial sectors. It is also helpful in promoting the initiatives of financial institutions and strengthening management and operation so as to improve the efficiency of financial institutions and make more effective use of capital. At the same time, it is also conducive to the suppressing of the underground financial activities and inhibiting usury behaviour. However, in a recent term, one of the biggest disadvantages of marketising interest rates is that it will have an impact at various degrees on financial activities of small and medium-sized banks, or the so-called "grassroots finance" – making them find it difficult to adapt to market changes shortly. Some weak financial institutions may even be caught in trouble. Of course, this pressure also has a role in forcing small and medium-sized banks and "grassroots finance" to upgrade their own market competitiveness and forcing them to reform and work harder. This is what is called "first be desperate to death and later come to life". Therefore, it is very hard to judge whether the marketisation of interest rates is good or bad to them. Opportunities are equal; nevertheless, achievements rely on human efforts.

In a medium and long term, the marketisation of interest rate has three advantages: first, it makes the Chinese banking industry integrate with the international banking industry, promote the competitiveness of the Chinese banking industry in the international market and accelerate cooperation between Chinese banking sectors and international counterparts so as to improve the status of Chinese banking sectors in the international market; second, upgrade the resource allocation efficiency of the Chinese banks to ensure the full and effective use of the capital, which is positive for the further development of the Chinese economy and third, increase the overall risk-resistance ability of the Chinese banking industry. Large, medium and small-sized banks have long been relying on the state. By benefiting from the interest rate differentials between deposits and loans, they have relaxed their attention to business management and risk prevention. As a matter of fact, they have lived on the control of interest rates and become numb financial institutions, which is extremely unfavourable for the growth of the future banking industry. Therefore, marketising the financial interest rates must be enforced and, the advantages of marketisation will be most prominent particularly in medium and long terms.

Therefore, what are the disadvantages of marketising interest rates in medium and long term? There will be some, of which the most important is the growing fluctuation in the domestic economy and enhanced impact from international financial turmoil in post-marketisation. This is because the government's control of domestic interest rates and restrictions over the differentials between deposits and loans can reduce the fluctuation of the domestic economy and lower the extent of the domestic economy fluctuation. However, after marketisation of interest rates, the domestic economy, whether it will be influenced by internal or overseas factors, will witness fluctuation on a larger scale. It is still not easy to judge whether marketisation will do good or harm to the Chinese economy. Deepening the reforms of the Chinese economy involves not only financial reform, or the marketisation of interest rates. Reducing the fluctuation in the domestic economy and alleviating the impact of international financial turmoil on China's economic fluctuation await coordinated reforms in other domestic economic areas and the exertion of reform outcomes, rather than taking marketisation of interest rates as the sole factor. Furthermore, even if marketisation of interest rates has some negative impact, lessons should be drawn from actual situations to make it more complete. Practice has provided prerequisites for perfecting marketisation of interest rates. In this sense, the so-called advantages and disadvantages should be rediscovered.

The discussion also involves the overall evaluation of marketisation of interest rates. It is not the only reform in deepening financial reforms. As has been previously mentioned, it also involves many other accompanying measures, such as strengthening banks' risk-resistance capacities, raising small and medium-sized banks' management and operation levels and risk-resistance capacities, and no more practice from all the banks in harvesting profits by relying on differentials between loans and deposits through interest rate control etc. Only in this way can the marketisation of interest rates be evaluated in an appropriate and overall sense.

What should not be ignored, as mentioned earlier, is that marketisation of interest rates by no means equals liberation of interest rates. Nor does it mean that the government turns a blind eye to the issue. Instead, the government regulates at a higher level and should do what the market is unable to do. If the financial market fluctuates too intensely, the economic shocks caused by the fluctuation are no longer what the market can adjust automatically, and then it is necessary for the government to make macroeconomic regulation by means of administrative measures to deal with fluctuation, particularly under urgent conditions. There have been precedents in America and other developed countries in Western Europe.

When we discuss the reform in interest rate marketisation, two more points need to be mentioned. That is, marketisation of interest rates should not be first piloted in a certain area and when currency is regulated, the loose and tight regulation should be symmetrical; otherwise, it would be adverse to the implementation of the marketisation of interest rates. Now I elaborate the two points as follows:

(1) Why shouldn't the marketisation of interest rates be first piloted in a certain area and then promoted after outcomes in other pilot areas have been achieved?

The problem, like the price reform, is not appropriate to be first piloted in one area and then promoted to other areas. The reason is: commodities and currency have high mobility. As long as flow channels are smooth, it is difficult to block the market and forbid the flow of commodities or capital. Prices and interest rates are not restricted in one particular area, unless obstructive measures are taken. In that case, the harm to the economy should not be neglected. For instance, if the price reform, here the liberation of price, was first carried out in a certain city or a province, businessmen in other cities or provinces would send and sell their commodities there through different channels. Thus, the normal market order would be disturbed. How should the next price reform be boosted? The same would occur if marketisation of interest rates was first piloted in a certain city or province. Capital in other cities and areas would flow irregularly, resulting in the flow of capital into non-piloting cities and areas or attracting capital to a certain non-piloting area. Wouldn't the normal capital market order be broken?

(2)   Why is the asymmetry in tight-or-loose monetary policies unfavourable to promoting marketisation of interest rates?

Let me first explain the asymmetry in monetary policy regulation. The asymmetry means: when the Central Bank makes monetary regulation, the effects of a currency policy that tends to be tight are asymmetric to those of a policy which tends to be loose. That is to say, when the monetary policy is tight, not only deposit-reserve ratio but also the benchmark interest rates will increase; when the monetary policy is loosened, not only the deposit-reserve ratio but also the benchmark interest rate will decrease. They are all normal. But in present-day China, what we have seen in recent years is: when the monetary policy turns from loose to tight, it is easy to turn the deposit-reserve ratio and the benchmark interest rate from low to high. The adjustment speed is fast. Nevertheless, when the monetary policy changes from tight to loose, it is much more difficult to turn the deposit-reserve ratio and the benchmark interest rates from high to low and the adjustment speed is much lower. This is one of the performances of the tight-or-loose asymmetry in monetary policy regulation. The asymmetry hinders the promotion of marketisation of the interest rates. The reason is: the prerequisite for the implementation of marketisation of the interest rates should be the flexibility that the market requires of the interest rates. That is, the interest rates should rise or fall correspondingly with the changes in the market. The difficulty of turning from loose to tight and the slow adjusting speed indicate the inflexibility and insensitivity of the interest rates under market conditions, thus reducing people's degree of confidence in the market and interest rates. Consequently, people will think that the macro economy regulation excessively controls the market, leading further to the suspicion of the true effects of marketising of interest rates. The reason for the monetary policy regulation to be asymmetrically loose or tight may be attributed to the guiding ideology of the Central Bank as a monetary policymakers and an operator, who values capital stability more, thereby preferring tightening polices, than placing economic growth and employment issues at the same equally important positions.

Another tight-or-loose asymmetrical performance in monetary regulation is: when the monetary policy is loose, small, medium and large -sized enterprises all benefit but large state enterprises benefit more; when the monetary policy is loose, large state enterprises, particularly oversized enterprises still benefit, but small and medium privately owned enterprises, particularly micro and small enterprises become victims, for it is very difficult for banks to be looked after and continuous phenomena like losses, stopping production, and bankruptcy occurred to micro, small and medium-sized enterprises. In the asymmetrical situations, the promotion of the marketisation of interest rates will be affected negatively. This is mainly because people previously thought that the marketisation of the interest rates will facilitate the formulation of fair competition environments in the financial field. Nevertheless, the asymmetry of the tight-or-loose monetary policy regulations makes the state oversized and large enterprises benefit and the privately owned micro, small and medium-sized enterprises are despised and harmed. Is this a fair competition environment? People's confidence in the marketisation of the interest rates drops.

3 Development of "grassroots finance"

The part of finance, previously mentioned in the discussion of Chinese financial structure and its adjustment, lies at the bottom of the Chinese financial system and is usually called "grassroots finance". Actually, if divided further, "grassroots finance" can be categorised into two types: the ground type and the underground type. The former type is formal grassroots finance, operated transparently or under the sun, while the latter is informal grassroots finance, operated covertly or in a black box. The latter type can be further divided into two subtypes. One is ordinary underground finance and the other gangster-involved or monopolised underground finance. Several years ago, the Economic Committee of CPCC went to some of the towns in *Guangdong* to investigate the financing of small and medium-sized privately owned enterprises, finding that some grassroots usury had a surprisingly high interest rate and was monopolised by folk gangsters. The monthly interests for some short-term loans were as high as 10% or above. There even occurred such incidents as breaking debtors' fingers or kidnapping the debtors' wives and children to force debtors to repay principals and interests. Even if loan activities were ordinary underground events, the majority of them had the high usury nature and the annual interest rates could be as high as 40–50%.

Underground "grassroots finance" will be further discussed in later chapters. The discussion here focuses on ground "grassroots finance", particularly on how to bring them into financial reforms, make them develop steadily and healthily and better serve the medium-sized, small and micro-enterprises and farmers.

Why is there survival and development space for "grassroots finance"? The folks need financing. For instance, micro, small and medium-sized enterprises and farmers have the need for investment and hot money in production and business operation. Banks usually do not have credit businesses in this aspect, or bank loan indexes have been used up. Enterprises and farmers with this need have no other choice but to turn to "grassroots finance" to meet their desperate need. Additionally, ordinary urban and rural residents are sometimes in urgent need of money, too. For instance, where can they raise funds in emergencies like marriages, funerals and interments, a seriously ill patient at home, children's education, working or studying abroad, family disasters or accidents of family members etc.? They can only resort to "grassroots finance". It is reasonable to say that the farmers have land and housing. Nevertheless, the land is contracted land or homestead and cannot be mortgaged. They have houses but houses without property ownership warrants cannot be mortgaged, either, let alone be transferred. Can there be any other way out apart from "grassroots finance"? This remark was often said in the countryside: "The loaner has done us a great favour, so does it matter much if the interest rates are a bit high?"

The ground part of the "grassroots finance" has agencies. When doing a survey in several counties in the *Linyi* City, *Shandong* Province, we found that there were generally four kinds of formal agencies for "grassroots finance", i.e. village banks, small-loan companies, financial support companies and small-loan guaranteeing companies. In some places, there were also formally listed pawnshops. In a survey of some towns in *Guizhou* Province, we found that in addition to the earlier-noted local grassroots financial agencies, rural credit cooperatives were also penetrating into the bottom of this market, developing grassroots financial services, and making outstanding achievements. This indicates that "grassroots finance" has been developing rapidly in recent years with scope of services extended and more and more agencies joining in.

Many experts have suggested setting promoting "the grass-root finance" as one of the most important future tasks in deepening financial reforms. The reason is well-founded, as this is closely related to the advancement of urbanisation, the establishment and growth of new micro, small and medium-sized enterprises, the expansion of family farm operation and the development of farmers' professional cooperatives etc. Grassroots financial agencies play an important role in increasing the income of low and medium-income families, alleviating rural poverty and promoting development and increasing employment etc. Nonetheless, at the moment, there are too few grassroots financial agencies; there have been in many places no such agencies as village banks. Many medium and large-sized banks have not gone deep into the general public at the grassroots level to carry out small-loan businesses that cater for their needs. This needs to be made up as soon as possible. Nevertheless, the more important reform task is to support grassroots financial agencies with policies.

First, moderately widen the access threshold of grassroots finance and permit more private capital to enter the bottom of grassroots to set up micro, small-sized financial agencies, which includes establishing village banks, small-loan companies, capital-supporting cooperatives, small-loan guaranteeing companies and formally listed pawnshops etc. These grassroots financial agencies should be given appropriate capital support and efforts should also be made to enable them to make proper profits without suffering loss in the business operation.

Second, set up insurance companies that particularly guarantee grassroots financial agencies' operating conditions to prevent debtors from suffering in poor business operation and in the meantime, make grassroots financial agencies have greater confidence in carrying out their businesses.

Third, strengthen guidance and regulation towards grassroots financial agencies by consider setting up local supervision offices that particularly regulate grassroots financial agencies in local financial supervision departments, and carrying out business guidance and supervision according to actual situations of grassroots finance.

Fourth, help "grassroots finance" on the basis of their own capital and capacity to open up new financial services, for instance, mortgage services for stock and inventory lists, property ownership mortgage service and small credit loan businesses etc.

Fifth, allow grassroots financial agencies with a certain scale, good performances and reputations to be listed in the existing small and medium-sized enterprise board market, and in the third board market to be set up in the near future.

Sixth, take a city as a unit and organise its specialised grassroots financial association to promote the mutual cooperation and self-discipline between the grassroots financial agencies.

With regards to underground grassroots finance, it should be differentiated and countermeasures corresponding to its categories should be taken.

If ordinary grassroots finance is still at an underground and covert state, measures should be taken to try to remove people's concerns and guide them to come to the ground and register themselves as grassroots financial agencies and carry out open loan businesses. If their concerns have not been eliminated, or they are unwilling to publicise their own identity and thereby come to the ground, we should be patient. As long as they do not do illegal business or make high-interest loans that exceed regulation, they should not be banned. As long as there is a demand, the underground grassroots finance will have businesses. What is more, sometimes neither creditors nor borrowers are willing to publicise their own identity, for they have their respective privacy.

As to underground finance involved with gangsters in the underworld, for instance, debt relationships with the nature of extortion and forced repayment of principals and interests by illegal means like breaking fingers and kidnapping hostages, it must be banned and severely punished according to the law.

4 Engaging experience of medium and large-sized stock-holding commercial banks' in small-loan businesses

This part discusses issues relevant to medium and large-sized stock-holding commercial banks' engagements in grassroots financial activities.

The grassroots, i.e. medium-sized enterprises, especially small enterprises, farming households and farmers' specialised cooperatives all have financing needs, thus needing financing. Who can provide them loans? It is difficult to meet their demand by solely relying on grassroots financial agencies. It is still difficult, even if grassroots financial agencies are increased. This is because supply and demand are interactive: after fund supply satisfies financing, the economy becomes active. Then with the economic growth, the grassroots demand more financing and it once again calls for the increase in financing supply. Thereby, apart from adding grassroots financial agencies, it is a must for large and medium-sized stock-holding commercial banks to enter the grassroots and conduct the grassroots finance business, no matter whether this is approached from the perspective of promoting the economy of the less-developed regions, increasing employment, promoting the vitality and growth of medium and micro-sized enterprises, enforcing the efforts of alleviating poverty and development or from the perspective of enlarging the enterprises' own business and improving the efficiency of the enterprises.

As noted earlier, there have been two major issues with loan work in the field of grassroots financing: great risks and high costs. Therefore, if large and medium-sized stock-holding commercial banks are engaged in grassroots finance, they must appropriately solve the earlier-noted issues, i.e. how to reduce risks and lower costs.

At many seminars held by the Economic Committee of the CPPCC, superintendents of China's Merchant Bank, *Minsheng* Bank and Bank of *Beijing* introduced their practice, including their experience of reducing risks and lowering costs, accumulated in carrying out grassroots financial businesses. The experience is as follows:

First, quantisation. Quantisation, mentioned here, means that loan businesses should be effectively categorised by nature of the loan and based on this, a quantified and scaled business-handling model should be adopted to deal with businesses with the same standard category in order to reduce costs. For the sake of convenient operation, the approach is specified as adopting a bank-government coordination mode, where banks and the government cooperate with each other, enabling banks to establish cooperative relationships with communities, markets and malls and supporting small and micro-sized enterprises, individual businesses, family farms and other grassroots economic units to further cultivate a large number of reliable customers and reduce both loan costs and risks.

Second, specialisation. Specialisation, mentioned here, means that after knowing about the customers' financing needs through rigorous investigations and classifying them into specialised categories, banks provide specialised financing services. This kind of business still needs to be combined with branch banks' regional economic features so as to provide "tailored" services. For instance, for tea businessmen, there are financing services that meet their needs and likewise, there are financing services appropriate for ceramic and so on. Thus, both loan risks and costs are reduced.

Third, invest coordinately to support small businesses to make science and technology innovation. The specific practice is: banks vote in small businesses that have good science and technology innovation and development records, invest capital after differentiating private equity funds, then coordinate with of science and technology departments to offer discounts and also consultation services, help them to be listed in the market, evade risks and retain values etc., thus setting up an initial cooperation platform between commercial banks, the science and technology-innovative businesses and private equity funds.

Fourth, strengthen intermediary businesses and adjust banks' earning structure. This is the strategic adjustment after competition between banks has intensified and their engagement in private grassroots loan businesses increased. The adjustment, however, needs to be made as early as possible in order to stop downgrades in earning rates. The intermediary businesses of banks include high value-added businesses like financing agencies, insurance and securities business. Even in the traditional deposit and loan businesses, operations with special features should be reinforced, customers appropriately oriented and markets well segmented to formulate a diversified profit-making pattern.

To summarise, with more and more medium-sized stock-holding commercial banks engaged in "grassroots financing", the earlier-noted four basic pieces of experience have not only referential but promotional values.

Note

1 The Chinese version is "*guo tui min jin*". [Trans.]

3 Changes in the mode of economic development

Section 1 The return of the real economy

1 A definition of the return of the real economy

The return of the real economy (or so-called "return to the real economy" in some articles) is usually associated with the hollowing-out of the economy. In other words, the hollowing-out of enterprises gives rise to the call for the return of the real economy (or the return to the real economy), that is, the request for monetary funds to return to the real economy.

The hollowing-out of enterprises refers to the withdrawal of monetary funds from the real economy to the virtual economy, namely the hollowing-out of the real economy. It means that the funds are withdrawn from an enterprise, reducing it to an empty shell. In China, the hollowing-out of the economy started after the 2008 American Subprime Mortgage Crisis. The outbreak of the European Debt Crisis between 2009 and 2010 had a great impact on the Chinese economy and intensified the issue. It then caught the attention of the government, the business and economics circles and news media. The trigger of the issue was accidental. It was likely because private enterprises that had engaged in the export business in *Zhejiang* areas experienced ineffective capital turnover and could not pay off debts because of the recession in the international market, so that owners simply escaped. It was known as "*paolu*".[1] The situation involved a chain of entrepreneurs and owners with whom the owners had loan or supply-and-sale relationships, which left economic order in some places in a chaotic state by the end.

During this period of time, many manufacturing enterprises, especially the small, micro and medium-sized enterprises in the manufacturing industry, experienced difficulties in getting loans and doing financing. They continuously appealed to banks not to "give cold shoulders to the poor" or disregard private enterprises. At several economic situation analysis conferences held by CPPCC's Economic Committee, the committee members all reflected that the issue of financing difficulties was pressing and if the issue was treated as laissez-faire and no counter-measures were taken, the foundation of the Chinese economy would be shaken, for only the real economy was the reliable and solid foundation of the Chinese economy. Thus, the importance of the return of the real economy has become the consensus among the government, enterprises, economists and the media.

2   *Reasons for funds to be withdrawn from the real economy*

The issue why funds are withdrawn from the real economy can be approached from three aspects.

(1)   Temptation of profit rates

The fund withdrawal in recent years has been mostly related to earning performances of Chinese enterprises in the real economy. In the 1980s, the virtual economy had just come into being in China and did not attract investors' attention. Meanwhile, the Reform and Opening-up had started, and various kinds of trades and businesses in the real economy were confronted with good opportunities, so it was normal for funds to access the real economy. In the late 1990s, the Chinese economy entered a rapid growth phase. Quantities of various products greatly increased and market competition became increasingly fierce. It was no longer that easy for enterprises to gain profits. After entering the 21st century, the quantity of production continued to grow, market competition became much more intense and manufacturing enterprises increasingly felt that there were only narrow profit margins. If they wanted to keep the original market shares, they must choose the path of independent innovation, while innovation was not so easy to achieve. It required talent, funds and time. So enterprises gradually transferred part of the business funds to the field of the virtual economy, holding that they could make more money in a quicker way. This practice had demonstrative effects in manufacturing enterprises. Lured by profit margins, capital has flown continuously out to the virtual economy.

According to our survey in some cities and provinces, large manufacturing enterprises in some places felt that as production costs were rising, competition was intensified and profit margins were small, they decided that it would be better to keep large manufacturing enterprises as platforms so that it would be easier for them to get large sums of loans for real estate speculation so as to make more money.

(2)   Comparing difficulties in field entries

The kind of industry an investor is to enter does not merely rely on his own choice, but also on suggestions of his relatives and friends. The author once led CPPCC's Economic Committee Research Group and conducted surveys in certain cities of the Pearl River Delta. According to the reflections of business and commercial figures, it was more difficult for new investors to enter the real economy than the virtual economy. Specifically, the difficulties in accessing certain fields of the real economy are as follows. There are high thresholds for entering an industry. Enterprises need a huge amount of capital as initial investment and good social relationships in the local areas. The investors themselves are supposed to have some business experience and specialised skills in this industry; some familiar core staff who can contribute to the enterprises' establishment and management. There are also complicated registration procedures. On top of those, investors should have accessible channels of financing; otherwise, capital chains would be easily broken. By contrast, it was much easier to enter the virtual economy. Take stock trading for example. As long as one has a sum of available money, he can earn some money with a more flexible mind and better luck. For another example, as long as one trusts the borrower, one can loan money to an acquaintance or an acquaintance's acquaintance. Naturally, there are risks in doing stock trading and loaning money; nevertheless, does investing in the real economy not bear the same risk? There is some truth in the remarks made earlier by industrial and commercial figures at *Guangdong's* symposium.

The comparison of risk degrees in investing in the real or virtual economy should be approached more from comparing the withdrawal mechanism and the ease of withdrawal. Let us now turn to the next question.

(3) Comparison of degrees of ease in withdrawing investment
    from the real economy

With regards to investment in the real economy, as has already been discussed, entry into the field is more difficult than entry into the virtual economy. Now, let us analyse degrees of ease in relation to withdrawal.

The comparison of the degree of risk between investing in the real economy and investing in the virtual economy is not directly related to risks in the business management process, for in business management, activities engaged in either the real economy or the virtual economy will both encounter a variety of new situations. The objective economic conditions will change and great changes will occur unexpectedly worldwide as well. From this perspective, the risk magnitude in investing in either economy is almost the same. It all depends on whether risk prevention measures that an investor has made are appropriate or whether his judgement of the economic tendency is correct or not.

The real risk is related to the withdrawal mechanism. In other words, it is related to the degree of difficulty in exiting from an investor's ongoing business activities. The degree of losses that an investor suffers generally depends on the degree of difficulty in withdrawing investment from business activities in progress. It is like a person who has a premonition that business activities engaged in will bring him great losses and he wants an early exit. However, withdrawing from the real economy is much more difficult than withdrawing from the virtual economy. It is self-evident that a difficult withdrawal is accompanied by greater losses.

Why is it difficult for an investor to withdraw from the real economy? This is mainly because in severe economic situations, the prospect for the manufacturing industry is not good enough. When one sells a plant, it is difficult to find a buyer. Furthermore, when the economy tends to be prosperous, with bright manufacturing prospects, one who intends to invest in the manufacturing sector and buy a ready-made plant cannot find a seller.

Since it is difficult to sell or transfer an existing plant, an investor can only apply for bankruptcy but the application for bankruptcy requires specific cumbersome procedures. Furthermore, clearing debt relationships, dismissing employees and dealing with the aftermath etc. take time, energy and money and these factors continue to make the investor suffer losses.

By contrast, it is far easier for a person engaged in investment and business activities in the virtual economy to withdraw from the field when he foresees unfavourable changes in the economic situation. This actually means that from the perspective of risk aversion, it is easier to deal with changes in the current situation by investing in the virtual economy than investing in the real economy, because when an investor withdraws from the virtual economy, he does not have many residual issues with which to deal.

Here, we can also give some supplementary information. As has been mentioned earlier, it is difficult for a new investor in the real economy to access the real economy, and once the access is successful, it is difficult to withdraw from it in the event of the deteriorating economic situation. Later, once the economic situation improves, it is even harder for the investor to re-enter it after the earlier withdrawal. This is because in the manufacturing sector, especially in the same trade with which an investor himself is more familiar, he will be misunderstood by his peers in various ways and a diminished reputation will make it difficult to carry out business activities.

To sum up, these three aspects result in a phenomenon where investors prefer to have funds to access the virtual economy rather than accessing the real economy.

3 Serious consequences due to fund transfer from the real to the virtual economy

The real economy is the economic foundation upon which a powerful industrial country can survive and develop. The more solid the foundation is, the broader the development prospect will be in the future. So if policymakers don't hold back the trend of fund withdrawal from the real economy, the sum of the fund withdrawal will increase, resulting in the previously mentioned hollowing-out phenomenon in some enterprises which incur serious consequences on the national economy.

Generally speaking, the following three consequences are very serious.

(1) Serious capital supply shortage in the real economy

Capital flows frequently between the real economy and the virtual economy. There are inflows from both the field of the real economy into the field of the virtual economy, and from the virtual economy into the real economy. Each has its respective in-flow and outflow. This is a normal state, and will not have significant impact on the entire national economy. However, it becomes abnormal when funds continuously flow out from the real economy into the virtual economy over a long period of time. As the news media has rightly commented, this equals hollowing-out the real economy step by step, ultimately making the real economy hollow.

One of the serious consequences due to the shortage of capital supply in the real economy is that research development and independent innovation become difficult, for both need funds. Enterprises must raise funds, but due to the lack of capital supply and the subsequent rise in financing costs, enterprises which want to conduct research and development and make independent innovation feel caught in a dilemma, as two popular sayings go, "Not to be innovative is to wait to die; to be innovative is to die early". It means that if an enterprise is not engaged in research development or ready to make independent innovation, it will sooner or later be cleaned out. If an enterprise decides to be engaged in research development, or is ready to make independent innovation, it will do its outmost to raise funds through various resources. As the cost for financing is so high, this enterprise is crushed due to the overload of debts before it sees achievements from the research development or innovation. This is what it means by "to be innovative is to die early."

Another serious consequence due to insufficient funds in the real economy is that many enterprises have difficulty in maintaining the normal capital chain, which in turn affects whether a normal industry chain is unobstructed. This is the problem that some export-oriented enterprises in some coastal provinces used to encounter several years ago. At that time, I was leading the Private Enterprises Research Group of CPPCC's National Economic Committee and making investigations in *Liaoning* and *Guangdong* provinces. We held private enterprise symposiums subsequently in *Dalian, Anshan, Shenyang, Guangzhou, Foshan, Zhongshan* and *Shenzhen* etc. The reflections that we collected were: the most heavily affected private enterprises were those engaged in export businesses. Due to reduced orders, overstocking of commodities and limited cash flow, those businesses had to rely on usury to keep themselves running. Later, as debts and interests piled higher and higher, they could no longer sustain themselves and had to close down. The fund chain broke; this immediately got many private enterprises involved and was quickly followed by the break-down in the industrial chain. Channels of commodity supply and distribution which used to link one to another could not be maintained any longer, and some of the local markets were close to being paralysed. Ultimately, it was through government funding and loans issued by the government through banks that the private enterprises experienced stock release. The hard lesson should be learned; however, that damage has been done.

(2) Abnormal asset price rises and after-effects due to bubble growth and burst in the virtual economy

When insufficient capital supply occurs due to the withdrawal of funds from the real economy, the influx of too much money will cause abnormal asset price rises in the virtual economic area.

A proven example is that since the middle of the first decade of the 21st century housing prices in big cities like *Beijing, Shanghai, Hangzhou* and *Shenzhen* have been rising at a surprising speed, becoming unprecedentedly high. Where did the buyers come from? A portion of them were buyers motivated by normal housing needs. They bought houses probably because each person in a family did not have enough housing space and they wanted to improve their family life. Those people involved would be newly married couples or couples ready to get married or even parents whose children were about to graduate or work in big cities. The other portion was so-called speculative buyers who stockpiled houses and drove up prices. The two categories of people influence each other. As demand grows housing prices rise. The higher that housing prices rose, the more ready people were to buy them. Those who stored or speculated on houses earlier all earned money. Even if purchased residential houses or villas were unoccupied, they still increased in value, because the demand was strong and the prices were climbing. Where did the money of stockpiling buyers, who rushed to buy houses, and speculative buyers come from? Some was transferred from the real economy, others borrowed from different channels or banks. If it was borrowed from banks, did this actually mean that the amount of loan put into the real economy was reduced which would have left capital in the real economy even more depleted?

The issue does not stop here. Once the virtual economy inflates in an unusual way, bubbles will boom and attract more investors into the area. The more it is like this, the more likely the time for the bubble to burst will come soon. Dangers accumulate and wait until they reach the limit. Once bubbles burst, it will definitely generate chain reactions. First, the capital chain breaks and the debt chain takes shape. The debt crisis in the virtual economy will inevitably affect the real economy, as with cost rise in the real economy, market competition will become more intense and profit rates will decrease with even an increase in deficits. Some manufacturing enterprises turn to invest in the virtual economy and others take advantage of their own platforms, get loans from banks and operate them in the virtual economy. Alternatively, they either establish subsidiaries or under-lease capital to their cooperative partners to share profiteering. Once bubbles in the virtual economy burst, it is inevitable that pertinent enterprises in the real economy will be involved. Such cases occurred several years ago.

(3) Adjustments of macroeconomic regulation policies and greater uncertainties in the national economy due to debt crises from bubble burst in the virtual economy and involvement of the real economy

For the government, neither the hollowing-out of the real economy nor the uncontrolled expansion of the virtual economy is conducive to the healthy development of the national economy. The government cannot but pay close attention to further changes in the situation. Once the bubbles in the virtual economy burst, debt crises will expand to the real economy, the fund chain will rupture everywhere and will evolve into a debt chain, throwing the whole market order into chaos. The government is determined to take powerful macroeconomic regulation measures to eliminate the debt chain, of which the most common measure is to "throw in capital and release stock". A debt chain is also known as triangle debts or polygonal debts. "Throw in capital and release stock" means that the government injects funds into an enterprise in the debt chain through banks and request that it pay off its debts with them. In this way one chain is linked to another. When some enterprises are relieved from a debt chain, others will be relieved from stock traps.

However, the measure "throw in capital and release stock" can only be a temporary and emergency solution, because it can neither change the hollowing-out tendency of the real economy, nor can it help to inhibit the virtual economy from growing bubbles again in the virtual economy.

If bubbles burst in the virtual economy and debt chains come into being, the government in the market chaos adopts inappropriate macroeconomic regulation policies. This instead will create more trouble in the economy and make further governance much more difficult.

For example, when large sums of money flow from the real economy into the virtual economy, speculation on all kinds of assets occurs which causes asset prices to rise and the government tightens monetary policy to curb rising asset prices. As a matter of fact, this is an inappropriate regulatory policy, for the rise of asset prices in this case is not due to excessive money on the market but to the low profitability of the real economy, leading the capital to flow out from the real economy into the virtual economy. Thus, assets are highly touted and asset prices rise one after another. Instead, the victim suffering most from the government's tight monetary policy is the real economy, which already felt a greatly insufficient fund supply due to capital outflow. Isn't life more difficult for the real economy which is experiencing profit rate decline and is then caught in monetary tightening? Therefore, careful studies should be made of which appropriate policies facilitate the return of the real economy and how the real economy should be revitalised and continue to grow.

Next, we turn to the discussion on basic countermeasures for the return of the real economy.

4 Basic countermeasures for the return of the real economy

To let funds flow into the real economic areas, profits must be ensured after the in-flow; otherwise, neither new nor original investors will remain in the real economy: new investors will be reluctant to enter, while original investors will be unwilling to continue to make expand their investments.

So, in this sense, two key issues exist that need to be effectively addressed. They are: first, how can the real economic areas be turned into profitable investment areas? This includes how to attract new investors to access the real economy voluntarily, how to make sure that investors in the real economy will not only not withdraw from the entity economic field but are willing to increase investment and expand their production scales. Second, how can the financing issue that faces enterprises in the real economy be solved? Now, let's address those issues respectively.

(1) Making real economic areas profitable investment areas

In the last few years, research groups of the CPPCC's National Economic Committee have conducted surveys on the private economy in four Chinese provinces: *Shandong, Chongqing, Shaanxi* and *Liaoning*. The preliminary view of those investigations was that the major reasons for private enterprises to be unwilling to invest in the real economy were heavy tax burdens, rising labour, land and housing costs and irregular conduct of the government. As a result, the profit margins were excessively low and there was even no profit for a long period of time. It was prohibitive for new investors and also difficult for old investors to step down. They felt like riding on a tiger's back and could not wait to get rid of the big burden as soon as possible, i.e. transferring out the plant.

At a symposium composed of industrial and commercial figures and private entrepreneurs, we gathered attendees' comments on the above issues. They said that within taxes and fees, the more burdensome are fees, because taxes have "bottoms", while fees might be "bottomless pits". In addition to stipulated fees, there are also provisional fees, like "sponsorship fees" and "public welfare donations" etc. all of which should be included in the costs of private enterprises.

One increasing phenomenon in recent years has been the rise in labour costs, and the phenomenon has not been limited to a particular city. The enterprises reported that workforces were unstable, as backbone workers were often unable to be retained. When employees requested enterprises to solve the housing problems of their families, enterprises, though willing, failed to do so.

The rise in land and rising housing prices has been a common phenomenon in recent years. Enterprises generally believed that this situation was not conducive to the expansion of plants. Even if they had intended to do so, they were forced to call it to a halt.

At the symposium, what was most strongly reflected by the attendees was the irregular conduct of the local government. For example, after the former city or county leaders negotiated with the preparatory personnel of an enterprise on the building of a factory somewhere in a city or a county, construction work soon started. However, when the former city or county leaders were replaced, new leaders did not recognise the previous agreement, demanding some additional fees. The preparatory personnel had no other choice but to agree; otherwise, the project could only be aborted. In another example, a municipal and county government head in charge of a department often handed over slips of paper or made a phone call, recommending a certain person to work in an enterprise. The enterprise could only accept; otherwise, there would be unpleasantness between the two parties in the future. In regard to these issues, enterprises would endure them. Over time, these emerged as the reasons why enterprises became reluctant to continue to expand their businesses there.

Seen in this light, the primary task of creating the perception that the real economy is a profitable investment area is to create favourable market environments where laws are fully observed, strictly enforced and lawbreakers are duly punished. Government officials and enterprise staff all act by laws, rules and regulations so as to reduce the randomness of government sectors.

The randomness of the government sectors can most easily cause disorder to enterprise expectation. Not knowing what will happen under conditions caused by the randomness in the governments' decision-making and management, enterprises have no idea how to make plans, or enact countermeasures. Disordered expectation makes it difficult for enterprises to set a particular area, industry or certain kinds of product as a long-term predetermined target. Everything changes according to changing circumstances and this is the unchangeable principle.

Some of the issues, like the rise in factor cost cannot be solved by government sectors, of which enterprises have also had knowledge. If the government can really control the price and stop it from rising, the government must restore all sorts of practice under the planned economic system. Do enterprises want the government to resume the previously "omnipotent status"? Moreover, commodities actually bear the cost of each other. The government alone can control prices of certain commodities. The control can be effective in the short term, and in the long run there will be other consequences. The cost of labour is more difficult for the government to keep under control in a rigid way. Under the market economic conditions, it is usually not possible to have a wage freeze. This has been proven by the practice of different national economies in the last few decades. Therefore, enterprises do not expect the government to exercise very tight price-control by freezing wages; rather, they only expect the government to rationalise prices and not let some interest groups damage the market rules for the sake of their own gains.

In face of rising factor costs, the best countermeasures for enterprises are to be committed to research and development, independent innovation and industrial upgrading, to set out a new path. Nevertheless, this relies on improving financing conditions. Next, let us analyse how to solve the issue of financing difficulties.

(2) Making the real economic area the investment area accessible to multi-channel financing

Investors in the real economy need good financing conditions, whether they are to expand the production scale or have a sufficient flow of funds. It is particularly so when they conduct research and development. Independent innovation, industrial upgrading, exploiting a new market or increasing market shares all need financing. Good financing guarantees that investors are reassured and will do long-term business in the real economy, and it also provides the confidence that new investors need so as to create businesses in the real economy.

Therefore, another basic countermeasure for the return to the real economy is to solve, as soon as possible, the financing issue that enterprises in the real economy are confronting.

First of all, we must figure out one issue: when banks loan, they should first review the borrower's asset conditions and operation achievements; second, review whether the borrower has a good credit history; third, review the use of loans and the risk degree of the given use. From the general situation, as the earlier-noted three conditions are better for enterprises in the real economic areas than those in virtual economic areas, the former should be more likely to get loans. Nevertheless, what we see in real life is another result. That is, some financial institutions are more willing to be engaged in loan business with enterprises in the virtual economy (especially the subsidiaries of state-owned enterprises).

Why is it like this? Here we leave aside personal factors, which involve friendships and personal social contacts between relevant business personnel who receive loans in the virtual economic area and the relevant personnel in a financial institution etc. but focus on objective changes of the economic conditions in recent years. Such changes can be generally divided into two categories:

One category of change is: the real economy is largely affected by the international market. A change in the international market will quickly affect import and export of Chinese manufacturing sectors, increasing investment and operation risks in the real economy and further topping up concerns of financial institutions. They would rather be more cautious than be involved in it.

Another category of change is: the real economy is largely affected by domestic macroeconomic regulatory policies. Whenever there are big adjustments in the macroeconomic policies, they will quickly affect the order, prices and the quantity of the stocks of the Chinese manufacturing enterprises, thus increasing investment and operation risks in the real economic areas, which will further increase the doubts of financial institutions, and make them cautious with their actions.

Then, people cannot stop asking: "Since changes in the international market and domestic macroeconomic regulatory policies will not only affect the operation of the real economic areas, but also that of the virtual one, why would financial institutions in issuing loans favour virtual economic areas and give the cold shoulder to the real economic areas?" This, as mentioned earlier in this chapter, is related, to some extent, to difficulties in the entry into and the withdrawal from real economic areas. As has already been pointed out, as soon as enterprises or individuals saw the investment opportunities in the virtual economic area, they could gain access with ease and withdraw with ease after foreseeing forthcoming fluctuations. The reason why financial institutions are interested in loaning to enterprises or individuals who are conducting investment activities in the virtual economic area is just out of consideration of their flexibilities in the entry into or the withdrawal from the area and they generally end their businesses with profits. The financial institutions are assured about these and render them their support. Thus, enterprises and individuals engaged in the virtual economic areas can easily get loans for speculation. By contrast, enterprises and individuals engaged in the investment or management in the real economic areas are in a passive state, and unable to withdraw their investments, unavoidably suffering loss when economic situations are about to make great changes or show fluctuations. They generally and inevitably suffer losses for the lack of similar flexibility.

Additionally, in the real economy, many of those engaged in investment and management are large state-owned enterprises, which indeed have a large fortune, financial strength, and a close relationship with big banks. They generally do not have the intention to withdraw, so when their funds are tight, the banks will try to provide loans. As to private enterprises in the field of the real economy, especially small and medium enterprises, it is very difficult in this case to get loans from big banks, or even small and medium banks. Normally, they will turn to usury as a means of emergency relief.

It should also be noted that, among those engaged in investment activities in virtual economic areas, some are state-owned enterprises specialised in this area, or subsidiaries of state-owned enterprises which are engaged in manufacturing in the entity economic areas but are now engaged in investment and management after entering the virtual economic area. As they are state-owned enterprises, notably subsidiaries of large state-owned manufacturing enterprises, they have far more financing channels. These are objective aspects, for which private enterprises admit that they are not qualified. They also admit that they feel indignant at them.

Given that, in order to make the real economic area into an investment area through multi- channels, we must emphasise reforms in the financial system and pioneer new and direct financing.

Issues like deepening reforms in the financial system, and opening up new and direct financing channels, have been discussed in Section 3, Chapter 2 of this book. Before this section comes to an end, I further discuss several points on the return and the transformation of the real economy.

(3) A centralised account of the return and the transformation of the real economy

A top priority for China at the current stage is to return to the real economy and the virtual economy undoubtedly needs further development and standardisation. But we must be soberly aware that in a big country like China, its national economy must be founded solidly on the real economy. People's attention should be drawn to this issue to avoid the hollowing-out of the real economy, namely the hollowing-out of enterprises.

However, it is far from enough just to return to the real economy. With the advancement of technology, if enterprises in the real economic area do not pay close attention to changes in production mode, take the road of independent innovation and industrial upgrading, they will sooner or later lose, and ultimately be eliminated from the market economy. The importance of the real economy transformation lies here.

Since the 2008 financial crisis, enterprises in the economically developed countries like the United States, Japan, France, Germany and the UK have realised the need for transforming the real economy. Their consensus is that control of the future market depends on who can lead the new trend of technological progress, and occupy the commanding summit of world science and technology. The understanding is in line with the big trend of the world economy.

In China, in fact, many private enterprises which are engaged in the investment and management of the real economy and have vision, have come to recognise the future trend of the market economy. They do not only stick to the real economy, but are also committed to innovation and transformation. Among them, there has been a popular saying: China, for a longer period of time in the future, will not only continue to be the world's manufacturing centre, but will also strive to become the world centre of creation, and also the world marketing centre. Entrepreneurs are willing to contribute their efforts to achieve this goal.

This is delightful. The delight lies in this: more and more prescient people, including these entrepreneurs, have shared this understanding. China is called the world's manufacturing centre, which is definitely not a derogatory term. As a developing country which is being transformed from an agricultural to an industrial society, China through years of hard work has finally become the world's manufacturing centre. This indicates China's achievements. But since it has become the world's manufacturing centre, it is necessary to keep this position rather than lose it. More importantly, it should be given new meanings and enrich its technical connotations. China is seeking to become the world creation centre. Be aware that there is still a long distance before China achieves this goal. However, since there have been clear objectives, there should be no hesitation; rather, we should go ahead and reach the goal. It is indeed right to say that morale should be kept up.

In striving to become the world creation centre, it should also seek to become a world marketing centre. It is through marketing that the value chain can be completely achieved and the added value fully realised. This will be an important achievement which combines developmental and system transformation.

Section 2 Creation of consumption need: the core issue of expanding domestic demand

1 The urgency of expanding private consumption

Since the outbreak of international financial crisis in the United States and major Western European countries in 2008, Chinese export orders have been drastically reduced. Since then, to prevent the economic downturn, the appeal for the expansion of private consumption demand has been growing among domestic economic circles and there have appeared more and more relevant policy proposals. In general, the viewpoints of those who advocate policy proposals include: according to the analysis of macroeconomists, to spur economic growth, we rely on nothing more than the "troika", namely investment, consumption and export. Currently, export orders have dropped, export markets are weak. It seems that it is difficult in the near future to rely on exports to drive economic growth, for it has been very difficult to maintain exports at its previous speed. It will be even more difficult to make exports contribute more to economic growth. As for the role of investment-pull economic growth, it is not easy to sustain it. The reasons are: what China is currently in urgent need of are structural adjustment, structural optimisation and increasing the quality of economic growth. If a large number of investment projects are carried out without carefully examining them, repeated constructions will occur as before. As a result, it may spur the economic growth in the short term. Nevertheless, it will exacerbate structural imbalance but also lead to the waste of resources, so that resources shortage becomes even more serious. Some enterprises with excessive production capacity will leave huge future problems and make structural adjustment even more difficult. Meanwhile, repeated construction, particularly low-level repeated construction will not only accelerate structural imbalance but will also lead to the waste of resources, making resources shortage even more serious. Additionally, substantial investment accompanied by the expansion of credit leads to excessive amounts of money in circulation, which in turn is bound to the consequences of inflation caused by excessive investment demands, forcing the government to shift to the macro-tight policy. This makes the economy fluctuate wildly, which is not conducive to economic growth. Therefore, we must learn carefully from experience and the lessons of those years, making the practice of using investment demand to stimulate economic growth moderately, rather than overdo it. The economy must not suffer "investment dependency syndrome"; otherwise, there will be re-occurrences of "the weird investment impulse circle."

What is left is to spur economic growth with consumption-pull measures. Consumption needs can be divided into two categories. One is government consumption need, and the other private consumption need. Under normal circumstances, expanding government expenditure is constrained by government budget, so the expansion of government consumption does not take place randomly. What we mean here by saying expanding consumption by stimulating economic growth refers to the expansion of private consumption, in other words, expanding the role of private consumption in economic growth. How to expand private consumption in China currently? This is a profound question, for the expansion of private consumption is rooted in people's income rise, private purchasing power and their willingness to purchase, as well as their increased inclination to consume, namely the rise of people's consumption expenditure rate in their income.

Therefore, answering the aforementioned question regarding the expansion of private consumption must be based on China's actual situation at this stage.

2 The impact of income distribution and social security institutional reforms on private consumption

Undeniably, the income distribution system reform and the social security system reform have obvious impacts on private consumption. There are two fundamental factors that affect the expansion of private consumption.

First of all, let us analyse the impact of the income distribution system on private consumption. China's ongoing income distribution system reform, based on the current level, aims to facilitate a steady increase of family income with low-and-intermediate earnings. Meanwhile, it works to narrow down gaps in social income distribution, so that the income gap between the rich and poor continues to narrow down and ultimately the pyramid-shaped income distribution pattern changes into an egg-shaped or olive-shaped income distribution pattern.

Therefore, we must realise that there are different reasons at the present stage for the poverty of China's low-income families and their lack of purchasing power. For rural residents, the biggest issue is that they have no property rights. They can only live on the crops grown on the contracted land or on the sales of poultry and livestock bred on the land. Among the rural residents, many go out to be migrant workers. Although they are likely to get some wages the payment is still very low. In recent years, wages have increased; nevertheless, so has the cost of living and pay adjustments usually lag behind. How can they not be poor?

For urban residents, what they fear most is to lose their jobs or become jobless adults. It is particularly so for poor families. For them, once they lose their jobs or cannot find jobs in the long term, they would not be able to live on in environments where living expenses rise year after year, should it not be for social welfare or aids from relatives and friends. What kind of purchasing power do we expect of them?

To put it simply, the fundamental measures for increasing low-income families' wages are to let farmers have property income, let rural residents who lose their jobs and the jobless have jobs to do, payment to gain or other gains (for earnings from doing small businesses and handcrafts).

Migrant workers from urban residents and from towns and cities share one common problem, that is, lower wages compared with commodity prices. Commodity prices always increase first, while wages lag behind. There are two main reasons: first, the working units that hire migrant and urban workers are usually enterprises and public institutions; those employed as urban and rural workers are individual workers. When pay standards are negotiated, the former has a strong status while the latter has a weak one. Their market status and strength in negotiating prices are asymmetrical; second, the majority of migrant workers, no matter whether they are urban or rural residents, lack specialised skills. They are merely labourers, who cannot get more wages for their specialised skills. This is also why their wages are less than normal. Thus, government and trade unions need to step forward and ensure that vulnerable individual employees are cared for, the minimum wages should be raised based on actual situations, wage arrears eliminated and unfair treatment against employees corrected.

In regard to the factors affecting farmers' income, we should protect farmers' interests from the perspective of agricultural sales and procurement. This is because an individual farmer as a seller of farm products has a weak status, while purchasing enterprises have a strong status. The status and bargaining power of both parties are also asymmetrical and bargains are unequal. Farm and pasture products are generally low in prices, thus affecting farmers' incomes from the sale of these products. It also depends on two remedial measures: one is to make farmers organised and establish husbandry cooperatives, and then the cooperatives step forward to negotiate with buyers, so as to increase the bargaining power of farm and pasture product sellers; second, the government needs to step forward to speak for the weak party and prevent farmers from being treated unfairly in farm and pasture product sales.

In terms of social security, there are broad areas for social reform. Here, let us look back at a debate which emerged in the Western economic circle after the capitalist economic crisis in the 1930s. At that time, the mainstream of the Western economics was neoclassical, with two representatives, one Cannan (Edwin Cannan), and the other Robbins (Lionel Robbins). Both were professors of the London School of Economics. Their views were consistent: the major way to solve the serious unemployment was non-intervention of the government in the market or enterprise behaviour to ensure that one employee's job was done by two, one employee's wage shared by two, and one employee's food eaten by two. At the same time, Myrdal, a young Swedish economist and his colleagues submitted a research report to the Swedish government, proposing that measures addressing common people's concerns should be prioritised to alleviate unemployment in Sweden. Specific measures include building a large number of houses with average sale prices, and low-rent houses for leasing, enabling everybody to have houses to live in; implementing an unemployment benefit system, free education and free medical services and pension security system.

Those measures were ushered in Sweden as a welfare state. At that time, Keynesian economics had not yet been issued. It was only until 1936 that the masterpiece of Keynesian economics *The General Theory of Employment, Interest and Money* was published.

After World War II, Western economists met to discuss the disputes between two parties of economists over unemployment countermeasures in the early 1930s. Which school was right, the Neoclassical or the Swedish School? After the discussion, it was agreed upon that the Neoclassical was wrong and that the Swedish School was right. What was wrong with the Neoclassical? We know that the proposal of one job shared by two people, one person's wage shared by two and one person's food eaten by two were simply ways that enterprises used to resolve internal overstaffing, and it was impossible to solve the unemployment problem, because the purchasing power of the society did not increase.

Why was the proposal of the Swedish school right? This is because the policy advice of the Swedish school and its welfare and social security policy which was adopted by the Swedish school lifted concerns of families with low and intermediate income. People lived in peace and had the confidence to consume. Consumption played a large role in economic recovery and alleviating unemployment. This formed a virtuous cycle in the social economy. That is, after people's concerns are lifted, consumer expenditure grew – employment grew – people's income grew then consumer expenditure re-grew – employment re-grew . . .

In other words, employment is expanded by employment. Some people were employed and gained incomes and used it for consumption, which increased employment. When the income is spent again, more people were employed.

Likewise, for China at this stage, improving people's livelihood, reforming the social security system, achieving the goal of integrating urban and rural social security in the near future and removing the worries of families with low and intermediate incomes are important countermeasures for the expansion of consumption.

3 Consumption-orientated economic growth not achievable in the short term but achievable over a transitional phase

Chinese economic growth was and is for a long period of time mainly pulled by investment. Consumption-pull economic growth (also called the consumption-oriented type) is the direction of future efforts, which requires a transitional phase. If the growth is now changed from investment-pull to consumption-pull, the strength of consumption is not sufficient. If people insist on doing so, economic growth will decline and it is likely to drop below 5%, which is not conducive to the Chinese economy. So we need to change from an investment-pull stage to a stage when investment-pull and consumption-pull are equally valued and then move gradually to a consumption-pull stage.

Take economic growth in Western Europe after World War II for example. After the war, the economy there needed to be established from scratch. Large-scale constructions were needed and investment inevitably occupied an important position. At the same time, following the capitalist economic crisis in the 1930s, World War II broke out. Individual consumption was suppressed during that period of time. After the War, it happened that new household electronic appliances were popularised when every family needed to rebuild houses, buy new furniture and cars. The post-war birth rate had an overall increase. In the 1970s, the so-called postwar period witnessed young people's "marriage tide" and "baby boom" so that consumption demand was greatly expanded. Then it changed into a phase when investment and consumption demands both spurred the economy. This situation lasted for about 20 to 30 years. Later, with the gradual increase in income per capita, the growth changed into a phase when growth is mainly pulled by consumption. Therefore, in the future, China, in the process of continuously expanding private demands, should transit from being mainly pulled by investment to equally weighing investment and consumption and then gradually transiting to be mainly pulled by consumption. This is in line with reality and is also feasible.

Moreover, the expansion of private consumption is a gradual process. We should not be too anxious for success. Nor can it be achieved primarily through the government issuing subsidies and grants. This kind of approach is not conducive but harmful. There are two such lessons from history.

One lesson took place in the late 4th century BC. After Alexander, the Macedonian king, (later known as Alexander the Great) regained the control of the whole territory of Greece. His army crossed the sea and made an eastward expedition. They defeated the Persian army and exterminated the Persian Empire. Gold and silver treasures accumulated over years in the Persian Empire and palaces all fell into the hands of Alexander the Great. How were those treasures consumed? A portion was divided among Alexander the Great's veterans who had followed him and fought in different places for a decade as their retirement awards, rewards or household allowances for the newly married. Another portion was divided among retired officials and the officials then holding office as their awards and allowances. Still another portion was given to different city-states in the Greek territory (Sparta is an exception, for the Spartans refused to comply with Alexander the Great's commands) as patronage for helping Alexander the Great in the crusade with human resources, ships and supplies. As a result, a large amount of gold and silver flew into the private sectors, giving rise to inflation for as long as 100 years. How could it be like this? The supplies could not keep up with demands. What those who received patronage from Alexander the Great wanted to buy was a variety of handicrafts, food, building materials, clothing, etc. How could the supply keep pace with such a great demand? Everywhere, currencies chased commodities and continuous price rises were inevitable. The lesson was documented in history.

There was another lesson in history. It took place in some Western European countries in about the16th-17th century AD and it extended in individual countries even to the early 18th century. Initially, Spain occupied Latin America (an exception was Brazil which was occupied by the Portuguese), some local gold and silver ores were mined by the Spanish colonists. Some Indian kingdoms were destroyed, and everything in Indian palaces, towns and villages was looted and a large amount of gold and silver was shipped back to Spain. So up until the present day, shipwrecks loaded with silver and gold from that time have been discovered at the bottom of the Atlantic. Treasure shipped back to Spain then became the private property of royal families, nobles, officials and military officers. They were mainly used to buy consumption commodities. As Spain's industry was not developed, it could not supply so many consumption commodities, so gold and silver of the Spanish quickly flew into nearby Britain, France, the Netherlands and some other Western European countries. They were used to buy a large quantity of local handicrafts and food, causing a substantial price rise in Western European markets, and the price rise lasted as long as 200 years. This is "the Price Revolution". The example also tells people that a sudden increase in purchasing power along with a serious supply shortage in consumption goods definitely causes severe and persistent inflation. Only supplies that grow hand in hand with purchasing power can steadily expand domestic demands.

4 Relative stability and volatility of the consumption commodity market

When it comes to the expansion of private demands and allowing consumption to be a major factor that pulls China's economic growth in the future, we need to analyse two basic characteristics of China's consumption market: first, the relative stability of the consumption market and second, the volatility of the consumption market.

Let us start with an analysis of the relative stability of the consumption market.

First, private consumption expenditures are inevitably affected by regular income, while regular income, whether it is current regular income or expected regular income over a longer period of time in the future, is all known. People usually arrange regular expenditure based on known income, so the consumption market tends to be relatively stable, or to increase relatively evenly and this in general will not change much. Of course, apart from regular income, there may be contingent income, such as the prize won in a lottery, great awards, or received inheritance and gifts and the like. Nonetheless, incidental income is hard to predict, as there is no law to follow. Moreover, even if there has been contingent income, most of it is used for contingent expenditure and it will not cause great fluctuation in the consumption market. The promotion of consumption credits may change consumers' spending arrangements but generally speaking, this is simply using the future income for current consumption expenditure and it will not exceed the range of expected income.

Second, private consumption expenditure is inevitably constrained by household consumption commodity stock. In general, a household has a consumption stock adjustment programme, which is based on stock adjustment of household consumption commodities and the expected regular income of the family. In the face of a gradual price rise, some aspects of the stock may be adjusted in order to avoid losses, for instance, updating some durable products in advance or increasing the number of non-durable products reserved by the family, but it will not depart from the big regular income framework.

Third, for any individual, consumption, savings and investment are transferable with each other. The three have different objectives: consumption is to satisfy demand; saving is either for future consumption expenditure or investment, maintaining value, obtaining interests or being spared for future use; investment is to make profits. Three of them can be transferable. In this sense, saving can be left out of our discussion and the main focus is placed on the transfer between consumption and investment. This kind of transfer is more of a universal feature. Take residents' purchase of houses for example. Buying a house for accommodation is consumption behaviour, while buying a house for renting or resale purposes is investment behaviour. However, as long as a resident has bought a house, whether it will be used for renting or resales, it is initially shown as consumption behaviour in the market. Therefore, this basically doesn't go beyond the range of an individual's current and expected regular income, so it is still relatively stable.

Fourth, personal spending habits are generally relatively stable. Such spending habits are likely to be under the influence of grandparents, family members or the social circle. It can also be said to be under the influence of an individual kind of culture, habits or convention. The spending habits are not easily changed. Among those, the influences of the social circle are increasingly greater. Changes in an individual's residence, career and progress in age bring about corresponding changes in the social circle. But generally speaking, an individual's spending habits are neither easy to develop, nor are they easy to change. As it is not easy to change a person's spending habits, some researchers insisted on calling consumption habits "inertia of life", which is not without reason.

Next, let us talk about the volatility of consumption commodity market.

First, the industrial society is not the same as the agricultural society. Nor is the modern society the same as the traditional society. China is experiencing a dual transformation. The changes in society are unprecedented. For example, in the process of urbanisation, farmers continue to move to towns and cities. Their living environments change, and so do the people with whom they are acquainted and in daily contact. Their spending habits will also gradually change, which prompts the consumption commodity market to change accordingly. Furthermore, more educational opportunities and improved knowledge and technology will also bring changes to the consumption commodity market.

Second, the rise in individual consumers' ages can also bring about changes in the types of commodities needed in the consumption market and this type of change is also related to changes in customers' living environments. For example, if farmers live in a rural area, there will no great difference between commodities they buy when they are young and when they are middle-aged or older.

By contrast, once they move to cities, the types of commodities they buy when they are young will be different from those they buy when they are middle-aged or older.

Third, the purchases of customers are, to a considerable extent, affected by fashion, social trends, advertisements and the media. A person, in a more remote place, less well paid, older in age and less educated, is less influenced by fashion. Nevertheless, after he moves to a city, his consumption behaviour and consumption options will change with growing income and social interaction.

Fourth, attention should also be paid to the impact of pre- and after-sale services on a person's choice of commodities. New services have been included in the marketing of new products. This is greatly attractive to consumers in their choices of commodities. An obvious example is the accompanying tourism consumption service. The higher quality of service an enterprise offers, the more attractive tourism becomes to tourists.

Fifth, changes in consumption attitudes also affect people's consumption behaviour, thereby affecting the consumption commodity market. Why do people consume? The most basic consumption concept is to satisfy their own basic demand and rigid demand. The basic demand (food, clothing, shelter, transportation) refers to people's demand for life necessities; the rigid demand is the demand that a purchaser feels for something they will have to buy. It includes demand for the life necessities mentioned previously, but the scope is bigger than this. For instance, customers, whether they are farmers in the countryside or urban residents, can act according to their expenditure capacity in handling birth, old age, sickness and death and such expenditures cannot be omitted, thereby belonging to the rigid demand. In view of the consumption concept since the development of an industrial society, the impact of consumption concepts on consumer behaviour can never be neglected. For example, the craze of viewing each other's choices changes consumer attitudes. Such a trend exists not only in the countryside but also in the cities. Take the craze of showing-off to another for example. It also changes consumption attitudes, as it drives consumers to pursue luxury and excellence so as to express their distinctness from ordinary people

It is because consumption attitudes are undergoing changes that the consumption market shows relative stability and volatility.

5 Feasibilities in creating consumption demand

In the process of expanding private demand, it should be understood that consumption demand can be created through efforts. That is to say, a consumer commodity market can be created. This can be elaborated by answering four questions.

(1) The role of desire alternation

Demand refers to demand with paying capacity. Therefore, demand originates from two aspects. On the one hand, demand comes from desire and with desire, there is demand; on the other hand, demand must have paying capacity, which includes current income and expected income. When combined with paying capacity, desire can satisfy demand.

Paying capacity is determined by income levels and conditions of income growth. After the income distribution system was pushed forward, income levels of low-income families improved. The number of intermediate-income families within the country's population and the proportion of the income of intermediate-income population within the total income of urban and rural residents will gradually increase nationwide. These trends have created premises for the consumption commodity market and also conditions for people's desire alterations. Be aware that people's desire alterations are caused by many factors. First, it depends on people's income growth, and next, it depends on the changes in residence locations and living environments, gradual changes in personal consumption habits, and changes in personal social circle etc. Thus, new consumption demand can be naturally created.

(2) The supply of new products and new services

It is not sufficient to simply rely on demand increase with paying capacity and peoples' alteration of desire. There must be supply increase in new commodities and services, for they strongly attract customers. This can be summarised in a simple way: growing demand with paying capacity and alteration of people's desires are a force that pushes the expansion of private consumption, while the supply of new products and services equals a pulling force. When pushing and pulling forces function together, private consumption is expanded.

Supplies of new commodities and services rely on market forces and enterprises' conduct. There is intense competition among enterprises. Enterprises know best about the kind of commodities and services that current customers of different ages, with different income and levels of knowledge, wish to buy. Old-fashioned or unattractive commodities and services make consumers' purchase intentions fall and only new goods and services that can keep up with fashion and meet consumers' interests attract consumers and they became the first customers. So due to demonstrative effects, new products and new services come into fashion.

Given this, enterprises, through research and development, constant market surveys, continuous promotion of new products and service programmes will broaden sales channels and expand private consumption. Often there are such sales modes. That is, when displaying new products and production (such as household electrical appliances), a manufacturer who introduces new products and production, as well as the market that sells the new products, instructs customers how to use them safely and maximise their efficiencies. So this creates conditions for the entry of new types of products into the homes of ordinary people. This is a reform in the way of marketing. It is people's desire for alternation that leads to the research and development of new products and it is the introduction of new products that attracts consumers, thus expanding private consumption.

In the 1970s, Galbraith, an American economist, studied the marketing methods outlined earlier and proposed the concept of "producer sovereignty". He thought that a "consumer sovereignty" phenomenon already existed. That is, enterprises produced whatever consumers wanted to buy to satisfy customers' needs. Now the situation has changed from "consumer sovereignty" into "producer sovereignty". That is, enterprises tend to first develop a certain new product, then promote this kind of new product by advertisements or demonstrative operation and invite customers to come and buy it. Galbraith called the case "producer sovereignty", which might not be appropriate because it was only under the planned economic system that there was real "producer sovereignty". That is, consumers could only buy whatever state-owned enterprises produced. However, he pointed out that "supply can be created". That is, the increase in the supply of new products and new services can expand private consumption.

(3) Upgrading consumption levels

Gradual upgrading of consumption levels from a lower level, comparatively low level, a medium level, comparatively higher level to high level is related to all kinds of the factors mentioned previously (such as income rise, changes in residence living environments and life circle(?), the impact of general consumption mood and fashion, the degree of education and levels of knowledge etc.). They will not be repeated here; however, there is a point that needs to be raised: inertia of consumption levels. That is, customers are more adapted psychologically and physically to the changes from a low level of consumption to a medium level, or from a medium level to a high level, while it will be more difficult for consumption levels to drop from a high level to a medium level or from a medium level to a low level, because it is more difficult for customers to adapt to such changes psychologically and physically. People generally have a consumption inertia of "it is better to be high than to be low".

The reason why people can easily adapt psychologically and physically to the upgrading of consumption levels is directly related to people's income rise. One would like to think that as the income has risen, it is natural to raise consumption levels. As to why people find it more difficult to adapt psychologically and physically to downgrading changes, the most important reason is that most of the downgrading is forced and involuntary. For example, a long-term nationwide social unrest, sharply-reduced income, high unemployment and severe inflation forced people to lower their consumption levels; otherwise, people will not be able to survive. In this case, how can people adapt to it? Some people or families want to maintain their previous levels of consumption and can manage to sustain themselves by living on savings for some time, but that cannot be a long-term solution.

It is people's adaptation to the upgrading of consumption levels and their increasing willingness for consumption that naturally leads to the expansion of private consumption. This is also the best opportunity for the extension of private consumption. It is necessary for the government to take measures to eliminate sources of social unrest, to avoid high unemployment and rampant inflation in economic operations and to promote the steady growth of income.

In general, consumer behaviour per se has a pattern to follow. The mastery of its development will not only ensure that customer demand can be created but also the goal of expanding private consumption will be steadily achieved.

(4) Deepening the understanding of luxury commodity

Luxury and luxury commodities are understood differently in different societies and ages. They have even been defined by law. There are also different moral criteria for what normal consumption is and what luxury consumption is in different ages and among different communities and the criteria are closely related to people's consumption concepts and habits. Legal and moral constraints are combined to become constraints on customer behaviour.

Why is the government often involved in constraining consumer behaviour so as to use laws to make mandatory provision? For instance, this is forbidden; so is that and so on. The government also makes moral regulations and stipulates that people should observe them. For instance, condemning certain consumer behaviour or recognising a certain type of consumption behaviour plays the role of a consumption director. In general, this is out of three considerations. First, whether the power of a nation can afford high private luxury consumption and avoid using limited resources for luxury consumption; second, concerns about whether social conduct will be downgraded and then corrupted by seeking a life of pleasure; third, fear that luxury consumption will highlight the social wealth gap, resulting in social unrest. Additionally, forbidding people from transcending their social hierarchy was also one of the factors that those in power took into consideration in the centralised feudal era.

Putting the last point (transcending the social hierarchy) aside, there are still merits in successive governments' legal and moral constraints on luxury consumption. Nonetheless, definitions of luxury and luxury goods in fact are changeable. Take what we experienced for example. Thirty years ago, it was considered to be a luxury or living a luxury life for a woman to wear a gold or pearl necklace, put on slightly better cosmetics, or for a couple to take their children to scenic spots to enjoy leisure time. Now, things have changed: wearing jewellery, putting on high-end cosmetics, making high-end residential renovations on newly-bought houses, raising pets, and especially travelling abroad to buy handbags and clothes with famous brand names in overseas supermarkets are all considered normal phenomena. As long as a customer does not use public funds to buy personal items, almost no one thinks that the consumer behaviour should be condemned. Isn't it right to say that the concepts of luxury and luxury goods have already changed?

It is worth noting that these expensive handbags and the like can be purchased abroad and also in China's big stores. Why do tourists travel to a foreign country to buy them abroad rather than buy them in China? It is said that first, they are worried about being cheated by handbags with fake foreign brands, that are being sold in Chinese markets; second, due to heavy import duties, buying imported products in China's stores is more expensive than buying them overseas, so those who go abroad prefer buying them overseas to buying them in domestic stores.

With people's changing consumption concepts and a deeper understanding of luxury goods, why not reduce import duties on certain consumption commodities according to the actual situation? Note that when people buy imported goods in China's stores, what is expanded is Chinese consumption demand, and what is raised is employment in China. The outcome brings about growth of China's Gross Domestic Product (GDP). Instead, if Chinese people buy goods in overseas stores, what is expanded is foreign consumption demand, and what is increased is overseas employment, leading to the growth of foreign GDP. In that case, why not reduce relevant import tariffs to promote domestic consumption?

Finally, we should remember that private consumption behaviour is the object of market regulation, but the expansion of private consumption demand needs coordination between the government's regulations, particularly in the reform of urban and rural residents' income distribution system. It should be executed by the government. Of course, legal constraints on private consumption behaviour and guidance on consumption trends and fashion cannot be ignored. Nevertheless, the government should show respect to the consumers' own rights of option but promptly discourage traditionally corrupt customs. In the process of expanding private consumption, the market order must be maintained and the security and reliability of consumption products must be ensured, which are obligations of the government at all time.

Section 3 Construction of ecological civilisation from the perspective of reforming forest right system

1 The "belated reform"

The reform of the collective forest system was already mentioned in the introduction section of this book and will be expounded in this section.

The earliest Chinese economic reform was the reform of the rural land contract system carried out between 1978 and 1982. The enacting and promotion of the reform mobilised farmers' enthusiasm and increased agricultural production. Based on that, the system of supplying necessities with coupons was finally cancelled after having been implemented for many years.

According to the logic of reforms, the reform of the collective forest right system should be introduced at the same time. Actions were taken first in some places, and the collective forest land was contracted to farmers. But at the beginning of the Reform and Opening-up, many farmers did not trust the policy of the Party. Based on their past experiences, they held that the Party's²policies were changeable. As forest land was contracted to them, they followed the trend and cut down trees, believing that it would be alright to plant new trees after getting the old ones cut down. Otherwise, once the policy changed, would the joy not be futile? In this case, the Central Committee urgently stopped the collective forest land household contracting practice. It was after it had stagnated for 20 years that the government relaunched the reform of collective forest land right system. Thereby, the reform of collective forest land right system is called "the belated reform".

In 2003, after *Decision of the CPC Central Committee and State Council on Accelerating the Development of Forestry* was issued and implemented, the reform of collective forest right system subsequently started in *Fujian, Jiangxi, Liaoning, Yunnan* and other provinces to explore paths for the reform of collective forest land system. Based on accumulated experience from pilot reforms, the CPC Central Committee and State Council issued "*Views on Comprehensively Promoting the Reform of Collective Forest Right System*" on 8 June 2008, which meant that a far-reaching reform began to be launched.

While the collective forest land contract occurred 20 years later than the farmland contract, it cannot but be recognised that the collective forest land contract, like the farmland contract which began in 1979, matters to the overall national economic reform, for the area of China's collective forest land was preliminarily estimated to be about 2.5 billion to 2.7 billion acres, and 90% of forestry resources were in mountainous areas, where the population under the poverty line clustered: 496 out of 592 state-level poor counties were distributed in those areas. Only through the set of figures can we gain some understanding of the significance of the reforms to the collective forest right system.

The reform of the collective forest right system is carried out by modelling on the farmland contract system. The core issue of the farmland contract system was to clarify use rights of contract land, management rights and benefit rights of contracted farmland. The farmland was still collectively owned, but with clarified use, management and benefit rights, farmers could safely cultivate the land and harvest thereafter. The importance of the benefit rights lies in its clarification that the owner of crops on the contracted land is the one who cultivates the land, and the rights could not be grabbed by others. It was the same with the collective forest land after contract: the woods in the contracted forests belonged to the contractor and a contractor can benefit from them. The rights cannot be grabbed by others. Contracting households have actually become operating entities of family forest farms, i.e. family forest land owners.

Nevertheless, the forest land contract does after all come more than 20 years later than the farmland contract. The collective forest land contract can fully take in experience and lessons from implementing the farmland contract system. So as was pointed out in the introduction of the book, the collective forest land contract system, while modelling the farmland contract system, broke through three aspects of constraints from the farmland contract, i.e. going beyond the farmland contract system.

First, unlike the farmland contract system which had a short contract term, the term for collective forest land contract was set as no change for 70 years right from the time when it was implemented nationwide. While farmland contracts were later changed to "no change over a long term", how long was "a long term"? The farmland contractors did not have a clear idea of the term, and did not feel assured. Nevertheless, "no change over 70 years" was defined for forest land contract households. With the contract unchanged for 70 years, the third generation will have grown up. Is there anything to worry about? So the remark "let the trees planted by the grandfathers be cut down by the grandsons" has become a mantra in forest areas. So contracted households enhanced their initiatives on afforestation, and their enthusiasm for loving and protecting forests was greatly enhanced.

Second, the contracted forest land and trees on it can be used as mortgage to obtain loans. As a result, the economy of contracted forest households became active, which was another major breakthrough. Note that when farmland was contracted, farmland and crops could not be used for mortgage. It was about 20 years later that the mortgage of farmland and crops was implemented in experimental reform areas, while this restriction or prohibition has not been lifted in other areas. Nevertheless, when the reform in collective forest right system started, it was stipulated in documents that the contracted forest land and woods on it can be mortgaged to gain loans. This enabled the financing function of financial institutes in the forest areas. The features of the mortgage are: a mortgager can continue to manage the forest land during the forest land mortgage term. It is only when the loan is due and the mortgager fails to redeem the mortgage debt that the mortgagee can deal with the mortgage legally. This can not only enhance the efficiency of farmland management but also guard against financial risks, making both forest land contractors and financial institutes satisfied.

Third, the forest land contract was directly contracted to farmers. This approach was initially controversial. At some symposiums, some held that in the reform of forest right system, characteristics of forest land must be taken into consideration. For instance, there were more people in rural areas while there was less farmland. It was feasible to let farming households cultivate contracted farmland; however, that was not applicable to forest land. If an individual forest farmer was allowed to make a contract, saying "contracting the hills to farmer households", then would it not enlarge the gap between the rich and the poor if a farmer could contract thousands of *mu* or at least hundreds of *mu* of forest land? Moreover, the farmland could be harvested within in a year, while it took at least eight or 10 years, or even as long as several decades or a hundred years to harvest forest land. Was it feasible to let forest land to be contracted by individuals? So others suggested that the forest land should be contracted to towns, villages or forestry cooperatives organised by farmers. Nevertheless, the decision of the Party Central Committee was to implement the forest land contract, to households, as it was to farmland, which greatly mobilised initiatives of forest land contractors. Forestry cooperatives were voluntarily established by contractors after the forest land was contracted to the households. This is a decision made in China's unique reality and the contract practice was welcomed by forest farmers.

In short, the biggest inspiration that the reform of the forest right system brought about was: great entrepreneurial initiatives were hidden amongst folks and through the forest contracting, this kind of initiatives has been fully mobilised. That is to say, under the planned economic system, although there had been human capital, it had long been sluggish or had no vitality. The exertion of the role of human capital was completely passive, which failed to exhibit its own strength. It occurs through a combination of the realisation of the reform of the collective forest right system, the establishment of appropriate institutional mechanisms or systems where human capital becomes vigorous, and the encouragement of entrepreneurial initiatives in private sectors. On top of that, the stock of human capital has greatly increased. This increase in human capital stock can be reflected in the following three aspects.

First, the number of people engaged in forestry labour and management has increased. Forestry has become a field that attracts labour. According to a survey, between 2009 and 2011, there appeared the phenomenon where some young workers who went off the forest land to be migrant workers returned and undertook the forestry labour and management. With progress in the reform of the collective forest right system, contract households felt that family labour was inadequate, so they passed word in succession to their migrant family members or relatives, asking them to give up their jobs, and do entrepreneurial work at home. When these workers returned home to conduct forestry work and management, they also brought some colleagues and friends along to work on forest land. In 2011, when conducting a survey on why there was an insufficient supply of migrant workers in some towns of the Pearl River Delta, we found that the reform of the collective forest right system was after all an important reason for the reduced supply of migrant workers in the nearby provinces.

Second, farmers greatly enhanced their knowledge, skills and abilities, for they were dedicated to setting up their own family forest land, and running businesses in relation to the minor forest products, they actively learned about forestry and under-forest breeding, and also gained marketing-related knowledge of minor forest products. Note that the increase in labourers' and managers' enhanced knowledge, skills and abilities is also an increase in the contents of human capital, which will be beneficial to the development of family forest land and the accumulation of family wealth.

Third, initiatives of forest contracting households and their family members were running high, which meant that the quality of human capital had increased. This can be seen as an embodiment that greater energy in human capital has been exerted within the given stock of human capital. When conducting surveys in *Bijie* City, *Guizhou* Province, we found the following case: in recent years, in places where *Yunnan* Province borders with *Guizhou* Province, there had been serious spring droughts. Fires often broke out in spring time. In the past, farmers used not to hurry up the hill to extinguish fires but would say: "This is the task of the village cadres", because collective forests were burning. If government militia at the county and township levels were organised to put out mountain fires, forest farmers would also follow orders and go up the mountain to extinguish fires. Now, the situation is quite different. Farmers' degrees of concerns over assets have increased substantially. As could be seen on collective forest land of *Beijie*, farmers knew that every piece of forest land was contracted land of their folks, neighbours or acquaintances. Once there was a fire or once villagers found a fire, they would call out for help with the fire and everyone went up the mountains to extinguish the fire, for what was burning could be their own forest land or that of their relatives or neighbours. At one call, hundreds would go into action. There was no need for the county or village government to give orders. They would voluntarily go up the mountains to extinguish fires. It was a kind of self-rescue and mutually-aided fire-fighting operation. There was no need for the county or village government to first issue an order and then people move up the hill to extinguish fires. From this we have known that enhanced concerns over assets fully reflected increased initiatives of forest farmers after the reform collective forest right system. This is was fully in line with the reality of forest land.

2 The development of the under-forest economy

Before the reform of the collective forest right system, mountains are collective mountains and forests collective forests. Farmers did not care about the under-forest economy. This is because farmers thought that since forests were collectively owned, did it have anything to do with me? If I raised chickens in the forest, would I not be taking advantage of the state-owned property? If I developed herb-farming in the woods and was known by the collective, would I not be accused and the herbs be confiscated? There used to be in some places collective under-forest chicken farms, and collective edible fungus production bases, but the majority of them were run with a low efficiency and were not profitable. Farmers did not care about them and after a period of time, they died out. It was right after the reform of collective forest right system that the forest economy took on a new life. The key lies in that the management system of the forestry economy has changed from then on. It is no longer a collective poultry farm or a collective plantation but an inseparable part of the family forest farm, which was invested and managed by households. In many places, the loans of financial institutions (including credit and mortgage loans) gave much support to the family under-forest economy.

The feature of family forest economic activities was its adaptation to local conditions. They have no established patterns but bear great flexibility. When an activity was appropriate, its scale would expand; otherwise, it would be shrunk or even its production and management were stopped until they were turned to livestock breeding or farming. This results from the flexible mechanism of family forest land. When surveying in some counties in the south of *Wan* (*Anhui* Province), we found that some collective forest contractors carefully ran their forest farms and meanwhile, to cater for tourists' need, they also ran "Happy Farms", an inn which offered catering and accommodations for tourists. Meanwhile, under-forest chicken, duck and goose farms and under-forest mushroom and fungus farms were managed by contract households. In the meantime, it satisfies catering needs of the "Happy Farms" but also sells other self-produced local specialties like mushrooms, fungi etc. Other contractors ran the bamboo industry and had their own products such as fresh and dried bamboo shoots to supply customers.

Thus, the development of family under-forest economy has increased farmers' income, and farmers are more confident with the increase of wealth. They are attaching increasing importance to the maintenance of the forest, as it is their source of wealth. They understand that only by increasing benefits of the forest land, can they safeguard the forest and that only by developing the under-forest economy, can they really get rich. This is called "the green path to riches". "Green wealth" is a welcome phenomenon that appears on forest land. While excessively cutting down trees can increase some income in a short term, it can never be a long-term strategy. If the ecological system is damaged, the road to wealth is destroyed. How can we talk about sustainable development and sustainable property income?

The under-forest economic development has in fact expanded the arable forest land, because the contracted forest area is fixed. However, if the forest economy is vigorously developed, for instance, raising under-forest chickens, mushrooms, Chinese herbal medicine etc., would it not be equivalent to an increase of forest area? Under-forest area is a land not fully exploited. Under family businesses, forest land is fully used. What else can it be but the expansion of the forest land?

Furthermore, the development of under-forest economy is an important component of the economic development mode shifts. This is because the traditional economic development mode threw environmental protection and growth into an opposite polarity. It seems that both of them are inherently irreconcilable. That is, if environments are protected, the economy will not be able to grow sustainably; to achieve sustainable economic growth, environments are bound to be destroyed, so people can only "choose the greater one when two benefits are weighed but choose the less harmful when two harmful ones are weighed". Often the outcomes are: a developing country should prioritise economic growth and that the GDP target surpasses all. So it can only follow the path of "governance after contamination". A good many developing countries just followed suit.

Practice has clearly told people that severe losses have been caused by the traditional mode of economic development. Ecological damages have resulted in many irreparable losses. Note that an overriding emphasis on GDP regardless of the depletion of resources and damages to environments will inevitably result in such consequences.

Thus, the quality of economic growth is more important than the speed of economic growth. Economic growth must be combined with the construction of ecological civilisation, both must be symbiotic and taken into account. This is the biggest reason for the urgent transformation of the economic development mode. Moreover, in recent years, significant changes have taken place in society's views over environmental protection. In the past, for the sake of human survival, people's focus of concern was the emission of toxic fumes, wastewater and residues should be forbidden in production and daily life, for the emissions could harm people's health, pollute environments and even incur deaths. Therefore, people demanded cleaner production and environments. Now, the focus of the environmental protection was not only to halt emissions of fumes, wastewater and residues. For instance, carbon dioxide is not toxic, but it cannot be emitted in unlimited amounts, for too much of it will lead to climate change and cause damage to environments that human beings rely on for survival. A low-carbon economy has become a common emission regulation by which countries around the world should abide. This is a new problem that China, a country which is still ranked among developing countries, has to face.

Specifically speaking, in order to adapt to the low-carbon economic requirements of the international community, China should not only take measures to close down plants not meeting environmental protection requirements, making new breakthroughs in new craft and new product designs, speeding up research and development of cleaner energy and new materials, we must also vigorously develop environmental protection industries. The environmental protection industries can be interpreted in both narrow and broad terms. The narrow environmental protection industry mainly refers to the manufacturing industry that produces environmental protection equipment, instruments, a wide range of monitoring means and various environment-purifying items. It also includes industries which use environmental protection equipment to purify environments and restore damaged environments. The environmental protection industry in a broad sense also includes afforestation, developing the under-forest economy, improving soil and slowing desertification and rocky desertification, purifying rivers, lakes and coastal tidal flats, and the recycling and reusing of resources. It can be seen clearly that the reform of the collective forest right system is of great significance to the construction of an ecological civilisation, for the reform has straightened out collective forest land relationships, mobilised the enthusiasm of the majority of forest land contractors, which are conducive to turning economic low-carbon forestry, forest maintenance and development of under-forest economy into farmers' conscious behaviour.

Here, there are some beneficial interactions between forestry, the under-forest economy and the low-carbon economy. Forests are the most important carbon sink resource. The better the quality of a forest is, the more solid a base will be provided for the under-forest economic development, and the more income people can get from the under-forest economy. "Living a good life without cutting down trees" has been the consensus among farmers. It is understood that forest mushroom cultivation requires good vegetation conditions to help mushrooms to grow, while the mycelium from mushrooms does not only increase soil carbon sequestration capacity, but also provides more nutrients for the growth of forests. So does the role of under-forest chickens to the forest protection. Chickens can remove the forest weeds and pests, loosen the earth and fertilise forest land, all of which are helpful to the growth of trees. The trees in the meantime provide appropriate environments for the growth of chickens. This is a typical model of the cyclic economy.

Currently, collective forestry economic activities have just begun. The developed under-forest economy only occupies 4% of the collective forest area. Under-forest planting and breeding have not yet achieved their expected scale-up, intensification and full scientific focus. Additionally, forest infrastructure is relatively less-developed, which has become one of the obstacles that stops the under-forest economy from further expansion. Another obstacle is forest farmers' insufficient capital investment to the under-forest development. Generally speaking, labourers who undertake under-forest activities lack sufficient knowledge, skills and abilities. Neither are they familiar with the market. This is the third obstacle to the further expansion of the under-forest economy. If the government, financial institutions and vocational and technical training sectors can increase their support and help provided to forest areas, I believe that forestry (including the under-forest economy) will certainly be able to play a greater role in the "green growth" and ecological civilisation.

It should also be noted that on the one hand, the realisation of the low-carbon economy depends on the active promotion of various energy-saving and emission-reducing measures; and on the other hand, it relies on the increase of the total amount of carbon sink. The reform of forest right system and vigorous afforestation are effective ways to increase the total amount of carbon sink, because the development of forestry can not only increase the gross carbon sink but can also provide the impetus for China in international carbon emission negotiations.

3 Prospect of forestry cooperatives

In order to let forestry exert a better role (including the under-forest economy) in Chinese economic growth and its construction of ecological civilisation, it is necessary to start with forestry industrialisation.

Forestry industrialisation is to treat forestry as an industry, making overall plans and integrating different aspects of production, circulation, distribution and reproduction. Forestry industrialisation covers both individual and independent household forest farms after the reform of collective forest right system, and also all the state-owned forestry units which have not formally adopted the reform of forest right system. Both the household forest farms and state-owned forestry units are market operation entities appropriate for the market. They should become active market participants through clearly defined ownership.

In regard to the system of state-owned forests and the future mode of operation, they will be further discussed below. Here, we shall first focus on the mode of farmland operation after the reform of the collective forest right system. After the implementation of contracting farmland to households, there are roughly three types of operation mode:

Type I: family forest farms

For a long period of time, household forest farms will be the main operation units on the collective forest land. With forest deeds issued after the farmers had contracted the forest land, they can assuredly operate the collective forest land, undertake afforestation on the contracted land, maintain forests, carry out under-forestry breeding and cultivation businesses and fell trees in accordance with regulations. They rely on sales of timber, fruit tree and oil tree products (fruits, nuts, tea, olive oil, palm oil etc.) for earnings. Their additional incomes are from under-forest breeding farms and plantations that they are running, so that their living standards will gradually improve. As the land, after having been contracted, can be circulated, forest farmers might take over the forest land through leasing, subcontracting and other forms from forest land contractors who intend to be migrant workers and do business in cities, thereby expanding their forest management areas. While some of the family-run forest farms can become big forest land contractors, a big forest land household still falls into the category of household-run farmland

and its nature has not been changed. They have terms to conduct operations and production of scale, improving efficiency, increasing minor forest products so as to increase incomes.

Type II: forestry cooperatives

Before the reform of collective forest right system, it would be impossible to establish the model of forestry cooperatives in its real sense on collective forest land. Even if forestry cooperatives were set up in some places, they were nothing but another form of the collective economic form. Just like brigade-run or community-run businesses set up before the farmland contract system, they were also listed as "cooperative", when they actually did not have the nature of cooperatives, because farmers did not possess property ownership and could not become the cooperative investors.

After the collective reform of the forest right system, forest land was contracted by farmers. So they set up forestry cooperatives based on "*The Law of the People's Republic of China on Farmers' Specialized Cooperatives*" and investors of such forestry cooperatives were contractors on the forest land, namely household forest farmers. These investors voluntarily joined the cooperatives. A cooperative set up in this way is an independent market entity with cooperate capacity. The newly-set up forestry cooperatives coexist in different places in a wide range of forms. Some are made up of shares turned from the contracted farmland by each investor (forest land contractor); others were not made up of the contracted forest land of each investor (land contractor) in the form of shares, rather, they are composed of shares converted from cash. There was still another type, that is, many investors (forest land contractor) not only converted their contracted forest land into shares and invested in the cooperatives, but also converted a certain amount of cash into shares and invested them in forestry cooperatives. The general capital of such forestry cooperatives was mixed with shares converted from both forest land and cash.

Whatever form a forestry cooperative took, it must be constructed on "*the Law of the People's Republic of China on Farmers' Specialized Cooperatives*". General Meeting of Shareholders (or members of the General Assembly) is the highest authority of a cooperative. The Board of Directors elected by members of the General Assembly is the executing agency. The president, equivalent to managers, trusted and commissioned by General Meeting of the Shareholders and the Board, presided over the daily production, business and management of forestry cooperatives. Accounts are open to public inspection; when the Board's term of office expires, re-election will be held on a due date and management should be democratic. Those are rules and regulations with which cooperatives must comply. The greatest advantage of forestry cooperatives lies in their harvest of scale benefits, which is conducive to investors' income rise and the development of cooperative businesses.

The existence and development of forestry cooperatives are not contradictory to the existence and development of family forest farms. The relationship between the two is not only cooperative, that is, being partners to each other, but also competitive, namely, making the best use of their own respective advantages in mechanisms and the conduct of their business activities.

Type III: forestry enterprises

Normally, there are four types of enterprises, which can be called forestry enterprises.

Type I enterprises take forestry management as their main businesses, which include planting trees, maintaining forest woods, felling and selling trees. For example, some forest industry enterprises operate both businesses. They consider forest land as their own forestry bases, and their main business is the wood processing industry, where they produce all kinds of products based on wood-material.

Type II enterprises provide services for forestry production, such as enterprises that provide specialised machinery for forestry, and enterprises that provide all kinds of production materials needed by the forest land, as well as transport enterprises that deliver the felled trunks and timbers from the forest land to the outside world.

Type III enterprises provide with all kinds of living materials for forest dwellers and forest labourers, as well as those that provide a variety of life services.

Type IV enterprises provide services for forest dwellers and labourers, and serve the construction of small towns, including the construction of architecture, roads and public utilities.

All four types of enterprises are likely to expand their businesses after the reform of collective forest right system, be involved in the production and management of forestry per se, and cooperate in different forms with household forestry cooperatives. For example, it is possible that these forestry companies may cooperate with family farms, particularly big forestry contractors by means of providing capital or forestry machinery, so as to be engaged in forestry and under-forest activities. Moreover, it is also likely that these forestry enterprises may cooperate with forestry cooperatives and be engaged in forestry and under-forest activities by means of holding shares. Of course, though purchase behaviour is against the regulations of the collective reform of the forest right system, we cannot say that it is definitely impossible for these forestry enterprises to acquire the ownership of the contracted forest land by purchasing, subletting or subcontracting and undertaking forest land businesses. While forest enterprises were restricted from taking over or directly managing forest land contracted by family farmlands (including big contractors), these may be ignored by local forestry enterprises, or violated intentionally or the restrictions may be breached. Generally speaking, after the reform of the collective forest right system, family forestry farmland and forestry cooperatives should be maintained as much as possible. Forestry enterprises are not advised to sublet or subcontract collective forest land. They should also be restricted from purchasing household forest land or the contracted forest land of forestry cooperatives.

But forestry enterprises (regardless of what kind of forestry enterprises they are) can still get access to the collective forest areas by various means and can establish and consolidate cooperative relationships with their family farms, large contractors and forestry cooperatives. All those forms like "forestry cooperatives with family farms and large contractors", "forestry enterprises – forestry cooperatives – family forest land and big contractors" are promising. This can increase the income of family forest land, big contractors and forestry cooperatives, and it can also help promote forestry industrialisation.

4 Exploring the state–owned forest farm reform: "one forest farm with two systems"

Up to now, the reform of the state-owned forest right system has been at an exploratory stage. How should the state-owned forest farms be reformed? Generally speaking, the following methods have been tested: for instance, the contracted management by forestry industry enterprises, the management of national forest parks, converting state-owned forest farms into public institutions, "one forest farm with two systems" and so on. Each of them has its respective applicable scope. Those trials need to be summarised and outcomes of the trials need to be further tested in practice.

From the perspective of practice, "one forest farm with two systems" may have greater applicability. "One forest farm with two systems" refers to the coexistence of two systems on a state-owned forest farm, i.e. the coexistence of direct management system by the state-owned enterprises and the contracted management system of state-owned forestry workers.

What the direct management system of state-owned forest farms operates is large ecological and public welfare forests. They are directly managed and operated by state-owned forest farms. Operations include afforestation and forest maintenance. At the same time we must strictly control the amount of logging, of which the aim is not at growing income, but better protection of forest ecology. In the direct management system of state-owned farms, financing is often allocated by recurrent cost. Under the forest economy this can also be carried out. The development of the under-forest economy aims not only at safeguarding the state-owned forest land, but also at increasing income to make more funds and improve the livelihood of the workers, providing reassurance about working on forest land.

The contracted management system of the state-owned forest land staff was piloted mainly by referring to the experience from the reform of the collective forest right system. The highlight of this approach is to take out part of the state-owned forest land, divide it into plots and have it contracted out to all the staff including employees who directly work on state-owned forest land, and all the staff who work on the forest land under the state-owned forest farm management system. The plots are contracted by individuals. Each has his share; otherwise, it would bring about conflicts and barriers between the state-owned forestry workers, and barriers and dissatisfaction due to the income gap caused by the state-owned forest farms under the state-owned forest land operating system.

After implementing "one forest farm with two systems", under the contracted management system for state-owned forestry staff, those who were allocated forest land according to the forest land contract system could all set up household forest farms. Forest land that they contracted to operate was state-owned forest land; what the staff obtained was its use rights and contracted management rights. Thus, there might be three issues.

First, should the state-owned forestry staff on this part of the forest land continue to receive pay? There are two kinds of opinions. One view is: they are still state-owned forest farm staff. Theoretically, their identity has not been changed; meanwhile, they still need to perform certain tasks like afforesting, protecting ecological forests, felling trees etc. as state-owned forestry staff. Thus, they should receive payment as usual. The other view is: they should receive payment as usual, but unlike collective farmland that farmers contracted after the reform of collective forest right system, their contracted forest land is state-owned, so contractors, i.e. the state-owned forestry staff (household forest land owners) are still staff of national forest farms. They should pay certain contract fees to state forest farm administration sectors. The proportion of contract fee to the pay that they received was negotiable. Nevertheless, it is reasonable to pay a certain amount of contract fees, whether it is small or large.

Second, can the land contracted by staff under the state-owned forest farm contract system be sublet or subcontracted? Can it be transferred? After the reform of the collective forest right system, those are feasible for forest land contracted by households but there are some restrictions on state-owned land after they are contracted. The restrictions are: if staff need to subcontract or sublet forest land, they should target other state-owned forestry staff on the forest land who are willing to accept the sublet and subcontract but not at non-state-owned forest farm staff. Otherwise, it will change the nature of state-owned forest farm and be contradictory to existing laws. In regard to whether state-owned forest staff can transfer the contracted forest land, it should be said that no matter to whom forest land is transferred, it is inappropriate.

Third, as has already been mentioned, when the state-owned forest farm contract system was implemented, all staff on the state-owned forest farms had contracting rights. Staff considered it appropriate to contract farmland close to their accommodation. If some forest land was far from where they lived, those who had an elderly, young or sick or insufficient labour force could subcontract or transfer their land to other staff and collect subcontract fees or rents. In particular, those still working directly under the state-owned forest farm management system could also subcontract or sublet their forest land to other staff due to busy work schedule, insufficient family labour force or the travelling distance from their accommodation. Similarly, they have rights to take subcontract fees or rents.

In short, the reform of state-owned farms under "one forest farm, two systems" still needs to be further tested to gain experience. Though the trial of "one forest farm, two systems" has comparatively higher applicability, it is not to deny that various other reform explorations and trials may be applicable in certain circumstances. Different experimental modes have different application areas, which actually suggest that each of them has their respective advantages.

For instance, the contracting management mode of the forest industry enterprises may be applicable to state-owned forest farms where commodity forests are major forests and public welfare forests and ecological forests are supplementary. Some forest industry enterprises have already had many years of business practice. They are already familiar with situations here. Those enterprises per se were profitable. Therefore, it was feasible for them to contract and manage forest farms. Both parties, the state-owned forest farms as the party awarding the contracts and the forest industry enterprises as contractors write their agreed-upon conditions down on contracts. Each contract has a certain term. When it expires, a new contract is to be signed. If the party awarding the contract feels that the contractor has not adequately fulfilled the contract, it can modify the contract or alternate the contractor.

Additionally, the national forest park management mode may be applicable to some scenic spots. Though the spots only take a very small part of the forest park area, tourism income from the spots helps with the maintenance of national forest parks. On every account, national forest parks should prioritise ecological and social benefits. Economic benefits are also important but should not be put above ecological and social benefits.

Furthermore, turning state-owned forest farms into public institutions may be applicable to some cities at the district level, which have small forest land areas. From the perspective of administration, this is an easier way. Though state-owned forest land does not have a large area and is comparatively more scattered, its management is effective, for funds are guaranteed and staff are stable. What deserves our attention is how to develop the under-forest economy in the future. Thus, it will not only promote initiatives and income of forestry staff but it will also use their collective strengths to better maintain the forest land.

There are various modes of managing forest land; it is impossible to have simply one mode. Nonetheless, they should all be tested in practice and tests through practice usually lag behind time, for which we also need patience and time. Hence, there is no need to rush into a conclusion for the moment.

Notes

1 *"Paolu"* means "escaped to avoid paying off the debt". [Trans.]
2 "The Party" here refers to the Communist Party of China. [Trans.]

4 Macroeconomic regulation and control

Section 1 Fine-tuning as the keystone of current macroeconomic regulation and control

1 Limitations of macroeconomic regulation and control

Grasping the right opportunity to launch or end macroeconomic regulation and control is very important. Though the launch of regulation and control is likely to drag behind the right opportunity, what is more likely to fall behind is the completion time. Both types of "lagging behind", nonetheless, can bring about losses to the national economy and even induce ensuing difficulties to economic operation.

It should be noted that that macroeconomic regulation and control used to be measures that targeted at the regulation of aggregate demand. They were mostly applicable to short-term regulation against unemployment and inflation. After the 1970s, the US economy underwent stagflation. Simply regulating aggregate demand became invalid; nor did the short-term regulation function. Afterwards, macroeconomic regulation and control started to pay equal attention to aggregate demand and aggregate supply, aggregate regulation and structural adjustment, short-term as well as mid-term regulation. So ever since then, the focus of macroeconomic regulation and control in some countries has taken into account a combination of all three: inflation control, unemployment alleviation and structural adjustment.

The most important reason for the lagging-behind is due to the lack of knowledge of economic development trends. Relevant sectors were inclined to being deceived by the illusion of "all good news and no bad news" in report materials. Apart from that, some economic phenomena could not be reflected through statistics. Two obvious examples are investor and consumer psychologies. With respect to investor psychology, the purchasing managers' index can only reflect part of the story, while investors' estimation of the investment prospect and their prediction of earning prospect in various trades are not necessarily (or at least not totally) reflected in purchasing managers' index. It is the same with consumer psychology. Normally, consumer expectation of the perfect degree of the social welfare system is one important factor that affects customer psychology. So are the household stock of consumption commodities (mainly durable consumption commodities) and the fashion of commodities. Therefore, the analyses and judgement on economic tendencies by relevant sectors are always erroneous. What they did was do their outmost to make prediction errors as small as possible. Since those errors are inevitable, it is hard to avoid the lagging behind of macro-regulation and control. This is often a common error of macro-decision-making sectors.

Thus, caution is needed before macroeconomic regulation and control is steered substantially. Policies should be consistent and normal expectations of investors and consumers should be undisrupted so as to avoid big fluctuations in the economy. Generally speaking, macroeconomic regulation and control should not rise dramatically or fall sharply, be greatly loosened or strongly tightened, unless there occurs an acute inflation or a high unemployment rate, or co-occurs inflation and unemployment. Otherwise, a big fluctuation would either cause many bubbles in the economy or cause them to burst suddenly, hence being greatly unfavourable to economic operations.

When macro decision-making sectors find abnormal signs in economic operations, they should adopt timely fine-tuning measures. The premises for fine-tuning are that sectors should be able to make predictions and establish early alerting mechanisms in order to take preventive measures. Just as soon as there are alarms of mountain fire, early measures must be taken before it spreads and becomes pervasive. Otherwise, it will be difficult to extinguish it quickly. So fine-tuning has to be given sufficient attention.

Fine-tuning measures involve structural and detailed adjustments. That is to say, in order not to let over loose or over tight phenomenon take place in macroeconomic regulation and control, structural and detailed adjustments can help to avoid big deviations and also prevent bigger future trouble. Do not be anxious for quick successes in this aspect. The best solution to the resumption of a normal economy is fine-tuning, as progressing steadily is much better than seeking quick fixes.

Macro decision-making sectors should understand that certain problems will occur in economic operation, such as structural imbalance, production capacity surplus, increasingly limited product supply, insufficient supply of skilled workers, commodity price rises under certain circumstances, even environmental degradation and ecological damages etc. Usually, solutions to those issues should not rest upon macroeconomic regulation and control. As a result, one should not assume that macroeconomic regulation and control measures instantly generate outcomes. Even the rise and fall of the real estate or stock markets will not necessarily be effective by relying solely on macroeconomic regulation and control. Therefore, under this circumstance, lowering or raising the deposit-reserve ratio, adjusting the benchmark interest rate, or even changing budget revenue and expenditures will complicate the existing issues.

For example, if some institutional barriers make it difficult for rural migrant workers to find jobs or make them not feel not at ease to continue working in original work units, or make them unable to run their own small businesses even if they are willing to do so, the issues cannot be treated as ordinary employment measures. Rather, efforts should be made to resolve problems in the urban-rural binary system or issues that arise in related reforms. Only in this way, can employment and entrepreneurship difficulties of migrant workers to cities be eased.

For another example, under circumstances of cost-push inflation, suppressing price increases cannot rely solely on measures such as tightening aggregate demand from the macroeconomic aspect. Tightening aggregate demand cannot solve the cost-push type of inflation. In face of a general rise, high price levels caused by increased labour cost or increased production cost due to a lack of raw materials and fuel, or even rising food prices, are caused by a short supply of pork and vegetables and so on. As such, adopting the measure of raising the deposit-reserve ratio is not only ineffective but also makes the supply tighter. Previous experience has confirmed this.

Additionally, commodity prices affect each other because they bear the cost of each other. In macroeconomic regulation and control, sometimes in order to control the price of a certain item, adopting the traditional measure of limiting the price is equally ineffective. Take resource price adjustments for example. Price control on certain goods will only make economic structural imbalance more prominent and serious. When prices of other related products fluctuate, the prices of some goods have been regulated to eradication, which made the regulated industries have no choice but to reduce production and supply dropped, which eventually resulted in economic operation with a series of aftereffects.

Thus, experience based on the above demonstrates that the mutual cost relationship among commodity prices cannot be broken up by administrative means. Macroeconomic regulation and control must respect the laws of the market. Control measures deviating from the law of the market will sooner or later be revealed as invalid.

The question is: why are there always macro-regulation and control measures that do not respect the laws of the market and are introduced mainly at the will of superiors? This can neither be completely attributed to a lack of experience in macroeconomic regulation and control nor to the wrong analyses or judgement of the macroeconomic policy-making sectors, which was accused of rushing into regretful decisions. It should be pointed out that to a large extent, this was largely related to democratic and scientific principles in the macro decision-making procedures as well as a lack of an effective policy-correcting mechanism. This is the usual error that a government sector can easily commit under the planned economic system.

2 Seeking progress in stability and making structural adjustments

To understand the falling tendency of China's economic growth rate since the fourth quarter of 2011 requires analyses of the macro-regulation and control process during this period. The reason why economic growth decline has aroused concerns from people of various walks of life is because the Chinese economy is thought to be unable to withstand the downturn of the economic growth rate. Like the fourth quarter of 2008 and the first quarter of 2009, when the economic growth rate fell continuously to about 6%, local fiscal revenue, business bankruptcies and unemployment became public concerns. According to experience, China's current economic growth rate should be maintained at around 7% to 8%. If the growth rate falls below 7% and even below 6%, it means that economic growth has fallen beyond the alert level.

Why so? This is related to the dual transformation stage that China is currently experiencing. Profound changes have taken place in the urban-rural binary structure. A large number of migrant workers have moved into cities or towns as migrant workers or to live there, and the employment pressure has increased instead of decreased. Additionally, among many factors resulting in inflation, the cost-push factors and international input factors are playing a more obvious role, and it has become increasingly difficult to achieve a desired result by curbing rising prices with traditional measures. Side effects brought about through tight measures have become more and more prominent, making the employment problem difficult to alleviate. This is precisely why China needs to ensure an economic growth rate between 7% and 8%.

However, there are many methods that prevent the decline of economic growth rate and maintain a maximum growth rate between 7% and 8%. Some of these measures can effectively promote economic growth rate in a short period of time, but its damage to the national economy is incalculable, for instance, indiscriminate deforestation regardless of ecological environments, building high-pollution and high energy-consuming enterprises, spreading non-urgent traffic route construction with no regard for needs of the real economy; disregarding cost-and-benefit relationships, expanding the scale of production even by enterprises which are running in deficit at the sacrifice of state subsidies. All are short-term behaviours and economic growth rate elevated by those measures will not only be unsustainable but also show no end to further difficulties down the road.

During the 2008 international financial storm, measures such as up-bursting investments and loans were implemented to stimulate economic growth. Five years later, we should make a sober summary of advantages and disadvantages of this approach. The advantages were that it promoted economic recovery and alleviated employment pressure while the disadvantage was that the rapid expansion of investment demands made inflation at the end of 2010 difficult to curb, and excessive investment demand was precisely one of the reasons for increasing money in circulation. It is worth discussing that first, there was no progress in the adjustment of the economic structure. First, the economy was increasing under a pattern which showed virtually no changes in economic structure. Second, independent innovation and industrial upgrading did not receive enough attention, and many enterprises did not adopt these solutions as their strategic objectives. Rather, they were only satisfied with changes in the improved economic situation or the upturn of the situation, but ignored the fact that the gateway to long-term business survival and development in the long run was to increase market competitiveness.

Given this, steady growth must be combined with structural adjustment. Progress in "progress in stability" does not mean breaking through the 8% growth rate or "the higher economic growth rate, the better". Instead, it refers to making substantial progress in structural adjustment on the premise of a stable economic growth of 7% to 8%, thereby finally enabling the quality of economic growth to improve significantly.

What are signs of improved quality in economic growth? According to China's economic development experience in recent years, this has first been reflected in a structure that is gradually rational structure, gradual elimination of overcapacity and alleviation of structural insufficiency. Next, this shows that environmental protection and control has achieved greater effectiveness, and the objective of a low-carbon economy has been achieved. Moreover, the economy and society have been steered towards the track of sustainable development. Again, new achievements have been made in innovation and industrial upgrading as enterprises have been committed to the endogenous power of independent innovation and industrial upgrading, and converting them into the competitiveness of enterprises. Finally, the economic growth model has changed from a mainly investment-led model into one that lays equal importance to both investment and consumption, which after a period of time will result in a consumption-pull economic growth model. Thus, a vicious cycle, as follows, will appear in China's economic growth: residents' income rise → a growing proportion of medium-level income earners within the income distribution → improved consumption → elevated market purchasing power of enterprises → rise in enterprise development and employment rate → continuous growth of residents' income.

The emergence of a vicious cycle is what we have been expecting, but the combination of steady progress and structural adjustment cannot be ignored. In other words, if there are no efforts made to adjust the structure, there will be no progress in stability. It will be even more difficult to maintain 7% to 8% economic growth, for under structural imbalance, we have to rely on government investment to ensure growth. In that case, would we not revert to the old path five years ago?

Macroeconomic regulation and control emphasises fine-tuning precisely for the purpose of achieving the combined principles of "progress in maintaining stability and making structural adjustment". The major experience is that, if we adopt the approaches of "excessive looseness or excessive tightness", "dramatic rises and drastic falls" will make the economy unable to get out of this vicious cycle of sometimes making excessive expansion and sometimes making great contractions. That is, this throws the macroeconomic policy-making sectors into a state of always being tense and being so busy handling emergencies that they have no time to consider how to perform the required strategic tasks. This will result in significant turmoil with violent ups and downs, incur severe inflation and a high unemployment rate and make increases in residents' income difficult to achieve.

3 Fine-tuning as a major measure similarly required in macro-regulation and control for the low-carbon economy

How to adapt to low-carbon economic requirements of the international community and how to ensure the stable growth of the Chinese economy in low-carbonisation both need fine-tuning as a major measure in macro-regulation and control. This accords with Chinese national conditions.

Note that the current Chinese economy is facing the dilemma of protecting ecological environments and continuing sustainable economic development. This is because if we only care about economic development at the expense of the environments, it may be difficult for the present generation to survive. Nevertheless, if we just care about ecological environments, then, how should developing countries like China develop? This question has been puzzling us. After many years of exploration, we found a way out, that is to say, combining both to achieve a low-carbon and green economy. Therefore, the following two claims are both correct: first, economic development resides in the construction of an ecological civilisation; second, economic development resides in environmental protection. In view of combining economic development and a low-carbon economy, the following arrangements should be made.

First, significant breakthroughs need to be made in process design and new products development. The most important method is to make our new products practical and safe. That is to say, there should be technological innovation and breakthroughs in technological products, for instance, the research and development of new energy resources, transport vehicles with new energy resources, and the promotion of new energy-saving facilities etc.

To this end, we must research and develop solutions to bottleneck issues in exploiting new energy and materials. Assuming that there are breakthroughs in finding new energy resources, they will spur power supply and transportation development and improve the quality of life, thereby providing strong impetus for the economy. New materials and equipment should both be in accordance with environmental standards but also be effective and affordable. At the same time, breakthroughs in new materials will enable the entire equipment-manufacturing industry to embark on a completely new path. These all reflect our emphases on ecological construction and environmental protection.

There is an important issue to be addressed here, namely the cooperation between state-owned and private enterprises. The advantages of state-owned enterprises lie in their strong technical strengths, sufficient capital and advanced laboratory equipment. The advantages of private enterprises are a flexible mechanism, assuming full responsibilities for profits and losses and boldness in making decisions on technological innovation. By contrast, state-owned enterprises face obstacles at various levels in the decision-making procedures and are subject to many constraints and dare not shoulder responsibilities, especially when they are caught in repeated setbacks. Therefore, the best option is for state-owned and private enterprises to take advantage of their own strengths, participate in major national projects and collaborate in low-carbon research and technology promotion under unified state arrangements.

Second, we must vigorously develop environmental protection industries, especially the renewable resources industry. When we conducted research in *Guangxi* in 2010, a nonferrous metal recycling plant was under construction. Raw materials were shipped in containers from abroad, screened and classified on a site in *Guangxi*, so that copper and other nonferrous metals would be separated. As a result, there would be less mining and smelting. Why did overseas enterprises not do this by themselves? It is because China has many advantages, for instance, qualified technical workers and an enormous domestic market. After nonferrous metals were produced in *Guangxi*, they would be directly sold in China. The recycling of metal was completely in line with environmental requirements. Therefore, this is an important environmental protection industry. Environmental protection in a broad sense also includes afforestation, gardening, forestation, soil improvement, controlling desertification and stony desertification, improving wasteland and tidal flats. These industries will attract a great number of labourers. They are not only conducive to the development of China's environmental protection but also deal with the employment issue that China is facing.

Third, we must develop a well-established capital market system. Investment funds from the government are always limited and cannot be used directly to update enterprise devices. To achieve a low-carbon economy, we need to rely on the capital market for financing. Enterprises with independent innovation and achievements in low-carbon technology should be tested by markets and then listed. They can also issue corporate bonds, which would address the capital supply issue in the low-carbon economy. One important issue in capital markets is that we must take the following aspects into account: on the one hand, we must stop deceivable behaviour to the public; on the other hand, we should support good enterprises which have favourable conditions and are capable to be listed. The strength of a state is not represented by the total number of enterprises but by high-quality enterprises. It is invalid to rely on the total number of enterprises. It is only with more high-quality enterprises, that our economy can grow stronger.

Fourth, regarding tax policy, we should adopt differentiated tax rates towards low-carbon enterprises. Taxes for enterprises with a good low-carbon economy should be alleviated; taxes for those with a bad carbon economy, however, should be increased. In addition, preferential tax policies should be granted to resource-recycling enterprises to urge their further development.

Fifth, the unemployment issue should be properly handled. To reduce emissions, small coal mines, steel mills and chemical plants should be closed. Measures in this area have to be tough and should be resolved in stages. More critically, means of living should be identified for laid-off workers in the process. The proportion of tertiary industry in China is too low. It accounts for more than 70% in developed countries while only 40% in China. There is much development room for China's tertiary industry. The acceleration of its development can alleviate the current unemployment issue.

Sixth, new business opportunities must be identified in low-carbonisation. In a global low-carbon economy, to make our products more accessible overseas markets and at the same time enhance domestic market, work in the following four areas must proceed carefully: First, when other countries do not have a certain product, China does. That requires us to rely on independent innovation; China possesses products that overseas counterparts want. Second, when other countries all make something, China makes the best of it. For the same product, the one made in China is better than that produced in a foreign county. Third, when a foreign country makes the best of something, China has new equipment, new technology and new thoughts. In this way, we can be innovative and make our mark on the international market with "made in China". Fourth, when a foreign country has the best of something, China has a complete set of it. This means that products of a particular trade can be made in cooperation with foreign products and China can also make accompanying products for a foreign country. As there is a huge market in China, this becomes a promising prospect and provides new development opportunities for us.

Seventh, ecological civilisation construction and low-carbon economy should be added to corporate style and enterprise spirit. The corporate culture used to refer mainly to corporate style and enterprise spirit, which was right. Now, the construction of an ecological civilisation and achieving a low-carbon economic path should be placed in the construction of an enterprise culture, so that we can mobilise more enterprise employees to oversee whether enterprise production meets environmental standards. This can not only guide enterprise employees to understand the significance of low-carbonisation but also encourage them to be consciously engaged in environmental protection. It is also a way to build a new corporate image.

Eighth, emphases should be placed on the development of consumer civilisation. The realisation of a low-carbon economy is not just an issue in production areas but also an issue in the field of consumption. The waste of resources exists within families, so there is a great potential in saving resources. Families can contribute a lot by recycling household waste. In addition, new living habits, consistent with an ecological civilisation, need to be formed: e.g. changing traditionally irrational, uncivilised and anti-hygienic consumption habits. This should start with individuals within each family. Hence, our low-carbon economy will have a favourable mass base.

Seen in this light, to move along a low-carbon economy pathway, we should, on the one hand, strengthen administration and develop various realistic laws, regulations and bylaws; and codes, on the other hand, take appropriate measures in macroeconomic regulation and control to enable enterprises and individuals to adjust their own production or lifestyles. For example, to save energy and reduce emissions and protect environments, enterprises with a high-energy consumption and heavy pollution should be closed. This may result in workers' unemployment in some factories. In such an event, unless it is an emergency situation or an unexpected event, it should generally be fine-tuned by developing rational disposal programmes and then gradually introducing them to society and thus reduce social unrest. Again, in order to change residents' traditional consumption habits, it is not impossible to take administrative means or macroeconomic regulation and control measures, but these should also focus on fine-tuning. Otherwise, it might cause public misunderstanding, offence and harm instead of traditional consumer habits.

4 Consistency of macroeconomic regulation and control with national conditions of China

According to the demand management principles of Keynesian economics, developed countries in the West summarised several decades of experience in implementing macroeconomic control policies after World War II, of which some were effective while others were ineffective. Whether effective or not, they were regulation and control measures corresponding to their respective national conditions. That is, their experience of success or lessons of failure are all related to their own national conditions. None of the types that broke away from their specific conditions and were copied from foreign country macroeconomic control succeeded. For instance, the monetary policy in macro-regulation and control is generally aggregate control. It is based on monetary flow analysis: when there is a larger monetary flow, control measures are introduced to reduce the flow; when the monetary flow becomes smaller, control measures are taken to increase monetary flow. The conventional practice in monetary policies is nothing but to raise or lower deposit-reserve ratio, raise or lower benchmark interest rate, increase or decrease public market operations and sometimes directly regulate the volume of credit, such as increasing or compressing aggregate credit. The reason for conventional aggregate control in monetary policies is based on the monetary flow analysis that in economic operation, the amount of capital in circulation, whether it is big or small, an increase or a decrease, will directly affect aggregate demand, thereby influencing macroeconomic situations at large.

While aggregate control in monetary policy is useful, its limitations cannot be ignored. They are mainly reflected in the following four aspects.

First, the foundation of macroeconomics is microeconomics, and given their respective situations, microscopic units vary widely. Aggregate control in monetary policies tends to form the defect of "one- size- fits -all', which has serious consequences for the Chinese economy at the economic transformation stage.

Second, aggregate control of monetary policies acts upon the expansion or compression of aggregate demand while its impact on the overall supply is not obvious. This is because aggregate supply control will inevitably involve adjustments to industrial, product and regional economic structure and the restructuring of technology, labour restructuring and investment. Aggregate control of monetary policies has salient limitations.

Third, so far, the Chinese economy remains in disequilibrium. The market has not been perfect with limited resource supply and an immature resource pricing mechanism, which is under constant reform. Moreover, there has been asymmetric information. All of those make aggregate capital control in monetary policies unable to play the same role as it is in a full market economy.

Fourth, in developed market economy countries, it is possible to adopt aggregate control at the macro level; for instance, by reducing monetary flow, curbing inflation or by stimulating aggregate demand by means of expanding monetary flow, thereby reducing unemployment. However, once the economy is caught in stagnation, namely economic stagnation and the concurrence of rising unemployment and inflation, aggregate control in monetary policies is paralysed.

Additionally, regulation and control of monetary policies are based on monetary flow analysis. The analysis, as an aggregate analysis, tends to conceal contradictions, creates a false impression, causing people to be misguided regarding economic situations, thereby leading further to wrong judgements. An obvious example is that monetary flow analysis will lead people to have unrealistic expectations of inflation, while inflation expectations will accelerate the arrival of inflation. This means that: when inflation expectations occur to a society, it spreads far and wide; and when everyone says that inflation is coming, individual consumers as well as businesses who are both supply and demand parties will change their consumption modes and investment behaviours. If each household stores one more bag of grain to guard against rising grain prices, grain prices will end up increasing. If enterprises expect steel and coal price rises, enterprises being the supply party will temporarily reduce sales due to the psychological idea of treasuring their products and wait for opportunities to sell them. Thereby, the market supply of steel and coal decreases. If enterprises as the demand party are willing to reserve some production materials whose prices may rise, so prices of steel and coal go up.

Moreover, even from the perspective of monetary flow analysis, the "normal level" in the calculation of the monetary flow is usually based on the experience of developed market economy countries, which require full marketisation and perfect market environments as preconditions. What needs to be considered is nothing more than data such as population growth rate, economic growth rate, inflation rate, and monetary velocity etc. It needs further study on whether this analysis method is entirely applicable to the present stage of the Chinese economy. This is because China is still at the stage of transforming from a planned economic system to a market economic system. As such, a rural-urban dual system continues to exist; so does monopoly in some industries. Moreover, the monetary flow mechanism is not as flexible and effective as that under perfect market conditions; there are many middle links in the distribution channel, and they are often not smooth; all of which increases the demand for currency. Moreover, in the past few years, farmers produced and lived under the influences of the planned economic system and were seldom involved in the market economy. They did not have great demand for currency. Nevertheless, in the process of system transformation, farmers were more and more involved in the market economic trends and their demand for money continued to rise. Therefore, copying the experience of developed countries' monetary flow analysis often leads to such a result: the calculated "normal level" of the monetary flow is indeed tight. In other words, the "normal level" of money flow in the Chinese economy is truly higher than the normal level of capital flow calculated on the basis of capital flow analysis. Thirty years of experience in China's Reform and Opening-up have illustrated this point.

The experience from China's practice also suggests that, in analysis of the country's current inflation and its industrial structure, ownership and regional economic structures may be more revealing than an aggregate index and the actual amount of money in flow. Returning the monetary flow to "normal levels" should be combined with analyses of industrial ownership and regional economic structures. This is because, through the analysis of industrial structure, we can know which industries' product supply and demand are roughly balanced; the proportion of those with serious shortages in production capacity and those with production capacity surplus; and that different types of industry have different demands for goods. No matter whether it is the adjustment of loan rates or of the deposit-reserve ratio, it should vary according to the structure of the industries. The "one-size-fits-all" approach can possibly lead to the opposite of intended results, thereby harming the normal economic operations and the coordinated development between economy and society. From the analysis of the ownership structure, it can be learned that large state-owned enterprises, private enterprises (especially private, small and medium enterprises), individual businesses and farmers with contracted land have different financing needs and completely different financing channels. Even though we can calculate the normal level of the total monetary flow in China, it is likely to have no effect on the large-scale state-owned enterprises, and private small and medium enterprises are subject to greater influence as individual businesses and farmers with contracted land have to endure higher private loan rates. The results from regional economic structure analysis can also illustrate the same problem. Assuming that the "normal level" of the monetary flow must be calculated by the flow of developed countries is bound to make life in the east of China uncomfortable, while conditions in central and western regions of the country become even more difficult.

Be careful of enterprise capital chain rupture. The capital and supply chains are linked; therefore, the rupture of corporate capital chain will also result in the rupture of the supply chain. In the current situation, the implementation of returning the monetary flow to "normal levels" is very likely to cause breaks in product supply and business capital chains; thereby leading to ceased production of some enterprises in the economy, bankruptcy, laid-off individuals and unemployment. It may also make individual, industrial and commercial households shrink, and the income of farmers with contracted land decline. This is because, as previously mentioned, different industries, enterprises and regions under the name of the return to normal monetary flow were subject to impacts of different extents. Some industries, enterprises, areas and populations are greatly affected, resulting in breaks in the product supply and business capital chains.

Conversely, it should also be noted that when the monetary flow is relaxed, enterprises all benefit, regardless of their economic scales. Large enterprises may benefit more and the interests of small and medium enterprises may be less. When the monetary flow is compressed to "normal level" or below "normal level", the degree of damages between large, small, and medium enterprises is much greater. Large enterprises can still survive but many small and medium enterprises will not. This is the asymmetry of monetary policy effects.

According to the above-mentioned circumstances, we cannot but reach this conclusion: at the dual transformation stage, macroeconomic control must be in line with China's national conditions; otherwise, it would be difficult to achieve the desired results.

Section 2 Different types of unemployment and respective countermeasures

1 Particularities of the employment issue in China's dual transformation

In November 2008, I was lecturing in Western Europe shortly after the international financial storm, when a European economist asked me: "Generally speaking, as long as the annual economic growth rate in developed Western European countries remains around 2% to 3%, the job market will be basically stable and there will not be a significant unemployment issue. Why must China's recent economic growth rate be maintained above 9% to 10% in order not to have a serious unemployment issue? If the economic growth rate drops below 7%, the unemployment issue will become quite prominent. Why?" The question from this European economist made me think.

Indeed, this was the case. China's economic growth rate in the fourth quarter of 2008 and the first quarter of 2009 was a bit over 6%, which really threw the whole country into a mood of uncertainty, exclaiming that migrant workers were laid off and were about to return home. How should we handle this? What should be done if the laid-off migrant workers were unwilling to return home, or when they returned home, there was no longer arable land? What if they stayed in the city? So, a detailed analysis must be made of the employment issues under Chinese dual economic transformation.

First, it needs to be pointed out that upon comparison with developed countries in Western Europe, the employment situation in China is very distinct. Industrialisation in developed Western European countries has been ongoing for more than 200 years. The process of migrating into cities to become workers has ended, and hunting for jobs in cities used to be what their great-grandfathers' and grandfathers' generation did before. Now farmers remaining in rural areas have their own family farms, small shops or workshops, as well as their own houses, gardens, or cars. They are living a peaceful life and there is no rural-urban dual system. The social security system covers both urban and rural areas. Why should they pour into cities to earn a living? Moreover, the urbanisation rate has reached 80% or even higher. What are the benefits of moving into cities? There is urban congestion and traffic jams. The quality of life in urban areas is not as good as that in rural areas. Additionally, the birth rate in those Western European countries is low and the population growth rate is close to zero. Each year, many employees retire and the newly-added young people reaching working age can fill vacancies. If there is only 2% to 3% economic growth rate, immigrants from North Africa, West Asia, South Asia and Eastern Europe could be provided with employment opportunities. Would this not ease the unemployment problem?

The situation in China is different. China is still a developing country experiencing a dual system transformation: the rural-urban dual system continues to exist; the integration of urban and rural social security is still ongoing; going into the cities in search of employment opportunities is still one of a farmer's options. Therefore, the employment pressure on society remains great. It is right under this circumstance that China at this stage must pay attention to its current economic growth rate. Of course, this does not mean that the higher an economic growth rate is, the better it will be, for too high economic growth will bring a series of issues, such as excessive investment and credit expansion, incurring inflation. In addition, if we only pursue high economic growth rates, this could lead to sequels such as neglecting the quality of the economic growth, thereby resulting in increasing structural imbalance, environmental pollution and a decrease in resource use and the like. Therefore, at this stage, apart from maintaining a high economic growth rate (7% to 8%), China should also classify unemployment as part of dual transformation so that specific countermeasures can be made accordingly.

Next we classify unemployment and also propose corresponding countermeasures, as follows.

The first type of unemployment in contemporary China is aggregate unemployment, namely unemployment due to lack of employment opportunities and insufficient posts. The second type is structural unemployment, namely unemployment due to coexistence of both overstaffing and lack of labour for some posts. The third type is individual career-based employment; that is, job seekers for various reasons select working posts and they would rather wait before they find jobs with which they are willing to be engaged.

Different types of unemployment have different countermeasures, which will be discussed respectively.

2 Aggregate unemployment and countermeasures

Aggregate unemployment refers to unemployment in the economy triggered by insufficient employment opportunities and posts. Under the planned economic system, farmers were under the governance of the peoples' communes and had land to farm, so they were considered to be in "full employment", and thereby not counted as aggregate unemployment. The government only needed to consider and arrange the employment of urban young people at an employment age, as well as middle-aged urban adults who were jobless, and thus incomeless (including some jobless and incomeless youth). There were two important measures at the time. One was that youth (at that time generally referred to as "educated youth" because they graduated from junior or senior high school) went to the countryside to join the work brigades or to the Production and Construction Corps on borders to work there. While these approaches could accommodate a large number of urban youth, this phenomenon, however, is called in economics "covert unemployment" and "covert unemployment" and is counted as unemployment. The second was to settle the jobless, incomeless urban middle-aged adults and a portion of young people to do casual work such as afforestation, road-repair and garbage cleaning removal. Though the jobs were temporary, those people finally became employed.

After the Reform and Opening-up, China entered the dual transformation phase. Communes were dismissed and the rural household contract system was promoted nationwide. The approach that required educated youth to join the brigades was abandoned. In addition, it became pervasive for farmers to go to cities and become migrant workers or engage in small vendors' activities. Nevertheless, aggregate unemployment continued to exist, relaxing for a few years but pressing back for some other years. They were all related to the level of economic growth.

Given the actual situation in China, there are five countermeasures to help relieve unemployment. They are as follows

First, economic growth should be maintained at a higher level and not reduced in the near future to 7% or less. This is because new jobs typically emerge during economic growth, while the continuous decline of economic growth will certainly make aggregate unemployment rise. This has been confirmed in China's dual transformation progress. It should also be noted that there is not only a time gap but also asymmetry between unemployment rate change and economic growth rate change. For instance, when enterprises reduce orders, their production values fall, thus causing the economic growth rate to decline. The employment rate is not reduced immediately; rather, it lags behind for some time, because enterprises still hope that orders can be restored. If enterprises lay off their staff in a hasty manner, what should they do once orders arrive? Therefore, enterprises first hold up for some time and must decide whether to lay off their staff in view of the status of orders. This means laying-off staff fall behind the decline in the economic growth rate. On the other hand, when the economy recovers, enterprises that have laid off staff will generally not recruit staff immediately; rather, they will remain at a waiting stage. At this time, most enterprises will permit existing employees to work overtime to meet the urgent production needs. They will not recruit new staff until there are indeed more orders and the economy rebounds. This is indicative that the rise in new employment lags behind the economic growth rate. Thus, with respect to economic growth, the increase in employment lags behind. This is the asymmetry between changes in the unemployment rate and those in the economic growth rate.

Second, wages of low and intermediate income families should be raised to improve their income levels, change their consumption structure and promote the development of the service industry. Traditional service industry will undoubtedly increase jobs, and more importantly, the development of modern service industry will add more jobs. That is, there exist significant employment potentials in the service industry. It will be an important field in the future that will attract graduates from colleges and universities; additionally, it will also accommodate employees with a secondary education.

Third, employment should be boosted by encouraging entrepreneurship. In the processes of industrialisation and urbanisation, the rise of the information economy and agricultural modernisation, urban residents and farmers both had enthusiasm for entrepreneurship. This is because policies and measures that the government uses to encourage business pioneering greatly stimulated urban and rural residents' initiative, for instance, creating self-founded small and micro-enterprises, setting up breeding farms and developing tidal flats and sandy wasteland. Family farms, ranches and forest land are micro and small enterprises. Not only do owners and their families undertake production and management activities here, the farms also receive local and foreign labourers for employment. This is "employment promoted by entrepreneurship".

Fourth, currently, private enterprises are a territory that accommodates the largest number of newly-hired employees. They should also be the territory that the government must give a primary account when enacting employment policies, mainly in terms of protecting private investors' ownership of their sectors and addressing difficulties faced by private enterprises. Specifically, those difficulties include constraints on access to some fields, financing difficulties, obstacles to fair competition, overburdening fees and taxes, and some other issues. Owing to their appeal to employment, private enterprises should be granted certain tax prefer-ences. For instance, any enterprise that enables a member of a "zero employment family" to be employed should receive a certain reward; and any enterprise that enables a certain proportion of "zero employment families" to be employed fami-lies should enjoy some amount of tax relief. Thus, private enterprises that accom-modate more members of the zero employment families will be encouraged.

Fifth, the government should take concrete measures to encourage enterprises (including state-owned and private enterprises) to migrate to high unemployment areas. This practice is not only good for enterprises but also aids these new areas, thereby alleviating local unemployment, increasing local revenues and raising the local economic growth rate. The key is that the local governments must honour credibility, abide by their commitments, and act on the agreement with immi-grating enterprises. This is also the conventional measure that Western market economy countries use to increase local employment.

3 Structural unemployment and countermeasures

Structural unemployment means that some jobs are understaffed while others are overstaffed. Why can't the surplus labour fill the vacancies caused by the short-ages in manpower? This is mainly due to the uncoordinated structure. The lack of structural coordination is manifold. Take the lack of coordination in the industrial structure. For instance, the skills and expertise of job seekers do not match needs of career vacancies; the age and gender of the job seekers do not match the avail-able vacancy that needs recruitment of new employees, or when there is a great distance between job seekers' residence and the location of recruiting enterprises or public institutions, job seekers are reluctant to go and work in a comparatively faraway place.

Structural unemployment exists for various reasons so the countermeasures to alleviate it should be specific, definite and detailed. In general, the follow-ing five measures could be effective in alleviating structural unemployment: first, strengthen vocational and technical training; second, make appropriate adjust-ments to wage differences and encourage youth prepared to be employed or in employment to consciously learn new knowledge and techniques and improve professional standards; third, give equal attention to knowledge and technology-intensive enterprises, capital-intensive enterprises and labour-intensive enter-prises; do not neglect but rather continue to develop labour-intensive enterprises; fourth, implement national industrial policies, adjust the industrial and product structures and encourage independent innovation, transfer products to suitable areas, and achieve industrial upgrading industrial transfer; fifth, encourage rural and urban residents to make innovations and exercise their enthusiasm and exper-tise. It needs to be pointed out here that the measures for addressing the structural unemployment issue often overlap with those for addressing aggregate unem-ployment. That is, those measures, for instance, include enhancing vocational and technical skills; encouraging young and middle-aged people to learn knowledge and techniques, improving professional standards; adjusting industrial and product structures and encouraging enterprises to transfer, stimulating urban and rural residents to bring into play their expertise and setting up their own businesses. Those measures are conducive both to solving the aggregate employment issue and addressing the structural unemployment issue. That is, although causes for aggregate unemployment and structural unemployment differ, the same measure can help alleviate both types of unemployment.

Furthermore, with progress in industrialisation, economic growth, science and technology, structural unemployment in the future will become increasingly prominent because professional requirements for prospective employees and those in employment have become increasingly demanding. If people preparing to be employed or the unemployed do not pursue continuous studies, they will be unable to perform their job tasks, and it is possible that they will be eliminated from their jobs. This is a tremendous pressure and deserves the concerns of enterprises, staff and the government. Moreover, continuous learning and lifelong learning are necessary for employees in any occupation; otherwise, one will change from being adapted to the previous job to being narrowly adapted, and then to being ill-adapted.

Similarly, there is a need for continuous and lifelong learning for household farmers and micro and small business owners with their own businesses. They should realise that the consequences of not learning new knowledge or technologies are not just the loss of customers and suffering deficits, but they are likely to be squeezed out of the market and ultimately be eliminated from it. We conducted surveys on micro and small business owners, small industrial and commercial businesses, as well as farmland contracting households and family breeding households in some small towns of *Zhejiang* and *Shandong* provinces. The surveys showed a consensus: technologies update at a faster pace. If these small businesses do not learn, they will not able to remain current with changes in the market. If they do not start to study hard, they will surely be out of date and it will be more and more difficult for them to catch up. This is a good sign. Technological innovations and market changes put those who establish their own businesses under greater pressure, which is not necessarily a bad thing.

4 Individual career option-based unemployment and countermeasures

Individual career option-based unemployment is sometimes conceptualised in Western economics as "voluntary unemployment" to differentiate it from "involuntary unemployment", which means being willing to be employed but unable to find jobs. As a matter of fact, the saying "voluntary unemployment" is inaccurate. For instance, if someone wants to be employed but fails to find a satisfactory job, this is called individual career option-based unemployment. He should be differentiated from one who enjoys welfare benefits (such as living allowance or unemployment benefits) provided by the government or social security system and is reluctant to go to work. He should also be differentiated from the "neet" group (not in education, employment or training), those who are continuously sustained by parents and unwilling to work.

The reasons for unemployment due to personal career options are as follows.

First, individuals have their own job evaluation criteria for what is indecent or despised occupation in which they are reluctant to be involved. For example, attending an employment condition survey conducted in a coastal city, we heard a presentation by the city's labour market sector: "In our case, street-sweeping and public toilet-cleaning workers here are mostly migrant workers from a medium-sized southwest city, while workers in the same work in that city are migrant workers from another southwest province." We asked migrant workers performing the cleaning job: "Is your hometown not short of street-sweeping workers and public toilet cleaners? Why don't you do the same job in your native land?" The answer was very simple: "If we did this kind of job in our native land and were caught by an acquaintance. What a shame." Thus, vocational evaluation is an important reason for job-seeking people to be unwilling to work but instead continue to wait for jobs.

Second, with relatively narrow personal expertise or technology, it is difficult to find relevant jobs. This greatly reduces the scope of individual career options and therefore, job seekers continue to wait. To some extent, this is the superimposition of individual career option-based unemployment on structural unemployment.

Third, there is a change in individuals' employment concepts. A person, when his search for relevant jobs to his expertise or techniques does not go well, has the idea of being reluctant to continue seeking jobs (at least unwilling to do so in a short term) and is more willing to be engaged in "freelance". "Freelance" is a fashionable term. It does not include setting up one's own business, such as starting micro and small enterprises, operating household breeding farms, household forest farms etc.; as a matter of fact, it refers to no fixed job. One sometimes speculates stocks in the stock market and conducts futures businesses; sometimes writes proses, comedies and even novels; on other occasions attends college courses or offers suggestions to friends and acquaintances. In relation to their living, to be employed or not can also be determined by family financial situations, either being wealthy or being frugal. If the family is wealthy, the person would rather continue to look for the right job than pick up a job and "make do". There are still some other young people who fancy "irregular employment" due to their changed concept about employment. Sometimes, they are "freelancers" or on other occasions, they are employed in a particular unit and do some casual work. They can also be categorised as unemployed due to personal career options.

By this token, countermeasures against individual career option-based unemployment are mainly related to career evaluation criteria, an individual's knowledge and technical training that feature a "solid-foundation-and-wide-calibre", and changes in an individual's concept of employment.

In regard to career evaluation criteria, it is not simply how an individual evaluates career options; rather, it is also to a large extent affected by society, family, relatives, friends and classmates. When society is popular with various kinds of bias and discrimination against a certain occupation, individuals will be unwilling to be engaged in such jobs and unable to break away from or correct these occupational biases. Conquering those occupational biases and discrimination needs joint efforts from the society and this may take a long time.

In order to meet career requirements of job seekers, disciplines in universities should not be over refined. The training involving "thick-foundation and wide-calibre" is useful in employment. At the postgraduate level, majors can be further specified. Practice has proved that this is good for specialised talents. Different people have different ambitions. Let those willing to wait for the arrival of employment opportunities suitable for their interests and aspirations wait for them. Before they come across jobs that meet their own interests and aspirations, let them wait for their arrival. Do not impose our employment concepts on them. As long as they can live a decent life, "freelance" is not necessarily bad. As long as there is an appropriate prompt "time waits for no man", then let them alone. Be aware that those who would rather wait than take a job have their right to make career options. The government cannot force them to work in certain type of jobs.

5 Unemployment as a long-term issue in China

In the previous section, we analysed reasons for three types of unemployment in China's dual transformation process and discussed their respective countermeasures. Given the above, we can draw a preliminary conclusion that alleviating China's unemployment is definitely not an easy task. We should be fully aware that unemployment will be a long-term issue in China.

In the final analysis, China in the near future should still improve the quality of economic growth and meanwhile keep a comparatively high economic growth rate (for instance 7%-8%), because new jobs will emerge in the economic growth process.

In a longer term, the urban-rural binary institutional reform is underway. The reform lifts various types of restrictions on farmers' rights, urging more rural labourers into towns seeking jobs. The paralleled promotion of the urban-rural institutional reform and the construction of urbanisation provide many job positions for farmers who move into the towns. Otherwise, urban and rural employment pressure will be tenser and tenser. This is the institutional reason that makes addressing the employment issue in China difficult.

Again, when we refer to countermeasures against aggregate unemployment, structural unemployment and individual career option-based unemployment in the previous section, we have pointed out the necessity of perfecting and developing the vocational and technical training system. It includes treating vocational and technical education as lifelong education and continuously improving technical levels of job seekers and people already in employment to enable them to adapt to continuous updates of technologies and so on. Nonetheless, the difficulties in implementing those countermeasures should not be ignored by any means. According to surveys, there are four main difficulties.

First, lack of teachers. There are not many teachers in vocational and technical education institutions who are competent and qualified, who have both practical experience and sufficient professional knowledge, and who continue to keep pace with advancements in new technologies. There are too few such talents. What is more, some competent teachers are unwilling to be teachers in vocational and technical colleges or schools.

Second, lack of funds. The government's education funds are mainly concerned about compulsory education, high school education, universities and their affiliated research institutes. It does not cover any additional funds for vocational and technical education. Meanwhile, the funding demand for vocational and technical education is increasingly high and the supply of funds has difficulty in meeting consumption demand.

Third, society does not pay sufficient attention to vocational and technical education. Many parents are hoping to send their children to elite universities, especially top universities, and also expecting their children to pursue postgraduate or overseas studies in the future. By contrast, only those with poor academic records or family financial situations are willing to apply for vocational and technical colleges or schools, so that they can easily find a job after graduation.

Fourth, outsized and large enterprises are both aware of the importance of vocational and technical education but based on past experience, they would rather set up a new pre-job training agency for new staff or an agency that trains in-service staff in rotation than operate vocational and technical colleges or schools with their own funds since graduates of these institutes are in flow. They may flow to other enterprises after graduation. If vocational and technical schools are founded by the local government, they will encounter the issues of insufficient supply of teachers, funds or other difficulties. Due to this, improving and developing China's vocational and technical system requires a long process.

Furthermore, there have emerged in recent years "green growth", "green employment" and other concepts. It will require a long time to promote them and get them accepted by the public, while implementing them will take an even longer period of time.

What is "green growth"? What is "green employment"? These two concepts appeared in the process of a low-carbon economy. "Green growth" means that economic growth should comply with requirements of a low-carbon economy. If enterprises cannot prioritise energy-saving and emission reduction as primary concerns of economic growth, thus being unable to reach requirements of a low-carbon economy, measures should be taken to close them down and stop their production. As to new projects, if they cannot reach low-carbon requirements, they will not be approved for construction. Those that have been in production, or about to be in production, should stop their development and be rectified according to low-carbon economic criteria. "Green employment" refers to a person who has already been employed in an enterprise that has not reached low-carbon requirements; this person will be in the state of "waiting for employment" due to the closing down, stopping production, merging and transferring of the enterprise. Any newly built enterprise in accordance with the low-carbon requirements is approved of production and the staff in this enterprise is ranked among the "green employment". Naturally, low-carbonisation is a process and should be realised according to the actual situation of China. Nonetheless, "green growth" and "green jobs" as the direction of efforts will not be shaken.

As previously mentioned, China is under great employment pressure and the pressure should be alleviated by a faster growth pace. The proposal of such concepts as "green growth" and "green employment" and their implementation are bound to affect the pace of economic growth. This is because requiring current enterprises not having reached criteria of saving energy, reducing emissions and controlling environmental pollution to close, stop production or be transferred, and the newly built enterprises, not having reached the low-carbon standards to cease construction and suspend production, will not only affect economic growth but also unemployment. It is, thus, clear that these in turn determine that solving China's unemployment will be a long-term issue.

6 Dual-labour market

The dual-labour market is not only a common phenomenon worldwide but also a system that is condemned by people in the market economy; it remains a deep-seated concern of many economists. Under the Chinese planned economic system, the issue of a dual-labour market was not prominent. First, because employment was controlled by the government under that system; jobs were not hunted by an individual; rather, they were allocated at the foundation level according to an employment quota. Hence the dual feature of the labour market was not salient. Second, because there was "covert unemployment" at that time, the existence of "covert unemployment" made the dual issue of the labour market unobvious.

After China entered the current stage of economic transformation, namely transition from a planned to a socialist market economic system, the dual-labour market phenomenon gradually took shape and eventually became obstacles to or constraints on people's income growth at the grassroots level.

So, what on earth is a dual-labour market? I can give some brief explanations. In economics theories, labour market can be classified by a worker's social ranks, which can at least be divided into two categories. One is called the top market, also known as "good jobs" in the labour market, and the other the inferior market, also known as "bad jobs" in the labour market.

The features of top labour market are: jobs here are all called "good jobs" as the basic salary is high with many additional allowances and benefits, better working conditions and higher technical requirements. There are also more opportunities for in-service training and further study and chance of being promoted is higher.

The features of inferior labour market are: jobs are called "bad jobs", as the basic salary for these jobs is comparatively lower. There are fewer additional allowances and benefits, with poorer working conditions and lower technical requirements. There are also fewer opportunities for in-service training and further study. Moreover, there is less chance for employees to be promoted.

Although the division of two categories of labour market is not formal, it has been a conventional way of categorising the market for a long time. In society, people generally show respect to those who have "good jobs" in the top labour market, considering them to be "promising" and "prospective". Instead, people generally do not show respect to those in "bad jobs" in the inferior labour market, holding a "despising" view that those employees are "good for nothing" or "have no future". Over time, this has become a kind of discrimination, or bias.

One more type of discrimination should be mentioned regarding China at the transformation phase. That is, the two types of household registration systems that came into being over half a century ago (the coexistence of urban and rural household registries). The vast majority of famers held rural household registry. Their rights and employment opportunities were restricted, so they could only enter the inferior labour market and sought for employment in "bad jobs". They would work in those jobs for a long time and rarely had a chance to be transferred into the top labour market and it was also difficult for them to be employed in "good jobs".

So in China, the social vertical flow channels for employees in the inferior labour market are very narrow and even blocked. This has resulted in fossilised social classes, forming in some sense "hereditary occupations". That is, if the father's generation worked in inferior labour market, the great majority of sons will also work there.

Thus, it is of practical significance to discuss the desalination of dual features of the labour market and measures that break through the social vertical flow channels in relation to alleviating China's employment pressure at the current phase. Next, we will approach the issue from three perspectives.

First, the possibility of cross-market flow. This is the most basic condition, because the cross-market flow here refers specifically to labour force's flow from inferior market to top market. It has nothing to do with a labourer's flow from top market to inferior market. The latter situation is rare and often there are particular reasons for the flow: for instance, in economic recession, some professionals and technicians are laid off. While they want to find another job in top market, but fail, they have no other choice but to find a job in the inferior market. As another example, some professionals or technicians were excluded from their working units due to errors they committed. They have no other choice but to find a job in the inferior market. These are all exceptional cases and thus will not be discussed here. What needs to be discussed here is: an individual has been employed in inferior labour market but hopes for an opportunity to be transferred to top market. Is there any normal way to go? The only normal path is to study hard, delve into technology, pass examinations through fair competition, be verified by recruitment units as being qualified and then enter top labour market. Real life does not lack such examples.

Second, "good jobs" in top labour market receive social attention, make rapid development and need additional staff. This kind of opportunity is also common. For example, the growth of service sectors in recent years has created many new jobs and requires additional professionals and technical personnel. This provides newly-graduated job seekers more opportunities to enter "good jobs" in the top labour market, and allows people in "bad jobs" of the inferior market to achieve cross-market flow through certain procedures. Opportunities are always there. It depends on whether job seekers have the corresponding capacity to seize them.

Third, as noted above, differences between "good jobs" and "bad jobs" lie mainly in the gap between salaries and benefits, good or bad working conditions, more or fewer learning opportunities and a high or low rate of career promotion. If all these aspects of "bad jobs" are improved, there will be fewer differences between the "bad jobs" and "good jobs" as there were previously. Will it be necessary not to rush into the "cross-market flow"? It is known from the progress of the developed market economy countries for nearly a half century that workers in many types of jobs are not working as arduously as before after the promotion of modernisation and automation. People engaged in manual labour in a factory do not feel as tired as they were before. Also, with the establishment of social welfare system, the income differences between practitioners in different sectors have shrunk. Thus, the number of people who require a change in careers is reduced.

Regardless of motives in requesting to move from the inferior labour market to the top market, the primary issue is still that the social vertical flow channel should be smoother. The discrimination and bias with various kinds of unhealthy practices in employment should vanish. Only by means of employment through fair competition can learning and working initiatives of each labourer be fully mobilised.

Section 3 Different types of inflation and countermeasures

1 Demand-pull inflation and countermeasures

The earliest and most frequently-occurring inflation in economic life is demand-pull inflation. In contemporary Western economics, economists who made the earliest studies of demand-pull inflation were Keynes and his followers.

In Keynesian macroeconomics, the basic function of an economic policy is to maintain economic stability, which is composed of two aspects: one is eliminating or alleviating unemployment and the other suppressing or relieving inflation. The reason for unemployment is insufficient aggregate demand and the reason for inflation is excessive demand. Assuming that there is serious unemployment, the government should stimulate the economy and relax its fiscal and monetary policies, since as long as aggregate demand increases, unemployment will be relieved until it disappears. Given that inflation is serious, the government should suppress aggregate demand and implement tight fiscal and monetary policies. As long as demand is reduced, inflation will be relieved.

About 20 to 30 years after World War II, the governments of Western market economic countries generally maintained economic stability largely according to Keynesian economic theories; that is, maintaining steady economic growth by using loose or tight fiscal and monetary policies to stimulate aggregate demand on some occasions or suppress them on other occasions to maintain steady economic growth. They were more effective then. In terms of controlling inflation, the reason for said effectiveness was because the inflation that emerged then was the demand-pull type of inflation.

Demand-pull inflation can be subcategorised into two types: one is investment-demand-prioritised expansion, namely investment demand-pull inflation, and the other is consumption-demand-prioritised expansion, namely consumption demand-pull inflation. Within the two pull types of inflation, the former, i.e. investment demand-pull inflation is more commonly known.

In 1958, Professor Phillips of the London School of Economics, UK, published a paper entitled *"The relation between unemployment and the rate of change of money wage rates in the United Kingdom, 1861–1957"* in the November issue of the *Economica* journal. In the paper, he compared the rise of money wage rates and the unemployment rate. He concluded that there was an alternative relationship between the two. In other words, a high money wage rise rate was always accompanied by a low unemployment rate; a low money wage rise rate was followed by a high unemployment rate. Phillips drew the above conclusion based on empirical data. The inflation rate is generally represented by price rise rate, while the price rise also causes the money wage rise; so changes in money wages can represent changes in inflation. The relationship between the wage rise rate and unemployment rate is expressed as an alternative relationship between growth and decline, advancement and retreat. In 1960, two prominent economists, Samuelson and Solow, published a co-authored paper entitled *"Analytical aspects of anti-inflation policy"* in the May issue of *American Economic Review*. In the paper, they named the curve proposed by Phillips the Phillips curve. Thereafter, the concept was widely disseminated. At that time, Samuelson and Solow modified the curve slightly and later, the academic and government decision-making sectors all interpreted Phillips curve as the alternating curve between inflation rate and unemployment rate.

The proposal of Phillips curve facilitated the control of demand-pull inflation. Just on the basis of the curve, bringing forth grounds for enacting fiscal and financial policies became convenient. The contents are: first develop "the social acceptable level" towards inflation rate and unemployment rate; then based on specific situation, try to control the rates within the "the social acceptance level". At that time, there is no need to take government intervention measures. If the inflation rate exceeds the level, the government can take tight measures. It would rather have a high unemployment rate and supress inflation; conversely, if unemployment rate exceeds the level, the government can take a loose policy. It would rather have a higher inflation rate and supress the unemployment rate.

Theoretically speaking, the Phillips curve did not have sufficient theoretical ground. Neither did Keynes, by the original intention of Keynesian economics, explain scientifically the real cause for inflation and unemployment in Western market economy countries. Insufficient demand and excessive demand are still two phenomena. Their institutional cause fell out of the scope of Keynesian studies. It was the same with Phillips, who never really explored the deeply-rooted cause for inflation and unemployment. Is the unemployment rise caused by lower or slower inflation? Isn't the decline in unemployment due to greater or faster inflation? Those are difficult to be convincing.

As expected, in the early 1970s, the Keynesian economics crisis took place, because from then on, "stagflation" occurred in the United States. That is, complications of inflation and unemployment took place. Neither Keynes' demand management theory nor Phillips Curve's interpretation could function properly.

2 Cost-push inflation and countermeasures

As described above, the major points of Keynesian demand management theory can be summarised into the following two points. First, the cause for inflation is excessive aggregate demand, so a tighter policy should be adopted to suppress aggregate demand; second, the cause for unemployment is insufficient aggregate demand, so a relaxed policy should be adopted to simulate aggregate demand. But the theory cannot any longer explain the complication of inflation and unemployment, nor is it possible to implement tight or loose policies. This is because: how can two completely opposite phenomena such as excessive and insufficient aggregate demand occur at the same time? How can we adopt both tight and loose policies spontaneously? Thus, people feel that the Keynes' demand management theory failed to work appropriately.

When discussing the cause for "stagflation", some economists held that inflation at that time might be the investment/consumption demand-pull inflation; rather, it was another type of inflation, also labelled as cost-push inflation. At the time, many economists called it a "new type of inflation." So they initiated discussions on the cause for the new inflation and proposed countermeasures

Cost-push inflation is considered to be caused by wage cost rise, while wage cost rise and price cost rise facilitate each other; they both take turns rising. Wage rise pushes up rise in commodity price and then the commodity price rises drives wage rate rise. Thus, the spiral rise of the two is endless. Some economists proposed the following explanations: in economic life, there came into being two monopolies, i.e. trade unions and large enterprises. Both sides are equally matched. Trade unions controlled the wage rise rate and supported wage rigidity. That is, wages could only be allowed to increase but not decrease. Large enterprises controlled price and enabled price rigidity. That is, prices could only be allowed to increase but not decrease. It was just like two kids playing "leapfrog". The leapfrog game is also called "frogs' jump". It is played like this: one of two children puts his hands on the ground and bends his body like a frog. The other child who stands jumps over the one with a bent body. Then the child who has jumped over bends his body in the front and the one who has bent his body stands up from the ground and jumps over the child who has bent up his body . . . they take turns jumping over. The jump can continue by taking turns. Wage and price were just like two children playing leapfrog with one taking turns to jump over the other. No matter how the government tried to "persuade" both trade unions and large enterprises to stop jumping, the persuasion did not work.

How should the government handle this? Since "persuasion" did not work, it had to take tough measures, i.e. taking a mandatory "income policy." That is, if a child was held down by hands and not allowed to stand up, there was at most one jump and then the game was over. If the two children were held down with two hands and neither of them could stand up, frog jumps stopped at an instant. Based on this reasoning, US President Richard Nixon followed the advice of some American economists and implemented wage- and price-control policies in the 1970s. Wages and price levels were frozen and neither of them could be raised at free will. Obviously, this completely infringed upon rules of the market and could undoubtedly be effective only for a short term, and it could not be sustained for long.

In the late 1970s, there came forward a school of supply-side economists in the United States. In Western economics circle, supply-siders were considered as proponents to conservative economics theories. They proposed that under the conditions of allowing the market mechanism to fully play its role, easing supply should be the basic policy for solving cost-push inflation and "stagflation" in the United States. They also held that only by increasing supply could the component cost-rising tendency be suppressed, while only through tax cuts, could supply be raised. Proposals of supply-siders were completely different from the demand management theory of Keynesian economics. To supply-siders, the inflation issue could not be addressed by demand-tightening policies. If that was the case, the insufficient supply would be intensified, while shortage was the right reason for inflation. "Standstill" in stagnation would not disappear with tightening, while "expansion" in it would continue to exist due to insufficient supply.

Regarding the advocate of Keynesian economics that taxes should not be cut but raised during inflation, supply-siders insisted that followers of Keynesian economics simply reverse measures that should be taken. This was because increasing taxes during inflation would suppress supply, and insufficient supply would be intensified and inflation would be further pushed up. Hence, supply-siders spared no efforts in proposing a maximal tax cut, which would result in stimulating enterprises to increase production, so as to achieve the objective of suppressing inflation.

Debate between the supply-siders and Keynesians continued with neither side succeeding in convincing the other. Then, how had the United States, by the mid-1980s, alleviated the complication of inflation and unemployment and made "stagflation" gradually disappear? At that time, the US government recognised that the most important strategy was to encourage enterprises to make independent innovation, industrial upgrading and embark on a new path of developing new and high-technologies. It was difficult to say that the US government accepted theories from one particular school of economists; rather, it integrated economic propositions from various schools. In regard to Keynesian recommendations on demand management, the US government continued to adopt them as ground rules for macroeconomic regulation and control. As to supply-siders' proposal on tax cuts, the US government adopted them as measures encouraging technological innovation and supporting the development of high-technologies. Regarding the monetary school's proposal of stabilising currency growth rate, it also became one of the US government's ground policy rules. But more importantly, the United States was inspired by world scientific and technological progress, and many successful American enterprises owe their success to scientific and technological innovation, holding that those were where the future hope of the US economy lay.

Breakthroughs in science and technology finally enabled the United States to gain a world-leading position in high- and new-technology industries. This is more convincing than the preaching of any economic school. Technological innovation is the best solution to cost-push inflation. Reducing the tax burden, developing capital markets, promoting equity incentive system, mobilising initiatives of science and technology research and development personnel and deepening reform in the higher education system etc. were all considered to be effective measures for the development of high and new technology industries.

For about 40 years since the 1970s, people from different walks of life in the United States debated countermeasures against cost-push inflation. Historical experience has shown the debate has been very instructive to many other countries, including China.

3 Internationally-imported inflation and countermeasures

Internationally-imported inflation has a relatively long history. A very obvious example was the "price revolution", which occurred to Western Europe countries between the 16th and 17th centuries. The revolution originated in Spain, because the Kingdom of Spain occupied Latin American territories other than Brazil. In the occupied Latin American colonies, they plundered Indians everywhere, palaces and nobles' mansions in some countries, and exploited captured Indians to mine precious metals, and transported a large amount of gold and silver from the Americas to Spain. So prices in Spain soared high. Very quickly, soaring prices spread to other Western European countries like France, the Netherlands and Britain. Commodity supply in those countries became greatly inadequate for the expanded demand due to impact from Spain, and thus all became victims of the "Price Revolution".

Economists call inflation originating from a foreign country and later having a profound impact on other countries internationally-imported inflation. Such inflation is exported from one country to another primarily through two channels: the channel of commodity flow and the channel of capital flow, regardless of whether the country that exported inflation is the source inflation country, and whether the country was the first export (meaning the source country that exports inflation), or the second or the multi-export following the second.

Inflation imported through the channel of goods flow means that when a country has domestic demand for some goods but cannot provide sufficient domestic supply, the prices of those commodities go up, leading to inflation through the commodity flow. This has been clearly demonstrated in the price rise of imported bulk commodities such as petroleum, natural gas, iron ore, nonferrous metals, cotton, grains, soybeans, cooking oil and other commodities.

Inflation imported through the channel of capital flow refers to the following four cases.

The first case: there are differences between international interest rates, which can be lower in some countries but higher in others. As capital always chases a higher interest rate, it flows from a lower interest rate country to one with a higher rate. Once capital flows into a higher interest rate country, it makes the country with a high interest rate possess excessive capital, thus raising the prices of commodities.

The second case: the degree of economic development varies among countries. Some have more investment opportunities than others; some have higher

investment income profits than others. Yet, capital is always chasing more investment opportunities and a higher investment rate, so capital flows from a country with less investment opportunities and lower investment profits into one with
more investment opportunities and higher profitability, thus causing the latter to
receive more in-flow capital and also rises in commodity prices.

The third case: the currency of some important countries, especially big countries
like the United States, also serves as an international reserve currency. To alleviate their economic recession, those countries have adopted a loose monetary policy,
resulting in an in-flow surplus. At the same time, the capital of the United States flows
into other countries. This is the so-called intentionally-exported inflation behaviour.
It is this behaviour that passes on inflation and makes other countries victims.

The fourth case: the balance of payments plays a part in internationally-
transmitted inflation. While surpluses and deficits in international payment both
have impacts on the internationally-transmitted inflation, their role is not the same.
If a country has a continuous payment surplus, its foreign exchange reserves rise
(usually known as the increased foreign exchange). This is just one of the reasons
that brings about inflation of the country. Additionally, in this case, the currency
of that country faces appreciation pressure, so when overseas capital expects the
appreciation of this country's currency, they will further intervene in the country.
Internationally-imported inflation accelerates the occurrence. If a country continues to receive payment deficits, its foreign exchange reserves will be reduced and
the country is urged to speed up the introduction of foreign investments. It is also
possible that they will devalue their currency, which is a precursor of inflation of
a country. Given this, successive surpluses and deficits in international payment
will give rise to inflation in different aspects.

So, how can a country guard against the in-flow of overseas inflation? In the
case where internationally-imported inflation has occurred, are there any effective
countermeasures? Generally speaking, the options discussed below are feasible.
However, before discussing alternative measures, we need to first assume that
the imported commodities (such as oil, gas, ore, crops and cotton etc.) are rigid
demands and that their imports will not dramatically decrease due to rises in international prices. Optional countermeasures are as follows.

(1) Control of foreign exchanges

In order to prevent the flux of international capital into a country, one of the
optional countermeasures is to tighten the control of foreign exchanges, i.e. raising the dam after foreign capital flows into the country to prevent it from flowing
back to its own country. Note that different types of capital can be discriminated
through screening. Special attention should be paid to the flow of non-oriented
international capital (known as international hot money) into the country.

(2) The Structuring of the monetary policy

A monetary policy which is too loose or too tight is not conducive to alleviate
the pressure incurred by internationally-imported inflation. A prudent monetary

policy is usually feasible and requires the total control to be combined with structural regulations in the monetary policy. This will also achieve the objective of both maintenance and oppression, making the amount of money in circulation return to normal and at the same time avoiding the side effects presented by implementing either a tight or a loose policy.

(3) Using foreign exchange reserves rationally

To use foreign exchange reserves rationally, particularly when prices of imported goods are expected to rise substantially, it is necessary to let enterprises import more goods as super-normal reserves. At the same time, enterprises must be encouraged (including state-owned and private enterprises) to make overseas investments, to purchase overseas assets and to make cooperative investments in management with its counterparts. These measures are helpful in alleviating the symptoms of internationally-imported inflation.

(4) Using tighter fiscal and monetary policies appropriately

One of the objectives of using tighter fiscal and monetary policies is on the one hand, to moderately reduce flow ability and ease too large of a flow ability; on the other hand, it is to suppress an excessively modest economic growth rate, reduce the quantity of imported raw materials and fuel, reduce dependence on imported raw materials and fuels, and force domestic enterprises to improve their use of raw materials and fuel. Even if domestic demand for these imported goods has a certain rigidity, rigid demand is not inelastic.

4 Comprehensive inflation in current China and proposed integrated countermeasures

Under the planned economic system, although there was inflation, inflation was covert. It was not primarily manifested in price increases; and yet it was reflected in the promoted use of quotas, and increased commodity varieties based on quotas. That is, the variety of commodities needed to be acquired with coupons increased. It was only after China's Reform and Opening-up, and its gradual transformation from a planned to a socialist market economic system that inflation became obvious and overt.

However, before the 21st century, China's inflation was mainly investment demand-pull inflation. The same was true in the early and mid-1980s. So was it in the mid-1990s. In 1988, due to the rumour of a price breakthrough, residents rushed to buy consumer goods and enterprises hoarded raw materials and fuel. This was when there was the first outbreak of inflation, jointly pulled and pushed by investment and consumption demands.

At that time, measures against demand-pull inflation were intended to implement tight financial and monetary policies. As soon as the fiscal and credit gates were closed, inflation stopped, though there were some side effects. That period of history remains fresh in our mind.

After entering the 21st century, the situation changed. Apart from the demand-prioritised investment demand-pull inflation, we also had internationally-imported inflation and particularly cost-push inflation, a new type of inflation in China. It can even be said that this type of inflation first occurred.

In the 21st century, there were three new factors in cost-push inflation. First, wage costs rose. Prior to this, China's labour costs had been low since the country had abundant cheap labour resources. But after two or three decades (from the 1980s to the early 21st century), living costs continued to rise. So did the cost for farmers to work outside the home as migrant workers. Migrant worker demands for higher wages were reasonable. Second, housing costs rose, which was very rare in the past. This was revealed in rising costs, not only in production, space and land use, but also workers' living quarters. They all contributed to rising wage costs. Third, financing costs rose. This was mainly due to the unsolved financing problem. The suspended financing issues left private enterprises with no other choice but to resort to private credit. High interest rates were rampant. More and more private enterprises found themselves in the mire, unable to break away from it.

Take the most recent period of inflation (2011–12) for example. It was a comprehensive inflation, where demand-pull, cost-push and internationally-imported inflations coexisted. In view of cause, what was the primary type of inflation? Generally speaking, while worldwide, there were intermittent price rises in important commodities, far fewer than in previous years. Demand-pull inflation could not be ignored, since both central and local governments all had the investment impulse to promote economic growth by relying on increasing investment and expanding the scale of credit. But the most important and also greatly unexpected inflation by the government decision-making sectors was cost-push inflation. Plainly stated, when government officials learned that many private enterprises were complaining about "difficulties in surviving on", they thought they were merely repeating the old sayings like "financing difficulties", "too heavy fees and taxes", "export difficulties", "too few orders", without realising that private enterprises were appealing to the government: "wages are soaring higher"; "it is difficult to hire suitable migrant workers"; "migrant workers are reluctant to come to my plant"; "workers just recruited were dragged away by another enterprise with higher wages." Such "weird things" occurred between 2011 and 2012. They were not what private enterprises had expected, nor had they been expected by the government. As a matter of fact, there was nothing weird about this. What was strange about farmers' call for a pay increase due to the fact of a handsome increase in living costs? Since the farmers felt the pay was too low to get them adapted to urban life, why couldn't they call for increase in pay and benefits?

Since farmers felt that wages were so low that it was hard for them to get used to their urban life, why shouldn't they call for an increase in wages and benefits? Those were significant signs of cost-push inflation on the Chinese territory.

As the most recent inflation in China (2011–12) was comprehensive, the experience can be summarised as follows: do not simply implement demand-pull, especially investment demand-pull anti-inflation measures. Simply raising the deposit-reserve ratio or raising the benchmark interest rate, or simply compressing the size of credit, would not ensure obvious effects. Unified planning should be used to take different cases into full account; moreover, cases should be differentiated and dealt with according to their corresponding category. This means that policies and measures should be made to adapt to cases in different areas: economically developed, moderately developed and underdeveloped areas. Similarly, policies and measures should be made to adapt to those different types of industries: those with production capacity shortages, those with balanced production capacity and those with production capacity surplus. Those are the effective measures that can cope with the comprehensive types of inflation.

Worldwide experience in dealing with cost-push inflation is emphasising independent innovation, industrial upgrading and optimising structure. China must draw on its experience in dealing with cost-push inflation. In relation to the above are two sets of supporting policies and measures. The first policy or measure is to strengthen the technical training of workers to let more workers become professionals, technicians, or skilled workers so as to meet the need of high-tech industries, and maintain their advantages and leading status in international competition. This is also in line with the call for wage increases and spontaneous productivity growth.

The second policy and measure is implementation of a proper incentive system that would let more workers become human resource investors who share equity and profits. This would further mobilise the enthusiasm of employees, especially enabling professionals, technical experts and skilled workers to play an active role. Note that raising their wages would increase business costs, but this can be offset by the simultaneous growth in labour productivity. Unlike raising wage costs, implementing an incentive system, property right-sharing system and profit-sharing system are more effective and more able to mobilise the creativity and enthusiasm of broad masses of workers and increase staff's corporate identity.

5 *Several focal issues in dealing with inflation*

(1) *Prioritising incremental adjustment to promote the adjustment of industrial structure on the premises of achieving higher economic growth*

Industrial restructuring needs to be conducted continuously and there is no limit to this. When the government takes various macroeconomic measures to control inflation, it should not relax industrial structuring, particularly not letting the industrial structuring work to come to a halt.

There are two basic types of industrial structure adjustment: the first is "incremental adjustment" and the second "stock adjustment." The "incremental adjustment" should be prioritised between the two. Let's assume that "stock adjustment" was prioritised in inflation control. Though it could be effective instantly, increasing social turmoil would follow and as a result, the practice was not conducive to the promotion of industrial restructuring. Meanwhile, local governments' concerns are: once a batch of enterprises are closed, stopped, merged or transferred, the local economic growth rate will decline, the unemployment rate will increase, local revenues will be reduced and their commitment to improving certain aspects of the people's livelihood will not be honoured. So in some places, there will be the following phenomena: some enterprises will have been closed officially but not in practice and the production of some enterprises will have been stopped in the public's eyes but actually not in operation.

By contrast, although the speed of adjustment slows down with incremental adjustment, it allows for less social turmoil and local governments would be under less pressure. All the factors weighed, effects of adopting industrial restructuring which prioritises incremental adjustment may not necessarily be small.

The premise of implementing "incremental adjustment" is to maintain a higher economic growth rate and enable revenues to grow continuously. Thus, the government can take advantage of new investment, make use of increased social purchasing power, continue to rely on market regulation so as to accelerate the development of new industries, and meanwhile, allow enterprises unable to adapt to the market to make their own industrial upgrading, introduce new technologies and reform their outdated production and management modes.

(2) Awareness of inflation alert levels and some knowledge of the alert level division

There has never been a common alert level applicable to all countries. Based on specific circumstances of each country, alert levels are determined by the country's economic growth, and its residents' degree of tolerance towards inflation.

Level 1 inflation rate alert is definitely not a zero inflation rate. As long as the economy grows fast, it is not possible to have a zero inflation rate. Roughly, it can be assumed to be half of the economic growth rate. When the inflation rate is less than half of the economic growth rate, the government should pay close attention but does not need to tighten its policy immediately. In this case, the government usually only makes fine-tuning or pre-set measures. Level 2 inflation rate alert is when the inflation rate surpasses level 1 inflation rate alert and comes close to the economic growth rate. Tight measures should be used to deal with inflation in this case. However, this is restricted to demand-pull inflation. In the event of comprehensive inflation, simply relying on a tight policy is not enough and there must be other measures to go with it. For instance, tight measures could be coordinated with loose measures or tight monetary policy is coordinated with a relaxed fiscal policy. Furthermore, if the cost-push inflation occupies an important position in comprehensive inflation, then adopting an appropriate tight policy must also be coordinated with an industrial policy that either fosters or encourages independent innovation, industrial upgrading and the development of new industries. Additionally, we can make more use of foreign exchange reserves, for instance, by expanding the import ratio of commodities in shortage and implementing policies that support enterprises to "go abroad". Foreign exchange reserves can also be used to reduce the amount of money in circulation.

(3) Understanding two characteristics of the Chinese economy
through the "cycling principle"

Why do we use the "cycling principle" as metaphors? This is because in the dual transformation phase, China's economic operation is like riding a bicycle. The speed must be slightly faster, so that accumulated social problems can be resolved in growth. Riding too fast will make the bicycle roll over but riding slowly will make the bicycle shake and no riding it makes it fall. Those are characteristics of Chinese economic operation.

Why should we remember "it is easier to brake than to start"? As mentioned previously, we take automobile industry for example. The Chinese economy at the transformation phase is like driving a car. This car has very good brakes; it stops instantly upon braking; however, it does not have a good starting mechanism. Even if power is burst, the car is often belatedly launched. This is because the initiative of braking is under the government's control. When revenues are tightened, credit is tightened and the car is braked. Nonetheless, the initiative of "starting" is not under the government's control but within the hands of private investors and consumers. If the private investors do not have enough confidence, they will wait and see without making investments. What action is required? If the private investors lack confidence, they will not buy. The government cannot force private investors to do so, nor can it force private investors to buy commodities or services not absolutely necessary. So, it is difficult to start. Furthermore, ordinary people do not only have inflation expectations but also investment prospect and employment expectations. Assuming that neither their investment prospects nor employment expectations are good, how can the economic situation be made prosperous?

(4) Inappropriateness in using Western market economy countries'
criterion to judge whether the amount of currency
in circulation in China is at a normal level

This was mentioned at the beginning but here I will make some additional remarks.

It is very clear that currently, China is still at the phase of dual transformation. The situation in China is different from that of developed Western market economy countries. The normal level of currency in circulation stipulated by Western market economists is suitable for Western market economy countries but unsuitable for China's current situation. The reasons are as follows.

First, China remains in a dual transformation phase. Farmers have broken away from their previous mode of production and ways of life. Even if they are still living in rural areas, they have been increasingly involved in the market and are using money more and more often. This must be taken into account in judging whether the amount of currency in circulation in China is normal or not.

Second, current distribution channels in China are not as smooth as those in developed Western market economy countries. In China, there are many links in the middle of the circulation, and transaction costs are high, which could definitely affect China's monetary circulation speed. This is another reason why there is a gap between China's and developed Western market economy countries' normal level of amount of currency in circulation.

Third, China's urbanisation is speeding up. Farmers have been successively moving to towns, setting up small business shops and workshops, or doing migrant work. Their living and working environments are changing and this is bound to increase Chinese society's demand for currency.

Fourth, financial activities in China's small towns and rural areas have failed to be carried out in line with economic development. Private enterprises, in particular small and medium private enterprises, have encountered loaning difficulties. In order to prevent capital chains from breaking up, they have the view of "cash is king". As a result, they all reserve excessive amounts of cash for emergency. Thus, the amount of currency in circulation multiplies.

In view of China's reality, it is not difficult to draw the following conclusion: the normal amount of currency in circulation for many developed Western market economy countries is a level slightly tight for China at the current phase.

According to China's economic fluctuation experience since 2008, neither a surplus nor a deficit of capital in currency circulation has been unfavourable, but a tight amount of currency in circulation has more negative impacts than a slightly greater amount of money in circulation. Why has it been like this? The most important reason is: the hollowing-out of the real economy, the hollowing-out of the manufacturing industry in particular is a phenomenon that cannot be ignored at the dual transformation phase, i.e. the withdrawal of a significant amount of currency from the real economic areas, from the manufacturing area. In case of a slightly tight amount of money in circulation, not only does returning to the real economy become more difficult, but also small and medium enterprises and private enterprises experience more setbacks and self-innovation and industry-upgrading are more difficult to achieve. Thus, a slightly tight monetary policy has a greater negative impact on China's dual economic transformation. From the perspective of "taking the less harmful one when two harms are weighed", it is better to have a greater amount than a tighter amount of currency in circulation.

Section 4 Thoughts on the national security of foreign exchange reserves

If security issues occur to a country's foreign exchange reserves, there are basically two reasons: first, there have been continuous deficits in foreign exchange balance, so that foreign exchange reserves decrease substantially; and second, foreign exchange reserves being held are experiencing continuous depreciation and the value of foreign reserves has been reduced. Therefore, to ensure the security of foreign exchange reserves, we should approach the issue from two aspects simultaneously.

1 The decline of foreign exchange reserves

International balance of payment accounts are divided into current accounts and capital accounts with equal importance. The primary issue in the current account is the balance of trade. How to avoid a balance of payment deficit has much to do with the competitiveness of export commodities. If an enterprise has no export competitiveness, it will affect the balance of payment and reduce trade surplus, eventually turning surplus into a trade deficit. Since the 2008 financial crisis, the United States and some other Western countries have regarded technological innovation as a post-crisis warranty on whether a country can gain a foothold in market competition. As a result, they have spared no investment or human resources, aiming at major breakthroughs in technological innovation. If we miss the opportunity or if we do not seize the opportunity to make independent innovation, complete industrial and product upgrading, we will regret it in the future. In current accounts, on-trade balance is also very important. For instance, tourism industry is an important industry in increasing foreign exchange earnings. So is the service industry. Clothing outsourcing is also an emerging channel that helps to increase foreign exchange earnings. There is not much room for development in these areas. We must not miss the opportunity.

According to discussions based on recent scientific community research, future significant technological breakthroughs will be made worldwide in the following four aspects:

First, new energy. Future development can be boosted by new energy, since it can reduce a country's dependence on imported energy and meanwhile spur technological renovation in the entire automotive industry. Moreover, the improvement in new energy technology will not only continue to enlarge the domestic market of the automotive industry, it will enable it to occupy part of the international market.

Second, new materials. This is also an important area, since the use of new materials will drive technological renovation in manufacturing industry, real estate and light industry, so prospects for developing new materials are good.

Third, biotechnology. Major breakthroughs in the field of biotechnology will not only promote the development of agriculture, animal husbandry and aquaculture, but also greatly boost the pharmaceutical industry, making products in these industries more competitive.

Fourth, environmental protection industry. There will surely be major breakthroughs in this area, since it affects not only export competitiveness but also whether there will be a sustainable export issue.

When I was lecturing in Europe in 2008, I had discussions with European economists. They made the point that to consume less was to protect the environment. For example, using less paper is environmentally friendly; using disposable chopsticks is not environmentally friendly; an energy-efficient home is environmentally friendly since the production of any product results in carbon dioxide emissions. From this perspective, families have great energy-saving potentials. It is much more the case for enterprises. If enterprises emit more carbon dioxide, their products will not be able to be exported and they will lose the international market.

Breakthroughs in industries make products more competitive. Even labour-intensive industries need innovation. When conducting surveys in several provinces, we found that many entrepreneurs still believed that innovation was relevant to knowledge and capital-intensive industries but has nothing to do with labour-intensive ones. However, some entrepreneurs suggested that labour-intensive industries can also make innovations. For example, innovation in labour-intensive industries can be approached at least from the following five aspects.

First, innovation in design. Be original and the design will be innovative. For example, innovative design is most important for the production of clothing, footwear and toys.

Second, there can be a breakthrough in the selection of raw materials. If you can choose new and more environmentally friendly materials for a fashionable suit, a pair of shoes or a toy, what will happen? They may become more popular.

Third, energy saving. It can reduce costs and meet environmental standards.

Fourth, innovation in marketing. There can be a big breakthrough in marketing. It is the same for the labour-intensive industry.

Fifth, innovation within enterprise management systems. Private enterprises, after family-run enterprises, have reached a certain scale and need to be standardised. A property dispute will affect the effectiveness of the entire enterprise.

Given the above, any type of enterprise requires independent innovation and has the potential to be innovative. Independent innovation capability is an important factor that impacts the current account of balance of payment, particularly in the trade balance current account.

In the capital account, two important measures should be taken to ensure that foreign exchange reserves do not drop substantially. First, we must adhere to reforming and opening-up, and creating more suitable environments for the entry of foreign capital. For example, we should honour creditability, improve investment environments and perfect basic infrastructure, and make our policies stable so that overseas capital will continuously enter and there will be no case of evacuation on a large scale. Second, stop large fluctuations in capital account to stop private capital from abnormally flowing out. The abnormal outflow of a huge amount of private capital will affect foreign exchange reserves. Therefore, policies pertinent to the development of the private economy must be continuous.

In February 2005, the State Council enacted the *Several Opinions of the State Council on Encouraging and Guiding the Healthy Development of Private Investment*, namely the so-called *"36 Non-public Economy Articles"*; however, to date, the *"36 Non-public Economy Articles"* have not been fully implemented. Private entrepreneurs are very sensitive to policies. If they find that policies have fallen backwards, capital will flow out of China abnormally. This will affect foreign exchange reserves.

2 The depreciation of foreign exchange reserves

Depreciation of a foreign currency can result from a country's domestic economic fluctuation. So, what can we do? Here are five points.

First, what proportion should any kind of hard currency, including the dollar, Euro, British pound, Swiss franc and sometimes Japanese yen, take in our foreign exchange reserves? It should be given an overall account. We can't overemphasise it or belittle it. The composition of currency types in foreign exchange reserves was formed historically and should not be changed too quickly or too dramatically; instead, we should have a clear idea of how we should gradually adjust, rationalise and optimise foreign exchange reserves.

Second, the scope of foreign exchange reserves should be expanded to foreign exchange reserves of gold. In the current situation, even if gold prices fluctuate, the trend is still appreciation due to the limited supply of gold. So we should increase gold reserves along with foreign exchange reserves. Putting them together is advantageous in ensuring the safety of our foreign exchange reserves. When gold prices fall, we can seize the moment and purchase more gold.

Third, we must establish the concept of foreign asset reserves. Foreign exchange reserves are made up solely of a foreign currency. In fact, from the perspective of national security, we should not only have foreign exchange reserves composed of foreign currencies but also foreign exchange asset reserves that can be quickly realised as foreign currencies. If foreign assets can be quickly realised in that way, it will be better than reserving foreign currencies. China's share of foreign assets is not better than that of Japan, whose foreign reserves are made up less of foreign currency and more of foreign assets. So we need to find ways to increase our foreign assets: for instance buying land, mines or enterprise shares that have good stock returns in foreign countries. Those are all foreign assets. In all, increasing foreign assets is very important since the hedging function of foreign assets will be much more obvious.

Fourth, use foreign exchange reserves as credit funds. Foreign loans can drive exports of assets, contracted engineering and labour output. So we can make use of our country's foreign exchange reserves to boost our domestic economy.

Fifth, even if foreign exchange reserves are composed of foreign currencies, we can enliven our reserves. Leaving so many foreign currencies there without using them is a loss in itself because the opportunity cost has increased. Additionally, some foreign currencies are being devalued, causing greater losses. So foreign currency reserves should be enlivened by importing advanced equipment, raw materials and fuel in shortage, as well as making overseas investment.

Let's imagine that our foreign currency reserves were reduced or even we did not have enough foreign reserves, could we import so much edible oil? Our supply of our edible oil has fallen behind our production. To make enough edible oil produced domestically, how many acres of land would be needed? Billions of acres of land might not be enough. Where would the land come from? With so little land, how could we plant beans to produce edible oil? If we increase foreign currency reserves, we could build farms abroad. We could plant soybeans, process soybeans and produce edible oil. What would be transported back was edible oil that our farms and processing enterprises could produce. Therefore, foreign exchange reserves should be enlivened.

If the earlier-noted five aspects are addressed, the national foreign exchange reserves will have anti-risk capabilities.

It is also necessary to propose the concept of "hiding foreign currencies among the people". What has been discussed above is about national foreign exchange reserves, while "hiding foreign currency among the people" refers to private reserves. It is more comprehensive if the domestic and foreign exchange reserves are divided into two sectors. One is national foreign exchange reserves and private foreign exchange reserves. Private foreign exchange reserves can also play a role in stabilising the economy. Note that private foreign currency reserves have a strong anti-risk capacity due to its mechanisms of being flexible, holding currencies in a scattered way and diversified sources of information.

Upon troublesome signs in the foreign exchange reserve market, civilians (whether enterprises or individuals) are always ready to take countermeasures and strive to preserve the values and avoid losses. The more foreign reserves a country has, the more a country's finance will be assured. Of course, if civilians hold more foreign exchange reserves, market risks will increase, but this is mainly an issue of policy guidance and financial regulations. As long as the system is improved and sound, "hiding foreign currency among the people" is more beneficial than detrimental from every perspective.

3 Further study on the security of foreign exchange reserves

Regarding the security of current foreign exchange reserves, I bring forth important questions for discussion and further research.

The first question: under the condition of a managed floating exchange rate, a substantial appreciation of RMB or its rapid increase in value is clearly undesirable. Setting a hard rule for the exchange rate, however, is even more undesirable. Then what are the advantages and disadvantages of the appreciation of the RMB in small steps? We need to make comparisons. Thereby, we need to proceed with the discussion from here: if RMB appreciates in small steps or rises in value slowly, will it bring unfavourable impacts as well? In that case, how should we remove them? What measures will be valid and feasible?

The second question: is there a ceiling or floor limit in the amount of foreign exchange reserves? How did we get the idea of optimal foreign exchange reserves? What is the optimal proportion of foreign exchange reserves in GDP? Would it be better to calculate foreign exchange reserves along with other national economic indexes? This also needs to be further explored. Maybe the idea of "the optimal amount of foreign reserves" is not valid or reliable. So can we establish sound foreign exchange reserves standards compatible with current situations in developing countries at the transformation stage?

The third question: foreign exchange reserves are not only a quantitative but also a qualitative concept. Designing an early alerting mechanism by the amount of foreign exchange reserves is relatively easier. For example, supposing foreign exchange reserves consecutively fall over several months, then what is the amount that indicates the fall has been close to the alert levels or has gone beyond them? However, do foreign exchange reserves have quality indexes? Where are the quality standards? How to determine quality indexes? How to make an integrative study of both quantitative and qualitative indicators and establish an early alerting mechanism related to foreign exchange reserves in the future?

The fourth question: study the currency fluctuation tendency of other countries that have a lot of economic contact with China. Since the appreciation and depreciation of foreign currencies in foreign exchange reserves are related to the security of China's foreign exchange reserves, we should carry out studies on i.e. short, medium and long-term analyses of the currency fluctuation tendency of the countries that have a lot of economic contact with China. Take changes in the dollar and Euro for example. It needs specialised research institutes and researchers to conduct the work and submit research reports. Such research has the same referential value as preparing overseas investment and preparing to expand the proportion of foreign exchange reserves.

The fifth question: strengthen the theoretical study of exchange rate determination. The traditional exchange rate determination theories (such as the Balance of Payment Theory, Purchasing Power Parity Theory, Interest Rate Parity Theory etc.) are clearly not sufficient to explain the current exchange rate determination issue. That is, in terms of new exchange rate determination theory, the more popular one is the fluid exchange rate model based on monetarism theories. However, the model over-emphasises the role of currency supply and has a bias towards money-flow analysis, and takes fully elastic commodity market prices as a basis. To what extent can this be adapted to the current exchange rate determination, particularly under the conditions that governments in different countries to a large extent intervene in the demand and supply of its own country, trade protectionism gains ground worldwide, with prices of key commodities still under monopoly and control? It is highly doubtful that such a model can explain foreign exchange determination and the reasons for changes in exchange rate. Therefore, it is necessary to carry out research on exchange rate determination theories.

5   Reform of the income distribution system

Section 1 Reasons for the expanding income gap between urban and rural areas

China's planned economy was established in 1958. The rural-urban dualism, based on the coexistence of urban and rural household registration systems implemented in 1958, was a major structural overhaul that consolidated the planned economy nationwide. Since then, the vast rural populations have become *de facto* "second-class citizens" who do not enjoy equal rights with their urban counterparts. The coexistence of two household registration systems has evolved into two different statuses. Rural status binds the peasantry to their land and prevents free migration. This seriously restricts the flow of social production factors, and severely hinders economic development.

Although China ushered in its reform by experimenting with and promulgating the rural household responsibility system in 1977 as pointed out in Section 2, Chapter 1, the rural-urban dualism was left essentially untouched, except in its extreme forms such as the base-level rural political organisation founded on people's communes and the combination of communes and villages. The separation of the two household registration systems and the restrictions on residence status remained unchanged. The income gap between urban and rural areas continues to widen even 30 years after China's Reform and Opening-up.

The widening income gap between urban and rural areas is a serious obstacle to social stability and harmony. To effectively narrow this gap we must first understand its main causes in recent years.

We start by discussing the three types of capital.

1   Three forms of capital: material capital, human capital and social capital

Three forms of capital are conceptualised in economics.

The first is material capital, according to traditional terminology. When economists discuss material capital, they always regard this capital as the most, if not the only, important type. There will be no production without production material – no land, no tools, no products. However, given the presence of the market, money can make up for the lack of material capital. Investment can be converted into the means of production, including factory buildings, equipment, raw material and so on. These all belong to the category of material capital, from which products can be made.

The second type of capital is human capital. Even if a labourer possesses no technical skills or knowledge, his bodily strength constitutes a type of human capital, although it is the lowest type and we can say that it almost amounts to zero. According to its definition in economics, human capital consists of a labourer's technical expertise, knowledge, wisdom and experience. The theory of human capital was developed in the 1960s, and since then it is generally accepted that wealth is created by both material and human capital and that the latter is often more important than the former. For example, many factories, bridges and ports were destroyed in Germany and Japan during the World War II, but their post-war economies recovered rapidly. The reason for this is that, although their material capital suffered damage, they still retained their human capital, which played a major role in revitalising the economy.

There are various ways to increase human capital, the most important being education. Only by attending school and acquiring knowledge and skills can one add to one's human capital. Other measures include increasing competence by continuing to study and accumulate experience after one has begun working, improving healthcare and medical services to ensure the well-being of workers and to maintain high attendance rates, and introducing skilled workers and professionals from abroad to boost domestic human capital.

The third type of capital is social capital. The theory of social capital was developed in the 1970s. This term is often used by journalists but carries a different meaning. The social capital mentioned in newspapers refers to non-governmental capital or funds. In economics, on the other hand, social capital denotes an immaterial capital such as one's social network and reputation. After the Reform and Opening-up, the economy of *Guangdong* thrived thanks to its rich social capital in the form of its connections with Macau, Hong Kong and the overseas Chinese. Similarly, the rapid economic development in *Zhejiang* province relies on the social capital held in families and fellow townsmen.

In a market economy, whether or not one has access to social capital and how much social capital one has makes a significant difference. Why is it increasingly popular to establish societies of alumni, former classmates and fellow townsmen, as well as other clubs? Why is there a resurging interest in rural areas in maintaining and adding to the records of family trees and building ancestral shrines? Many factors contribute to this trend, one of which is to secure more social capital. Many people are realising the importance of social capital, since more connections means more opportunities.

Wealth is created from the combination of material, human and social capital. Right now, urban areas are superior in all three types of capital compared with rural areas.

(1) Material capital

Material capital remains fundamental to anyone who wants to start a business or increase his earnings. The possession of land, houses and capital for investment is key to raising income and accumulating wealth. The importance of land and house property for farmers needs no elaboration, but it is precisely here that we see the glaring differences between urban and rural residents.

Take land and property as an example: the urban land is state-owned; the title deeds are inherited with the property and can be used for mortgages. If an urban resident wants to start a business, he only needs to mortgage his title deeds to gain cash for investment. He can then use the cash to open a workshop, a store or other small enterprise. This is an advantage urban residents have over their rural counterparts. As pointed out in Chapter 1, even now, with the exception of pilot reform zones, land in rural areas is collectively owned, and neither contracted nor homestead land can be mortgaged. No matter how fine a house a farmer can build, he cannot mortgage it if he does not have the title deeds. Therefore, farmers lack material capital. In the past few years, I have led the Subcommittee of Economics of the CPPCC to conduct research in rural areas annually. The farmers ask how it is that inherited or newly purchased commercial properties on state-owned urban land can be used for mortgage and transfer, whereas the houses they have built on the homestead land cannot. It is even difficult to rent houses out because the owners feel insecure without property rights and title deeds. If an outsider rents a house, they fear that he may continue to occupy it after the term has expired, or refuse to pay rent. Therefore, they only rent houses to their friends or relatives, but at a substantially lower price. Some farmers leave their villages to find work in cities and towns. Once they have a stable job, they will take their wives and children with them, and lock the doors of their houses. This is where the story of "two mice" originates: when the migrant workers' wives and children have left for the cities and locked up their houses, they become populated by mice – this is the first "mouse". When the migrant workers arrive in towns, they have no possessions and nowhere to live, and so they stay in the basements of apartment buildings. As a result, they are called "the mice people" due to their living underground – here is the second "mouse".

In the mid-19th century, industrialisation and urbanisation accelerated in France and large numbers of farmers poured into the cities. At the same time, real estate mortgage banks were established. The economy in France then was a small-scale peasant economy. When the farmers migrated into the cities, they mortgaged their land and property to gain capital, with which they could start a business, rent a house or perform labour. Consequently, urbanisation and industrialisation in France proceeded smoothly, without disruption to the social order.

How can we help Chinese farmers gain material capital? In addition to the capital accumulated from their agricultural activities, the most important factor is to determine their land rights, as has been discussed in Section 2, Chapter 1. This will protect the interests and rights of the farmers, and prevent the arbitrary occupation of their land. In addition, determining land rights is the premise for land transfer. Following the establishment of land rights, three associated rights and three corresponding deeds should be implemented. The three rights are the right to operate on contracted land, the right to use homestead land and the property rights of houses on homestead land. They have corresponding deeds, which can be mortgaged. There is a difference between a mortgage and a pledge. The pawnbroker is a typical example of a pledge: to get a loan one has to pawn personal items such as clothes or jewellery. Mortgaging is different in that one can continue to use the land and the house after the title deeds have been mortgaged. If one fails to pay the loan, the court will resolve the case by auctioning the property to pay the bank. This is a crucial way to help the farmers gain material capital. Therefore, currently in China the most important task is to determine land rights and implement the three rights and deeds for every rural household. The farmers will not only be able to gain capital to start a business but will also have income from property.

(2) Human capital

Next, we turn to human capital. How can we address the meagre human capital in rural areas? The main cause of the problem is the imbalance in educational resources. Schools in cities benefit from more investment and funds, and superior teachers and equipment. Schools in rural areas, by contrast, are inferior: they have poor equipment and lack teachers. Consequently, the number of students who can attend senior high school is proportionally lower in rural areas than in cities, and even more so in terms of college education.

To change the situation, the allocation of educational resources must be balanced.

Some children of migrant workers want to start working earlier, and this demand can be fulfilled by opening technical schools in cities and towns to train technicians and other professionals. They can attend these schools free of charge, and will be able to obtain an income proportionate to their skill levels. If a city or town can afford to, it can provide free accommodation and catering to the youth in rural areas admitted to the technical school.

As of now, many local governments are preparing education reform plans. A moderately developed county has formulated the following plan: from now on only kindergartens will run in the villages, and occasionally some elementary schools as well but restricted to grades one to three; both are day schools. They run in villages because the children are still too young to go to more distant schools. Students attend elementary schools or higher grades and junior high schools in the county seat and local towns. These are either day schools or boarding schools. Students living too far away can lodge with their friends or relatives or choose school accommodation. Children from families with financial difficulties can enjoy free school accommodation and catering. Safe and convenient school buses take boarding students home and back to school once a week. Senior high schools only run in the county seat and are all boarding schools. This facilitates management and improves the quality of education. In this way, the gap in education between urban and rural areas can be gradually reduced. Children in rural areas will have more opportunities to access higher education, which in turn will improve their job prospects. In 2012, the Subcommittee of Economics of the CPPCC conducted research in Jarud Banner of *Tongliao* City in Inner Mongolia. They found that all of the children of the herdsmen living in the mountainous or remote areas attended boarding elementary and junior high schools in the city free of charge. They called these schools the pilot education zone. This had an unexpected effect: as commercial properties in the city were affordable, after some children from remote areas went to boarding school in the city, the elderly people such as their grandparents accompanied them from the countryside. They purchased commercial properties and settled down to look after the children while the children's parents remained in the villages and pasturelands to continue to grow crops and graze animals.

(3) Social capital

How can the social capital of the farmers be increased? Urban residents have more social capital than those living in rural areas. When they want to venture into the market or start their own business, they can turn to their distant relatives or their friends and acquaintances for help. Farmers, especially those in the mountainous areas, have little social capital. They have few acquaintances and are not familiar with the market economy. In this respect we ought to emulate the strategies of the *Wenzhou* people in *Zhejiang* Province and the *Chaozhou* people in *Guangdong* Province: we should encourage the farmers to venture outside and undergo the trials of the market so that through hard work they can start their own businesses.

In short, it is up to individuals to seek and accumulate their social capital. The key is to have a good reputation. Reputation has to be earned and is the greatest social capital. Only when one obtains other people's trust can he navigate the market economy and fulfil his potential. It is a wise saying that small wealth comes from diligence, moderate wealth from good opportunity and large wealth from wisdom. Now we can supplement this saying by adding that wealth, be it small, moderate or large, needs reputation, without which one can expect neither trust nor help. "A person who starts out by deceiving everyone will eventually end up deceived by everyone." Thanks to their good reputation, the *Wenzhou* and *Chaozhou* people receive assistance from their fellow townsmen wherever they go, be it at home or abroad. One needs to accumulate social capital, and the same applies to reputation. We will further elaborate on this topic in Chapter 8.

2 The role of secondary distribution

Distribution by the operation of the market is called primary distribution, while the distribution by government regulation is called secondary distribution. Generally, in developed market economies, the deficiency in primary distribution is compensated for by secondary distribution. In other words, if distribution by market operations leads to a substantial income gap, it can be remedied by government regulation. However, due to the dual household registration system in China, secondary distribution further widens the gap created by primary distribution.

The cause of this phenomenon lies in the difference in social security systems. Up till now, employees in cities have enjoyed publicly funded medical care while farmers have cooperative medical care, and herein lies one of the differences. Secondary distribution also includes the allocation of funds for education, healthcare, culture and public services. Cities have higher allocations per capita than rural areas. This adds to widening the income distribution gap between urban and rural areas, which is obviously unreasonable. Therefore, it is necessary to accelerate the integration of the social security systems in urban and rural areas, and to balance the allocation of funds for education, healthcare, culture and public service.

Section 3 will discuss secondary distribution in greater detail, so here we will only give a brief outline. Practically speaking, reform in the following three respects is worth considering.

First, we need to integrate the social security systems in urban and rural areas as soon as possible. This means that the differences between the two social security systems are to be gradually diminished. All those with Chinese citizenship, whether they have rural or urban household registration, will be entitled to equal social security arrangements regardless of their status. In this way, once the social security systems in urban and rural areas have been integrated, the two household registration systems will lose their significance, so that all residents can access social security using only their standard identity cards.

Second, the allocations per capita for education, healthcare, culture and public services should gradually adopt a single standard. Although the realisation of this aim may be a lengthy process, with some effort we can approach this goal.

Third, if primary distribution results in too substantial an income gap, the wealthy can be made to shoulder the burden of higher taxation, so that the low-income families can receive more subsidies. This is why developed countries often adopt secondary distribution.

3 The outflow of the capable and the accumulation of the weak

The present situation in rural areas involves the outflow of the capable and the accumulation of the weak. Those who are competent, or have connections to urban residents, migrate to the cities to perform labour, open workshops or run businesses, leaving behind the old, the weak, the sick and the disabled in rural areas. If they engage in agricultural activities, production and incomes will fall. This inevitably leads to the expansion of the income gap between urban and rural areas.

How do we find a solution to the income gap? The outflow of the capable is reasonable. If they migrate and decide to work permanently elsewhere, we should respect their choice. If they are willing to return to the rural areas and start a business, we should create more favourable conditions to support and attract them in doing so. For example, we can help them start small businesses by providing loans, reducing tax, assisting in staff training, simplifying the process of registration and opening bank accounts and so on.

What should we do about the accumulation of the weak? If the old, the weak, the sick and the disabled remain in the rural areas, the best way is to transfer their land, because if they do farm work, the rate of return and the efficiency of land utilisation are too low. If we can properly resettle them when transferring the land, they will have a higher income than when they farm the land themselves.

The accumulation of the weak is likely to become a common phenomenon in rural areas in the future. That the old, the weak, the sick and the disabled remain in the rural areas is a social problem worth noting. The questions are who will provide for their living expenses, who will look after them and who will arrange their affairs when they pass away. Migrant workers have not only left behind the old, the weak, the sick and the disabled in the family, but also their wives and children when they first went away. During this period, at least there are people to look after the old, the sick and the disabled. However, later, when the migrant workers take their wives and children away with them, and even the land is transferred, what should be done to take care of the old, the weak, the sick and the disabled? When we were conducting research in *Pingli* County of *Ankang* City in *Shanxi* Province, we found that elderly care homes and welfare homes run by the villages and towns provided a good solution. There, the old, the weak, the sick and the disabled received sufficient care, had small bedrooms and common canteens. Special personnel were assigned to tend to the disabled. This seems to be a viable solution that we should try to implement.

4 Who will farm in the future?

Now that the capable have migrated to cities to perform labour, open shops and workshops, and the weak have subcontracted, leased or transferred their land, who will farm in the future? We should be aware that, in China, unorganised individual farmers will always exist, and it is up to them to decide whether they will migrate to the cities or work the land. Those who farm in the future will mainly fall into the following three categories.

The first are farming experts and large plantation households. Through subcontracting and leasing, they have increased the scale of their farming. A study in *Hubei* Province showed that some large plantation households have rented up to 20,000 *mu* of land. They employ a few or even tens of workers, fully mechanise their farming and have realised large-scale operations. After the farmers have leased the land, they seek work in cities, run businesses or work as employees for large plantation households, by which means they receive rent, wages or other income if they work elsewhere. These farming experts and large plantation households are based on family farms. Family farms differ from the small farms of the past. These planters are more connected to the market. With the increases in scale and levels of industrialisation, productivity has risen significantly. Not only do they engage in production, but they also rely on logistics and other service industries to organise marketing activities. They are key market players, active participants and promoters of the modernisation and industrialisation of agriculture.

Should we set an upper limit to the scale of large-scale planters; namely, how many *mu* of land are they allowed to acquire? Research shows that this regulation is unnecessary, because they facilitate large-scale operations and improve efficiency. As long as they can improve efficiency when they expand, there is no reason to set an upper limit, and when they see efficiency dropping, they will automatically stop expanding. We should leave it to the large-scale planters to make decisions based on the "optimal" scale. In other words, the determining factor should not be the scale of operations itself, but whether or not they adhere to market principles and achieve efficiency – the latter will place a limit on them. Moreover, large-scale planters acquire their land by means of subcontracting and transfer, and therefore they have contracts with the farmers who have rented or subcontracted their land. When the contracts expire, decisions concerning their extension will also set a limit on the planters.

Another matter of dispute regarding large-scale planters is how to prevent them from using the land for non-agricultural purposes. When they sign contracts with the farmers to lease or subcontract the land, the contracts should include supplementary conditions that restrict the usage of the land: cropland should be used for crops, and agricultural land must not be turned into industrial land arbitrarily. Only by doing so can we ensure the development of agriculture and the growth of crop output. We have analysed this issue near the end of Section 2, Chapter 1.

The second category is the specialised farmer cooperatives, each with its own specialised area. In 2007, 2008, 2010 and 2011, I led the research team of the Subcommittee of Economics of CPPCC to conduct research in *Jiangjin, Changshou, Liangping, Zhongxian, Fuling, Wulong, Pengshui* and *Shizhu* counties of *Chongqing* municipality. There we saw cooperatives that specialised in citrus fruits, watermelons, tea, flowers, traditional Chinese medicine and so on. The farmers formed these cooperatives. They pooled their land and ran the cooperatives democratically, publishing accounts and electing cooperative leaders. Under these conditions, the farmers can better utilise their land. In order that the specialised farmer cooperatives can be true to their name, they should not be government-based as in the past. During the research, when we discussed the specialised cooperatives with the farmers, they emphasised the following two points: first, everything should proceed according to the rules and regulations passed in voting, and no one should be exempt from them; second, the specialised cooperatives should confer real benefits on all members, realised in the form of dividends. Regarding the profit of the cooperatives, accounts must be published to ensure the delivery of the dividends promised from the pooled land, together with the fact that profit belongs to cooperative members. Empty promissory notes would not be accepted. The farmers further added that no one was allowed to acquire profit in private, or take the lion's share. Both would be regarded as fraud.

The third category is the agricultural enterprises that extend into the countryside. They rent land, employ new and advanced technology, invest in the construction of irrigation systems, improve the soil and introduce new species from abroad. We will give two examples. The first example, *Xuwen* County in *Zhanjiang* City, *Guangdong* Province, is located at the southern end of our country, with *Hainan* Province on the other side of the strait. This county suffers from dry weather, has no access to rivers and relies on typhoons for agricultural water supplies. A *mu* of land can only yield three to four hundred Yuan's worth of crops.

After the agricultural enterprises, including privately owned and foreign ones, arrived, they rented land from the farmers and achieved large-scale operations. And what did they decide to grow? Pineapples, since the land is most suitable for tropical fruit. As of now, *Xuwen* County grows one-third of our country's pineapples. The rent for the land is several hundred kilos of crops per *mu*, and can be converted into cash payments if needed. After the land is rented to the enterprises, the farmers can choose to work elsewhere while receiving the rent, or they can remain and work for the agricultural enterprises as contract workers, and get not only payments in proportion to their skill levels, but also rent at the same time. In this way, their lives are improved. The enterprises provide investment for drilling deep wells and installing sprinkler irrigation. In the suburbs, an area of over 10,000 *mu* is now called "MeditePinean Sea". The second example is the *Qixingguan* District in *Bijie* City, *Guizhou* Province. One private agricultural enterprise grows Korean pears on the hillside. The owners have told us that they earn 50,000 Yuan by growing pears, compared with 1,000 Yuan when growing crops.

Therefore, it is important for agricultural enterprises to extend into rural areas because they bring capital and technology with them. In order to encourage more agricultural enterprises to invest in agriculture, it is necessary to transform one-way integration into the two-way integration of urban and rural areas. That is to say, in addition to the migration of farmers into cities seeking employment, the enterprises in cities should also be willing to run business in the countryside. In this way, agricultural productivity will rise and the income gap between urban and rural areas will diminish.

During the research, we have also discovered other problems that need further discussion.

First, after the agricultural enterprises come to the countryside, can they become shareholders in the specialised farmer cooperatives? I think that, as long as they follow the rules and regulations of the cooperatives, this can be feasible within certain parameters, and has already happened in some places. We learn that after the agricultural enterprises arrived in the countryside, they were willing to become shareholders in specialised farmer cooperatives mainly to better integrate into the local society and to garner support from local farmers. They are willing to finance cooperatives to upgrade infrastructure, improve the soil and the quality and quantity of output and increase farmers' income. Some specialised cooperatives have become good partners with the agricultural enterprises, and this is beneficial to both sides and a good foundation for a win-win, long-lasting situation. As for how the cooperation between agricultural enterprises and specialised farmer cooperatives may change, this depends on their mutual consultations and the discussion in the general meeting of cooperative members. This should not be resolved unilaterally by a handful of persons, or new disputes will arise.

Second, are urban residents allowed to rent contracted land in rural areas to farm and sell the harvest? Again, the key is mutual benefits and consent. At present, we can experiment with the idea, and decide what to do next based on the results.

New solutions require pioneers. The result of such experiments still needs to be tested in practice.

Section 2 Reforms of primary distribution should be the focal point for the reform of distribution system

1 The primary distribution of income should be based on market distribution

In deepening the structural reform of the Chinese economy, the reform of the income distribution system is vital and requires urgent implementation. This will have major implications for social stability and harmony, and whether or not domestic demand can be effectively raised and the economy can continue to grow.

Income distribution generally involves the following three layers: primary, secondary and tertiary distribution. In economics, primary distribution is defined as the market's allocation of income based on the quality and quantity of productive factors people provide. Secondary distribution is the government's adjustment of primary distribution using taxation and social welfare policy. At this point, the income distribution by the market and the government is complete; the income everyone receives is after-tax income or income after the implementation of social welfare policy. Tertiary distribution is based on the result of secondary distribution. Being non-compulsory and completely voluntary, tertiary distribution is a morally guided distribution of income, including donations from individuals, private poverty relief measures and private foundations for public welfare. The role of the government in these situations is to introduce sound laws and regulations that encourage individuals to donate willingly and prevent relevant organisations and personnel from acquiring donations by fraud.

What should the focal point of the income distribution system be? There is little disagreement on tertiary distribution, which is mainly because China was transformed into socialist market economy not long ago, and tertiary distribution has yet to exert a major influence on the economy. It might still take some time before tertiary distribution begins to play a bigger role if we compare the situation in China with that in the developed market economies. Nonetheless, quite a few people in our country have started to note this issue, and almost all agree that an early introduction of laws granting tax relief on donations will make more people enthusiastic about public welfare.

At the moment, the debate on the reform of the income distribution system revolves around whether to emphasise primary or secondary distribution. Even if both are crucial and deserve attention, we must still decide which is more important and should be prioritised.

This book argues that, regarding the present stage in China, the reform of primary distribution is more important. The reason is clear: it is fundamental and the basis for secondary distribution.

In a market economy, primary distribution of income should generally be the result of market mechanisms. As long as operation of the market is sound, and as long as the distribution of income corresponds to people's contributions of productive factors – or, in other words, corresponds to the quantity, quality and the impact of the productive factors – we can say that this distribution follows market principles. Income distribution gaps are inevitable under the operation of the market. On the one hand, this is due to market flaws, such as monopolies, and imbalances in power between suppliers and buyers, with one side occupying a more advantageous position and thus altering the distribution landscape. On the other hand, income distribution gaps are due to the unequal possession of production material caused by historical factors; in other words, since people differ greatly in their possession of material, human and social capital when they enter the market, they are not at the same starting point in market competition, resulting in relatively large income gaps. This shows the necessity of secondary distribution, whose goal is to diminish income differences through government taxation and social welfare adjustments. In this way, secondary distribution can compensate for the deficiencies of primary distribution.

However, the actual situation in China is that, during the period of the planned economy, the plans exerted a much greater influence on primary distribution than did the market. The results of primary distribution were not mainly determined by the market but by government regulations under the planned economy. One of the most conspicuous examples is that under the planned economy wages were regulated by the government. Partly as a result of the "supply system", actual incomes differed substantially from the apparent wages on the books. This was especially true regarding the actual incomes of some senior officials, who received more support in everyday life and enjoyed other privileges. The wages on the books did not reflect actual living standards. A second example is that the incomes of the farmers were divorced from market mechanisms. Under urban-rural dualism, farmers did not have property rights; the so-called collectively owned land belonged to the people's commune, which was also a political unit. The income of farmers was the portion allocated to them from collective production, but it had nothing to do with the market. They only engaged with the market when they sold their poultry, livestock and limited products such as eggs for meagre personal incomes.

Therefore, primary distribution under the planned economy was not regulated by the market, but was decided by the government, including at base-level administrative units such as the people's communes. After the Reform and Opening-up, the market has become more accessible and farmers have had greater autonomy in their economic activities. Their incomes have been increasingly determined by market mechanisms, but the most important income, that is, the rightful property income from their land, has been excluded from primary distribution, because the farmers do not have actual property income. The incomes according to primary distribution under market operations only includes the incomes of individual urban workers, merchants, employers and employees of private enterprises, freelance workers and, in addition, individual investors.

In the sections above, we have summarised the present situation of primary distribution in China prior to the launching of structural reform in income distribution. The situation differs greatly from the economic principle that the market should regulate primary distribution. We must not overlook this reality when discussing the forthcoming reform of the income distribution system.

2 Difficulties that need to be tackled in the reform of primary distribution

Again, we need to begin with the imbalance in the present Chinese economy.

According to *Chinese Economy in Disequilibrium* (Economic Daily Press, 1990; Guangdong Economic Press, 1998; Encyclopedia of China Press, 2009), there are two types of economic disequilibrium: type I and type II. Type I refers to disequilibrium in a flawed market, and the economic disequilibrium in some contemporary developed countries falls into this category. Type II refers to the disequilibrium caused by the lack of market entities in addition to the flawed market. The Chinese economy in transition from the planned economy into a market economy belongs to this type. Therefore, the problem the Chinese economy has faced since the Reform and Opening-up is first and foremost the reform of ownership to transform enterprises into true market entities and investors with clear ownership. With this, the Chinese economy can shift from type II to type I disequilibrium. Afterwards, with gradual improvements in the market, type I disequilibrium can approach equilibrium. This is the thesis of *Chinese Economy in Disequilibrium*, which has been summarised in Chapter 1.

Now in 2013 it has been 24 years since the publication of that book in 1990. How has the disequilibrium in the Chinese economy changed over the years? Generally speaking, with ownership reform, the reform of state-owned enterprises has seen substantial progress. Most state-owned enterprises have become market entities and investors with clear ownership. Of course, as has been pointed out previously in this book, the reform of the capital system of state-owned enterprises must be deepened, and the achievements made in the last twenty-four years has laid a solid foundation for further change. However, we cannot deny that China has yet to completely shake off the difficulties of type II disequilibrium, because the property rights of the farmers have not been determined. Although farmers are involved in the market, they have not become market entities with clear ownership because their property rights, including the right to operate on contracted land, the right to use homestead land and the property rights over their houses, have not been implemented for every household. Therefore, even though China has put much effort into pulling itself out of type II economic disequilibrium and has made considerable progress, we must not suppose that China has completed its transition from type II to type I disequilibrium.

In addition, flaws still exist in the market, and the influence of market mechanisms over primary distribution is restricted by many factors. We still cannot suppose that the market is playing a fundamental role in the primary distribution of income in China at the moment.

The problems facing urban and rural areas in primary distribution can be summarised as follows:

(1) Historically inherited problems. This includes the unbalanced economic development in different areas across China due to the influence of cultural

traditions and customs. In addition, the maturity of the market differs from area to area. Traditional customs dominate some areas and hinder market growth.

(2) Different degrees of monopoly exist everywhere in economic life. In terms of each industrial sector, perfectly competitive markets do not in reality exist. Some say that the agricultural market is perfectly competitive, but this is not the case. Monopoly still persists, though perhaps to a lesser extent in relation to many types of product. Monopoly severely disrupts the formation of a fair competitive environment. To the detriment of some markets in agricultural products and small merchandises, a few people, some of whom are connected to local organised gangs, dominate the market by bullying competitors. This shows the flaws and confusion in the market, as well as a lack of law and order.

(3) The ongoing influence of primary distribution under the planned economy in terms of wage standards and differentials. The wage standards and differentials within and between different industries may have been set down according to circumstances and prices in different areas during the planned economy. After all these years, the situation has changed and it is obviously unreasonable that those regulations still apply to the present.

(4) The imbalance of power between the buyers (employers) and sellers (employees) in the labour market. In most cases, the employers are enterprises and institutions while the employees are individual workers, including migrant workers. The unequal positions of the two often result in disadvantage to the employees. If there is a surplus of supply in the labour market, employees can only suffer in silence when their demands are not met.

(5) The separation of high-level and low-level labour markets. If we analyse the structure of the labour market, we can divide it into two categories. High-level labour receives higher wages, superior welfare, more allowances and better opportunities for promotion. Workers often learn more from their jobs and, with the acquisition of professional knowledge, they are more likely to improve their technical expertise. These jobs are regarded as "good jobs". Low-level labour has lower wages, inferior welfare and allowances and fewer opportunities for promotion. Jobs often involve simple, repetitive manual work. Workers acquire few skills and little professional knowledge. These jobs are considered "bad jobs". The coexistence of two types of labour characterises what can be called a dual-labour market. Employees who lack skills and a good educational background generally can only enter the low-level labour market. They face discrimination and their low wages are unlikely to rise. The existence of a dual-labour market is common in developed Western market economies and also in developing countries. We have elaborated on this point in the last part of Section 2, Chapter 4, so here we will only give an outline.

This phenomenon appears to result from the structure of the labour market. Since the Reform and Opening-up, many job seekers from rural, and especially poorer areas, take up unskilled, simple labour. If they seek job in the low-level labour market they receive more unfair treatment.

According to the above analysis, we can clearly see that it is impossible to achieve wage rates that are fundamentally regulated by the market in China at the moment, or, in other words, wage rates under economic equilibrium.

(6) The primary income distribution for farmers is formed under disequilibrium. The most obvious case is their lack of clear ownership rights, which so far prevents them from becoming true market entities. They do not have formal property rights over contracted land, homestead land or the houses built on homestead land and, consequently, these cannot be mortgaged or transferred. In addition, the transfer of farmers' land is largely influenced by factors outside the market, and the farmers are not properly compensated for their loss of land. Without property rights, unable to secure their rights to use and profit from their land, farmers find their land income limited by many factors and they cannot make plans based on the expectation of future profit. This leads to uncertainty in the prospects of income from the land. There are many types of "rent-seeking" in land usage that often damage the interests of farmers. That is to say, it is the farmers themselves that suffer losses from rent-seeking.

(7) Although farmers can leave their homes and work in towns and enterprises, they are the most underprivileged group. On the one hand, this is due to the dual household registration system in urban and rural areas. Farmers have different household registration and status from urban residents. Their rights are restricted, while the enterprises and institutions that hire migrant workers are in a more powerful position. The disparity between employers and employees is conspicuous. Migrant workers are in an even more unfavourable position compared with urban residents. On the other hand, because migrant workers leave their homes to work in urban areas, and some have even brought wives and children with them, they have to rent a house and shoulder more living expenses. These factors increase the cost of working in towns and cities. Compared with urban residents, migrant workers have a greater financial burden and less income, and this does not even include the cost of travelling back to visit their homes and relatives.

(8) In agricultural markets, if farmers as suppliers face individual, unorganised buyers, it is difficult to decide who has the edge over the other. However, if farmers face organisational buyers of agricultural products, they tend to be in a disadvantaged position. During negotiations, farmers who grow crops and rear livestock often get lower prices than the market average. This situation results in lower income in primary distribution. Even though in some places farmers create specialised cooperatives and thus have somewhat better leverage in negotiations with buyers of agricultural products, they nonetheless cannot avoid losses. Compared with big enterprises, the specialised cooperatives are still in an unfavourable position. The situation is different in some developed market economies. According to our observations in Denmark, the Netherlands, New Zealand and other countries famous for their agricultural products, farmers form cooperatives, and the cooperatives further unite to form joint cooperatives. These joint cooperatives possess impressive strength

168 Reform of the income distribution system

and scale. They boast their own trucks, ships, docks and warehouses. They have their own sales channels and even sign sales contracts with domestic and foreign supermarkets directly. All these factors help ensure higher incomes for the farmers. In addition to cooperatives and joint cooperatives, organisations such as farmer's associations stand up for the rights of farmers. All these factors are still beyond the reach of farmers in China at the present stage.

(9) Farmers' lack of social capital in terms of primary distribution partly results in their disadvantageous position. As has been pointed out earlier, the existence of the dual-labour market means discrimination for farmers who are job seekers. They can only enter the low-level and not the high-level labour market. In this regard, farmers face more discrimination than rural residents. This is due not only to their inferior educational background and expertise compared with rural residents, but also their lack of relatives, friends and acquaintances in the cities, which is especially true for those from remote or mountainous areas. When they are in dire need, no one offers a helping hand. If social capital requires accumulation, the farmers do not even have the chance to accumulate any, let alone to make use of it.

These nine points all show the necessity of prioritising the reform of primary distribution in the reform of the income distribution system. Without the reform of primary distribution, secondary distribution alone has limited impact.

3 Suggestions for the reform of primary distribution

How can we effectively initiate the reform of primary distribution? From the analysis above, we give the following suggestions.

(1) Improving and perfecting the present market

Since a reasonable primary distribution cannot be separated from an improved and perfected market, this should be the chief mission in the reform of primary distribution. More specifically, the improvement and perfection of the market includes the following aspects:

(i)   Removing the influence of the planned economy on primary distribution, such as in ownership discrimination and monopolies in certain industries.

(ii) Creating an environment of fair competition as soon as possible for the suppliers and buyers of productive elements and the producers of merchandise, in order to institutionally prepare for the adjustment of the primary distribution landscape.

(iii) Scrutinising the existing wage standards and differentials within and between different industries as formulated under the planned economy that still influence primary distribution, in order to decide which should be cancelled and amended so that market-regulated primary distribution can be implemented as a fundamental principle.

(iv) The following is a further analysis of the problem of current wage differentials within and between different industries in China. These differentials are due to, on the one hand, the market mechanism being obstructed and unable to fulfil its adjustment function, and on the other hand, the monopolies in certain industries and the restrictions on market access developed under the planned economy. The greatest obstacle we inherit from the planned economy is the special franchising system. This not only excludes fair market access and competition, but also leads to price controls and insider manipulation. This is detrimental to the interests of private enterprises, their investors and the whole country. This situation must change.

(2) Making farmers true market entities

The unreasonable nature of primary distribution is largely associated with the inequalities farmers face concerning household registration and status.

According to statistics, the urbanisation of China now exceeds 50%, but, after careful consideration, we do not think this figure reflects the actual situation. This is because, in the calculation of urbanisation rates, farmers who reside in rural areas for more than half of the year are treated as part of the urban population. This means that the figure includes migrant workers who are actually rural residents. According to the numbers in some cities, these migrant workers account for around 20% of the total urban population. Therefore, we estimate that the urbanisation rate of China, namely the percentage of the population that holds urban household registration status in the total national population, is below 40%, and that the population with rural household registration status constitutes more than 60% of the total population. This means that more than 60% of the population lacks individual or household property rights and property income, which is an important factor contributing to the weakness of primary distribution in contemporary China.

Therefore, in order to tackle the present unreasonable landscape of primary distribution, we must enact a series of measures based on determining land rights in rural areas.

First, the determination of land rights should cover a greater area. Up till now, we have only experimented with the determination of land rights in a limited number of counties. Nonetheless, according to information from those areas, this has achieved impressive results. The farmers show great enthusiasm in their agricultural activities, and the income gap per capita between urban and rural areas has significantly declined. The main reasons for this narrowing income gap include the possession of property rights, the addition of property income, greater enthusiasm in their agricultural activities and the accumulation of capital, which in turn increase the scale of production and productivity. All these result in a more advantageous primary distribution for farmers.

Second, once land rights have been determined, farmers have the three types of rights and three certificates. With these and given mature financial institutions in rural areas and small towns, farmers can acquire mortgages and capital to help develop agriculture, aquaculture, handicrafts and commerce. The farmers can also demolish old houses and build new ones on the certificated homestead land. The new houses can be used by the farmers themselves or rented to urban residents. This is beneficial to urban residents and profitable for the rural residents.

Third, after their determination, the land rights of farmers are protected by the law. Without going through legal procedures, the government cannot occupy the contracted land or homestead land of the farmers, nor can it demolish houses built on homestead land. The orderly transfer of land requires that it be carried out in consultation with farmers, based on their free will. This will protect their income. When researching in some areas, we find that farmers use their contracted land, with their rights to it being determined, as a share in specialised farmer cooperatives or other enterprises, or rent it to enterprises or other farmers as farmland. This expands family farms and facilitates large-scale operations, or generates dividends and regular rent income. Thus, the income for farmers from primary distribution will rise.

Fourth, after the land rights have been determined, the farmers' income after primary distribution shows signs of diversification. According to our investigation, farmers receive income from the following six channels: agricultural income; income from jobs outside rural areas, such as performing labours, opening workshops and shops and working in logistics; dividends coming from their pooled land; rent from their land; wages from working for specialised cooperatives or agricultural enterprises that specialise in crops, livestock or fruit; and rent from letting houses built on homestead land to urban residents. There may also be other sources of income. Generally speaking, the farmers' income after primary distribution will be much higher than before the determination of their land rights. The key factor is that the farmers then become true market entities.

(3) Creating equality between buyers (employers) and sellers (employees) in labour market

This equality is a crucial element influencing primary distribution. There are many reasons why it is difficult for employers and employees to have equal positions. We will discuss the solutions to these difficulties in turn.

(i)   In the labour market, a surplus of supply is often the reason why the labour suppliers are in a disadvantaged position. Yet, we must not end our analysis there. The structure of the labour market is a problem that must not be overlooked. As has been mentioned above, the labour market can be divided into two categories: the high-level labour market and the low-level labour market. Jobs in the former are considered "good" while those in the latter are considered "bad". Both labour markets can be further divided into several sub markets according to different professions. When discussing the supply and demand in the labour market, we should analyse the sub markets that correspond to these different professions. This might be more effective than a sweeping discussion of the whole market. Through the analysis of sub markets, we can better understand the changes in supply and demand in the labour market in recent years in China, that is, 30 years since the Reform and Opening-up. We see that the supply of simple labour is in surplus and, the simpler the labour, the higher the supply, as is the case with unskilled workers, porters, quarry workers, road workers and canal workers. On the other hand, regarding skilled workers, there is greater demand and hence a diminishing gap between supply and demand. However, in recent years, the situation has greatly changed. The supply of simple labour is declining, and this may be due to rising living expenses. The wages for simple labour are so low that many people are unwilling to become porters, quarry workers, road workers or canal workers. Another reason for the fall in supply is that fewer young people in rural areas are inclined to leave their homes and perform such unskilled labour. In comparison, there is an increasing supply of college and technical school graduates who have received higher education, but a shortage of positions suitable for them, so that they find it hard to get jobs. Supply and demand in sub markets are undergoing change, and the respective positions of employers and employees are tipping in the opposite direction. This means that suppliers and buyers are experiencing changes in their negotiations for wages that may shift the landscape of primary distribution.

We still need to point out, that although changes in supply and demand in the labour market may affect the negotiations for wages between employers and employees, the former still have the upper hand over the latter, and this will not be reversed, not only because the employers are often enterprises and institutions while the employees are individuals, but also because the employees are on the defensive compared with the employers. The employers have their own bottom line: the cost must be lower than the profit, or they will not be hiring staff. The employees, too, have a bottom line: the wages must not be lower than local living expenses, or they will not work. The problem is that the bottom line of employers is inelastic, as they will never, except under special circumstances, accept costs that are higher than the associated profits. On the other hand, the bottom line of the employees is flexible. There is no absolute standard for local living expenses. It can be higher or lower. When there is a surplus of supply, the employees will make compromise after compromise to reduce their living costs, as long as someone is willing to hire them. This is the true bottom line for employees.

Problems like this have existed in Western industrialised countries in the past two centuries. How does the superior position of the employers over the employees change? The supply of labour may play a part, but does not solve the problem. Instead, its solution depends on the power of trade unions. More and more employees join unions, so in representing the rights of the employees, unions gradually become a significant force facing employers. The strength of the unions comes from their efforts to raise awareness of employee's rights, and they at times even call for industrial action. Of course, there are many problems that need to be discussed regarding trade unions in Western developed countries. Their government often gets involved. The government, the enterprises and the unions form checks and balances. Only in this way can the position of employees be improved.

Nowadays, China needs a fresh understanding of unions, since they are a force to be reckoned with in primary distribution.

(ii) Since the dual-labour market will not disappear in the near future, we should stimulate the transformation of the low-level labour market into the high-level labour market, and upgrade "bad" jobs into "better" ones, and "good" jobs into "even better" ones. This includes raising wages for some heavy and dirty labours, improving the benefits for certain jobs and offering more opportunities for promotion and further education. Meanwhile, with technological innovation and industrial upgrading, jobs in the high-level labour market can constitute a higher proportion of the overall job market, so that more people will have better jobs.

At the same time, in order to adapt to technological innovations and industrial upgrading, we should devote great effort to developing mid- and high-level technical education, cultivating mid- and high-level technical professionals and training employed workers. We ought to provide free catering and accommodation, and in the case of senior high school and beyond, scholarships and financial support for compulsory education students coming from areas or families with financial difficulties. This will allow them to study without anxiety and acquire technical and professional expertise so that they can have a better chance to seek higher incomes. This is also a way to increase household income from primary distribution.

In addition, we should encourage and help job seekers to start their own businesses, such as small enterprises, so that they can do their best to contribute to society, create wealth and increase their incomes.

4 A tentative idea: let the providers of human capital also share in profits

In the 1980s, in the American economics academic world, there once emerged a theory of the "share economy" or "shareconomy". This means that profit should not belong to the investors of material capital alone, but also to those who contribute their human capital, for the following reasons.

Wealth, income and profit are jointly created by material and human capital, and therefore they cannot come into being without the latter. If so, why should all the profits go to investors of material capital while the income of the investors in human capital comes only from wages, which is listed as a cost? This does not make sense according to economic theory. Therefore, based on the principles of the "share economy" or "shareconomy", profits should be distributed among the investors of both human and material capital.

That is to say, if the investors of material capital become managers of the enterprises, they participate with a double status in the creation of wealth, income and profit. They get profit as investors of material income or shareholders, and receive wages as investors of human capital or managers of the enterprises, although both incomes should in principle belong to the wage or the cost of production. Regarding the employees, they too participate in the creation of wealth, income and profit with a double status, and thus, in theory, they should also receive both wages and profit. They receive wages because they are employees and invest their human capital in production and sales; they should receive profit from shares because, according to the principles of the "share economy" and "shareconomy", wealth, income and profit are created jointly by material and human capital. Employees of enterprises should therefore receive a share of the profit as investors of human capital.

There are many ways for employees, as investors of human capital, to share in the profits. Enterprises can adopt solutions that best suit their specific situations. For example, they can share the profit with the employees by converting it into stocks or cash payments. In some cases, enterprises can offer stocks to employees who make a relatively large contribution to the development of the business as an incentive (the system of equity incentive), and offer cash payments to the others.

Regarding the question of how much of a share investors of human and material capital should have in profits, no fixed answer exists, and enterprises can make decisions based on their actual situations.

Anyhow, the shares of profit among investors of human and material capital can stimulate initiative among all employees, and would reflect the spirit of the reform of primary distribution, because profit share is theoretically sound and practically tested.

Section 3 Key points in the reform of secondary distribution

1 The integration of the social security system in urban and rural areas

In the current reform of distribution in China, primary distribution is the key, but this does not imply that secondary distribution is unimportant or that its reform can be delayed. In fact, secondary distribution is significant because its relationship with primary distribution in China is abnormal. As has been discussed in the previous section, in Western developed market economies, generally speaking, secondary distribution is to compensate for the deficiencies of primary distribution. In other words, the income gap resulting from primary distribution is diminished by secondary distribution. However, currently in China, there is a strange phenomenon where secondary distribution further widens the income gap created by primary distribution.

Why is this so? It is mainly due to the dual social security system in urban and rural areas. This dualism arises from the urban-rural dualism and the existence of the system of separate urban and rural household registration established during the planned economy. The urban-rural dualism and two different household registration systems which continue to exist today are the roots of the dualism in social security in urban and rural areas.

For example, for many years, healthcare provision has been different in urban and rural areas. Urban employees enjoy publicly funded medical care while the employees with migrant worker status have cooperative medical care.

In addition, for many years, conditions after retirement have differed for urban and rural workers. Urban workers have pensions but employees with migrant worker status do not.

Furthermore, the government funding per capita for education, culture, health-care and the construction and maintenance of public facilities is lower in rural areas compared with urban areas.

This situation has only started to change recently, but the gaps still exist. Secondary distribution remains unbalanced for urban and rural residents. Primary distribution causes inequality; secondary distribution expands it even further.

Therefore, right now in China, in order to reform secondary distribution, we should first and foremost integrate the urban and rural social security system. This can only be achieved gradually in stages, because China has a vast territory and a large population, of which 60% has rural household registration, and because there is a limit to government funding for social security. However, the overall goal is clear: the keys to the reform of secondary distribution are integrating the urban and rural social security system and reducing the income gap.

The integration of urban and rural social security is a huge programme, which can be divided into the following parts, namely, the social security for maternity, ageing, sickness, death, disability, education, unemployment and housing and so on.

(1) Maternity benefits. Women should receive social care starting from their pregnancy. This care would cover regular health checks for pregnant mothers at designated hospitals, commune hospitals and health centres. It further covers the period from parturition to discharge from hospital, as well as health checks for mothers and babies after discharge. The expenses associated with childbirth and care should be partly provided by the social security fund and partly paid for by the family, but families with financial difficulties should receive appropriate special treatment and some may not even have to pay. Mothers should be entitled to paid maternity leave. Some Western countries even grant paid paternity leave to fathers.

(2) Ageing. When people with regular jobs reach retirement age or, due to various reasons, have to retire early, they should be entitled to pensions that are commensurate with inflation. Elderly people who have lost either their partners or children can choose to go to elderly care homes. If the various levels of local government can afford it, they can build elderly care homes and encourage charity and welfare organisations to build them. Elderly people from families with financial difficulties can be granted concessions or go to care homes without charge.

(3) Sickness. This refers to the healthcare provided to urban and rural residents, including medical services at the nearest hospitals and commune hospitals, and touring medical organisations in rural areas to provide medical services to patients or regular health checks to rural residents. Urban and rural residents should receive equal reimbursement of any charge made. There should be healthcare aid to urban and rural families with financial difficulties to ensure that patients can receive timely treatment.

(4) Death. The welfare policies in Western developed market economies cover citizens from "cradle" to "grave". The government provides funeral grants to residents. The relatives of those in the armed forces who die in the line of duty receive compensation as a token of respect and commemoration for the departed. Both urban and rural residents should be entitled to equal treatment in this regard.

(5) Disability. This includes inherited disabilities and those caused by traffic accidents, earthquakes, diseases, medical treatment, falling, sports activities, industrial injuries and other factors. Social security for the disabled should correspond to the severity of the disabilities, their causes and the financial situations of their families. In general, the social security received should allow children to study, adults to find employment and the elderly to find a home. Families with financial difficulties should receive monetary aid. Both urban and rural residents should enjoy equal treatment in this regard.

(6) Education. Social security for education covers a large area. This can be broadly divided into pre-school education, compulsory education, senior high school education and above, adult education and technical education. The overall principles are that both urban and rural residents should have equal compulsory education, and that compulsory and technical education should be free. Regarding the other types of education, poorer families should receive subsidies, and students can receive scholarships or financial aid.

(7) Unemployment. The government should be responsible for helping the unemployed to find jobs. When people remain unemployed for a certain amount of time, they are entitled to unemployment benefits to ensure minimum living standards. In addition, the government should offer guidance on how to find jobs and provide information on job markets for job seekers. All the towns and cities should have employment centres. Moreover, we should help students that receive higher education find suitable jobs before or upon graduation.

(8) Housing. Housing is a crucial component of social security in Western developed market economies. It refers to the responsibility of the government to provide housing for low- to middle-income families. This will prevent them from becoming homeless and living on the streets, and avoid giving rise to shanty towns and slums like those at the beginning of the industrialisation and urbanisation process. In some countries, the government provides two types of housing: low-rent housing and affordable housing. To access low-rent housing, low-income families need to apply to the government and, if they meet the criteria, they can rent government-built houses. These houses are not big, but at least the families will have a place to live with low rent. Affordable housing, too, is limited in size but inexpensive and the payment can be made in instalments. With enough low-rent housing and affordable housing, the housing security system in urban areas is established, and shanty towns and slums can be gradually removed as illegal constructions. Right now in China, we can slowly promulgate the housing security system in cities and towns. Middle- to low-income families and migrant workers can access

low-rent or affordable housing if they meet the appropriate criteria, without discrimination according to status.

The above sections sum up the content of the integration of the urban and rural social security system. We should have a clear goal in mind, but be prudent and realistic in its implementation.

2 We should note the inelasticity of welfare during the integration of the urban and rural social security system

Welfare is characterised by inelasticity, which means that welfare measures that have been implemented are unlikely to be annulled, and that welfare standards are unlikely to be lowered. Therefore, there is a saying that "welfare can be easy to implement but difficult to annul" and that "welfare standards can be easy to raise but difficult to lower".

For example, a certain Western European country introduced a public welfare policy of free tap water, which pleased the residents immensely. However, this policy caused people to use more water than was necessary because it was free, leading to more freshwater being wasted. In addition, the policy placed a great burden on government and created an increasingly serious fiscal deficit. The government planned to cancel the welfare policy of free tap water, but upon hearing the news the whole country was opposed and so the government had to give way. The government explained that, in order to charge for tap water, every family had to install a water meter. The residents claimed that the free tap water should not be taken away and refused to install the water meters. If the government were to pay for their installation, it would require a large sum of money, which was outside the budget limits. As a result, as of February 2012 (at which time I was doing research in this country) the government was still providing tap water free of charge.

Therefore, when we try to realise the integration of the rural and urban social security system, we should plan the process carefully as a whole, do it step by step and take into account what can be realistically achieved within our capacity. Otherwise, the inelasticity of welfare may cause unnecessary disputes and even social instability. The sharp rise in government spending can also become too big a burden for the government to handle.

There is also a negative phenomenon that arises from the welfare policies of some Western developed countries. People react in two very different ways to rising welfare standards. First, the rise in welfare, including introducing more welfare policies and expanding the area of implementation, inevitably leads to tax increases because the funding for welfare comes from government revenue. As a result, the government has to face the negative impact of tax increases on economic growth, one of which is that rich people tend to migrate to countries with lower taxes. Second, too much welfare may discourage people from working. They would rather stay at home and live on unemployment benefits. The desire to work hard and start a business dies down. In Australia, some Southeast Asian immigrants, including those who had been smuggled into the country, live on various types of benefits and allowances. Local Chinese people say that there is a popular saying among those immigrants, that having two more children is better than a job. That is to say, by having an additional child, they can get a monthly allowance which is half the wage of a job. Have two additional children, and they can get enough money for their living costs.

These cases further illustrate the limits and negative consequences of welfare, which should give us food for thought.

3 Adjustment to secondary distribution with taxation

In the reform of secondary distribution, we must consider the reality of the present stage in China, and improve the adjustment of distribution by taxation. This includes four important measures concerning personal income tax, property tax, high-end consumption tax and inheritance and gift tax. To put it in a simple way, when implementing the reform of secondary distribution, in addition to the integration of the urban and rural social security system, we should also improve the four aforementioned measures of adjustment by taxation. This is equally important.

(1) Personal income tax

In order that personal income tax can fulfil its adjustment function, it is necessary to change the way it is levied.

First, when calculating levels of personal income tax, we should include all types of income, and then levy taxes using marginal tax rates. The advantage of this measure is to make sure that no personal income tax has been overlooked or omitted.

Second, when calculating personal income tax, we should reduce the sum according to the number of family members who require special care, such as those who have lost the ability to work and who suffer long-term illness, babies and small children and others who need long-term support. The cost of taking care of them and medical fees should be deducted from income tax. This is the proper application of the principle of personal income tax.

Third, how do we set the starting threshold for income tax? What is the marginal tax rate and what is the starting tax rate? These need to be determined after careful assessment of the actual situation. The overall principle is that income tax should narrow the income gap but not discourage people from working, starting a business or making innovations.

(2) Property tax

According to the current situation in China, it is necessary to levy property tax beginning from the second property owned, because the first property may come from various sources: it may be inherited, sold by enterprises and institutions to employees at specific prices based on their rank and age, or it may be newly purchased commercial property or second-hand houses. Levying taxes on the first property will cause disputes and, moreover, it is difficult to determine the value of the house and the appropriate tax rate. Therefore, it is prudent not to do so.

If we levy property taxes beginning with the second property, some problems still remain. For example, the first property may be small but many family members might live there. Even if we combine the size of the first and the second property, the living space per capita may not reach the minimum threshold for property tax. If we levy property taxes uniformly on a second property, this will lead to dissatisfaction and give cause for complaint among those who have many family members but only a small first property. Therefore, whether or not we levy taxes on the second property must be decided according to the specific situation.

In fact, the primary goal of property taxation in China right now is to prevent opportunism in the housing market. Some opportunistic buyers purchase houses when prices are low and hoard them for speculation so that they can raise the rent or resell the houses later for profit. Property tax can deal a blow to those opportunists who hoard and resell houses for profit so that the income gap can be narrowed. However, if the aim of property tax is to deter residents from purchasing houses to live in and to reduce their inelastic demand for housing, the tax will miss its true purpose. It is better to focus housing policies on two measures: adjustment through taxation so as to reduce housing prices, and a housing transaction tax that limits the reselling of houses but does not ignore the housing needs of residents.

To elaborate, adjustment through taxation works as follows: first, to prevent the driving up of land prices, the land should have a clear and fixed price, and construction on this land requires open bidding. Real estate investors should put in their bids according to uniform technical standards for housing. Based on the technical standards and the price of land, the company that offers the lowest price should win the bid. If it fails to finish construction on time or does not meet the technical standards, it will face severe penalties. This can prevent land price being driven up during bidding, which gives rise to "land kings" – developers who pay enormous prices for parcels of land. This measure is similar to the open bidding for equipment purchasing in major construction projects. The buyers publish the technical standards and the delivery time, while the suppliers offer their prices. The one who has the lowest price wins the bid. If the quality does not meet the technical standards required or if the supplier fails to meet the delivery time, they will face severe penalties.

Adjustment through a housing transaction tax works as follows: the buyers will pay a heavy housing transaction tax if they resell a house they have only recently purchased. For example, if they resell a house within one year after purchase, they will pay the maximum transaction tax. The transaction tax will decrease with each successive year after purchase until it reaches the normal rate in the sixth year. In this way, adjustment through taxation can prevent opportunists benefitting from the hoarding of houses and driving up housing prices.

(3) High-end consumption tax

There are three goals that high-end consumption tax tries to achieve as an adjustment in secondary distribution.

First, those who engage in high-end consumption, in addition to public servants who spend public funds, are either senior managers of enterprises, who regard this as spending on public relation, or members of high-income families. Therefore, high-end consumption tax can reduce the spending of public funds by public servants, the business spending of senior managers, business-government collusion and other types of corruption. Imposing high-end consumption tax on high-income family members may reduce the income gap, but its effect is limited. In any case, this can at least make high-income families pay more taxes and contribute more to the country.

Second, the implementation of high-end consumption tax, especially for food, may reduce the waste of food and save resources.

Third, it may help promote the practice of thriftiness and deter wasteful luxury.

Two more problems that have been discussed before need clarification and further elaboration.

First, the definition of luxury consumption, including the consumption of high-end entertainment, food and luxury items, is related to the perceptions of the public. Therefore, the implementation of a high-end consumption tax requires a definition of what counts as luxury consumption. Otherwise, this will dissatisfy domestic consumers and discourage spending.

Second, should we cancel or lower the import tax on certain merchandise? Statistics in recent years show that more and more tourists make purchases abroad. This is because, on the one hand, all the merchandise is authentic, and on the other hand, cheaper than in the domestic market. The comparatively low price is due to the high import tax. In fact, whether to impose import tax on this merchandise is a question that needs discussion. The government cannot prohibit tourists from making purchases abroad. Since the prices there are lower, consumers naturally choose to buy abroad. The solution is to lower or cancel the import tax on this merchandise so that the consumers can buy it in the domestic market at a lower price than abroad. It should be noted that, if consumers buy merchandise at home, this can add to the income from taxation, create jobs for China and bring commercial profit to domestic enterprises. Isn't this more beneficial to China? By contrast, suppose we retain the high import taxes on this merchandise. Aren't we forcing domestic consumers to spend their money on enlarging the foreign market? If we compare these two scenarios, it is clear which is more favourable to China.

(4) Inheritance tax and gift tax

Inheritance tax and gift tax are part of the property transfer taxes that some countries implement. They are considered effective measures in secondary distribution to narrow the income gap. At its present stage, China should fully prepare for the implementation of inheritance tax and gift tax, and introduce them when the conditions are ripe.

What, then, are the conditions for the implementation of inheritance tax and gift tax? There are three main preparations to be made.

First, the system of property registration and examination should be improved. To levy inheritance tax and gift tax, it is necessary to have a sound property registration system, which chiefly includes the registration of real estate, shareholdings in companies and other major changes in property ownership. In addition, there should be a property examination system, including the assessment of property. Otherwise, the levy of inheritance tax will lack proof, even leading to prolonged property disputes within families, and causing difficulties to the taxation department due to heavy workloads and lack of staff.

Second, residents should understand the meaning of inheritance tax and gift tax to better cooperate with the taxation department. If the residents begrudge or fear these taxes, they are likely to transfer their property and capital abroad, to a country where there are no or lower inheritance and income taxes. This is obviously disadvantageous to Chinese economic development. In other cases, if they do not transfer their property abroad, they may try to use it up or give it to their offspring and relatives, which is not beneficial for the stable development of enterprises either. Therefore, we must study the present situation in China before determining the starting tax threshold and tax rates and whether to adopt a marginal or flat tax rate. In addition, it is equally important to educate residents on the meaning and details of inheritance tax and gift tax.

Third, there is the question of whether to grant tax exemptions to donations in cases of charity and public welfare.

Section 1 of this chapter has already mentioned tertiary distribution. This refers to the donations of individuals of goodwill to promote charity and public welfare. They donate their property when they die to some charity or public welfare organisation, or to help with the construction of schools, hospitals, welfare homes, libraries and so on. These arrangements are set down in their wills and notarised, and should be carried out according to the wills, with gift tax and inheritance tax exempted. There are other methods of individual donation. If we can establish a connection between donations to charity and public welfare and exemptions to gift and inheritance tax, we can surely reduce residents' discontent regarding these taxes and their attempts to avoid them. In fact, from the perspective of reducing the gap between the rich and the poor, donations by the wealthy to charities and public welfare organisations may have the same function as the inheritance tax and gift tax imposed on them. However, they may feel less compulsion when they donate willingly, which is also a notable point.

6   Urbanisation

Section 1 Urbanisation that suits the Chinese context

1 Traditional urbanisation and urbanisation that suits
the Chinese context

By traditional urbanisation, we refer to the mode adopted by developed countries which first underwent industrialisation. Their urbanisation was in tandem with industrialisation and was characterised by the lack of overall pre-planning or scientific understanding of city size. A city's leadership did not take into account the sustainability of social and economic growth. When they noticed the deterioration in the residents' conditions of living, it was already too late to make effective changes. Although countries that industrialised later were aware of the problems that afflicted the pioneers during urbanisation, they often could not afford the large pubic investment needed to avoid repeating those mistakes. As a result, both the forerunners and late-comers in industrialisation and urbanisation suffered from the same "urban disease": the massive influx of rural populations into urban areas leading to shanty towns and slums, environmental degradation, air pollution, water shortages, traffic congestion, overcrowding, high unemployment rate and poor public security. These problems had repercussions in the form of counter-urbanisation: as the poor moved into the cities, the rich moved out to suburbs or rural areas. This further fed into counter-urbanisation, because the more the former moved in, the more the latter moved out.

In some developed market economies, the rate of urbanisation can be as high as 90% or more. After 200 years of urbanisation and industrialisation, the rate of urbanisation has lost its former significance and attraction to people for the following reasons.

First, if urban and rural residents in these market economies remain unequal in rights and are restricted by status, the rate of urbanisation can indicate social stratification. However, at the present stage, when neither of these applies to citizens in these economies, the rate of urbanisation becomes almost meaningless.

Second, if public services differ in urban and rural areas or social security has not been integrated in a certain country, urbanisation rate can show the gap in conditions of social security between urban and rural areas. Yet, few such cases remain today.

Third, thanks to improvements in national transportation networks, the convenience of telecommunications, the reduced cost of transport and information, and differences in land prices, a high rate of urbanisation does not necessarily imply the concentration of industrial activity as this may spread across rural areas.

Traditional urbanisation does not fit well into the Chinese context. According to the National Bureau of Statistics of China, the urbanisation rate in China is just over 50%. However, experts on China's urbanisation believe that the actual rate is lower than 40%. This is because of the dual household registration system that divides urban and rural areas: even if rural migrants reside permanently in cities, they remain registered in the rural households and retain their "farmer" status and, as a result, they cannot enjoy the same treatment as urban residents. Therefore, the rate of urbanisation remains meaningful in China at the moment, but this reflects the inadequate integration of urban and rural areas, which affects new generations of migrant workers in particular. Hence, it is imperative to find a mode of urbanisation that fits the Chinese context. According to research on migrant workers in *Zhejiang*, *Fujian* and *Guangdong* Province, children of migrant workers who began working in cities after the mid-1980s have reached working age. Although they have always lived and received education in cities, they still have rural status. Without a change in status, they will face discrimination and have limited opportunities in the job market. They have few other choices than to become migrant workers and marry within the same group. This situation needs to be changed presently, or the delays in urban-rural integration will incur greater costs.

From another perspective, China will definitely face a sharp decline in urban living conditions and quality of life if it strives for the same rate of urbanisation as in Western developed countries, with over 90% of the population concentrated in cities. Even though the rising urban population may create more jobs in the service industry, the job market will not be able to accommodate the influx of rural migrants.

Therefore, China needs to follow an urbanisation mode that suits the Chinese context. This new mode, also known as in-situ urbanisation in some places, consists of three elements: the old towns, the new towns and the new rural communities. *Gongcheng* Autonomous County of *Yao* Ethnics in *Guilin*, *Guangxi* Province, showcases this new, in-situ urbanisation mode. During my research in this region, I observed that the farmers had revamped their rural houses, and that their income mainly came from fruit farming and processing, together with pig farming and the initial processing of new pork products. The quality of life in the rural area was almost the same as that in the urban area. This is a good example of in-situ urbanisation. At the end of November 2012, I led a research team of the Committee of Economics of CPPCC to conduct research in the counties in the municipalities of *Hangzhou, Jiaxing* and *Huzhou* in *Zhejiang* Province. Local officials told us that urbanisation had been achieved without any disturbance: there were no large-scale programmes of demolition or relocation, and the village and town residents did not perceive much difference between living in urban and rural areas; in fact, there was even no large urban-rural income gap. Farmers in *Pinghu* County of *Jiaxing* City and *Anji* County of *Huzhou* City told us that water and electricity supplies, roads, schools, hospitals and community services in the rural areas were identical to those in urban areas. Some families might have had to relocate to somewhere nearby, but this did not give rise to any complaints. As long as they could enjoy better living standards, people were willing to cooperate. Their remarks give a realistic picture of in-situ urbanisation.

In the following sections, we will elaborate on the three components of urbanisation; that is, the old towns, the new towns and the new rural communities.

2 Renovation of old towns

The old towns refer to existing urban districts, some of which were established long before industrialisation. After the beginning of industrialisation, industrial enterprises were set up in these areas. The old towns started to expand, the number of residents grew and the narrow streets became overcrowded. The presence of industrial enterprises also accelerated the development of commerce and the service industry.

The development of old towns should focus on renovation. We must find ways to move industrial enterprises out of the old towns, as they have already caused pollution. Recent years have witnessed the implementation of the correct "secondary out and tertiary in" policy. This means that secondary industries ought to leave the old towns while tertiary industries should move in. This will transform the old towns into commercial and service centres and agreeable residential areas. The old towns are blessed with many historical buildings, including streets, alleys and commercial and public infrastructure from the *Ming* and *Qing* Dynasties and the Republic of China era. They can serve as cultural heritage after appropriate maintenance, restoration and preservation. In addition, some streets, wharves and shops should be preserved in their entirety to retain their historical character.

During the renovation and environmental remediation of old towns, we should pay attention to pulling down shanty towns. They were built in the early stage of industrialisation and suffer from bad construction quality. Residents in these shanty towns have poor living conditions. Most are poverty-stricken and under-educated. Some are retired, laid-off or jobless. The high unemployment rates in these areas lead to bad public security and high crime rates.

During the renovation of some old towns, we have accumulated experience on the demolition of shanty towns and subsequent relocation of residents. The key is to combine three factors in the planning process: constructing new towns, attracting business and investment and renovating old towns. Based on the practice in some cities, we can summarise the process as follows.

The first step is to construct residential buildings that meet quality standards on open land and to resettle shanty town residents there; meanwhile public facilities should be in place, such as public transportation, schools, medical facilities and sanitation, to make sure that new residents can settle down.

The second step is to provide jobs for unemployed residents by attracting business and investment, developing industrial companies in the new towns or establishing commercial and service companies on the sites of shanty towns in the old towns.

We can also help the unemployed to start their own businesses if they are willing to, whether it is an independent store, a small or a micro-enterprise. In addition, they could work in domestic service, cleaning, security and so on in the residential areas of the new towns. Some cities, including the old towns, provide strong support for small and micro-enterprises to ease unemployment. This is a good way to create jobs as it can incentivise urban residents and rural migrants who want to start their own businesses. During our research in *Chongqing*, we found that the government took the following actions to support these businesses: (1) reducing and exempting from taxes; (2) providing small, convenient loans; (3) offering the necessary funds to those who lack capital to kick-start small and micro-enterprises; (4) free training for small and micro-enterprise owners and employees and (5) simplifying business registration. These measures have been well-received.

During the demolition of shanty towns and the subsequent relocation, we can give urban resident status to rural migrant workers living in these areas if they have stable jobs, such as the ownership of shops or licensed stalls. We can take advantage of the opportunities of demolition and relocation to solve their household registration problem, since sooner or later they will become urban residents.

3 Planning new towns

Generally located in the suburbs, new towns may have evolved from industrial parks, high-tech parks, start-up hubs and logistics parks. With numerous factories and infrastructure in place, these areas have great development potential.

Inhabitants in addition to enterprises also reside in these new towns. Some used to live in rural areas; others, with rural household registration, are owners of small private businesses in towns, some of which have been integrated into either the old or the new towns. Because of the presence of residents and employees of new industrial enterprises, new towns incorporate commercial districts, service districts and residential areas besides industrial parks.

It is of paramount importance that the new towns attract industrial enterprises into the parks. This will furnish enterprises with the following four advantages: first, reductions in cost thanks to good infrastructure and transportation; second, easier regulation and remediation of the environment due to the concentration of pollution sources; third, convenience of communication and increased opportunities, as industrial enterprises are all closely gathered together in the parks; and fourth, good, timely government service and support for the enterprises provided by the management committees of the industrial parks.

In *Bijie* City, *Guizhou* Province, we conducted research in some start-up hubs for small and micro-enterprises and witnessed their establishment and growth. Besides the bases provided by the hubs, the greatest advantage was the sense of belonging shared by these small and micro-enterprises. They felt at home in these parks because they now enjoyed closer ties with the government and, when encountering problems in management, they could turn to the government for support.

The new towns often serve as a foothold for fast-growing, emerging industries. Industrial enterprises with local characteristics and enterprises in emerging industries are the powerhouse for the growth in the economy, employment and government revenue from cities or new towns.

Regardless of whether new towns are erected on open land or developed from the expansion of existing towns, they have less of a historical burden than old towns. This is precisely their advantage. The new towns offer more job opportunities. Moreover, they can function as vocational training centres for technical and professional service workers and even channel them into other new and old towns both inside and outside the city.

During our research in some new towns, we found a new problem: these new towns may struggle to retain skilled workers due to their high mobility. Some employers believe that the underlying reason for this is the young skilled workers' fixation with wages. If their demands are not met, or if other enterprises have more lucrative offers, they will job hop in spite of having signed contracts. The same also applies to base-level management. Besides this, some skilled workers and employees are reluctant to work in cities far away from their homes because living apart from their spouses would greatly increase living costs. While these demands are not unreasonable, it is very difficult for the enterprises to solve the accommodation problems for workers and their families at present. This issue can be addressed gradually during the new urbanisation process. In the future, we should try to help rural couples that work or trade in cities live together with their children.

4 The building and transition of new rural communities

(1) The requirements of building new communities

New rural communities with Chinese characteristics are emerging everywhere. In many places, they are built on the basis of natural villages by renovating old houses, or on open land near original natural villages. In the latter case, after the residents move into the new communities, the old houses are pulled down and the land is reused as farmland or construction land. Either way, these new socialist villages serve as the starting point for new rural communities.

The building of new rural communities generally includes the following five aspects.

First, we should build garden-like rural communities. Instead of just erecting a few tall buildings, we need to focus on creating agreeable residential areas with lush greenery.

Second, new communities must become clean residential areas, which are equipped with pollution control and rubbish recycling and adhere to low-carbon and energy conservation standards.

Third, public services must be in place in the new communities, including health centres, kindergartens, nurseries, primary schools, homes for the elderly, public transportation, tap water, telecommunications, cultural venues, public security and fire services – in sum, the same public services as in cities.

Fourth, new communities should achieve the integration of urban and rural social security systems as soon as possible, so as to abolish the status restrictions on rural or urban residents.

Fifth, in managing new communities, we should implement a democratic system, through which the residents can elect officials or remove unqualified ones from office.

People used to say that it was difficult to integrate farmers as urban residents. The underlying reason for this is the urban-rural dualism. Differences in household registration systems, status and social security treatment, plus the unbalanced allocation of educational, cultural and medical resources all widen the gap between farmers and city dwellers. As a result, migrant workers who have been working or running small businesses for one or two decades still cannot blend in with urban residents. This is a key issue.

Therefore, when we have achieved all of the above, village-level autonomy will transform into community-level autonomy. The new rural communities will become base-level city units incorporated into the urbanisation process. There will be equal rights between rural and urban residents and no more restrictions due to different status. By that time, we will have accomplished the *de facto* integration of the two types of resident.

(2) Various employment modes in communities

The employment situation in new rural communities varies and depends on the locality. During our research, we found that different places have come up with different solutions.

(i)   In some places, a leading company leads and organises the farmers. They contribute their farmland to the company and in return become its shareholders. The company then decides, based on the quality of the soil, to grow fruit trees, grain, grapes or animal feed on the land. Factories are built on the construction land, and cattle and sheep farms on grassland. In other cases, the land may also be used for pig farms and chicken farms. The farmers can choose to work outside, or if they choose not to, they can be allocated to factories, cropland, vineyards, orchards or animal farms. Every farmer can receive, in addition to their monthly salaries, dividends based on their shares. The leading company also builds dormitory areas for residents and adopts the community model in the management of these areas. The company further puts public services in place. We have seen this mode, known as "Company + Community + Rural Residents", in *Yantai* City, *Shandong* Province.

However, there is a concern that this mode might eventually come to an end and adversely affect the employment and everyday life of the farmers, if the leading company, due to various reasons, suffers losses in the market, closes down, restructures or becomes owned or taken over by another company. While there is no sign of this at the moment, we cannot guarantee that the leading company will not sustain losses in the future. A viable plan is to set up a dedicated risk guarantee fund from the company's annual profits in order to ease difficulties of the farmers if the worst happens.

(ii) In some places, specialised farmer cooperatives lead and organise rural residents. Different cooperatives specialise in different products, such as tea, watermelons and citrus fruits. Meanwhile, these cooperatives encourage farmers to refurbish old houses or build new residential areas on open land nearby so that farmers can move in. While the cooperatives organise production on farmland, village committees or community committees elected by residents manage the refurbished houses or the new residential areas. This mode is known as "Cooperatives + Communities + Rural Residents": cooperatives sign contracts with the leading companies, which provide technology and production material, such as seeds, chemical fertiliser and irrigation machines. These companies also organise unified purchase arrangements and resell the products. We have seen this mode in *Jiangjin*, *Changshou*, and *Liangping* in *Chongqing* City, among other places.

The major weakness of this mode is that specialised farmer cooperatives lack the trust of farmers. These cooperatives are organised by the farmers in local towns or villages and are hampered by their small-scale, weak foundations and inadequate marketing capabilities. In addition, without leading companies as partners, their achievements in the market are limited. As a result, these cooperatives have to face the following dilemma: either they overly depend on, and even fall into the control of, the leading companies, or they end up operating on a small scale with meagre profits at best. One viable way out of this is to form joint cooperatives. With better development potential, these can gain more trust among rural residents.

(iii) Under the supervision of the city, county, town or village governments, some localities organise the farmers to build new socialist villages, and offer construction subsidies to encourage them to build or renovate houses. Afterwards, the government will invest in infrastructure and implement community management, and the farmers will then engage in specialised production. For example, every household is equipped with vegetable or strawberry greenhouses. Intensive farming produces higher yields and incomes. While each household is responsible for production, the community provides professional logistics facilities to transport their products to agricultural markets for sale. Alternatively, the community can change the area into a tourism site. The farmers run rural tourism while local women engage in handicrafts activities to attract tourists, who may also buy fresh fruit, vegetables and other local specialities. This mode, named "Self-owned Business under Community Guidance", is seen in *Bijie, Guizhou*. This mode has several advantages: it allows the farmers to run their own businesses, advances the industrialisation of agriculture and offers the farmers various community services and guidance in production and management. Nonetheless, it suffers from the following two disadvantages. First, although the communities offer important, useful services and guidance, they are not economic entities that can organise the farmers. Therefore, the farmers remain individuals on the market, and are in an unfavourable position. Second, there are many stalls along the roads to the villages, leading to fierce competition and price war. In view of these disadvantages, some suggest a combination of community guidance and collective management, which gives birth to the following alternative mode.

(iv) City, county, town or village governments supervise and help the farmers start a collective business during the construction of new socialist villages. For example, all or most of the rural labour can be channelled into industry, construction or logistics. While the company organised by the residents and its elected board are responsible for the management of production, the community makes arrangements for issues in everyday life. The head of the community committee is also elected by the people. We have seen this mode, named "Community-guided Collective Business" in the *Binhai* New Area of *Tianjin* Municipality.

Yet, there is still doubt about this mode. Is the community-guided collective business a retrogression to the planned economy? In the planned economy there used to be collective enterprises supervised by village officials (these were initially called "commune and brigade enterprises" and afterwards, "township and village enterprises"). While some of them were quite competent, these officials had unchallenged authority to make arbitrary decisions, effectively reducing these collective businesses to family businesses. "Collective businesses" lack a standard company structure and legal support. Therefore, it is better for them to take up a standardised name, such as "specialised farmer cooperative" or "limited liability company" and operate according to rules and regulations. This will ensure the sustainable development of the new communities.

New rural communities are sure to have more modes than those mentioned above. Local governments are exploring new possibilities based on their own circumstances. No doubt there is more than one suitable mode in the vast territory of China. The emergence and coexistence of multiple modes should be regarded as a normal phenomenon in urbanisation that suits the Chinese context. It is also a very positive phenomenon because it shows that we have successfully awakened the long-hidden motivations of the people. Standardisation of those modes is necessary because only with standardisation can we avoid various flaws.

Let us approach this problem from another perspective. If we do not build new communities but rely exclusively on old and new towns when resettling the large numbers of farmers, we can hardly provide a comfortable life for everyone, maintain urban living standards and address the unemployment problem at the same time. The new communities stand out as the best solution.

Moreover, the implications of new communities are ever-changing. Due to the present urban-rural dualism, new socialist villages can serve as a suitable starting point for new communities. In the future, by building garden communities, promoting a circular economy, improving public services and integrating the social security systems, we can gradually transform new socialist villages into new communities. These efforts can only come to fruition if we make full use of people's vast motivations that have hitherto been hidden. Without their support, there will be no new community. This central role of the people is characteristic of China.

(3) The equality of rights and status for urban and rural residents

As has been discussed above, the urbanisation that fits the Chinese context consists of three parts; namely, the old towns, the new towns and the new rural communities.

While some experts agree with the three components of Chinese urbanisation, they have the following question: granted that urbanisation includes old and new towns, it seems to be inappropriate that urbanisation should further encompass new rural communities. They argue that we risk self-contradiction if we regard the new rural communities as part of the urbanisation process. They have a point when they question the suitability of treating rural and urban areas as one. We can address this question in the following way.

The urbanisation of China will take a very long time. At the beginning, or even for a relatively long period during this process, the dual household registration systems that divide urban and rural areas cannot be annulled, and the inequalities of rights and status will persist. At this stage, there will be farmers in the old and new towns, not to mention the new communities which consist mainly, if not wholly, of rural populations. This is the reality in China. Therefore, according to this analysis, it is fitting to use the term "new rural communities" to describe the situation.

As the economy advances and the structural reform of the economy deepens, those farmers residing permanently in the old and new towns will eventually obtain urban household registration. This is a general trend that no one can alter. In terms of the farmers who live and work in the new rural communities, with the development of the economy, the improvements in public service facilities, and especially the integration of social security, they will gain urban household registration in due course.

To be more precise, the dual household registration system will be transformed into a single national system. Residents in urban and rural areas will no longer differ in terms of status or rights. By then we can replace the name "new rural communities" with "new communities" and do away with the word "rural". "New communities" are a vital component of the urbanisation with Chinese characteristics within the Chinese context. The new communities will become the new towns of China.

In this sense, the urbanisation of China reflects the features of the dual economic transformation in China. As has been pointed out in the Introduction, the two transformations are the "developmental transformation" and "institutional transformation". The "developmental transformation" is from rural to industrial society, while the "institutional transformation" is from a planned to a market economy. Since the Reform and Opening-up in 1979, these two transformations have overlapped. The completion of China's urbanisation will also mark the success of the dual transformation, in which the abolition of the dual household registration system may be a crucial milestone. Only when urbanisation is adapted to the Chinese context can we achieve equal status and rights for urban and rural residents.

5 A stable source of funds for the construction of public facilities during urbanisation

Finally, we will discuss how to fund the construction of public facilities during urbanisation.

Practical experience shows that the system of "land finance" and local debt finance in China has come to an end and is no longer sustainable. No one can have the means to pay the local government debt if it keeps snowballing. How many people migrate to old towns, new towns and new communities every year? This new population will require enormous investment in new housing, roads, kindergartens, schools, hospitals, cultural venues, public service facilities, water, electricity, gas and heating supplies, public transportation, environmental protection, city cleaning, greenery and gardens. Without public construction funds, city planning will be empty talk.

Public utilities will develop with the advance of urbanisation. In terms of the ways to raise and use public utility funds, we can emulate the example of the "urban public utility investment fund" in Western developed countries. China has accumulated experience in industrial investment funds and there are professionals with the relevant expertise. The conditions are ripe for the establishment of urban public utility investment funds. To be specific, such a fund is an investment organisation that combines the strength of central government, local government and financial institutions. The Finance Ministry and the National Development and Reform Committee can take the initiative and invest government funds so as to guide and regulate the investment of public utility funds. The investors may include social security funds, state-owned development banks, insurance companies and other long-term investment organisations. After the establishment of the urban public utility investment fund, it can issue "urban public utility development bonds". As a long-term financial bond, this can attract enormous amounts of private capital to maintain a steady supply of funds for public utilities such as water, electricity, gas and heating supplies, public transportation, environmental protection and city cleaning. In addition, the bonds will serve as a long-term and reliable investment vehicle and offer new opportunities for private capital to participate in urban public utility construction.

In order that this strategic investment can achieve better results, we can first establish pilot zones in a few provinces and cities. Once we have the successful experience, we can then promote this measure in a wider area.

Western developed countries have been driving urban development with urban public utility investment funds in recent years. According to their experience, with its large scale and risk capacity, the investment fund often has high rates of return despite the long payback period, as long as it picks the right investment target and is under the proper management. Some international public utility funds also vie for the huge market in China's urbanisation and participate in the construction of urban public utilities. Therefore, to clinch the opportunity, China's own public utility investment fund should be established soon and start to channel private capital into the urbanisation process.

Section 2 Deeper analysis of the difficulties in urbanisation

1 The mutual support of industrialisation and urbanisation

Currently in China, industrialisation and urbanisation are not only advancing in parallel but also support each other. Industrialisation accelerates urbanisation, and *vice versa*. It is important that the mutual support of industrialisation and urbanisation is achieved in the dual economic transformation: both must go through the developmental transformation and the institutional transformation.

The institutional transformation of industrialisation refers to, on the one hand, the further marketisation of industrialisation. Through market competition, indigenous innovation, and industrial upgrading, we must simplify the long-standing complex approval process, and reduce and remove government intervention in the Chinese economy, so that the allocation of resources under market operations will become effective and fair, without ownership discrimination. The institutional transformation means, on the other hand, that urbanisation should gradually evolve beyond the urban-rural dualism and integrate the migrant workers, who have long been an integral part of the Chinese economy, into urban society together with their families. Urbanisation should gradually abolish the restrictions on their rights so that they can be equal to urban residents.

The developmental transformation means, on the one hand, that industrialisation should focus on the quality of economic growth, make headway towards new development modes and reaching a higher level. The developmental transformation means, on the other hand, that the leading role of urbanisation in the development of rural areas and agriculture should be prioritised, transforming the cities into economic centres and bringing about the industrialisation and modernisation of agriculture. If during urbanisation cities prosper while rural areas deteriorate and agriculture development stalls, urbanisation will have failed to achieve its original goal.

This is the true meaning of the mutual support of industrialisation and urbanisation. During the modernisation of the Chinese economy, institutional transformation and developmental transformation are interwoven with each other, and so too must be industrialisation and urbanisation. Their mutual support gives an overall picture of the dual economic transformation in China.

Reform and development are constantly going on and will never come to a halt. It is the same with industrialisation and urbanisation. As science and technology advances, new waves of innovation will arrive one after another. Modernisation is forever forging ahead and no one can point to when it will come to an end. The same applies to the improvement of the quality of life during urbanisation, which includes the quality of natural life and the quality of social life. The former encompasses the development of clean energy, the remediation and restoration of the environment and the reduction of carbon levels in the economy; the latter includes social harmony, a sense of well-being and security and a good moral atmosphere. All these areas will see constant progress. People will always strive for a better quality of life, which means that there will always be things waiting to be done for our generation and the next during industrialisation, urbanisation and modernisation. Besides this, each generation has their own understanding, experience and wishes. This generation can hardly claim that they understand what the next two generations will think, except that they will definitely think more and their thoughts will better suit their reality.

There is another issue that is worth noting: in which areas have industrialisation and urbanisation benefitted from their mutual support?

Let us first look at benefits for industrialisation. The industrialisation we talk about today is far from what it used to be when it first began in China. The industrialisation that took place between the 1950s and the 1970s still operated within the confines of the experience of early industrialisation. It focused solely on the construction of large steel companies, large mines and large electricity enterprises, with the belief that its only goal was to boost industrial output, and that industrial pollution could be dealt with later. Since the 1980s, notions of industrialisation began to change. Technological innovations necessitated the replacement of traditional industrialisation with new industrialisation and changed people's understanding. In the wake of new industrialisation, efficiency soared, products improved in quality and sophistication, market competitiveness increased and environmental issues attracted more and more attention. Amid these changes, high-tech and emerging industries gradually became the main driving force of economic growth. Right now in China, the emphasis on the necessity of a transition in development mode signals that the notions of new industrialisation are increasingly being put into practice. Urbanisation bolsters the new industrialisation mainly in the following three respects. First, urbanisation increases the income of residents and purchasing power as well as domestic demand, and thus expands the domestic market for the new industrialisation. Second, new towns provide a solid foundation for emerging industries and urbanisation supplies ample high quality technical and professional labour. Third, urbanisation creates favourable conditions for the development of modern service industries that complement the new industrialisation.

Next, consider the benefits for urbanisation. As has been mentioned previously, the ongoing urbanisation in China is different from the urban construction under the planned economy and the urbanisation that retained the urban-rural dualism in the early stages of Reform and Opening-up. The current urbanisation aims to abolish that dualism and integrate rural and urban areas. It is no longer limited to expanding cities, increasing urban populations, boosting the urban economy and increasing GDP. Instead, from the perspective of the "urbanisation of human beings", it seeks to improve the quality of life. Here lies the reason why urbanisation has to combine with the new industrialisation. The new industrialisation benefits urbanisation mainly in the four following ways. First, the emerging industries in the new industrialisation are based in new towns. They contribute to urban tax revenues and improve urban public finance. Second, the advancement of the new industrialisation and its accompanying modern service industry create jobs and ease unemployment in cities. Third, during the new industrialisation, the industrialisation and modernisation of agriculture will attract more attention, leading to increasing technological innovations and support for agriculture. This will benefit the rural areas and agricultural industries, producers and business owners, transforming the profile of rural areas and agriculture as an industry. These factors will all help fulfil the requirements of urbanisation. Fourth, in terms of the construction of urban housing, promoting the use of new forms of energy, materials and smart solutions and upgrading other household appliances will reduce building costs and everyday expenses. These measures will also conserve water and energy and reduce pollution, creating a more comfortable life for residents.

From the analysis above, we have a clearer grasp of the mutual support of industrialisation and urbanisation. This kind of urbanisation is the new urbanisation in its true sense.

2 Basic measures to ease urban housing pressure

As urbanisation progresses, high housing prices and housing shortages become a thorny issue. This is one of the most troubling problems that confronts rural residents who are planning to settle in cities. During our research in some cities and provinces, some rural migrant workers with years of working experience told us that they always felt adrift and could not settle or put down roots in the city. They added that having a home was more important than having a job; a job could be part-time work or it could be running a small shop, a workshop or a stall; but to feel at home, they needed a house, and it would not matter whether they rented or bought one; in fact, they could even make do in a shack in a shanty town. When discussing blending into cities, they became more forthright: "It is relatively easy to blend into a small town. If we rent a room, sooner or later we will get to know everyone nearby. Things are much more difficult in cities. We cannot buy a house with our wages. The high rent will eat up most of our income, leaving little to feed the family."

Why are urban houses so expensive and why are rents so high? In terms of housing as a commodity, the main reason is a shortage in supply. High housing prices are connected to high land prices, which are fundamentally caused by auctioning of land by local government. On the topic of rising housing prices, I told reporters my opinions during the CPPCC plenary sessions in three consecutive years from 2011 to 2013.

During the plenary session in 2011, I said to reporters that the government should replace land auctions with invitations to tender. My opinions were as follows. For a parcel of land allocated by the government for residential housing, if the government sold it through an auction, the bidding would keep surging due to the limited supply, giving rise to "land kings" – developers who pay enormous amount of money for land parcels. Local government could raise huge revenues by auctioning the land. Developers were willing to pay the highest price for a parcel of land because they could recover cost through housing prices. Consequently, rising land prices lift the price of houses and represent an increasingly large proportion of the latter. Therefore, I proposed to utilise the method of government procurement in land grants. In the procurement of mechanical equipment, the government would first publish the performance and quality standards for the whole set of equipment and then invite tenders from qualified manufacturers. The government could choose the bidder that offered the lowest price, provided that the products met the technological and quality standards required. Similarly in land grants, the government should set the land price and developers would put in their bids based on housing specifications and quality standards. Under identical quality standards, the one who offered the lowest price per square metre would win the bid. If the successful bidder failed to finish construction on time, if the houses did not meet the technical and quality standards, or if the bidder planned to sell the houses at a higher price than initially offered in the bidding, it would face penalties. These might include enormous fines and the revocation of qualification to bid. This would prevent land prices being driven up.

During the plenary session in 2012, I said to reporters that, on the issue of urban real estate, the solution at present was not to limit demand but to increase supply. Besides this, inelastic demand was a reality that none could evade. How could college graduates marry if they had nowhere to live? At least they had to rent a room. Migrant workers, too, needed housing to settle down in cities. They would buy or rent a home eventually and we should make sure they could afford to do this. I went on to say that: "Purchase restrictions are wrong but sale restrictions might work." The former would restrict house buyers; the latter would restrict resellers and impose taxes on the quick reselling of houses. The sooner they tried to resell the houses, the higher the tax would be. The tax rate would decrease with each successive year of ownership. Resale restrictions would render the hoarding of houses unprofitable and limit opportunism. Therefore, these measures could work.

In the plenary session of CPPCC 2013, I gave my frank answer to questions from the reporters. They asked, "What's your opinion on the five measures to strengthen the regulation of the property market released by the State Council this year?" I smiled and said, "Time will tell! These rigid measures aim at forcibly suppressing the demand. If they could suppress the housing prices in Beijing, we could throw economics out of the window." Some reporters asked, "American young people are not eager to buy houses. Many live in rented houses all their lives. Why are Chinese young people so fixated on buying houses?" I answered, "We should not take these cases out of their respective national contexts and compare them." It is more than 200 years since the United States began their industrialisation. All of the surplus labour has been released from the rural areas. The agricultural population in the United States currently accounts for fewer than 10% of the total. People in the agricultural sector have their family farms and their own houses, so they will not work in cities. But China is different. People with urban registration status only account for just over 30% of the total population. As industrialisation and urbanisation advance, many rural residents and their families plan to move into cities in the hope of settling down. This is the situation in China. Due to the high housing prices and the difficulty of renting a house, urban housing has inevitably become a vexed problem. How can this be compared with the situation in the United States? Besides that, the Chinese and Americans have different mentalities. For Chinese people, having a house in the city is like taking root there. A house is one's own property while renting is not a long-term solution. Therefore, people living in cities make every attempt to buy houses since they regard renting as merely a temporary solution.

How should we address the housing pressure in cities? I will repeat what I have said before. The government should build and provide social housing while the market will deal with high-end, spacious and comfortable housing. Let the government and the market each do their jobs. With higher supply, all social classes will be able to meet their housing needs. When people no longer stick to the expectation that housing will become ever more problematic, they will have faith and confidence in resolving housing issues. Concerns about high housing prices and the difficulty of renting will abate. Sooner or later, Chinese people will be equally disposed to rent and buy houses. They will rent before they buy, starting with small houses and then move on to more spacious ones.

3 Revisiting the increase in supply as a means to ease urban housing pressure

We have argued that, in order to ease the urban housing pressure, we should mainly increase supply rather than suppress demand. We will now give some further elaboration of this.

(1) There is still room for the expansion of housing construction land

Experience in recent years shows that, in the process of urbanisation, land available for housing construction is dwindling in rural areas near central city districts, yet there is still ample land if the rural areas are further away. Therefore, more and more residential housing will be situated in distant suburbs, where there is available wasteland, low-yield farmland, and hillsides for construction. Through land surveying and the determination of land rights, the government can revise or redraw city development plan to incorporate additional land available for construction. The government can set land prices and specify technical and quality standards for construction before inviting tenders. At the same time, it can work on planning roads and public transport infrastructure to turn the new building clusters into residential areas. According to experience in pilot zones, the actual volumes of agricultural land have increased after land surveying and the determination of land rights. Thus, we will not cross the farmland red line, or the minimum farmland threshold, of 1.8 billion *mu*.

*(2)   We should continue to renovate the old towns, demolish shanty
towns and old, crowded compounds, and construct new residential
areas on open land and replacement land*

For old towns within cities, demolishing old houses and building new ones is a
long-term project. On the one hand, due to tight budgets and huge costs, the renovation of old towns can only proceed step by step. On the other hand, the work
involves a great number of residents, including urban residents, migrant workers
and their families, the employed, the unemployed, solitary elders, the disabled
and the "left-behind children" of migrant workers. Demolition and resettlement
is very time-consuming because it takes scrupulous efforts to address the various
requirements of those relocated, some of which seem impossible to fulfil. Nonetheless, the work must be carried out.

According to our research in *Shenyang* and *Fushun* in *Liaoning* Province, the
demolition and renovation of shanty towns can achieve positive results if the
following conditions are met. First, the plan should be comprehensive and the work
meticulous. Second, the relocated people should be generally pleased with the new
residential areas. Third, there should be appropriate arrangements for people's
employment. We have also observed that the new residential areas can accommodate more people than the old.

(3)   High hopes for the building of new communities

The building of new communities is an innovation of China's urbanisation. Their
predecessors are the new socialist villages across the country. These new villages
evolve into new communities after the old houses have been renovated or replaced
by new ones. With the addition of green spaces, the control of the environment,
the establishment of public services, the integration of urban and rural social security systems and the shift to community management, the new communities will
finally take shape. To fit urbanisation into the Chinese context, the new communities must be regarded as a vital part of China's urbanisation and as new towns that
will accommodate a large number of rural residents. The new communities still
have great development potential. As commerce, the service industry, the specialty
handicraft industry, artisan workshops and factories flourish in the new communities, they will attract rural residents from other areas with job opportunities,
vibrant business and high incomes. Believing that they can make a better living
here than in the cities, rural residents will settle down in these new communities.

During our research in *Qianxi* County and *Dafang* County of *Bijie* City,
Guizhou Province, we found that after the local farmers had moved into the new
houses, the empty old houses were rented to migrant workers from outside, who
worked in vegetable greenhouses or ran small businesses. In this way, the old
houses generated more income for the locals and served as affordable homes for
migrant workers who performed labour or ran businesses.

In the new rural areas or new communities in the outer suburbs of *Beijing*, local
farmers run some "farm inns" and "farm restaurants" – together these are designated

"rural tourism" – to attract visitors. Because they need more workers, they put up notices saying "hands wanted". Some farm owners become chefs if they have culinary skills; others become managers and buyers if they have business knowledge. Non-local farmers often take up jobs as handymen or attendants. Some of them have even brought their families and rent houses in the village. We can see from this that the new villages or new communities have potential in accommodating more non-local farmers, and we should tap into this potential in the future.

(4) Properly addressing the problem of houses
   of limited property rights

In recent years, houses of limited property rights (HOLPRs) have emerged in the suburbs not far away from the city centres. We will discuss this phenomenon from the perspectives of supply and demand.

First, we look at demand. Who are the buyers of HOLPRs? Urban residents. Rising urban housing prices are unaffordable even for the middle class, to say nothing of lower-income families. Besides this, while some urban residents buy rural HOPLRs as their first houses, others buy them as their second homes. The latter stay in their small apartments in the city on weekdays, and travel to the countryside during vacations or in their leisure time. They may also live in their second houses in the countryside when they are writing or painting. Some non-local merchants who do business in large- or medium-sized cities also purchase rural HOPLRs as homes, because on the one hand, HOPLRs are cheaper than always living in hotels, and on the other hand, HOPLRs can be used as makeshift warehouses. Therefore, the demand for HOPLRs is great.

Next, look at the supply. Where do HOPLRs come from? Indeed, some people occupy additional land and build houses on it for sale. These people include former and even incumbent village officials and their relatives. This is illegal. Yet, in most cases it is farmers who build HOPLRs on their homestead land. Housing regulations prohibit selling these houses to non-locals, yet some farmers still do so for money despite the regulations. As suppliers, they do not need to promote or advertise their HOPLRs. They only need to wait at home and buyers will come to them. Once they agree upon a price, they have a deal. Due to the large demand, the price of HOPLRs is also rising.

Policies on HOPLRs centre on prohibition and mandatory retraction. These rigid measures leave no room for negotiation. Their enforcement, however, is often beset with difficulties and delays. For example, although it is easy to annul the sale contract on the HOPLRs between the buyers and the suppliers, it is very difficult to expel the residents (the buyers). Let us suppose that the contract has been signed and the payment has been made, but the buyer has not moved in. If we cancel the contract, the payment should be returned to the buyer. However, the seller may have spent the money elsewhere or is unwilling to return it. This will then become a problem. To give another example, the buyer and the seller only dared to complete the transaction on the HOPLR after acquiring permission from village officials. If higher level government reinstates the prohibition and outlaws

HOPLRs, who will be responsible for the results and the losses? Lastly, what if there are several disputes over the HOPLRs in the village, involving the interests of many farmers and buyers? Since those involved are all watching closely for the decision, the village official must mete out impartial treatment, but at the risk of undermining social stability. In the end, these cases generally remain unresolved.

All these disputes took place prior to the determination of land rights. After the determination of land rights, farmers will have the title deeds. Most people hold that, with title deeds, farmers should be allowed to freely make use of their houses on the homestead land and can even transfer them. Of course, there are opposing voices. Some local governments have come up with the following solution: they no longer question HOPLRs but ask whether or not the homestead land on which the house is built belongs to the farmer. If the answer is yes and the principle of "one household, one homestead, one house" is followed, there will be no restrictions on transactions concerning the house. This is because the transaction will not hurt the interests of others but will also help with the shortage of and pressure on urban housing.

4   The relationship between urbanisation and poverty reduction

If urbanisation does not remove the urban-rural dualism but focuses only on the expansion and economic growth of cities, it may raise the average incomes of urban residents but will not lift rural migrants in the cities out of poverty. Therefore, in order to reduce poverty in urbanisation, we should not only prioritise the reform of the urban-rural dualism but also devote great effort to narrowing the gap in social security systems between urban and rural areas. This is an important lesson we have learned in China's urbanisation in the 21st century.

We can analyse the relationship between urbanisation and poverty reduction from the following four perspectives.

(1)   Solving the urban employment problem in urbanisation

During urbanisation, urban employment problems consist of two areas. First, employment opportunities should be available to urban residents who newly reach working age. Second, employment opportunities should be available to farmers who move to cities, their spouses and their children who have reached working age and are willing to work. These are vital issues directly related to urban poverty reduction.

In order to give so many job seekers opportunities that suit them, a constantly growing economy that creates more jobs in cities is essential. However, economic growth alone is not enough. We must establish a proper employment structure. If the job seekers do not meet the skill and professional requirements of the position, corresponding professional training must be in place to support them. In addition, no discrimination against job seekers with rural household registration should be allowed. Any such discrimination is unfair.

To offer more jobs to people, we must vigorously support the development of small and micro-enterprises in cities, and encourage more talented urban and rural job seekers to start these types of businesses. In this way, new business undertakings will boost employment. As cities grow, public services and modern service industry will expand rapidly and absorb many job seekers. This, too, will meet the needs of society, providing more jobs for people and increasing their incomes.

(2) Agriculture, the livestock industry, and forestry will always require
*   labour: they can help with easing employment pressure and poverty*
*   reduction in urbanisation*

Currently in China's urbanisation, development should be coordinated between the rural and urban areas and the development of urban areas must not come at the cost of neglecting rural areas and agriculture. We must be aware that the income gap between rural and urban areas persists and has increased in recent years due to urban-rural dualism. The government should pay more attention to the widening income gap. From the experience of urbanisation in China, this gap can only be diminished through reform and development. The most important reform measure is to remove the restrictions on rural areas and rural residents. We should give the same rights to rural residents as their urban counterparts enjoy, grant them property and property income rights, eliminate discrimination in employment due to household registration status and integrate the rural and urban social security systems. These are structural supports for the reduction of poverty in rural areas and residents. The most crucial development measure is to support rural residents in performing labour, doing business and running small and micro-enterprises in cities so as to increase their income. Meanwhile, we should provide support to family farms, and organise specialised farmer cooperatives by introducing new technologies, promoting large-scale operations and raising productivity. These measures will also contribute to poverty reduction.

(3) Balanced distribution of educational resources and good social
*   mobility will help in the reduction of urban and rural poverty*

Due to urban-rural dualism, the distribution of educational resources is unbalanced and biased towards cities and urban residents. Take compulsory education as an example. For a long time, rural areas have had a smaller budget for schools, inferior equipment, fewer teachers and poorer learning results. Consequently, the senior high school and college enrolment rates in the rural areas are substantially lower than in urban areas. In recent years, we even find that the children of rural residents are unwilling to attend senior high schools after the compulsory education in junior high schools. During our research in *Chifeng* City and *Tongliao* City in Inner Mongolia, the local rural residents said to us: "What is the good of finishing high school? It is becoming harder to enter college. Our children might as well go to work in cities right after graduating from junior high schools. In this way they can save money for the family and make money earlier!"

This situation hinders the effort to reduce and end the poverty of low-income families in urban and rural areas. Junior high school graduates can only get low-salary jobs that involve simple labour, to say nothing of their difficulty in finding these jobs. This will not help them escape poverty. Therefore, in the process of urbanisation, it is necessary to balance the education fund per capita in urban and rural areas, so that the unequal allocation of educational resources can be remedied. Moreover, we should adjust the distribution of different types and levels of school in old towns, new towns and new communities, and provide low-income families with compulsory, senior high school and specialised secondary school education free of charge, with free catering and accommodation. This is crucial for poverty reduction and is an essential part of urbanisation.

(4) An important reason why low-income families relapse into poverty
is the long-term illness among family members: when building
towns and cities, we must note this problem

According to our research in *Wulong*, *Pengshui* and *Shizhu* County in *Chongqing*, not long after some low-income urban and rural families finally pulled themselves out of poverty thanks to their hard work and help from the government, their economic situations soon deteriorated. The reasons for that, according to the reports of village officials, included the following: sudden death or disability of the main labour force in the family due to car accidents, floods and the like; accidents of fire that destroyed their houses along with all their possessions; their sons' weddings, the expense of which incurred heavy debt; personal failings and addiction to gambling that led them to squander their possession; long-term illnesses of family members that overburdened the families. The latter was especially widespread. Additionally, some merchants were ruined by the fraudulent practices of others, and livestock farmers were driven to poverty by frost damage, or poultry or swine diseases.

The sheer number of causes of relapse into poverty posed a challenge to the village officials. The research team suggested that, while some cases were due to custom and personal failings, commercial insurance could be of help and the integration of urban and rural social security systems could alleviate relapses into poverty due to disease. Integration of healthcare system is a part of the integration of urban and rural social security systems, involving equal treatment in terms of medical charges and prescription fees for people with urban and rural household registration. It aims at both equalising the treatment of urban and rural residents, and balancing the distribution of healthcare facilities. Farmers often complain about difficulties when seeking medical treatment, such as unequal reimbursement for urban and rural residents, and the lack of healthcare facilities in the large rural areas forces them to spend much more time and energy in order to receive medical treatment. These problems must be taken into account during urbanisation to prevent the relapse into poverty due to disease.

5 The integration of household registration is a gradual process

Currently in China, urbanisation is a crucial component in the deepening of reform. Its key is to abolish the urban-rural dualism that has lasted for 50 years and to realise the integration of city and countryside. The dual household registration system is the cornerstone of urban-rural dualism. Therefore, this dual system must be integrated into a single system to do away with the urban-rural dualism.

We need to integrate the dual household registration system in urban and rural areas; that is to say, to transform the household dual-track system into a single-track system. However, there are debates in academia regarding whether or not this reform should be carried out first.

Those who say it should give the following reason. The establishment of urban-rural dualism in 1958 rested on the coexistence of urban and rural household registration systems that restricted population flows between urban and rural areas. Therefore, to abolish this dualism, we should begin with the household registration system. In other words, the urban-rural dualism will not survive without its cornerstone.

Those who oppose the prioritisation of the abolition of the dual household registration system, including me, argue that this measure would not be hard to implement but would have a limited effect on accelerating urbanisation in China. Can a single public announcement put an end to all the restrictions on the farmers formed over more than 50 years and solve all the difficulties? Supposing we announce that the two household registration systems are integrated into one, the urban social order will be severely disrupted by farmers pouring into cities due to the lack of restrictions on population flow. Similarly, what should we do when urban residents go to the countryside and ask to purchase the houses left by the migrating farmers? Therefore, the integration of urban and rural areas will be a long process requiring much work. If we rush the process, we risk destabilising society and obstructing the orderly process of urbanisation.

The reform of the household registration system cannot be forced. In recent years I have repeatedly stressed that only when all preparations have been made can we say that the conditions are ripe for the transformation of the dual-track household registration system into a single-track system. These preparations can be summarised as follows. The farmers have already begun migrating to towns and new communities and, when they arrive, they can find jobs for themselves and schools for their children. With the establishment of public services, these farmers can settle down and enjoy their normal everyday life. Only then can we say that the integration of household registration systems has begun: by that time, all Chinese residents, regardless of whether they used to live in urban or rural areas, will use standardised identity cards and will no longer be differentiated by urban or rural status.

This will be a gradual and orderly process that ends the discrimination against those with rural status and ensures equal rights among residents.

However, arguments still arise during the discussion of this problem. Cities can be divided into four categories according to their scale: extra-large, large, medium-sized and small cities. Many experts think that we can first implement the single-track household registration system in small to medium-sized cities to accumulate experience, before promulgating it in large and, eventually, extra-large cities. Their reason is that these types of cities differ considerably and that during urbanisation, extra-large cities have their own characteristics that require further research prior to the implementation of the single-track household registration system. Otherwise, with a population of over 10 or even 20 million, extra-large cities like *Beijing, Shanghai, Guangzhou, Shenzhen* and *Tianjing* will be overwhelmed by large numbers of migrant farmers if the household registration reform is hastily promoted. These experts certainly have a point when they insist on putting off household registration reform in extra-large cities. Yet, this gives rise to the further arguments that large and extra-large cities boast formidable government revenues, and so they, instead of poor, small cities, should act as the trailblazers and exemplars for the integration of migrant workers.

To conclude, which cities ought to first initiate household registration reform should be decided by the local government treasury, taking into account the housing and employment situation of migrant workers and the state of public service facilities. Overall, it is more realistic to first implement this reform in relatively wealthy small cities and new communities. Small, medium-sized and large cities should not rush or compete with each other in the implementation of a single household registration system, nor should they pursue speed at the cost of effect. Otherwise, we will repeat the old problems of urbanisation and suffer from their consequences and complications.

Here we need to reiterate the purposes of urbanisation: to realise the urbanisation of human beings and improve their living standards. These goals can only be achieved if we proceed steadily and step by step.

Therefore, we should always emphasise the significance of building "new communities". We must treat the new communities as cases of urbanisation within our national context, and achieve in-situ urbanisation. Otherwise, hundreds of millions of farmers will pour into old towns and new towns when we struggle to integrate urban and rural social security systems. How can China achieve the goal of urbanisation steadily in that situation?

Section 3 The urbanisation of pasture areas

1 Difficulties in the urbanisation of pasture areas

Urbanisation is in progress nationwide. Comparatively speaking, the urbanisation of villages proceeds relatively smoothly, but it is slower in pasture areas and faces many difficulties. In August 2011, I led the *Guanghua* School of Management research team of *Beijing* University to conduct research in *Chifeng* City urban district, *Heshigten* Banner, *Bairin* Right Banner, *Ongniud* Banner, and *Ningcheng* County. This section focuses on the urbanisation of pasture areas.

The difficulties of the urbanisation of pasture areas can be summarised as follows. First, pasture areas are sparsely populated, with few small towns except near municipal or league centres. Urbanisation involves the expansion of existing towns to attract more farmers and herdsmen and their relatives. If an existing town has good foundations, expansion will be relatively easy. Yet, most towns in pasture areas are small, lack basic facilities, and require new investment for expansion before they can accommodate more people. In some places, new towns have to be built from scratch, and this requires even greater investment, exceeding the fiscal capacity of local governments.

Second, residents of towns who have newly migrated from pasture areas have difficulty finding jobs. According to *Chifeng* City Commission of Housing and Urban-Rural Development, it is difficult to allocate jobs to new migrants due to belated town planning, the limited size of the town, the lack of basic facilities, low level of industrialisation and other problems when building small towns, regardless of whether these towns are expanded or newly built. If unemployment continues, these migrants will not settle down, but will plan to leave.

Third, during the urbanisation of pasture areas, the expansion of existing towns or construction of new ones often lacks an index of land, and even the limited index of land favours county seats where banner and county governments are located.

The situation is different in the urbanisation of farmland areas in certain provinces and cities. There, in order that the land needed for the expansion of towns or the construction of new towns can be acquired, farmers move to new villages, vacate their homestead land and reuse it as farmland. Meanwhile, another parcel of farmland with the same size as the homestead land is converted for industrial or urban construction. This process is called "land replacement". As a result, the "red line", or the minimum threshold for agriculture land, has been preserved. This land replacement is inapplicable to pasture areas, because the pastureland has been contracted to the herdsman and because there is no homestead land – the herdsmen live in yurts or build their own houses. Therefore, attempts to urbanise pasture areas by expanding existing towns or building new ones is often restricted by the lack of index of land.

Fourth, and perhaps most importantly, many herdsmen prefer not to migrate to towns because they think life on the pastureland is much more comfortable. As long as they manage their pastureland properly, they will enjoy higher incomes compared with working in a factory, and in addition they do not have to follow a rigid working schedule. If they settle in towns, they will have to abandon their grassland and pastureland, become underprivileged and face many uncertainties in jobs and salaries. Some elderly herdsmen are especially reluctant to give up their familiar lifestyle. For years they have relied on livestock farming for their living and as a means of production. They are unwilling to leave behind the simplicity, tranquillity and leisurely life on the pastureland and the culture associated with grassland and nomadic life. Of course, habits can change, and lifestyles can adapt to new environments, yet both take time and depend on two important conditions: first, life in towns must be more comfortable for the herdsmen than that on the pastureland, and second, they must have higher incomes after they migrate. If neither condition is met, herdsmen will lack the incentive to work and live in towns. They will resist the demolition of their homes and relocation and, even if they do migrate, because they yearn for their roots on the pastureland they often leave the towns and go back.

Due to the four reasons mentioned above, the urbanisation of pasture areas proceeds at a slow pace and urbanisation rates remain very low. First, the herdsmen will not settle in the towns, because they prefer not to migrate, and even if they do migrate, it tends to be the old and the infirm rather than the young and strong that choose to do so. Second, local governments do not have sufficient revenues to provide jobs for migrant herdsmen and their family members. The government cannot pressure the herdsmen to migrate, nor can they pull down their houses to force them. As a result, it is extremely challenging to increase urbanisation rates in pasture areas. Some local government officials complain that such low urban-isation rates place great pressure on them. Local government officials feel the strain of low urbanisation rates of the pasture areas, which hinders the progress of urbanisation in the whole region.

To address this challenge, we need fresh ideas and strategies.

2 Lessons from herdsmen who migrated from pastureland due to desertification

During our research in *Chifeng* City, we especially visited *Hailasu* County, located 62 kilometres from the government of *Ongniud* Banner. This small pastureland town covers an area of around 2.3 million *mu* containing 15 neighbourhood com-munities, with a total of 5,000 households and a population of 15,000. By the end of 2010, the town district covered an area of 3.6 square kilometres, with a population of 6,000.

The construction of *Hailasu* County in *Ongniud* Banner is an achievement. Some herdsmen in the vicinity are among those who migrated to the county dis-trict. One of the reasons why they are enthusiastic about relocating there is the rapid development of the county that is creating additional jobs. The young, the strong and even older people can find suitable work and gain stable incomes. For example, independent stores, restaurants, small repair shops, processing factories and other commercial or service businesses number a total of 300 with 1,300 employees. In addition, there are 13 institutions, including the *Hailasu* Water Authority and *Hailasu* Commune Hospital. The migrant herdsmen can choose to open stores, workshops and restaurants or work in enterprises and institutions according to their skills and expertise, which raises their income levels after migration. Another reason is the diversified investment that has accelerated the building of residential houses and infrastructure such as roads, green spaces, sew-age, water, heat, electricity and gas supply systems. The county government not only increased its investment, but also made good use of private funds and bank credit to support the construction of the town.[1] This substantially improved the living and working conditions there, which attracted more herdsmen.

However, while additional working opportunities and better living and working conditions affected the decisions of the herdsmen to migrate to the town, these factors were not the main reason. During our research in *Hailasu* County under *Ongniud* Banner, we discovered that the determining factor was desertification and the deterioration of the pastureland, and the subsequent decline in income from livestock farming. In addition, desertification led to failing water supplies for the people and their livestock. Therefore, relocation from desert areas became the first priority for them, or they could hardly sustain basic life and production. Against this background, the additional job opportunities and better living conditions in the town began to influence their deliberations on whether or not to migrate.

From this we can see that, in areas without desertification, herdsmen will still prefer their contracted pastureland. If they manage the land properly, maintain rich grass and water resources, and continue to increase their incomes, most herdsmen will not be keen on moving to towns.

We should understand that the herdsmen are extremely motivated after acquiring their contracted pastureland. This is reflected in the following three perspectives.

First, the herdsmen value their contracted pastureland and hold that they have inviolable rights over it. They will not give up their pastureland except in a scenario where they cannot deal with severe desertification on their own and have to migrate to the towns. Their major concern is whether or not their pastureland will be occupied. Therefore, during urbanisation, we must respect their rights over the contracted pastureland and should forbid anyone either to compel them to leave it without their consent or forcibly pull down their houses. These are the most effective measures to incentivise the herdsmen.

Second, the herdsmen are enthusiastic about managing the pastureland and increasing the quality of the grass. They are aware that overgrazing will cause the deterioration of the grass resources and directly reduce their incomes. In the past, before the household contract system for pastureland was implemented, overgrazing occurred because many herdsmen took advantage of collectively owned pastureland to graze more and thought it foolish not to make the most of it. Under these circumstances, grazing inevitably overburdened the grassland, causing it to deteriorate. After the implementation of household responsibility systems, clear borders divided the pastureland belonging to each household, and since no one would graze beyond their assigned areas, they took good care of their own land. They gradually moderated the feeding of animals and began to use pens so that the pasture grass could flourish. This shows how much attention the herdsmen pay to the grass resources.

Third, the herdsmen care greatly about the future of their children and grandchildren. When discussing whether or not to move into towns, they keep saying: "think more about our children". With this in mind, they often try to send their children and grandchildren to towns, even though they themselves are willing to live and work on the contracted pastureland. Sometimes they purchase a house in town for their children or grandchildren to live in, or have them lodge with urban relatives so that the young can more conveniently go to school and find a job in the urban areas. If the town has boarding schools, they tend to send the young to study there. Meanwhile, the parents remain in the pastureland, raise and graze cattle, and continue their habitual way of life with their incomes. They are enthusiastic about the education of their children and grandchildren, and hope that they can lead a better life. This is human nature.

The herdsmen regard the pastureland as their true home. They are unwilling to leave it, but instead carefully manage it to increase their earnings. When their children or grandchildren grow up, the herdsmen are willing to send them away and have them venture outside, but they always remind their youngsters that if they suffer setbacks during work, they can always return to the pastureland. How can they leave behind this home of theirs?

Considering how much the herdsmen value their contract rights over the pastureland, and how much care they put into its management and the future of their children and grandchildren who are ready to leave, we need to be attentive to two points in the urbanisation of pasture areas. First, urbanisation does not necessarily have to lead to reductions in the population on the pastureland, and we should respect the will of those who decide to remain; and second, we need to emphasise marketisation and level of social services, and as long as both are achieved, we have in effect attained the goal of urbanisation.

We will discuss this problem in the following section.

3 The marketisation and social servitisation of pasture areas: two major indices for the urbanisation of pasture areas

(1) The marketisation of pasture areas

Urbanisation is closely related to marketisation. In fact, by migrating to towns, farmers take part in the market. To some degree, marketisation and urbanisation are not only parallel, but also accelerate each other. Instead of the percentage of the urban population in the overall population of a country (or a province, city, county), we can use the percentage of the urban and rural population who engage in the market to measure the rate of marketisation so as to infer the rate of urbanisation.

This measurement should provide a better picture of the progress of urbanisation in pasture areas. For example, these areas are sparsely populated; the herdsmen value their contract rights, manage their land with enthusiasm and are reluctant to resettle in towns, not to mention abandoning their homes in the pastureland. In this case, it is preferable to judge the progress of urbanisation by the extent to which herdsmen participate in market activities; namely, the extent to which they participate in the urban economy, rather than the percentage they represent of the urban population in an area.

To be more specific, the extent to which herdsmen participate in the urban economy is reflected by the marketisation rate of the initial products, livestock product processing, the supply of goods and means of production. We should be aware that herdsmen used to have little contact with the market but afterwards, their initial and processed products, everyday needs and means of production are increasingly interwoven with it. Together these factors provide a picture of the ever-closer relationship between herdsmen and the urban economy. The herdsmen used to be self-sufficient, but now they rely more and more on the market and urban economy. Isn't this proof of the increasing urbanisation of pasture areas? The progress of urbanisation can be reflected in how many initial and processed products the herdsmen sell directly to the market, and how much consumer goods and production material they buy, instead of just calculating the rising number of herdsmen who migrate to towns.

Another useful index of marketisation and the participation of herdsmen in the urban economy is the development of pasture area finance (a component of rural finance), and the increase in lending transactions between herdsmen and pasture area financial organisations. In the past, herdsmen used to have few lending transactions with pasture area financial organisations. Instead, they turned to private funds or their friends and relatives for help. The business of the few financial organisations was concentrated around the county seats or large towns. Subsequently, financial organisations began to grow in number, and smaller ones, such as rural credit cooperatives and the Postal Saving Banks of China, established more branches. Some counties in pasture areas plan to build "grassroots" financial organisations including village banks, small lending companies, small bond companies and cooperative funds. If finance in pasture areas develops at a relatively rapid pace and provides support to the herdsmen, the marketisation of pasture areas and the participation of herdsmen in the urban economy will increase. This, too, should be regarded as an aspect of the urbanisation of pasture areas.

(2) The social servitisation of pasture areas

As has been mentioned before, out of consideration for their children's and grandchildren's future, some herdsmen send them to live in towns so that they can study, graduate and eventually find better jobs there. Meanwhile, the herdsmen remain in the pastureland, continue to raise livestock and treat the contracted pastureland as their home. Perhaps when they grow old, they will retire and resettle in the towns, and leave the pastureland to their sons to manage. As a result, middle-aged people and those who are strong stay on the pastureland, while the young and the elderly migrate to the towns. Regardless of how long the separation between family members will last, we expect this situation to continue without substantial change over the next 10 to 20 years, or perhaps even longer. During our research we have heard elderly herdsmen say that, when they could no longer work, they would like to move to the towns with their partners and leave the pastureland to their sons, because the towns have more accessible healthcare services and better doctors. This shows that the herdsmen will be still willing to migrate when they become old.

Therefore, even though not many herdsmen want to live in towns, they still care about social services.

This provides another possible angle when we consider indices of the urbanisation of pasture areas, which is the rate of social servitisation. In other words, during the urbanisation of pasture areas, we must integrate the herdsmen into the social services system which used to be separate from their lives.

The integration of social security is a major reform that is underway and we need to speed up its implementation. However, the integration of social security is unbalanced within our country and within different provinces, cities and districts. This integration is evidently more difficult in pasture areas than in farming areas.

Pasture areas, and especially larger ones, are mostly located in remote parts of the country or near the borders, far removed from provincial administrative centres. Moreover, because the pasture areas are sparsely populated, county and prefecture level administrative centres are also relatively far away. In addition, shortages of funds and professionals greatly restrict healthcare, education and provisions for the elderly. Nevertheless, without unified social security, it is hard to incorporate herdsmen into the social services system. As of now, we can promote health-care services, increase the enrolment of school age children and youngsters in education, open additional boarding schools and expand existing ones, increase the percentage of high school and technical school graduates within the same age group, and vigorously develop various social services facilities, such as sewage treatment, waste recycling, tap water supply and electricity supplies and public transport.

The integration of the household registration system is equally important in farming and pasture areas. This is the goal of the household registration reform. Even with household registration reform and the disappearance of the dualism of rural and urban households, urbanisation will continue because it will progress in accordance with economic development. Rural residents, including those in farming and pasture areas, will continue to flow into cities and towns. How can the percentage of urban residents rise within the total population of pasture areas if we take the specific situation there into consideration? Even now, many residents, especially the main labourers within families, prefer to live in their contracted pastureland rather than move to towns. Will this hinder urbanisation and become a bottleneck in the rate of urbanisation?

In the following part, we analyse the above questions with a new approach to the urbanisation of pasture areas.

4 How to increase the urban population of pasture areas

The percentage of rural and urban populations remains a key index. Although we have discussed marketisation and social servitisation in the pasture areas, and have suggested that these may serve as important indices of urbanisation, their significance does not diminish the importance of the urbanisation rate. To grasp the whole picture of the progress of urbanisation, we still mainly rely on meas-uring urbanisation rates; namely, the percentage of rural and urban populations within a certain area. The remaining questions include how we can increase the urban population if most herdsmen are unwilling to leave the pastureland for the towns, and how the urbanisation rate can be increased.

There are two ways to approach this. We will continue to use *Chifeng* City as an example.

The first is to coordinate the proportions of urban and rural population as a whole, with *Chifeng* city district as the focus, to increase the rate of urbanisation. This involves the strengthening of the city district, turning it into an industrial, commercial and financial centre, a base for new industries and a tourist city rich in culture. In addition, *Chifeng* must evolve into an important nexus that connects

eastern Inner Mongolia with adjacent provinces and the sea, and a logistics centre in eastern Inner Mongolia, northern *Hebei* Province and western *Liaoning*
Province.

Under this general arrangement, *Chifeng* city district will attract rural residents
from the farmland in local counties and banners, and from other cities, leagues,
counties and banners, because it will need a labour force for the industrial, commercial, services and logistic sectors and will have sufficient job opportunities
to accommodate them. In addition, as the prominence of *Chifeng* city district
grows, its radius of influence will gradually extend beyond Inner Mongolia, and it
will attract farmers from *Chaoyang* City in Liaoning Province, *Zhangjiakou* and
Chengde in *Hebei* and other cities and provinces to resettle, work and live there.
As a result, the urban population of *Chifeng* city district will grow continuously
and the urbanisation rate will increase.

The other approach is to increase the urban population of towns and banners in
pasture areas under the municipality of *Chifeng* City by building industrial zones,
and developing commerce, service industries and cultural and natural tourism.
These counties and banners should rely on local farmers and those from other
counties and provinces instead of local herdsmen to boost the urban population. As
long as these counties and banners develop their economy, they can create more
jobs. With the expansion of the towns in the counties and banners, they can accommodate migrant farmers and their relatives and the urbanisation rate will increase.

Whichever approach we take, we should note that the population and urbanisation rate of *Chifeng* City and its counties and banners will continue to rise in
spite of the reluctance of herdsmen to live and work in towns. This is because the
farmers who move into towns to work or start a business become urban residents
once they settle there.

That farmers will leave their provinces, cities and districts for their desired
towns is a nationwide trend. This will not affect these provinces, cities and counties because, when the farmers leave, the local rural population and its percentage of the total local population will shrink, regardless of where they decide to
migrate. In the case of counties and banners in the pasture areas that receive
migrants, although the herdsmen are reluctant to leave their contracted pastureland, and only send their children and grandchildren to live in towns for education
and employment purposes, provided that the farmers from other places boost the
local population, the urbanisation rates of those counties will rise. Therefore, the
above scenario is favourable for urbanisation.

In fact, we can clearly see from the history of the past one to two centuries that
the *Han* Chinese in *Chifeng* City of Inner Mongolia came from *Shandong* and
Hebei Province. In many cases, people from some counties move and resettle
there, which further attracted more fellow townsmen to the same area. Some of
them lived in villages for generations, while others lived in towns. Therefore, the
migration of farmers from other provinces is not just a contemporary phenomenon
but reaches back into the past.

In order that towns can accommodate more farmers from the outside, counties
and banners in the *Chifeng* municipality are making preparations. For example,

according to the *Chifeng* Bureau of City Planning, real estate developments have emerged in more than 50 small towns in recent years. On the one hand, this provides housing for the surplus rural labourers that flock into towns and helps increase the urban population. On the other hand, the sale of land supplies extra funds that town governments can in turn invest in infrastructure, effectively overcoming the bottleneck in town construction funds. In *Chifeng* City, there is a rising trend for farmers to move into towns because the wide implementation of modern agricultural technology is reducing the labour intensity of agricultural production and the number of workers required, so that a part of the rural population no longer has to remain in the countryside. In addition, living conditions and the environment are often far superior in small towns than in villages, and the housing prices are much lower than in the county seats or medium-sized to large cities, making small towns a realistic choice for those who can and want to leave the rural areas.

This situation proves the basic thesis we have put forward earlier regarding the urbanisation of pasture areas: we need to respect the choice of herdsmen to remain on the contracted pastureland, and must not compel them to move into towns; the increase in urban populations and urbanisation rates should mainly rely on local and incoming farmers resettling in towns to work, open businesses and workshop, or do other jobs.

Section 4 The urbanisation of forest areas

1 Comparison between the urbanisation of pasture and forest areas

In Section 3, we have discussed the basic ideas concerning the urbanisation of pasture areas. In this section, we turn to a consideration of the urbanisation of forest areas.

Forest and pasture areas have the following four similarities. First, both are sparsely populated. The progress of urbanisation is slow and urbanisation rates are low. Second, both are located in the borderlands, where ethnic minorities, who have had their own cultures, customs and means of living, work and live for generations. Third, both have a simple industrial structure. Forestry and livestock farming are the main sectors in forest and pasture areas respectively, accompanied by agriculture, manufacturing, hunting and foraging. Mining only emerges after the discovery and extraction of mineral resources. Fourth, the pasture areas have grassland while the forest areas have trees and other resources; both areas can provide relatively stable livelihoods. Consequently, during the Three Years of Natural Disaster, no one died of famine in these areas, unlike with farmers in the inland flatlands. Many *Han* farmers fled here to find a living. After these farmers, who were then called the "blind flow", settled down, few of them returned. They worked in the forest and pasture areas, claimed small pieces of land to grow crops and raise livestock, or started small workshops, businesses, restaurants or inns. In fact, this had already happened in the late *Qing* Dynasty and is common in forest areas in *Daxing'anling, Xiaoxing'anling* and the *Changbai* Mountains, and in the pasture areas in *Bayannur, Ulanqab, Xilingol, Chifeng* and *Tongliao,* hence the establishment of towns in these regions.

Yet, there are also relatively large differences between forest and pasture areas. Generally speaking, the differences can be summarised into the following five aspects.

First, pasture and forest areas differ in the nature of ownership. In contemporary China, state-owned forests and collectively owned forests cover roughly the same areas, each accounting for half of the total forest resources. After the reform of collective ownership of forests, areas under collective ownership have been contracted to rural households. They are now owners of family forest land and some have even become large forest contractors. Meanwhile, the reform of state-owned forest land is still being explored. Several different experimental plans have been formulated and applied, and the conclusions are yet to be drawn. In the case of pasture areas, while state-owned pastureland exists, it is much smaller compared with the areas which are collectively owned. Some state-owned pastureland has been transformed into ownership by joint-stock companies, some of which are listed companies, with dairy products, meat products and livestock as their main output. The collectively owned pastureland was contracted to the herdsmen in the 1990s, and became family pastureland. Therefore, comparatively speaking, the reform of state-owned forest land faces greater challenges than the reform of state-owned pastureland. Any mistakes could cause grave damage to the ecology.

Second, after pastureland has been contracted to the families, the ways of using it undergo significant changes. Some grow food for livestock and raise the livestock in pens. Others adopt rotational grazing on their contracted grassland to retain mobility. Trees and forests, on the other hand, have fixed locations. The contractors of pastureland, namely the owners of the family pastureland, say that they cannot leave the pastureland for a single day. To graze the cattle and sheep they have to leave their homes early and return late. They need to prepare places for cattle and sheep to live and store food for them. Livestock farmers fear the winter most, and when snowstorms occur, they have to take care of the livestock so that they do not starve or freeze to death. By contrast, forest land contractors or the owners of family forest land say that they do not have to go to the forest everyday unless they have a chicken farm there; a visit every few days will do. Of course, when there are wild fires they will rush there even at night. Otherwise, they can live in small towns. Thus, herdsmen and foresters hold different views on urbanisation.

Third, when we were doing research in the forest areas in *Daxing'anling* and *Xiaoxing'anling* and the pasture areas in *Chifeng* and *Tongliao*, the foresters on the forest land as well as the employees of state-owned forest land and their family members told us that the winters there were long; thick snow rendered roads almost impassable. With nothing to do, they considered it much better to get together with their families and stay warm in the towns than remain in the forest. The herdsmen, however, said that on snowy days they had to stay in the pastureland. If they moved to the towns, they would be concerned about their cattle, which were their possessions and livelihood. They had no choice but to remain.

This further illustrates the different attitudes towards migrating to and settling in towns.

Fourth, compared with the forest areas, people in the pasture areas are mostly ethnic minorities, while the people in forest areas are mainly *Han* Chinese, regardless of whether they are employees of state-owned forest land or foresters on collectively contracted forest land. The *Han* Chinese either moved to the forest areas during the Late *Qing* Dynasty or the rule of the Republic of China to make a living, or tried to find bare sustenance there after they had escaped the famines under the planned economy, especially during the Three Years of Natural Disaster. The ethnic minorities are used to living and working on the pastureland but are not accustomed to life in towns, while the *Han* Chinese in the forest land are comfortable with working and living in towns. In addition, for a long time, ethnic minority families did not pay as much attention as the *Han* Chinese to the education of their offspring; in terms of compulsory education, schools in towns have better buildings, teachers and teaching equipment, and so the *Han* Chinese would rather settle in towns for the sake of their children, while they work alone on the forest land. Ethnic minority families, on the other hand, would prefer to live on the pastureland. Although in recent years the situation has changed and they have become increasingly aware of the importance of their children's education, traditional way of thinking will not disappear very soon.

Fifth, employment is a problem that must be addressed during urbanisation. During our research in *Chifeng* City, the Mongolian herdsmen told us that they could only rear livestock and that, if they moved to towns only to do trivial work such as sweeping streets or carrying bricks, they would rather remain on the pastureland. Manual labour and small business are not their strong suit. After they moved to towns, there would be no jobs that they would be either willing or able to do, making employment difficult. By contrast, the *Han* Chinese earn a living in forest areas using their strength or skills. With this background, they and their children who are influenced by their parents can quickly adapt to an urban working environment. Even if they have stable jobs, regardless of whether they work on state-owned forest land, or are themselves contractors of a piece of forest land, they could still find work if they migrated to towns. While they may not be inclined to move into towns at the moment, their children might want to live and work there since they could accustom themselves to the working environment. They would also be happy to open stores, run small businesses and become small business owners.

We can see from this that urbanisation will meet less resistance in forest areas than in pasture areas.

2   *The birth and development of existing towns in forest and pasture areas*

While there used to be no towns in forest or pasture areas, fortresses had existed since long ago where garrisons were stationed to guard the borders. The larger fortresses were the seats of borderland administration and local government.

Commerce and manufacturing gradually developed, likely undergoing a phase of market transactions. Markets were held every few days; residents nearby brought their goods, sold them at stalls and purchased goods and production material as well as weapons for self-defence. Merchants from the inland also transported their goods to the markets and set up temporary stalls to trade. According to our research in western Inner Mongolia pasture areas, the earliest inland merchants mainly came from the provinces of *Shanxi*, *Shaanxi* and *Gansu*, while those in the pasture areas in eastern Inner Mongolia and the forest areas in *Daxing'anling* and *Xiaoxing'anling* were primarily from *Shandong* and *Hebei*. These inland merchants not only brought goods to trade, but also carried special local products to Inner China for sale, such as cattle, sheep and horses from the pasture areas, and mountain delicacies from the forest areas. These activities developed during the second half of the *Qing* Dynasty.

After the *Xinhai* Revolution, the Northern Warlords seized control over Inner Mongolia and Northeastern China. To raise tax revenue and fulfil the needs of the army, local officials and their families, they encouraged inland merchants from *Shanxi*, *Shandong* and *Hebei* to trade and open shops in the pasture and forest areas. Consequently, these places underwent many changes: for example, the fortresses where troops were garrisoned were expanded into towns, surrounded by newly built streets lined with stores, manual workshops, restaurants and inns. There were schools, theatres and hospitals. Permanent residents, including local people and migrants from inland, grew in number. The towns were relatively well-developed, especially the seats of government and the administrative centres of leagues and banners, and these evolved into commercial hubs in addition to political and military centres.

In the 1930s, Japan captured the Three Northeastern Provinces, and proceeded to seize Jehol, Chahar and eastern *Suiyuan*. In this period they intensified the exploitation of resources in the forest areas in northeastern China and eastern Inner Mongolia, for which purpose they constructed roads and expanded existing towns. On the other hand, much of the pastureland in eastern Inner Mongolia was retained by the Mongolian lords despite the presence of Japanese garrisons. Without their own grassland, the herdsmen, or more precisely the serf herders, grazed the livestock for their masters. The lord's residences or the puppet governments were located in some of the larger towns. Despite the existence of some shops, the economy was generally stagnant, and markets remained weak. The Japanese were keen on cutting down trees in *Daxing'anling* and *Xiaoxing'anling*. The grass in the pasture areas, by contrast, was of little interest to them. Therefore, the Japanese attached greater importance to the forest areas and the towns there tended to develop more rapidly during the occupation.

After the establishment of the People's Republic of China, *Daxing'anling* and *Xiaoxing'anling* became state-owned forest land under the management of the forestry department. The ownership of collectively owned mountain forest remained unchanged. After the land ownership reform in the pasture areas, the landlord's ownership was dismantled and the herdsmen were allotted grassland for livestock farming. Later, higher level farmer cooperatives and people's communes were founded. After the Reform and Opening-up, following the mode for contracted farmland, the contract responsibility system was adopted in the pastureland. In the 21st century, all collectively owned forests, whether in the pasture or forest areas, have been subjected to ownership reform and the mountain areas have been contracted to individual households. During this period, the urbanisation of pasture and forest areas has seen some, albeit slow, progress, because the dual household registration system is still in place, hindering the migration of herdsmen and foresters into towns. Moreover, the lack of jobs makes it difficult for them to settle, unless they secure stable incomes by opening businesses, performing manual labour or excelling in other skills.

To conclude the above discussion, having observed the long-term urbanisation of Inner Mongolian pasture areas and the *Heilongjiang* forest areas, we find that the process is accompanied by many challenges. However, this may serve as a reference for the urbanisation work in the next stage.

We have explored the urbanisation of pasture areas in the last section. We will now confine our discussion to the urbanisation of forest areas and their future, based on the examples of *Xiaoxing'anling* forest areas in *Heilongjiang* Province and *Daxiang'anling* forest area in *Heilongjiang* and eastern Inner Mongolia.

3 Construction funds for the urbanisation of state-owned forest land to be raised in multiple ways

The present towns on the vast state-owned forest land in *Daxing'anling* and *Xiaoxing'anling* have been formed over the years due to various reasons. Some were planned by forestry departments in different periods. Others took shape when migrants, including job seekers, the "blind flow", merchants and manual labourers, gathered and built houses and shops, and were completed by the addition of public services facilities. Due to the lack of earlier planning, the latter type tends to be more disorganised, a phenomenon we should try to avoid repeating. In the future we need to revamp and rebuild these towns and, to do so, we must first have a plan in place and carry it out step by step, focusing on refurbishing these towns so that they have agreeable residential and commercial service districts. Additionally, we must also take into consideration the prevention of floods and fire and improvements in public hygiene.

When we were on our way to *Mohe* County by train, we saw many small villages in the forest areas being revamped, rebuilt and expanded, which was commendable. The forestry employees have made great contributions to their industry and they and their families deserve to be resettled in standardised employee new villages instead of living in crude, shed-like houses. This is the shared wish of the research team.

These new villages have the same implications as the "new communities" mentioned in Section 2: urbanisation that fits into our national context consists of old towns, new towns and new communities. According to our observations in *Jiangsu, Henan, Shandong, Tianjin* and *Beijing*, some new socialist villages have sprung up in the rural areas, and these will serve as the template for future new communities. After the farmers resettle in the new villages, they will enjoy better housing conditions. As has been mentioned before, future effort should focus on the following four points. First, we should create more green spaces in the new villages. Second, the new villages should adopt a circular economy, which includes wastewater treatment and recycling, waste disposal and the introduction of the circular economy into agriculture. Third, various public services must be put in place, such as pre-school education, compulsory education, healthcare, water, electricity heat and gas supplies, public transport, cultural facilities, homes for the elderly, retail and sports facilities and financial and postal services; and fourth, we should achieve the integration of the social security systems, abolish the differences in household registration and status and transform the double household registration systems into a single system so that the new socialist villages will naturally turn into new communities, and the new communities will no longer be accompanied by modifiers such as "village" or "farmer". The urbanisation of state-owned forest land is identical to that in the inland rural areas.

Yet, in order that state-owned forest land can adapt to the needs of ownership reform, we need to further consider increasing the number of new towns distributed across the area, because state-owned forest land is sparsely populated, and existing towns are few and unevenly distributed. Therefore, it is necessary to add new ones so that towns can fulfil their political, economic, social and cultural functions. In addition, the industrialisation of forestry, scientific and technological advances in forestry and the application of research results to forest land also call for the addition of new towns. This is a general tendency.

The new towns in state-owned forest areas can be divided into the following three types. The first type refers to the bases for the development of new forestry industry. They adapt to progress in forestry, advances of science and technology and their major achievements. The new towns are built around the industrial bases and consist of residential areas for employees and their families, commercial services districts and complementary facilities such as employee training facilities, research institutions, logistics parks and other domestic and manufacturing services districts. We must come up with a detailed plan before building these new towns, as the construction of factories and towns will destroy part of the forest. A lack of planning would cause irreversible damage to the resources and the ecology.

The second type refers to the mining bases built after the discovery of valuable mineral resources and the towns around them with complementary facilities such as housing for employees and their families, and commercial, domestic and manufacturing service districts. The construction of this type of town also requires regulation to avoid damage to resources and ecology.

The third type refers to newly built towns that improve the management of state-owned forest land and the living standards of employees. Construction here often proceeds through three stages. Stage one, as has been mentioned before, involves building the new village. The sites of new villages for employees should be chosen appropriately to facilitate their daily commute, so that they do not have to live in scattered locations, far away from their workplaces and deal with the inconveniences in their everyday lives. In the second stage, as has also been mentioned before, we can gradually develop the new villages into new communities through the addition of green spaces, the implementation of the circular economy, appropriate public services and the integration of the social security systems; meanwhile, the new communities can emulate those in towns and establish community committees. In the third stage, we can slowly expand the communities and attract more non-state-owned forestry employees and their families to develop commerce, service industry and small businesses. In this way, the new communities will evolve into small towns. This type of new town will have great promise, if state-owned forest land can be reformed into "one land, two ownership systems"; namely, the coexistence of the direct management of state-owned forest land and the household responsibility system in which forest land is contracted to employees.

The first type of new town, which revolves around the bases for new forestry industry and the development of forestry, can raise their construction funds mainly from new forestry industrial enterprises, with some additional support from state-owned forestry departments. The second type of new town, which centres on mining, relies primarily on funds from the mining sector and secondarily on the state-owned forestry departments. As for the third type of new town, which aims at improving the management of state-owned forest land and the living standard of employees, it is only reasonable that it should obtain funds mainly from the state-owned forest land.

4 The urbanisation of collectively owned forest land after its ownership reform

The collectively owned forest land has been transformed into family forest land after the implementation of the forester responsibility system. The foresters welcome urbanisation due to the rapid development of the forest economy. As has been mentioned before, the family forest land owners are accustomed to urban life, and are willing to resettle in towns while continuing to work in the forest. These choices do not conflict and foresters are mentally prepared for this lifestyle. During the research, a forester who contracted collectively owned forest land in *Pengshui* County of *Chongqing* City told us that he would purchase a house in the town for his wife and children while he would in turn live in the countryside and in the town. He thought that this was an excellent arrangement. His neighbour said that the forester did not have to do much work and moreover he had hired a co-worker, his nephew, to help him. We heard many similar stories from contractors during our research in *Wulong* County of *Chongqing* City.

One of the achievements of the ownership reform of collectively owned forest land is the accelerating urbanisation of forest areas, which is reflected in the following three respects.

First, it is easier to deal with the employment problem with urbanisation. The family forest land has more development potential, and the owners of forest land and their family members who move to the new villages, which will gradually be expanded into new communities, already have jobs as either foresters or managers of forest land, so they are not in dire need of employment like the migrant workers. After they settle in new villages or future new communities, they can continue to work on the forest land, or they can stay there during weekdays and spend their vacation in the new communities. As long as roads are good, they can conveniently travel between these two places using private cars, motorcycles and goods and passenger double-service trucks.

Second, manufacturing companies that serve the family forest land will gradually emerge to cater to its needs, providing services such as pest control, the cultivation of new tree species, tree planting, logging and transportation. Similarly, domestic services companies that answer the needs of forest land owners living in the countryside and towns will also appear to provide door-to-door delivery, school drop-off and pick-up services, repair and cleaning. These developments will help ease the concerns of forest land owners and their families about moving to towns.

Third, for the family forest land after the ownership reform of collectively owned forest land, the forest economy will continue to develop. This will fuel the urban economy, including that of old towns, new towns and new communities, thanks to the growing income of foresters, their increasing buying power and changes in their consumption structure. The rise of domestic demand provides the necessary conditions for the advancement of urbanisation and is the backbone of the economic prosperity in the forest areas.

5 The urbanisation of forest areas will substantially advance the two-way integration of urban and rural areas

After the ownership reform of collectively owned forest land, the foresters will have benefitted from the establishment of family forest land and the increase in forestry efficiency and income. This will accelerate the development of collectively owned forests and urbanisation in forest areas, and help transform the one-way integration into a two-way integration of urban and rural areas. The latter will become the general trend. Of course, the transition is gradual and will not happen overnight. It must go through experimental stages in certain cities and counties. After drawing lesson from the results, we can then promote this mode, with government guidance, to the whole country.

The reform of state-owned forest land is underway. While each of the many experimental plans suits a specific situation, the "one land, two ownership systems" model may have wider application. All these plans help to benefit the forest ecology, society and economy, and support the transition from one-way to two-way urban-rural integration. This, too, requires experimentation, study and government guidance before it can be promoted.

The driving force behind the two-way urban-rural integration is the special role of forest areas in a low-carbon economy. The experience of Western developed market economies shows that urban-rural integration is not a one-way but a two-way process, in which not only are rural residents willing and able to move into cities freely, but urban residents can also migrate to the countryside as well. They are free to make their own decisions with few restrictions. From the economic perspective, this means that they can make free decisions after comparing employment, investment and income prospects in urban and rural areas. From the perspective of quality of life, they will take into consideration the differences in living standards. It is reasonable that urban residents do not want to remain in cities with inferior natural or social quality of life, including bad public security, overcrowding and traffic congestion. There is no doubt that natural quality of life is superior in forest areas, thanks to the fresh air and low-carbon environment. These factors cater to the needs of urban residents and it is understandable that they are inclined to move to resettle on the forest land.

Two-way urban-rural integration is not limited to enterprises that reach out to the countryside. Enterprises or private investors are willing to bring capital and technology to the countryside and rent a piece of land for commercial or industrial use, or as bases for animal, vegetable or fruit farming. Yet, this only covers part of the two-way integration. The voluntary choice of urban residents, including retired workers, to move to the countryside for tranquil, clean and beautiful living environment can better reflect the two-way urban-rural integration. In *Huairou* and *Pinggu* Districts of *Beijing*, we can see some retired employees who used to live in the old town rent houses in the countryside to enjoy their sunset years. Some even rent land to grow vegetables and fruit and to raise chickens. These activities, they think, can save on living costs, and moreover they are enjoyable and beneficial to their health.

In fact, with cleaner air, better scenery and a more tranquil environment, small towns and their neighbourhoods in the forest areas may be more attractive than those in rural areas. As long as there is a good transportation system and adequate supplies of goods as in other towns, urban residents may very well prefer the forest towns and their neighbourhoods to those in the rural areas.

People often ask whether or not the urbanisation of forest areas, and especially two-way urban-rural integration, will damage the ecological balance, reduce the size of forests, accelerate deforestation and consequently harm the economy. After researching in some new villages (future new communities) in the forest areas and investigating the management situation in family forest land after the ownership reform of collectively owned forest land, we find that deforestation may happen but can be prevented by strict regulation. We will summarise our findings as follows.

First, since the ownership reform of collectively owned forest land, there have always been strict regulations to protect the forests. The key is contracting mountain forest to the households. The long-term income increase from forest land encourages foresters to care more about the growth and maintenance of trees, and changes the short-sighted way of gaining wealth by logging. The foresters have realised the long-term benefits of the forest land, including the increase in income, and so they have a solid grasp of the importance of maintaining the forest. If the trees grow better, the forest economy will thrive and in turn support the growth of trees. This is a positive, mutually supportive relationship which the foresters understand through their practice. This further incentivises foresters to maintain and protect the forest land.

Second, there are strict regulations on logging, including fixed indices and quotas that must not be breached. The combination of strict management and the initiatives of the foresters to maintain family forest land provide effective protection of the forest.

Third, the choice of appropriate sites for new communities and the expansion of existing towns must be included in the general plan, and the use of land must not be changed arbitrarily. In other words, forest land and construction land must be clearly defined. If due to construction needs some forests have to be destroyed, there should be a strict approval process in place.

Fourth, there must be adequate reasons for the expansion of small towns, such as improving the housing conditions of the residents or building public facilities. No individual or enterprise can expand the amount of construction land at will.

Of course, the construction of new towns and the expansion of existing ones require reasonable and scientific planning, and, most importantly, must follow strict procedures and regulations. In this way, the urbanisation of forest areas will not come at the cost of environmental protection.

Note

1 People's Government of *Hailasu* County, Ongniud Banner, "Report Material on the Construction of Small Towns", August 2011.

7   Independent innovation and industrial upgrading

Section 1 Originality, innovation and entrepreneurship

1 Originality, invention and innovation

It is often said that invention is a scientist's business; innovation, that of an entrepreneur; and originality, that of a talent. The saying is usually appropriate but may not be so conventional. From a practical point of view, originality always precedes invention and innovation: any invention and innovation begin with originality, and any breakthrough resides in originality.

Originality is embodied in advanced concepts and leading designs. A real achievement is to design a new product, a new process flow or a new technology that no one else has ever created or even dared to imagine. What is a talent? A talent is a person with originality who leads invention and innovation by his imagination and practice. Only an enterprise with originality can indeed seize the commanding heights of its industry and field. So can it lead the trend of the industry or field?

In this sense, a person with originality is himself an outstanding inventor. Certainly, not all people with original ideas are inventors. It is likely that they only provide the original idea or remain at the stage of providing a new idea or design. It needs an inventor to turn the idea into a "finished product" and present it to the users. An invention needs to be beneficial to economic activities and needs to be promoted. Without the efforts of entrepreneurs, research findings will remain in laboratories rather than have a significant impact on the economy. It is an entrepreneur's performances that change the nature of production and leads to changes in people's lives.

A person with an original idea can become an inventor, and an inventor can become an entrepreneur. However, there are not many who are both inventors and entrepreneurs. There are several cases where a man with an original idea is also an inventor and entrepreneur. Similarly, by various means, an entrepreneur can also turn another person's original idea and inventions into his own. Of course, these must be accomplished without breaking the law. Everyone should respect other people's research outcomes and their intellectual property rights. It should be a win-win or an all-win scenario.

Starting a business involves converting original ideas into an invention, then turning it into innovation and finally implementing it in the market. The achievements of entrepreneurship are showcased in one or many market entities which possess core competitiveness and intellectual property rights and can capture and expand their market. That is to say, the ultimate result of originality, invention and innovation is an enterprise that provides society with new products, equipment and manufacturing techniques. The history of technology is also the history of the successes of numerous enterprises amid competition and monopolies (technological and market monopolies). A person with an original idea is important. So is an inventor or innovator. However, the most important of all is the entrepreneur. When China moves toward modernisation through a dual transformation, there is a short supply of persons with original ideas, inventors and especially outstanding entrepreneurs.

An entrepreneur must understand that he should not be good only at management but also in operation since the operation is more important than management. Management and operation are two different concepts. For an entrepreneur, management involves how to effectively allocate the limited human, physical and financial resources and how to raise production and resource allocation efficiency under the given stock conditions so as to increase profit margins. Operation targets at an increase in increment capital, seeking to increase the aggregate capital value of existing stock. The more the capital increases, the better an entrepreneur has achieved his objectives. A good entrepreneur values both management and operation but emphasise operation. Thus is the path to entrepreneurship.

Note that an entrepreneur needs to develop a market for his products while such a market can be created. Not only a market itself but also shares of the products in it can expand. Creating a market mainly relies on management and operation rather than operation alone. Although some experts hold that management is the foundation, innovative use of capital and increasing stock value count on the operation. A business will not have a promising future if management is divorced from entrepreneurship. It is a pity that many Chinese entrepreneurs have not grasped the principle yet.

2 Invention, innovation and entrepreneurship's demand for appropriate institutional environments

Profit margins are crucial for an enterprise, regardless of whether it is a joint-stock company, partnership or a family-based single proprietorship. The decline in profit margins or even losses will give rise to discontent among its investors, and as a result, the manager will lose their trust. Thus, when profit margins decline in successive years, an enterprise must locate the reasons behind the decline.

In fact, that is closely related to where an enterprise sits in the value chain with upper and lower ends. If an enterprise sits at the lower end and becomes a simple processor of products, a large portion of profits will go to other enterprises with original ideas and innovations since intellectual property rights belong to them. Such an enterprise ordinarily receives processing fees, but the room for profit margins in processing is narrow.

Thus, to increase profit, an enterprise with vision, ambition and strength must rely on independent innovation, accelerate industrial upgrading and obtain their intellectual property rights. The enterprise should try its best to occupy the upper end of the value chain. The situation of competition in the modern market is, "only the most excellent can survive and have a promising future", which means that those less desirable enterprises will be excluded and eliminated from the market. Given this difficult situation, the market is in the hands of top enterprises. Only those that seize the commanding position of an industry and operate at the high end of the value chain can become the trendsetter in an industry or field.

Enterprises should also be aware that occupying the top of the value chain will help improve the overall quality of the whole industry and result in mutual benefits. That is because all companies in the same industry are not only competing but also cooperating with each other by providing complementary and reciprocal services. Thus, the more a company achieves in independent innovation, the faster assets recombination will proceed in an industry or a field, thereby enhancing the overall quality of the industry. If a company is a forerunner in a field, it is more likely to incite other related companies in the value chain to upgrade and transform spontaneously. Of course, we cannot exclude the possibility that new competitors will emerge in the same industry; however, this is not a bad thing for the national economy.

That shows us from another perspective that no enterprise should be satisfied with its current situation in creativity, invention, innovation and entrepreneurship. Instead, all enterprises need to keep moving forward on their existing bases instead of being complacent.

Nevertheless, it is necessary to have a proper institutional support for this to happen. We will analyse this from the following five respects.

First, there should be a system that enables market entities to make investment decisions. Innovation and entrepreneurship both need investment. After successful innovation and some achievements, more investment is needed to expand the production scale. If a market entity does not have decision-making authority, it will miss the best opportunities due to the complex review procedures and belated approvals from the government. As a result, innovation and entrepreneurship will not yield actual results or increases in market share.

As a result, administrative approval procedures need to be simplified and governmental intervention reduced. As long as a market entity meets the national industrial policy, it should be allowed to make decisions. This will greatly encourage innovation and entrepreneurship in a market entity.

Second, there should be a fair and competitive market environment, especially without discrimination based on ownership and enterprise scale. Many market entities are conducting research and development and are ready to put their new designs into practice. They should share the same platform and have fair competition. Discrimination based on ownership and enterprise scale should be abolished. In a fair environment, enterprises share the same starting point and achieve different results due to competition.

Third, the government should have a complete set of favourable policies and measures in taxation, credit and incentives that help innovators and entrepreneurs.

By national economic development strategies and industrial policies, the government should treat enterprises in different industries, fields and regions differently and according to their degrees of priority. However, it must not neglect the following premise: all enterprises should be treated fairly without discrimination against their ownership and enterprise scale. They should be given support, concessions and incentives according to their innovative and entrepreneurial contributions as well as their role in the national economy.

Fourth, there should be a rigorous set of laws, rules and regulations regarding the protection of intellectual property rights. The lack of laws, rules and regulations that protect intellectual property rights is a serious blow to innovators and entrepreneurs. What is even more detrimental is that laws are not followed or fully enforced and that lawbreakers are not prosecuted. In this way, innovators and entrepreneurs would lose their confidence, which in turn would cause immeasurable damage to the national economy. Thus, the protection of intellectual property rights must be fully implemented to support innovation and entrepreneurship.

Fifth, there should be a property rights sharing system within an enterprise that encourages innovation and entrepreneurship. According to the experience of innovative overseas enterprises, such a system is an effective incentive. Enterprises adopt property rights sharing systems to motivate employees, research and development professionals in particular. In this way, both professionals and other employees can buy shares in the enterprise at an agreed-upon price over a given period of time, or employees who make contributions to the enterprise can be rewarded with certain shares. As a result, a wave of independent innovation will occur within the enterprise, creating a capable research development team, who will put forward valuable original ideas and contribute to the invention, innovation and entrepreneurship.

From the analysis above, we can draw the conclusion that a proper institutional environment is necessary for innovation and entrepreneurship.

3 Upgrading China's manufacturing industry

Manufacturing is the most important industry for major industrialised countries. Due to the effort over the past hundred years, China has finally become a global manufacturing centre, which is a momentous event worth celebration and the Chinese are proud of this achievement. We must not be convinced by those who claim that this is not beneficial to China as this gives China's cheap labour and resource-consuming products away to Western developed countries, and lets them enjoy real benefits. How can this be? Being a global manufacturing centre is a milestone for China. We need to put continuous efforts into making China a global centre of innovation. Meanwhile, we must not give up its status as a global manufacturing centre. It takes time to become a global innovation centre and prior to that, a large country like China has to become a global manufacturing centre.

However, some problems remain to be resolved in China's manufacturing sector.

First, costs, primarily the cost of wages, are increasing. Increases in wage costs are inevitable because once a certain level of industrialisation is reached, it is abnormal for wage costs to remain low. Other costs are also rising, such as the cost of land, factory building or renting, raw materials, fuel and transportation. This is due to slow supply growth and continuous strong demand, and it is a common phenomenon as industrialisation advances. Be that as it may, rising costs in manufacturing industry remain a difficult issue for Chinese enterprises.

Second, some in China's manufacturing have dropped due to the fierce international competition and the impact of the recent international situation, namely the stagnant market in some developed countries. In recent years, China's manufacturing industry has been increasingly struggling in the export markets due to the American financial crisis and the ensuing European debt crisis. Some manufactured goods such as textile products and food in light industries have suffered from falling orders due to competition from countries in Southeast Asia.

Third, China's manufacturing industry has long been at the low and middle ends of the value chain where profit margins are low. China's manufacturers are in a difficult situation. That suggests that manufacturers at the high end of the value chain will perform well under unfavourable economic conditions while companies at the low-middle end of the value chain will face more difficulties. This rule applies not only to China's manufacturing sector but also to that of other countries.

Fourth, China's manufacturing industry faces a financial strain and struggles to acquire funding, upgrade technology and seek development. These problems often beset China's manufacturing companies. Why is it so hard to raise funds? Generally speaking, it is due to the following two reasons. On the one hand, China strengthened its control over money supply by issuing a macroeconomic policy two years ago, making it difficult for manufacturers to obtain loans. On the other hand, China's manufacturing companies faced a difficult time and an uncertain future due to thin profit margins and competition from countries in Southeast Asia, which causes financial institutions to adopt a cautious lending approach to domestic manufacturing companies for fear of greater risks. As a result, private manufacturing enterprises shift away from this industry to overseas investments or virtual economies such as real estate speculation.

Fifth, due to the lack of internationally famous brands, Chinese manufacturing industries require popularity in the global market. Precisely because of this, Chinese manufacturing enterprises, especially those producing daily necessities, have low profit, which comes mainly from processing. A possible reason behind this is that China's manufacturing enterprises have neglected the cultivation of their brands. However, building a global brand can never be achieved in a short time.

Based on the above analyses, we can say with certainty that the hope for China's manufacturing industry lies in independent innovation and industrial upgrading. In every market economy, an enterprise is its market entity. Independent innovation and industrial upgrading both rest on the market entity. Enterprises, whether they are state share-involved, state, privately or mixed ownership, all have the responsibility to achieve independent innovation and industrial upgrading. The government should play the role of a planner, facilitator and coordinator, giving support to related companies in strict accordance with industrial policies, and treat each enterprise by the principle of fair competition.

There are three key points regarding the independent innovation and industrial upgrading of China's manufacturing industry.

First, we should enable some advanced manufacturing enterprises to move from the low and middle end to the high end of the value chain through independent innovation and industrial upgrading. However, this does not mean that we should overlook enterprises at the low and middle end of the value chain since those at the high end need partners from the low and middle end. Additionally, employment pressure has been high and deserved our attention. Much of the workforce needs to be absorbed by the low- and middle-end manufacturing enterprises. The manufacturing enterprises at the high end of the value chain are not necessarily large-scale sectors but they must be able to take the lead in technology.

Second, the independent innovation and industrial upgrading of the manufacturing industry must be administered by the optimisation and adjustment of industrial structures. We should solve the following problem as a whole at this stage in China: how should we promote the development of sectors with supply shortages and boost the supply of rare products? How should we deal with overcapacity? How should we achieve the return of capital to the real economy, especially to manufacturing sectors?

Third, labour-intensive small and medium enterprises at the lower end of the value chain also need independent innovation but how they create innovation remains to be discussed. As mentioned before, we once inspected some coastal cities and towns after the American financial crisis and held symposiums on independent innovation in small and medium enterprises. The experience of those enterprises can be summarised as follows. They innovated product designs and techniques, added new functions to products, selected raw materials with care, paid attention to energy conservation and emission reductions and cooperated with other companies in the same field to develop new products. It is clear that even small and medium manufacturing enterprises showed promise in terms of innovation and entrepreneurship.

4 Market prospects of China's manufacturing industry

When evaluating the market prospects of China's manufacturing industry, we should first avoid pessimism and remain confident and optimistic that the future of China's manufacturing industry will be promising, as long as it focuses on independent innovation and industrial upgrading. Also, we should notice the following points.

First, the manufacturing industry worldwide still has significant room for development, which Chinese enterprises can take advantage of international competitiveness, which is both an opportunity and a challenge for the Chinese enterprises. As long as China's manufacturing companies put in great effort, there are opportunities for further development. There is no reason for us to lose heart in this competition.

Second, rising costs such as increases in wages have always been alleviated by technological breakthroughs. They have not only reduced costs but also helped to build up a brand. A brand requires support from continuous innovation and it will serve as a key to opening new markets.

Third, to exploit new markets at home and abroad, apart from making considerable efforts in independent innovation and industrial upgrading, China's manufacturing enterprises also need to focus on marketing and pre- and after-sales services. New product supply can also boost demand. Market share can be increased by upgrading existing products and introducing new and attractive ones. We should value and motivate our research and development personnel as well as those who work in marketing and sales, since the latter play an equally important role in market development.

Fourth, domestic manufacturers, whether state, privately or mixed-owned, should work together in the cooperative development and form a win-win situation. Manufacturers with different ownership types have different advantages in exploring the market. For example, a state-owned manufacturing enterprise usually boasts its large scale, sufficient capital and abundant human resources. A privately owned manufacturing enterprise tends to be more flexible. It is more willing to take risks, making independent decisions and facing its losses and profits by itself. As for mixed-owned manufacturers, their flexibility and independence in decision-making are determined by their shareholding structures.

Generally speaking, state-owned, privately owned and mixed-owned companies have the following four cooperative modes to develop new products and technologies.

First, the vertical mode also called the industry chain mode, which means that enterprises with a diverse ownership and scale exist in an industry chain of a specific manufacturing industry. Some enterprises are willing to cooperate to address the weak links in the industry chain. Once progress is performed, it will not only help eliminate bottlenecks in the industry chain but also benefit all other enterprises in the chain.

Second, the horizontal mode also called the counterpart mode, which means that enterprises with different ownerships and scales make similar products in a specific manufacturing sector. Among them, some enterprises would like to cooperate with their counterparts to address the weak links in the industry. If progress is made, it will help eliminate bottlenecks and common challenges in the industry.

Third, the subsidiary mode means that complementary state-owned, privately owned or mixed-owned enterprises create an assistant company together based on mutual consultation and joint funding. This subsidiary will be concentrated on research and development to deal with the technical problems in manufacturing.

Fourth, the state establishes a certain key national project and invites tender from various manufacturing companies, research institutions and even higher education institutions. Or, the state can divide a key project into several subprojects and let tenders compete for them. That is a cooperative mode that combines production, teaching and research. This cooperation can also be achieved by establishing research colleges or institutes which will then operate conventionally.

In short, there are various cooperative modes in technological innovation, whether it is cooperation between enterprises or a combination of research, teaching and research. As long as there are manufacturing companies, goods and brands from China in the global market, it will not matter whether these are related to state-owned or privately owned companies.

5 Embracing challenges by applying China's strengths and avoiding our weakness

We should be clearly aware that the global manufacturing market has become increasingly competitive with countless strong competitors. As mentioned before, in the face of significant competitive pressure, we can only ensure the future of China's manufacturing industry by encouraging independent innovation and industrial upgrading and shifting from a low-middle to a high-end value chain. In the following part, we will further analyse the strategy of "applying our strengths and avoiding our weaknesses".

It took China's manufacturing industry more than 30 years, or an even longer period, of continuous effort to become the global manufacturing centre. In retrospect, there have been three major phases of China's export trade.

The earliest phase featured agricultural, mineral, light industry and textile product exports. During that phase, no other manufactured goods except those from the light textile industry could be exported.

In the second phase, the principal exports became mechanical products from the manufacturing industry. That was an important change for a developing country because it signified that China had started to transform from an agricultural to an industrial society. Although the mechanical products were of inferior quality during this phase, they were inexpensive and sold well. Some developed market economies also imported Chinese mechanical products, like lathes. They used the lathes as raw material, added some high-end equipment to them and then exported the finished product for profits.

In the third phase, China's import and export trade focused on electronic and high-tech products. This indicated that China had entered the middle phase of industrialisation, with exports that corresponded to this phase. China's electronic goods and high-tech products were not only exported to some developing countries but also to emerging and even some developed market economies. The achievements of independent innovation and industrial upgrading in China's manufacturing industry were shown in the upgraded export products themselves.

Apparently, China's manufacturing industry and the overall manufacturing level have seen rapid development. China's manufacturing development strategy that we have adopted over the years can be briefly summarised as "applying our strengths and avoiding our weaknesses".

The strategy of "applying our strengths and avoiding our weaknesses" means that we should not only consider the objective situation where numerous strong competitors exist in the global manufacturing market but also take into account the features and direction of development of China's manufacturing industry. In the past 30 years, we have made significant achievements. In the future, we should adhere to this development strategy and face the challenges of the global manufacturing market.

First, we need to grasp the meaning of "applying our strengths and avoiding our weaknesses". What on earth do the eight characters mean? What are "our strengths" and "our weaknesses" in their worthy names? A flawed understanding will mislead China's manufacturing industry.

Where are our "strengths"? For a long period of time, the abundant cheap labour force in China had always been considered as "our strengths". This opinion needs to be scrutinised. As will be elaborated in Section 3 of this chapter on the new and old population dividends, we cannot rely on cheap labour any longer for the following reasons. First, wage costs are rising. Second, migrant workers from rural areas are unwilling to take up low-wage jobs. Third, the birth rate is falling, and the population is ageing faster and, as a result, enterprises struggles to find suitable workers. Therefore, to some extent, the abundant cheap workforce is no longer an advantage of China's manufacturing industry.

In addition, for a long period of time in the past, China's manufactured goods had another "strength". That is, Chinese export products were sold on the low-end foreign market that catered to customers with limited purchasing power. Although this "strength" is unlikely to disappear for the moment, its significance is fading with the changing global competition. If Chinese manufacturing enterprises still believe that they are as popular among customers as they used to be, they should be warned that the situation will not last long because similar products in Southeast Asian countries are squeezing Chinese products out of the low-end market, In addition, China is finding it difficult for its products to enter the high-end consumer goods market in large quantities. If we still mistakenly take the above situation to be a durable advantage, we will mislead China's manufacturing enterprises.

Thus, in the future, we need to "focus on our strengths". What exactly are "our strengths"? In manufacturing, our strengths lie in the following three aspects. First, owing to independent innovation and industrial upgrading, the strength of China's manufacturing lies in its advanced technologies, the high-end position on the value chain and the upgrading of our brands

Second, due to professional and technical training, another strength of China's manufacturing industry is its adept technical workers who are hardworking, disciplined, highly skilled and competent. On the one hand, these technical workers have much better skills than the workforce from common developing countries. On the other hand, they have lower wages than their counterparts from Western developed countries.

Third, owing to innovations in marketing and improvement of pre- and after-sales services, the strengths of China's manufacturing industry include not only its versatility and flexibility in meeting the various demands of different markets but also the dedicated and meticulous pre- and after-sales services that satisfy foreign customers at different levels.

Next, we will discuss how to "avoid our weaknesses". We should have a clear understanding of the meaning of this phrase when facing global manufacturing competition shortly.

First, the manufacturing industry is a trade with a broad territory and great diversity. A country cannot ensure that all its products and trades are in advanced positions. Not all of its products may enjoy some advantages in the market, no matter how advanced the technology of a country is, how low the costs are and how dedicated and meticulous the pre- and post-sales services are. China is no exception. As a result, we must objectively evaluate the weak points of China's manufacturing in the global market. Here is the meaning of "our weak points". We should acknowledge these weaknesses rather than pose as a hero and devote great effort to overcoming them instead of turning a blind eye. On the other hand, we should not feel discouraged because we still have time to catch up and there are many examples where newcomers surpass the forerunners.

Second, according to the principle of trade, an increase in the number of global competitors will result in more countries and regions being involved in the global market. A significant number of countries and regions can serve as potential markets for China's manufactured goods and possible venues for setting up branches of China's manufacturing enterprises. However, do we have sufficient knowledge of the local people and their customs and practices? Are we familiar with their laws, taxation, customer behaviours and fashions? All of these factors may differ substantially from ours. It is often said: "Do not wade into water unless you know how deep it is". Our insufficient knowledge of the foreign market is our weak point. A lack of preliminary research and a good understanding of local laws and taxation will result in losses. We avoid our weak points in order to avoid risks.

However, avoiding our weak points does not mean that we dare not explore new markets or compete with strong participants in the global manufacturing market. That is to a large extent similar to how sports competitions work. Consider the example of table tennis. Soon after the founding of the People's Republic of China, the Chinese table tennis team was at a disadvantage, and their skills were not as good as that of other countries. How did we overcome this? Had we been afraid of defeat and only played against weak teams, our skills would never have improved. It was by frequently competing against stronger teams that our table tennis players gradually improved. The same applies to market competitions. Our strengths can be displayed in competition fields and promoted to another level. Likewise, it is only in competition fields that our weaknesses are improved and our weaknesses turn to be our strengths. Herein lies the hope of China's manufacturing companies.

Section 2 Industrial shifts and upgrading

1 Undertaking industrial shifts as a development opportunity for less-developed regions

The shift of industry between regions is a common phenomenon in industrialisation and mainly occurs to processing and manufacturing sectors. Shifts in those industries may occur between regions or even across national borders. The reasons behind this include not only administrative efficiency but also increases in costs. Enterprises that extract resources also face the issue of shifting their business to new areas due to the depletion of resources and difficulties in deep mining (e.g. high mining costs or technological limits). In this case, follow-up industries should be developed in resource-depleted regions to alleviate local unemployment, increase local government revenues and sustain economic growth. However, that is not the focus of this section. This section will discuss shifts in the processing and manufacturing industries and other related issues.

During cost-push inflation, it is increasingly necessary for industries to shift to less-developed regions. As to enterprises, they need to reduce the costs of labour, land, house purchases and uses and logistics. From a macroeconomic perspective, industry shifts present a chance to optimise the allocation of resources between regions.

There are various reasons for rising labour costs. These include increases in wage costs due to rising living costs in developed regions, a shortage of technical workers, insufficient labour supply and the promotion and implementation of social security measures. Generally speaking, wage costs in economically developed regions are higher than those in less-developed regions, so the shifts of industry from developed to less-developed regions are in line with the economic principle. The shortage of technical workers and general labour force can be understood as new situations that are part of the economic development. In recent years, technical workers and general labourers tend to work nearby because they believe that if they take jobs far away from their hometowns, they will be separated from their spouses and unable to take care of their children and the elderly. In contrast, if they take jobs in the nearby areas, they will not only have incomes but can also take care of their families and save on living costs. Conversely, if their spouses, children and elderly are brought over to the developed cities, expenses become unaffordable. In addition, people increasingly prefer opening their businesses and being bosses themselves to working for others. Capable villagers and skilled craftsmen who are good at management and running businesses prefer to open workshops and factories in cities and towns rather than become employees. This also weakens the shift of technical workers and the common workforce to developed regions.

It is understandable that under these circumstances, enterprises in developed areas, especially labour-intensive enterprises, will shift their companies from developed regions to less-developed ones, including shifting from developed coastal cities to less-developed inland cities in order to survive, develop and reduce wage costs. That is a great opportunity for less-developed regions, and they should make the most of this shift.

The second factor of the cost that promotes a regional industrial shift is for enterprises to reduce costs of land use, property purchase and construction. The increases in land and housing prices are not only the result of demand-pull inflation but also the cause of cost-push inflation. Rising land prices will increase property values, the living costs of workers and ultimately the wages. Rising housing costs means that enterprises also need to pay higher rents for factories, shops and office buildings. By comparison, the land and property prices in counties and cities in less-developed regions are lower than those in developed regions, which is also an important cause for enterprise to shift regions. When existing enterprises need to expand, or when investors plan to set up new processing and manufacturing factories, land prices, house construction costs and demolition costs are factors that enterprises give more concerns.

The third factor of the cost that causes a regional industrial shift is to reduce logistics costs. In recent years, enterprises have faced an increasing proportion of logistics costs in the total costs regarding raw material and fuel supply and the transportation of the finished products from enterprises to the market. Thus, enterprises will decide whether a shift is necessary by making a comprehensive analysis of the distance between their locations, the origins of the raw material and fuel and the place where the finished products are sold, and the transportation costs. Taking a long-term view, enterprises will consider it important to expand their markets. Industrial shifts should not only focus on the reduction of logistics costs but also take into account the benefits from expanded markets. If venues after relocation are close to raw materials, fuel supply and a potentially large market, the decision of shifts will be justified. Compared with logistics costs after relocation, a future market is more important. However, if logistics cost can be reduced after relocation, the shift will be more appealing to enterprises.

2 Advantages of less-developed regions in undertaking industrial shifts

Less-developed regions as receivers of industrial shifts usually abound in human, land and mineral resources, which are advantages of these regions. They should make good use of these advantages to undertake industrial shifts. That being said, it is important to note that, until now, these advantages have been to a great extent potentials waiting to be realised. So, an important task at present is to gradually transform these potential advantages into actual ones.

To realise those potential advantages requires capital, technology and talents. Capital can be introduced from the outside or raised locally; technology and talents can be introduced or provided, selected or cultivated locally. The key is to find the way to accomplish this. Commonly, it depends, first, on the system, and then on policy and the credibility of the government. In addition, it requires local infrastructures and a good environment for work, study and everyday life. For both introduced talents and those cultivated locally, working environments, living conditions for their families and the employment conditions for their children are equally important, without which it would be difficult for them to remain in their positions for long.

To change potential resource advantages into actual advantages, the system and policy are of primary importance. The system plays an especially significant role. It determines the policy released, and a good system will make sure that officials who are efficient, honouring government credibility and law-abiding will take important positions and have more impact. What is particularly noteworthy regarding system and policy is the protection of property rights (including intellectual property rights). Clearly defined and well-protected property rights are crucial if we are to introduce and accumulate capital, apply technologies, encourage innovation, and employ and cultivate talents.

Resources such as land, mineral, water, tourism and the wind can all be transformed into capital. Since resources can generate future benefits, the transformation from resources to capital means exchanging future resources for present capital investments. Take the construction of a highway for example. An investor would like to raise funds to construct a highway since he will be rewarded with years of road toll rights after the completion of the construction. Take the renovation of inner cities as another example. Property developers will gain from the remaining land after the renovation, so they would like to finance the renovation and expansion of the inner cities and then the renovation can be carried out. Similarly, the construction of new cities and industrial and logistics parks also exemplify the transformation from resources into capital. It is a model of market operation. The less-developed areas that are ready to receive industrial shifts from developed regions can follow this practice to turn resource to capital.

In the course of undertaking industrial shifts, less-developed regions must pay attention to ecological protection and environmental remediation instead of pursuing short-term benefits at the cost of environments. It is not only feasible but also effective in some areas to build industrial parks, commercial service zones and logistics parks to facilitate industrial shifts. The benefits of establishing those parks include the following:

First, those parks and zones make it easier for the governments to provide centralised services and reduce the intermediaries between government departments and enterprises. This both saves time and increases work efficiency because the governments and park management serve enterprises. Management is a form of service.

Second, not only relocated enterprises but also newly established and expanded businesses enter the parks. Being in the same park, they can exchange information faster, which creates more business opportunities.

Third, the parks and zones boost the efficient use of infrastructure, energy, heating, land and transportation. To enterprises, this means saving costs, while to the government, it means rationalisation of resource allocation.

Fourth, as mentioned earlier, parks and zones are conducive to environmental protection and remediation. If pollution is decentralised, its remediation will be more challenging and costly. From another perspective, by allowing shifts of enterprises into industrial parks, the regions receiving industrial shifts can have more efficient supervision over how these enterprises take appropriate measures to deal with sewage, exhaust gases, waste residues and reduce the discharge amount of carbon dioxide.

Less-developed regions have their advantages when receiving industrial shifts from developed regions. People only pay attention to resource advantages since they are on the surface, thus easy to be identified and utilised. As a matter of fact, their advantages are not restricted to However, apart from resources, there are other advantages in less-developed regions. Compared with the substantial potential advantages of resources, the following two late-developing advantages are more important and appealing.

First, less-developed regions can adopt the experience of developed regions and learn from their industrial development. That is one of the late-developing advantages of less-developed regions. Apart from this, less-developed regions should also try to find structural measures, that is, reforms of unreasonable existing systems in order to make breakthroughs in undertaking industrial shifts and upgrading. Note that in the process of deepening reforms, reforms of existing systems in industrially developed regions are much harder than those in less-developed regions. In other words, the less-developed regions that undertake industrial shifts are more likely to make progress towards economic system reforms. It is especially so for the pilot zones in Western and Central China. From a dynamic perspective, less-developed regions can pave the way for the introduction of the companies in the developed regions by reforming the irrational economic systems during industrial shifts.

Second, the late-developing advantages of the less-developed areas also lie in the great potential market which has not been effectively developed yet. On the one hand, these areas rely on low production costs to attract enterprises waiting for shifts and, on the other hand, they will, in the long run, attract those enterprises with their markets which are of great potential and wait to be exploited. The development of potential markets depends on increased individuals' purchasing power. If employment in less-developed areas increases during the process of shifts, the rural-urban income gap will be narrowed, and farmers' income will be increased. As a result, individuals' purchasing power will gradually rise, and the market will definitely and gradually expand. Meanwhile, there will be increases in local revenues and funds for local construction and urbanisation will accelerate. All of these have positive impacts on the market expansion in less-developed regions.

3 Conditions to be created for less-developed regions undertaking industrial shifts

Generally speaking, the urgent issues for less-developed regions to address in undertaking industrial shifts now and in the near future include the following: improving the quality of the labour force; integrating rural and urban lands; cultivating local private entrepreneurs; developing local finance, especially rural finance; and creating favourable cultural environments.

(1) Improving the quality of labour force

As mentioned before, the primary reason for some industries to shift from developed to less-developed regions is to reduce employment costs and hire qualified workers at a relatively lower wage cost. However, the reality is often that while less-developed regions have a greater labour supply than developed regions, the quality tends to be inferior. As a result, the advantage of lower wage costs is nullified by the inferior quality of labour and does more harm than good to enterprises shifting to less-developed regions.

Nevertheless, this will not prevent enterprise shifting from developed to less-developed regions because the poor quality of the labour force in less-developed regions can be remedied or improved. For example, during the process of the industrial shift, enterprises can provide technique training for recruited local employees as early as possible so that they can improve their technical skills and meet the corporate standards for workers. It is worthwhile for companies to pay the technique training fees. In addition, enterprises can transfer their original core staff, including skilled technical workers, operators in charge and experienced employees, to the industrial shift destinations, so that the enterprises can retain their technical advantages and the established unique features in management and marketing. For core employees to settle into their new working conditions, it may require extra costs, such as subsidies to those who move with the enterprises, and the rents or construction fees of the dormitory for core employees and their families. Nevertheless, these are worthwhile.

What is important is that labour supply in less-developed regions will remain strong for a long time in the near future, which is determined by China's national conditions, and also by the urban-rural binary system and the urbanisation process. Remarks such as "The age of China's cheap labour force has come to an end", "China's demographic dividends have been exhausted", and "The age of China's blue-collar workers is gone forever" do not conform to the reality in China. It is difficult to recruit young labourers in some cities of developed regions. That is because the majority of the local labour force already have their jobs as workers, farmers, businessmen or owners of small workshops. At the same time, young labourers outside the developed regions are unwilling to come to work because they think that the salary is not enough to meet local living costs, which is not economical. Moreover, they prefer working nearby to enjoy convenient family get-togethers to staying far away from their native homes and families for a long term. From a corporate perspective, enterprises prefer to hire migrant workers with a comparatively better education background, such as graduates from high schools or vocational and technical schools. This indicates that the era of a low-quality labour force has come to an end because their employment prospect is becoming increasingly limited. By contrast, the era of skilled technical workers has just begun in China. China is facing an era in which large numbers of low-quality workers need to be transformed into skilled ones. The governments in less-developed regions should be clearly aware of this situation, take advantage of it, continue to make good use of the regional advantages of an abundant labour force and make significant efforts to develop vocational and technical education to improve labour quality. In this way, they can prepare themselves for the upcoming era of skilled workers and industrial shifts.

(2) Centralised planning of urban and rural land

The key to unified development planning is the centralised planning of urban and rural land. This is in line with the national conditions of China. China has limited farmland resources. The utilisation rate of contracted land is low because farmers and young labourers leave their native lands and become migrant workers, which causes the following dilemma. On the one hand, the land supply is restricted or limited in urban areas. On the other hand, the land is idle, and yields are low in rural areas. While advancing urbanisation, the core issues of urban and rural centralised planning are circulation, re-planning and full utilisation of the land.

According to the experience of some areas (including developed and less-developed regions), after the circulation of contracted land and the replacement of home steads, a portion of rural house sites designated as rural construction land were vacated by farmers moving to new areas and reused as farmland. This expands the area of the farmland. The additional farmland can be turned through quota trades into urban construction land suitable for developing industries, commercial services, logistics and urban residential areas. In this way, we will not break the "red line" of the arable land. At the same time, we will be able to provide land for industrial parks, commercial service zones, logistics parks and residential areas. That will provide the necessary support and land for the less-developed regions that receive industrial shifts.

The centralised planning of urban and rural land also benefits agricultural development. In the future, there will remain some individual farmers in the countryside who would rather stay in the villages and manage their small plots of contracted farmland rather than migrate to cities. There will always be such individuals. We should respect their wishes as well as their land contract rights. However, apart from the individual farmers, three other categories of agriculture will further develop in the future. The first category refers to farming experts and large plantation households. They farm productively and are willing to do it. When farmers nearby leave the rural areas for work or business, those farming experts and large plantation households collect their contracted land by subcontracting or leasing and begin large-scale farming. The second category refers to specialised farmer cooperatives. Farmers voluntarily organise these cooperatives. To create a large-scale organisation, farmers contribute their farmland as shares. These cooperatives publicise their accounts, have democratic management and increase the land utilisation rate. The third category refers to agricultural enterprises. They contract or rent a certain area of the wasteland, sandy land, saline-alkali land, beach land or low-yield fields. Afterwards, they use high technology to convert them into arable land with increasing yields or into construction land. These have previously been discussed in the relevant sections and chapters.

Let us look into the future of individual farmers involved in farming and livestock breeding in the rural areas. Individual farmers refer to those who continue to stay in the countryside and farm but do not join specialised farmer cooperatives. After the establishment of land ownership, they have the option to work as owners of independent family farms. They can then develop crops or livestock farming by using small farm machinery to sow seeds or by hiring temporary workers to help with the harvest. They can also buy a second apartment in the city and send their elderly and children there. The elderly will enjoy a comfortable life, and the children can go to school. The farmers can work in the countryside and spend their vacations in cities. We should let the individual farmers choose how they want to live their lives.

(3) Cultivating local private entrepreneurs

It is necessary for less-developed regions to cultivate local private entrepreneurs and enterprises when they receive industrial shifts from the developed regions. This is because the partner enterprises in developed regions that specialise in production and marketing will not relocate with the enterprises that undertake industrial shift, unlike the core employees and managerial personnel with management experience. Thus, the enterprises that will be relocated to less-developed areas need partners who can provide support and service for them. This will depend on the efforts of local private entrepreneurs. Industrial shifts create many business opportunities, but these opportunities will be fleeting. If local private companies cannot seize them, they will soon be replaced by private enterprises from elsewhere.

Cultivating local private entrepreneurs is also important for the following reason. To attract more enterprises to move into less-developed regions, we must accelerate local urbanisation and increase the purchasing power of local residents. The process of urbanisation sees improvements in living conditions, facilities like schools and hospitals, urban environmental protection, hygiene of the environments, cultural facilities and market supply. These are important factors that attract enterprises to relocate. Likewise, there are many business opportunities in these areas that local entrepreneurs should not overlook. Greater buying power for local residents means an expanding local market, which, in the long run, can encourage enterprises to move from developed regions to local areas. As mentioned before, market expansion in less-developed regions is the appealing power in industrial shifts. Local enterprises should understand the truth in it.

Needless to say, the maturity of local private entrepreneurs is closely related to their good reputation. Reputation is an intangible asset. Only by establishing good reputation can local private entrepreneurs develop a lasting partnership with the relocated enterprises.

(4) Developing local financing, particularly rural financing

In recent years, the financial centre of gravity has been shifting upwards. There have been no medium and large-sized financial institutions at the county level or below. At least, large state-controlled banks are absent on the grassroots level. This condition is not favourable for less-developed regions in undertaking industrial shifts because both the relocated enterprises and the local private enterprises that supply supportive services need good financing conditions. Besides, urban construction also needs support and help from financial. A poor financing condition in a less-developed region will not only affect the relocation of enterprises from the developed regions and but also make it difficult for those relocated enterprises to survive and prosper in those regions.

Rural finance plays an important role in narrowing the urban-rural income gap in the less-developed regions, creating business opportunities for farmers and raising their incomes. This will pave the way for market expansion. As mentioned before, enterprises in developed regions are attracted to less-developed areas for the following two reasons: reducing costs and a broad future market provided by less-developed regions. If farmers in less-developed regions have their three rights secured (contracted land operating rights, homestead land rights and property ownership rights) and can use the three corresponding deeds as a mortgage for loans, the rural economy will come alive. Farmers can get a mortgage from banks or credit cooperatives as start-up funds. It is an important guarantee for an increase in farmers' incomes and the expansion of the market.

A practical difficulty is that banks are concerned that if farmers cannot pay off their loans before the due date after they have received the granted collateral loans, how should they deal with the houses and land mortgaged by the farmers? If this issue is unsettled, either banks will be apprehensive about providing rural collateral loan services, or they will get into trouble by the outstanding collateral, including the mortgaged land or houses. Thus, it is necessary to establish rural credit guarantee centres at the county level as well as rural property rights trading centres at the city level. County level rural credit guarantee centres can provide guarantees on collateral or credit loans to farmers by investigating an applicant's credit so that banks can have greater confidence in granting loans. Meanwhile, city level rural property rights trading centres can transfer the homes and land that farmers mortgaged, so that the banks can rest assured that they will get back the principal and interest. These are powerful measures that invigorate rural financing.

(5) Creating a favourable cultural atmosphere

Different counties, cities and provinces in less-developed areas have their cultural and historical backgrounds and ethnic customs. To become destinations for the industrial shift, they should fully develop their unique features and form a good cultural atmosphere.

Regional economic development requires both "hard power" and "soft power". They are indispensable. Infrastructures, capital, equipment, technology and plants are "hard power". Talents are "hard power", but their quality, professionalism, dedication, enthusiasm, initiatives and working relationships with other people are "soft power". Apart from these, "soft power" also includes the efficiency of the government, the results of the construction of legal systems, people's awareness of the law, the local cultural atmosphere and tradition, the modest way of life of the local residents and the local social harmony. Therefore, when introducing enterprises from developed into less-developed regions, we should not only focus on building the "hard power" but also the various types of "soft power" in the less-developed regions. Only in this way can we help the local economy reach a new level.

4 Undertaking industrial shifts and upgrading

For less-developed areas, undertaking industrial shifts from developed regions is only an intermediary stage instead of the ultimate objective of industrialisation or economic development. No province (city, region) can possess advanced industry and become economically developed by simply undertaking industrial shifts from developed areas. That is to say, less-developed areas, based on the actual conditions of the provinces (cities or regions), should seize this great opportunity of industrial shifts to develop high-tech industries so as to upgrade their local industries and achieve independent innovation. An assumption that a province (city or region) is only satisfied with undertaking industrial shifts from developed areas is far from enough for the realisation of local economic development objectives. With such an assumption, local enterprises will not be able to achieve independent innovation or local industrial upgrading, and particularly be unable to make use of their regional advantages and local resources to develop industries with their own characteristics. Thus, they can only remain at the level of industrial shifts.

Of course, industrial shifts in the current phase are still necessary to less-developed regions. They will stimulate local economic growth, create jobs, increase local revenues and incomes of local urban and rural residents and improve the quality of the labour force. At the same time, less-developed regions can take the opportunity of the industrial shifts to increase local employment rate, cultivate talents and private entrepreneurs, and develop local financial sectors, thus creating conditions for the establishment of new local industries and industrial upgrading.

Based on the discussion above, we will further elaborate on the relationship between industrial shifts and industrial upgrading.

First, even if new industries are established and upgraded in less-developed areas, they are not independently accomplished by relying on local enterprises (including state-owned and private enterprises). This is more likely to result from the capital, technical and personnel cooperation between local and non-local enterprises. The entrepreneurs of these enterprises organise and manage these types of cooperation. Industrial shifts and the subsequent cooperation between local and non-local enterprises facilitate mutual understanding. Based on this cooperation, they will jointly contribute financial and human resources and efforts to the establishment of new industries and industrial upgrading.

Second, as already mentioned, the decision of enterprises to shift from developed areas is based on the potential advantages of less-developed areas. However, these enterprises will gain a deeper and more comprehensive understanding of the potential advantages and market prospects during, and especially after the industrial shift. As a result, they will be keen on continuing or increasing their investment in these areas. The investment will help independent innovations and industrial upgrading in existing enterprises as well as the creation of companies with new and advanced technology. Local enterprises can provide support in the capital, technology, talent and marketing, and thus become close partners with the companies that undertake industrial shifts.

Third, when less-developed regions receive an industrial shift, the introduction of talents, the cultivation of local talents and the enhanced vocational and technique training will all benefit future industrial upgrading. If the number of local professional and technical talents increases and the increase is accelerating, this indicates that these less-developed areas will have better conditions for future development. These areas will be a preferred target of industrial shifts of enterprises in developed areas, and a good choice for non-local capital as a site for the establishment of new, high-tech industries, owing to rich human resources. In this way, the economic operation in these areas will enter a virtuous cycle. Governments in less-developed areas have an adequate understanding of this and make early preparations.

Fourth, for less-developed regions, what is more important is that by undertaking industrial shifts, the overall economic operation begins to enter a virtuous cycle. An indication of that are the above-mentioned increases in talents and technicians and their effects. The virtuous cycle of economic operation in less-developed areas as a whole refers to the following. As a result of the industrial shifts, the employment rate in less-developed areas increases, the total value of GDP rises, the industrial structure of the areas is adjusted, local revenues increase, the living conditions of the people have improved and the income of the residents and their purchasing power have increased. All of those lead to further increases in employment and GDP. Based on steady economic growth, the industrial structure will be further adjusted after the overall economic operation has shifted into a virtuous cycle. In accordance with the laws of economic development, prosperity is self-subsistent because prosperity naturally brings about growing investment and increased consumption, which in turn ensures continuous market growth, industrial upgrading and enhanced competitiveness of the enterprises.

To summarise, less-developed areas should pay attention to industrial shift, as this is the preparatory stage of industrial upgrading and the starting point for the entire economy to enter a virtuous cycle.

Section 3 Creation of new advantages and dividends

1 Explanations of the disappearance of initial dividends

The so-called dividends truly refer to the development advantages of a country or a region at a specific stage and the benefits these advantages bring. Demographic, resource and reform dividends (also called institutional dividends or system dividends), for instance, are the outcomes of development advantages and their applications.

The disappearance of dividends refers to the disappearance of development advantages. The disappearance of the dividends, whether they are demographic, resource or reform dividends, is regarded as a normal phenomenon in any country or region in the process of economic development. It will occur at a certain stage of economic development and is not restricted to a specific country.

What is important is that the economic development mode must change when it reaches a certain stage. Otherwise, the economy will gradually fall into a predicament after the initial dividends disappear. Therefore, every country or region faces the pressing issues of making corresponding changes in development modes, reformulating development strategies, and effectively adjusting industrial structures. This is what is commonly called economic transformation. If the transformation is timely and goes smoothly, the economy will go through this bottleneck. Otherwise, the economy will continue to be entangled by difficulties.

After reaching a certain stage of economic development, some Latin American countries were stuck in a long-term stagnation or recession because they did not undergo economic transformation in a timely or successful manner. This is a lesson to be learned.

If some developing countries do not realise the necessity of timely economic transformation, that is to say, if they rely heavily on their initial advantages and are reluctant to do their utmost to transform, this will result in the following three drawbacks.

First, they will lose confidence in continuing to develop the economy, because they think that, with the disappearance of the initial dividends, their development advantage is gone and they can hardly accomplish anything.

Second, due to the loss of confidence, investors in the real domestic economy will withdraw their investments or move their enterprises to late-developing countries. As a result, the gross domestic investment will be reduced, and the national economy will face a lack of investment. Meanwhile, the experts in the development of the real economy will go abroad, following the investors and the enterprises.

Third, if the real economy of a country is hollowed out, investors will regard the real economy as an industry with no development value. As a result, a lot of money will go to the virtual economy, creating bubbles and a deeper trap for the economy. The burst of asset bubbles will cause the economy to stagnate and hinder future economic development.

2 Progressing from the old to the new demographic dividends
from to the new

Demographic dividends refer to development advantages and their embodiments in the economic development of a country or region owing to the existence of human resources. The advantages of human resources, however, can change the course of economic development. At the early stages of a country or a region's economic development, the advantages of human resources were often embodied in a large number of cheap labourers. At this stage, four employment conditions applied to the cheap labour force in these countries, and as a result, cheap labour resources generated demographic dividends. These four conditions are as follows.

First, the domestic natural conditions were suitable for operating plantations supplying grain crops, tropical fruits, cotton, rubber and other agricultural produces. With abundant cheap domestic labour force, as long as people (either domestic or overseas investors) were willing to operate plantations, there were no concerns over being unable to hire cheap labour.

Second, there were rich domestic mineral resources, such as iron ore, nonferrous metals, coal, oil, natural gas, rare and precious metals, diamonds, precious stones and other stone material for construction use. If people were willing to invest in the mining industry, the abundant cheap local labour supply would satisfy investors' needs for cheap labour.

Third, at the early stages, developing countries prioritised labour-intensive industries like light textile and food industry in accordance with their actual national situations. Those industries needed a cheap labour force and were not technologically demanding. Thus, with preliminary training, labourers in those countries could meet the need of investors and enterprises could enrol employees Apart from that, a large number of handicraft workshops and individual small businesses also provide labourers with job opportunities.

Fourth, the construction industry at this stage was developing more quickly and also provided cheap labourers with job opportunities. For instance, the construction of roads, railways, port facilities, residences, shops, factories and other public facilities brought in dividends owing to the use of cheap labour. Again, this type of demographic dividends is inseparable from the existence and use of abundant cheap labour. At the early stage of development, abundant cheap resources were the major cause of low production costs. It was precisely relying on low production costs that some developing countries explored new markets and accumulated capital, further enabling those countries to raise their GDP from a low-income, gradually close to an approximately middle-income, and even to middle-income phase.

Nevertheless, situations changed. In countries or regions that gradually shifted from a low- to approximately middle-income or even to middle-income country, the advantages of cheap labour resources gradually disappeared and so did their initial demographic dividends. Cheap wages were no longer the unique factor that attracted investors, as there emerged some late-developing countries and regions with similarly abundant cheap labour resources but even lower wages and production costs. The latter countries and regions were, therefore, more appealing to overseas investors. Additionally, some countries or regions, which relied on the income from the use of cheap labour resources to break away from low-income countries, always neglected investing in human capital and remained complacent about providing cheap labour instead of improving the quality of their labour force. This led to the decline or even disappearance of existing demographic dividends, and eventually resulted in economic stagnation of these countries and regions. There are many such examples.

How should this issue be handled? Should those countries and areas lose confidence in future economic development? Losing confidence will not help solve the problem, as this issue needs to be addressed on account of appropriate understanding of demographic dividends.

Note that a country at different developing stages has different human resource advantages corresponding to each stage. With cheap labour force and old demographic dividends vanishing, the advantages of a skilled labour force will take their place. New human dividends will become the features of a new development stage. The economy will continue to develop in a newly-changed development mode. There have been precedents. Therefore, any country or region should have confidence.

Moreover, when the average income continues to increase with sustainable economic development, especially with the promotion of urbanisation and the rising urbanisation rate, the population growth rate usually tends to decline. The age-ing of the population and the proportion of the young within the total population declines. This explains the disappearance of the old demographic dividends from another perspective.

Now after a right understanding of the replacement of the old dividends with new ones, we will further explore this phenomenon by linking it with China's current situation.

Since the replacement is inevitable and accords with the general trend, we must strengthen our confidence and strive to achieve the replacement at an early date. New demographic dividends are created through our efforts. The creation relies on efforts in four aspects, and none of them is dispensable.

First, increase investment in human resources and expand vocational and tech-nical training so as to substantially raise workers' technical expertise. We should be aware that for China, the end of the cheap labour era is the beginning of the mechanical era. The cheap labour era was usually associated with low labour qual-ity, low technical levels and low efficiency. Why was labour cheap? This involved precisely low labour quality, low technical levels and low efficiency. Hence, it is necessary to transform this labour force into technical workers by investing in human resources. This is also the basic condition for promoting industrial upgrad-ing, independent innovation and improving product upgrading.

For example, wages in China's manufacturing enterprises are visibly higher than those in the neighbouring late-developing countries. As a result, while the old demographic dividends relying on cheap labour retired from China's stage of history, they still exist in the neighbouring late-developing countries. How-ever, if China replaces the cheap labour era with a technological age promptly, on the one hand, China will be in a better position compared with its neighbouring countries owing to its entry into the technological age. On the other hand, wages of technicians in China are still much lower in comparison with those in Western developed countries and it will take some time before the wages of Chinese tech-nicians with equal proficiency can catch up with those of Western countries. Thus, China will have its developmental advantages and new demographic dividends will come into being.

In the future, when China's neighbouring late-developing countries enter the technological age, China will have been ready for an advanced-technical or pro-fessional age and its advantages will remain. This will depend on continuous investment in human resources, which is essential to the promotion of the new demographic dividends.

Second, motivate the enthusiasm of workers in employment or to be employed to improve their technical expertise. On the one hand, both enterprises and staff should realise the significance of improving workers' quality to the survival and development of enterprises, and its role in changing "Made in China" into "Orig-inated in China". On the other hand, it also relies on both parties' acknowledge-ment of the significance in linking wages with work performances. If staff wages are not linked with work performances, many staff will consider it meaningless to make assiduous study and research efforts and improve their techniques, preventing them from exercising their desires and initiatives for keeping forging ahead.

Third, under the influence of China's existing binary household registration system, the unfair treatment of migrant workers is one of the major obstacles to the creation of new demographic dividends. This is mainly because migrant workers are restricted in rights and even receive identity discrimination in some aspects. Under such circumstances, some migrant workers are disappointed with their prospects. Their enthusiasm for hard work will be abated and even disappear.

Fourth, encouraging employees to delve into technology and improve their technical abilities; in the meantime, instruct them to be hardworking. To be more exact, give them instructions on professional ethics. Chinese workers have long been known as being diligent, working painstakingly under any circumstance and playing a rigorous role on their jobs. They have received consistently positive evaluations from overseas business people. Some investors with factories built in other developing countries (including the "going-abroad" Chinese enterprises) all prefer Chinese workers to the locals, since Chinese workers are hardworking, well-disciplined, and neglect no working time. This tradition should be carried on.

It is clear from our analysis of the above four aspects that it is prospective to create new demographic dividends in China. Given this, we need to understand one principle, i.e. valuing the role of micro and small enterprises in cultivating technicians in China's further economic development. The small and micro-enterprises here refer to the self-funded and self-established enterprises, of which the owners themselves are often skilled workers and advanced technicians. The British Industrial Revolution started in the 1770s. The earliest steam engines, machinery and equipment, rolling stock (including locomotives and vehicles that carried passengers and cargos) were unprecedented innovations. Who first designed and manufactured them? They were mainly invented by owners of small handicraft workshops or skilled artisans such as water millers, watchmakers and grindery millers, among others. Craftsmanship was handed down from the older generation of the family or obtained through an apprenticeship where masters taught apprentices by letting them become involved in doing. Thus, over time, the number of skilled workers with more and more refined skills increased. It was not until later that vocational and technical schools were established. Up until now, micro, small and medium-sized enterprises are still playing an important role in developed Western economies. They have not only alleviated the employment issue but are also partners of large enterprises, manufacturing parts for the latter. Many micro and small enterprises which are well known for their craft or expertise manufacture famous brand products and also provide society with highly skilled workers, including those who create merchandise based on customers' particular orders, and other skilled craftsmen specialising in repairing automobiles, motorcycles, yachts and home electrical appliances. Therefore, while shifting to a "technological age", China should not neglect the role of micro and small enterprises in those aspects.

3 *Progressing from the old to the new resource dividends*

Resource dividends refer to the resource advantages of a country or region in land and mineral, forest and freshwater, pasture and others. Those resources were relatively abundant in the early days of economic development. Take land resources for example. The amount of usable land at that time was comparatively larger, and the prices were lower. This is resource advantages, and their results were embodied in resource dividends.

It should be noted, however, that these were likely to be old resource advantages. If a particular country genuinely has a vast territory with abundant resources, resource dividends can exist over a long term. Otherwise, when the economy develops to a certain stage, some of the resources will become increasingly scarce and limited, and after a certain period of time, resources advantages and dividends will both gradually disappear. It is the right case for China.

Where do new resource dividends come from? New resource advantages and dividends both come from advanced science and technology and their application. Generally speaking, resources provided by nature can always be exhausted, and only intellectual and human resources are inexhaustible. Advanced science and technology derive from intellectual and human resources. Science and technology will only advance further through increasing investment in the development and utilisation of intellectual and human resources. Once the advanced research results are applied, new resources advantages come into being; so do the new resource dividends.

At the current stage in China, if the cost of desalination is reduced, this will be a huge breakthrough. Northern coastal areas will be able to use desalinated seawater. Of course, some technical problems remain to be resolved. For instance, the expenses for the transportation of desalinated seawater should be lowered and the steel pipes, susceptible to corrosion, need to be changed regularly. Those issues, however, can be solved.

As another example, developing and applying new energy, and improving sandy pastures and pasture grass varieties are all scientific research and development activities, conducive to the creation of new resource dividends.

In the summer of 2012, I led a research group of CPPCC's Economic Committee and conducted a survey in Inner Mongolia, feeling that the grass industry in Inner Mongolia was an emerging industry with a bright and promising future. The functions of the grass industry included, first, improving pasture soil, increasing vegetation and protecting ecological environments, all in accordance with the requirements of a low-carbon economy. Second, it developed new grass varieties that suited the Inner Mongolia grassland. These varieties had higher protein content and increased nutritional values in sheep and cow milk. This will help create national diary brands and expand market access. The grass developed by the grass industry enterprises could also save water and was welcomed by the herdsmen. Third, the enterprises in grass industry, the pastureland and the herdsmen all enjoy higher income.to promote new grass varieties; that is, by promoting the plantation areas of the new grass, enterprises in the industry were signing contracts with pastureland owners and herdsmen, sharing mutual benefits for the grass industry. Fourth, it helps lower the costs for afforestation in cities and golf course maintenance. The grass industry companies were promoting grass varieties that conserved water and had a longer green period. These varieties would prolong the use of grass in city green spaces, and could also be used in golf courses. This example clearly illustrates how new resource dividends were created.

In some aspects, new resource dividends are combined with new demographic dividends, especially with new reform dividends. One connection between them is that without a large number of scientific researchers, professionals and skilled workers, there would be neither breakthroughs in science and technology nor new resource dividends. Talent is a prerequisite for new resource dividends. In this sense, new resource and demographic dividends are both complementary to each other and inseparable from each other. The growth of research teams and technical staff embodies the new demographic dividends and is also the premise for the creation of new resource dividends.

On the other hand, new dividends, may it be new demographic and resource, all need to rely on new reform dividends to be realised. This will be discussed in the following section of this chapter. Here we will only illustrate their relationship with an example.

New demographic dividends rely not only on the training of professionals but also on a tremendous number of skilled workers and advanced technicians. How should new demographic dividends mature without necessary reforms to the current educational system and newly established and qualified vocational and technical education? How can they grow with vertical and horizontal channels for talents to become eminent in society blocked and an emphasis laid on the gradual increase of the proportion of education funding in GDP?

Similarly, new resource dividends also rely on institutional innovation and new reform measures; that is, relying on the exertion of the due role of new reform dividends and institutional dividends. Specifically speaking, this needs reform in the science and technology management system with special focus on incentivising researchers and those who promote research results, and ensuring institutional measures that gradually increase the proportion of research and development funds in GDP.

In order to achieve more breakthroughs in the field of science and technology, we not only need new inventions, but also their applications to the economic sphere, so that research outcomes can generate effects in the economy. The former task rests upon inventors and the latter, on entrepreneurs. Both are indispensable.

That is to say, society needs more inventors, entrepreneurs and people to join the ranks of successful inventors and entrepreneurs. Successful inventors may pursue lifelong scientific research and technological innovation. They may also engage themselves in entrepreneurial activities after scientific inventions, establish their businesses and become excellent entrepreneurs. There have been many successful examples at home and abroad.

May it be inventors or entrepreneurs, there must be an institutional environment facilitating them to make achievements. Such an institutional environment is created by the new institutional innovation and embodies the reform dividends. Otherwise, new demographic and resource dividends were nothing but empty talk. Steve Jobs' success was not mainly due to his personal wisdom, courage or resolution. Rather, the institutional environment where he grew up played a major role and enabled him to display his talent. That environment included an equity incentive system, a strict intellectual property protection system, as well as a relatively healthy capital market. As a result, around Steve Jobs was a huge scientific research and development team with mobilised enthusiasm and technology innovation thrived. It is precisely the most valuable experience that we have learned from Jobs and Jobs's type of new inventors and entrepreneurs.

4 Progressing from the old to the new reform dividends

As is clear from the discussion above, among new demographic, resource and reform dividends, the reform dividends are not only the most substantial but also the most significant dividends. Reform dividends, also known as institutional or system dividends, refer to more energy released to push forward the economy through reforming and adjusting system or institution. Every reform is issued in line with the specific situations in economic development. Reform dividends include the elimination of system or institutional constraints on productivity in order to support economic growth and development. For example, in the initial phase of China's Reform and Opening-up, three reform measures were implemented based on the then economic situations in China: the promotion of the rural household contract responsibility system, the rise of township and village enterprises and the establishment of special economic zones. These measures created enormous dividends. They are still fresh in people's memory as these measures ushered in a new era for the China's economy.

For example, the rural household contract responsibility system reflected the wishes of the majority of farmers and greatly incentivised them. A few years later, agricultural products bloomed. Poultry, meat, fish, rice, grains and rare goods like sesame oil could all be traded in the agricultural market and the number of buyers and sellers surged. Afterwards, food, oil, clothing coupons and other coupons which were implemented many years ago were cancelled. The above is one of the examples of reform dividends at the beginning of the Reform and Opening-up.

Again, after the implementation of the rural household contract responsibility system, agricultural productivity increased and surplus labour emerged in rural areas. As a result, township enterprises (then called brigade enterprises) were established. Those enterprises did not need government investment. The government did not allocate them any production material, nor was it responsible for the sales of their products. They totally relied on self-raised funds, organised production and were responsible for their sales. The 1980s witnessed a new phenomenon in China. People who looked like farmers could often be seen on trains or coaches, of whom some wore suits and ties and carried small and large bags. Those people were actually salesmen from township enterprises. They carried their samples and orders and endured the hardships of travels to promote their enterprises' products. Within a few years, township enterprise commodity markets emerged beyond the centralised planned economy and those enterprises flourished. The aforementioned is another illustration of reform dividends at the beginning of the Reform and Opening-up.

Let us give another example. In the early 1980s, a Special Economic Zone with new reform measures and regulations was established in *Shenzhen, Guangdong* Province. When other regions were still operating according to planned production and distribution, market-regulated measures were implemented in the *Shenzhen* Special Economic Zone. In other areas of the country, only individual- and family-based businesses were allowed. By contrast, though there was no such term as "private enterprises" then, private enterprises existed in the *Shenzhen* Special Economic Zone. When the number of employees in those enterprises surpassed the upper limit of individual or family-based businesses (no more than seven to eight employees), no one went to seize and ban those businesses. That was a characteristic of the *Shengzhen* Special Economic Zone. It also reflected the reform dividends.

It was precisely the above reform measures at the beginning of the Reform and Opening-up that brought in reform dividends. Thereby, a new atmosphere emerged in China in the 1980s. People had profound experiences with reform dividends at that time.

A new round of reforms was launched after Comrade *Deng Xiaoping's* talk in South China in 1992. The term private enterprise was formally adopted, and there was great enthusiasm in setting up private enterprises in many places. Some able-minded young people switched from within the system to outside the system and formed the increasingly influential group of entrepreneurs known as the "Ninety-two Group". In the meantime, the reform of state-owned enterprises began. Some managed to raise capital from different sources and were reconstructed into listed companies. With raised funds from different channels, they entered a period of significant development. Moreover, China's stock market became increasingly active after 1992. The *People's Republic of China Securities Law*, drafted over a period of six years, received overwhelming approval from the Standing Committee of National People's Congress in the late 1990s and was subsequently implemented. Despite some imperfections, the stock market began to have a legal basis. These are important achievements of the economic reform. After the mid- and late-1980s, a large wave of migrant workers emerged from the rural areas and substantially changed these areas. The land transfer became an irresistible trend and took multiple forms such as subcontracts, exchange, leases, share-based specialised cooperatives and the "enterprise + farmers" mode. Large-scale production, specialisation and diversification became a trend in the agricultural reform of different regions. Due to the reforms, China's economy not only withstood the impacts from the 1997–98 Asian Financial Crisis but also made great strides towards a healthy domestic economy. All of these were the gifts of the reforms, gifts of reform dividends or institutional dividends.

Nonetheless, after a round of reform measures were implemented for some time, the advantages or dividends began to diminish. That is evitable, and the reason is simple. Under a certain system, as new situations emerge, the old reform measures will become more obsolete. All reform measures aim at specific situations, and when they change, the effectiveness of those measures will naturally decrease. Thus, the disappearance of first reform dividends is a common phenomenon not limited to China alone.

The benefits and dividends generated by the primary reform measures are called old reform advantages or old reform dividends. Here, "old" and "new" are relative and are not related to the length of the effective period. Some reform dividends may exist for a long period of time while others may not and this simply depends on how fast the situation changes. When the old reform dividends are about to disappear, the potential advantages of the initial reform measures are close to depletion.

Reforms are institutional adjustments, which must be carried out in a timely manner. Only with the continuous introduction of new reform measures and institutional adjustments can new reform and institutional dividends emerge. The great enthusiasm hidden among the people is the largest driving force of the reform. Therefore, if we do not continue to adjust the system, we will be ignoring and even suppressing this enthusiasm. That is almost a consensus among supporters and advocates of reforms.

5 Creation as the origin of both advantages and dividends

We have explained the old and new development advantages as well as old and new demographic, resource and reform dividends. Given those, it is unreasonable to paint an unpromising future of the Chinese economy based on the disappearance of many dividends. We should have confidence that there will be new dividends and advantages in our future economic development.

Note that both development advantages and dividends originate from creation. Even the old advantages or dividends were derived from creation. They did not emerge "out of the blue".

For another example, even though we have a large population, if everyone stayed at home and was reluctant to leave their homeland to seek jobs, how could we take full advantage of the cheap and strong labour force in our country and bring about its dividends?

Moreover, how can China exert its resource advantages of vast amounts of cheap land, if none of the regions tried to attract investments from overseas, develop land or build factories? How can there be resource dividends?

Let us give one more example. Institutional barriers in economic development are objective realities. In primitive societies, if development obstacles had not been altered, there would not have been development or improvements in living conditions. That is to say, without people's efforts, the earliest reform dividends would not have come into being.

To sum up, even the earliest demographic, resource and reform dividends were inseparable from human creation. Undoubtedly, the same also applies to the replacement of old dividends with new ones. In neither history nor real life is there a single case where dividends appear out of thin air.

Since all dividends originate from creation at all times and in all land, what has been revealed to us can only be that we should not only have a new understanding of the dividends but also take actions. It is only through practice that dividends are turned into reality.

8 Social capital and corporate social responsibility

Section 1 Reputation is the most important social capital

1 Social capital in economics

The theory of social capital in economics became popular in the 1970s, but the existence of social capital, together with the attention it has drawn, far predates that. Since the emergence of market transactions and the beginning of productive and sales activities, people have noticed and utilised social capital, a phenomenon that can be summarised in the following three points.

First, social capital is discovered when there are market transactions – for example, bartering or transactions with money as medium that take place when people bring their products to the market. Social capital smooths the way for transactions. Only with the help of social capital can the buyer and the seller feel satisfied and convenient, and complete the transaction.

Second, in order to realise market transactions, people must first perform productive activities, the simplest being foraging, hunting and fishing. When the power of a single man cannot procure enough goods, he naturally cooperates with others, so that a group of several or tens of people can work together in these activities. Social capital influences the way people cooperate, how they can be more productive in foraging, hunting and fishing, and how the products can be satisfactorily distributed among the members so that they can continue in these collective productive activities. Social capital makes sure that all members benefit from the cooperation and are willing to maintain this relationship.

Third, the development of productive activities and the expansion of exchange activities give rise to specialised manual workshops, stores, restaurants, hotels, financial institutions and public institutions, making social capital even more important in these situations. When a person enters society, he must have reliable and usable social capital, or he will find it difficult to advance. When a person migrates from the countryside to a town or a city, he has to have some social capital to lean on, or he will be turned down wherever he goes and end up on the streets. Even if he is reduced to begging, he still needs social capital, without which he will face every humiliation and can hardly survive.

Although these situations may belong to the distant past, they contain some good common sense. Economists in the 1970s merely provided theoretical explanation and further elaboration of the function of social capital, which has existed since long ago.

What is social capital, after all? To put it simply, it refers to an immaterial capital that exists in human relations. The more comprehensive and better these relations are, the richer social capital one has. Human relations cover a wide range. Relationships with family members, fellow townsmen, classmates, teachers, students, colleagues and friends all contribute to one's social capital. One should make an effort to find, establish, solidify and develop one's social capital. Social capital is like a network and can snowball, encompassing the relatives of relatives, friends of friends, colleagues of colleagues, and acquaintances of acquaintances.

Wealth is created jointly by the three types of capital – material, human and social capital, as has been mentioned before. Social capital is important because, as an immaterial capital, it can better combine the other two. In other words, social capital is a necessary immaterial capital that can improve the union and efficiency of material and human capital.

2 Social capital and reputation

Since social capital consists of human relation, its core is the mutual trust between people.

Whether or not, and for how long, people can maintain their connections depends on their reputation. After a person enters a market, if he can behave with honesty and value his reputation, other people will regard him favourably and consider it worthwhile to get to know him. He will not be alone in the market and others will give him a helping hand when he is in need. In this way, his social capital begins to function. There is no doubt that reputation is the most important social capital.

When I was conducting research in Malaysia, Thailand and Indonesia, I met and held discussions many times with overseas Chinese. They would always mention how their ancestors came from *Fujian* and *Guangdong* Province and tried to make a living abroad. The most important lesson from their experience was that they were not apprehensive about the lack of possessions in a foreign land with no acquaintances. How did they cope with this? First, they worked diligently and endured hardships to make their living. Second, they prized honesty and trustworthiness so that when they needed help, they always received it from their fellow townsmen, classmates or colleagues. This is how social capital functions. When I researched in France, Germany and Britain, I also met overseas Chinese who came from *Zhejiang* Province. They, too, would tell me about how they, their parents or grandparents ventured out and started a business in Western Europe. Their experience was the same: they valued hard work and honesty.

All in all, those who venture into a market, be it at home or abroad, tend to reach the same conclusion. With a good reputation comes more and more acquaintances and friends. By contrast, if one already knows some fellow townsmen, classmates and colleagues, or friends and relatives in the market but he has a bad reputation, they will notice his conduct and dissociate from him, diminishing his social capital.

The accumulation and collapse of social capital may rest on a single incident. It may take several generations to build up the reputation for a business to flourish, but an inheritor's lack of honesty is enough to ruin it. These instances, while not common among overseas Chinese, do happen. Whenever the overseas Chinese in Southeast Asia or Western Europe mentioned these instances, they all sighed and said that it was a shame that some people should be unscrupulous and seize on immediate profit at the cost of long-term benefits. Afterwards, these people could no longer remain in the business circle and had to leave, crestfallen, for their hometown or some other place to start afresh; some even changed their names. They also said that, if these people did not repent, they would repeat their mistakes in the future.

We should be aware that all types of human relations can be seen as cooperative relations. This cooperative relationship may or may not be immaterial, consciously carried out or even felt. In the late *Qing* Dynasty, when the ban on northeastern China was lifted, many people in *Shandong* Province left their homes and travelled there by road or by waterway. This migration lasted for decades or even over a century. The migrants came from different prefectures, counties, towns and villages. Some of them knew each other; many did not. They remained in cooperative relationship over a long time span. Later immigrants to northeastern China should be grateful to them in every respect. Their ancestors built roads and bridges, reclaimed land, constructed houses and opened restaurants, inns and shops along the way. This was a cooperative relationship at the macro level. The earlier immigrants provided massive help to the later ones. However, the later immigrants might not be the kinsmen or offspring of the earlier ones, and they might not come from the same prefectures, counties, towns or villages either. Yet, there is no doubt that they were cooperating and helping each other and, since this is the case, they had to have mutual trust to maintain this relationship.

Mutual trust means that both parties treat each other with honesty. This is a basic principle that must be followed, the foundation for the growth of social capital on both sides, and the starting point for further cooperation and enterprise.

Everyone should take to heart a saying popular in Western society: a person who starts out by deceiving everyone will eventually end up deceived by everyone. This means that a person may succeed a few times if he lies and deceives others, but after a while, when they know that he always lies, they will lie to him as well so that he will end up being deceived by everyone.

If many people are unscrupulous and lack trustworthiness, society will suffer a crisis of trust. Supposing that this happens, then the economic operation of society will fall into disorder, and consequently everyday life will descend into chaos.

Human beings cannot live without forethought. Disorder confuses expectations of the future, and eventually renders it impossible to tell what will happen tomorrow. As a result, people will fritter their time away and the social economy will operate in the unknown. Society will stop advancing and even retrogress, leaving people in disappointment about their uncertain futures.

Therefore, it is vital for the survival of a nation to restore mutual trust among people. People often mention an "apocalyptic mood", but this refers more often to the collapse of social trust rather than religious prophecies or forebodings of natural disasters.

3 The bottom lines of society: the legal bottom line and the moral bottom line

Social capital requires years of accumulation. Anyone can rely on the acquaintances he has made over the years and his reputation to increase his social capital gradually. If you help others you will receive their help in return, and if you treat others with honesty they will treat you in the same way. Social capital is an immaterial capital and wealth because there are bottom lines in society by which everyone abides.

The accumulation of reputation is not accomplished by anyone in a day. One cannot hunt for it. The same applies to enterprises. For example, nothing is more precious than a brand, and the brand comes from reputation. An enterprise can only establish its brand after years of effort. Once it is established, it must be maintained and supported by reputation. People in the enterprise know that the brand and reputation do not come easily. Everyone in the enterprise, from top to bottom, understands that it is necessary to value the brand and reputation.

Reputation takes years to establish, yet it only requires a single incident for a reputation to change for the worse and collapse like a dam. Once this happens, years of effort will come to naught.

If this is so, why do some people and enterprises risk their reputation to engage in fraudulent practices? There are three main reasons. First, they think it unlikely that they will be discovered, so that their dishonest dealing will not be noticed if they only try it once. Second, they think that when they are discovered and have to be punished or pay fines as compensation, the penalty will be relatively small as a cost, so that the fraudulent practice may turn out to be profitable in the end. Third, they are tempted by high profit. These three cases share one similarity: they all rest on opportunism. Reputation is abandoned under the temptation of gain. In fact, any individual or enterprise that engages in fraudulent practices pays a very heavy price, because the loss of reputation means the bankruptcy of social capital and the collapse of human relations. Moreover, it is extremely difficult to rebuild a lost reputation. It may cost even more in time and effort just to partially repair it.

Trust is related to everyone's social responsibility. There are two bottom lines that no individual or enterprise can cross. One is the legal bottom line and the other is the moral bottom line.

The legal bottom line is no doubt extremely important. In social economic life, no individual or enterprise can cross the legal bottom line to engage in illegal activities. Any such activity is punishable by law, and will result in the loss of reputation. Of course, there is also the possibility of cases of misjudgement that condemn the innocent. However, when the truth is known, the public will restore the reputation of the wronged party. Yet, this does not mean that the legal bottom line does not exist.

The moral bottom line is equally important. Breaking promises, breaching agreements and deceiving others may not cross the legal bottom line but are not tolerated according to the moral bottom line. In social economic activities, crossing the moral bottom line is equally deplored and is a sure way to destroy one's social capital and social network.

Government staff, too, should stick to these two bottom lines as their basic social responsibility. We should be aware that government staff represents the image of the government. Therefore, they should have a stronger sense of social responsibility, of which the minimum requirement is to abide by the legal and the moral bottom lines.

To individuals, enterprises and government staff, social responsibility should not be confined to these bottom lines, although they are the last line of defence. They are a starting point, and people should strive for higher standards.

Regarding the punishment for breaking the legal bottom line, we must grasp the significance of upholding the principle that "where there are laws to go by, the laws must be observed and strictly enforced". It is important to strictly enforce the law due to the opportunism mentioned above. When people are tempted by profit into performing illegal activities that damage the individual or public good, they are opportunistic and think it impossible or unlikely that they will be discovered, or, when they are discovered, that they will be punished. Opportunism breeds fraudulent practice. We must enforce the law strictly to mete out the deserved punishment to those who engage in such practice.

4 Social capital can be created

When economists discuss market capacity, they often say that a market does not have a definite capacity but that instead it can be created. Who creates market? Both the supplier and the buyer.

The creation of a market by the supplier means that when there is no specific demand on the market or the demand has not crossed people's minds, the supplier develops some product, deploys it in the market and by means of advertisement and media promotes and introduces it to attract buyers. The consumers who have used this new product further promote it, and so a market comes into being. This is a newly created market. The electric shaver is often considered to be a classic example.

Thousands of years ago, men did not shave their beards. Then they shaved with knives and scissors, and afterwards with razor blades. Who could have thought of using electric shavers? People were concerned that electric shavers might cut the face. Therefore, the manufacturers that first promoted electric shavers had to hire people to display their usage in public to prove their safety.

In addition, trendy phones today have many more functions than the phones that were popular years ago. This is another example of the supplier's promotion of their innovations. People flock to buy the latest phone models because they are attracted by the new functions. This, too, shows that the supplier can create the market.

Let us now turn to the creation of markets by demand. The development of the tourism industry and tourism market is a convincing example. Due to people's desire to travel, the tourism market is ever-growing and attracting more and more consumers. Demand creates supply, and supply in turn further creates demand. This is an example of how demand and supply can influence each other and jointly create markets.

Now let us return to the topic of social capital.

A person who has never entered the market before does not, strictly speaking, possess social capital. If he was born into a prestigious family, the social capital belongs not to him but to his family, parents and grandparents. Since this person does not have any experience in the market, how can people judge his character, capabilities and trustworthiness? There is no doubt that the influence of his family still plays a part, but it only serves to prepare the way for him. Social capital must be earned through his endeavour and hard work.

The ability to create one's own social capital is crucial for anyone who ventures into the market. His reputation must withstand trials, and his character and capabilities must earn approval from the public. One must achieve these on one's own.

Of course, the creation of social capital requires opportunities as well. Whether or not one can clinch the opportunity and make the most of it has nothing to do with luck but depends on abilities and wisdom. If he has neither, he will miss the opportunity even if it presents itself. Therefore, abilities and wisdom are key to the creation of social capital for a person who ventures into the market.

If one can clinch every opportunity, he can acquire new wealth and income, but this is not the most important thing. It is more important that with every opportunity he gets to know new friends to increase his social capital. If they trust each other and treat each other with honesty, more opportunities and social capital will become available.

Social capital can be created by making more friends or through one's own search and discovery. The reason why societies of former classmates, alumni and fellow townsmen are valued is that people can find their former classmates, alumni and townsmen in the list of names so that they may meet and even be ready to help each other. This is also the factor that underlies the recent trend of composing, continuing the records of family trees and building ancestral shrines – they are ways to discover and increase social capital.

Nevertheless, all these connections must be maintained by reputation. Reputation is the most important social capital. A disreputable person may know many people but none of these acquaintances will be of any help to him if they all consider him untrustworthy. After all, social capital stands and falls by reputation.

We have mentioned in the discussion of material, human and social capital above that social capital is a special capital compared with the other two types. It is immaterial and exists within human relations, and it cannot be quantified. Material capital can be created with the proper use of existing material capital.

Human capital can increase with the accumulation of knowledge, experience and technical expertise. This is not the case with social capital. A person may know many people, but how many can he count on to give a helping hand when he is in trouble? Knowing many people is not enough. He can only rely on those friends, acquaintances and relatives who are willing to lend a hand when he is in dire need. Therefore, having more acquaintances and knowing more people may create social capital, yet to wield it depends on one's own character as well as that of the people he knows.

This is related to the moral atmosphere of a society. In a society where people value trustworthiness and treat each other with honesty, social capital is determined not only by the number of acquaintances, but also the quality of the relationships. If the moral atmosphere is good, and if people are trustworthy and willing to help others, the social capital is truly useful. If one finds oneself in a society with a crisis of trust, he can hardly find people who will lend a hand as they used to.

Section 2 Corporate social responsibility and the extension of social capital

1 Further analysis of corporate social responsibility

When discussing the structural reform of state-owned capital in Section 1, Chapter 2, we elaborated on the goal of the structural reform of the allocation of state-owned capital and the ownership of state-owned enterprises. When we mentioned the reasons for retaining state-owned enterprises, we pointed out that they should act more on their own initiative to realise our country's economic development strategy, thus fulfilling their social responsibilities. In other words, if state-owned enterprises do not consciously contribute to our country's economic development strategy, why do we have to keep them?

Here we will discuss corporate social responsibility in depth. We should be aware that there are two types of state-owned enterprise. One is non-profit organisations, meaning that these state-owned enterprises have special functions that do not target profit. These state-owned enterprises belong to special areas. The other type is profit-making organisations. They have profit goals to fulfil and are responsible to their investors, including state-owned investment organisations. This type of state-owned enterprise, including fully or partially state-owned enterprises, is special in terms of its social responsibilities, because within a market economy an enterprise as a profit-making organisation makes profit from production, operation, sales and other activities. Without profit, it cannot repay its investors, so that the investors will no longer run the enterprise. Therefore, the after-tax profit and its proportion in the overall capital are crucial for any profit-making enterprise, including state-owned enterprises.

The above is related to the basic views of corporate social responsibilities. As a profit-making organisation, the greatest social responsibility of an enterprise is to provide quality products and services to society to fulfil its needs. The more products and services the enterprise provides and the higher the quality, the more it caters to social needs, and in this way it fulfils its social responsibilities. Moreover, this must be done without crossing the legal and moral bottom lines during the production and operation of the enterprise.

During production and operation, the enterprise must also pay taxes according to the country's regulations. This, too, is a social responsibility it must fulfil. If it does not, it fails to meet the requirements of corporate social responsibility.

During production and operation, the enterprise hires employees from society and trains technical and managerial talent and skilled workers. This is another contribution it makes to society. We should not impose a quota on the enterprise regarding how many people it must hire or how many skilled workers it must train, because this depends on the specific production situation and technology level. It is up to the enterprise to decide how many and what kind of people they hire according to its circumstances. We must not and should not impose a rigid quota because the enterprise is, after all, a profit-making organisation and has to make its own decisions.

Are there other standards to measure corporate social responsibilities? How after-tax profit should be distributed to fulfil the requirements of corporate social responsibility remains to be analysed further.

The following four ways to use the after-tax profit of the enterprise are closely relevant to, and should be included within, corporate social responsibility. These are the improvement and repair of the environment during production and sales, the improvement of employee welfare, harmonious relations between the enterprise and local residents, and the relief of major disasters. The sections below will give further elaboration.

(1) The improvement and repair of the environment
during production and sales

During production and sales, the enterprise may cause various pollution to the environment, including by the disposal of wastewater, the emission of air pollutants, the accumulation of solid waste and the generation of loud noise. Some of the pollution and accumulation of pollutants has been dealt with by the enterprise during production and sales, and the cost is included in the production cost and the environmental remediation expenditure. Yet, the workload accumulated over the years on environmental remediation and restoration is related to the production scale of the enterprise, the time span of the pollution and the seriousness of the damage done to the environment. Some environmental remediation, such as the remediation of small drainage basins, costs huge amounts of money and time, and cannot be supported by the yearly production cost and environmental remediation expenditure, but requires large-scale funding. After so many years, enterprises, whether they used to be state-owned or not, have incurred debts in this regard, plus additional new debts in recent years, both of which must eventually be paid. Therefore, a portion of the after-tax profit should go to the restoration and remediation of the ecology and environment, and especially the inherited problems caused by state-owned enterprises in the past, which should be repaired partly with government funding. Since, according to the regulations, the profit of state-owned enterprises belonged exclusively to the government, the government today should be responsible for some of the spending on environmental remediation and restoration.

(2) The improvement of employee welfare

This, too, is an inherited problem. Some large state-owned enterprises, when they prioritised production over living standards, only built temporary shacks for employees. Afterwards, when the production of these enterprises rose, they did not pay much heed to the living standards of the employees, nor did they invest in improvements in their housing and quality of life. When I was researching in remote areas, I found that the housing conditions in some mining, forest and reclamation areas were extremely poor and crude. Some family members of employees told me that they had been living there for decades, and had not seen any new investment in the living facilities. This, too, is an inherited debt that has not been paid. Considering that the enterprises established there were all state-owned enterprises, and that their initial profit belonged exclusively to the government, the government should bear a part of the cost to upgrade the living facilities, including the employees' dormitories and the public service facilities. As for the enterprises, regardless of whether or not they have undergone ownership reform, they should take responsibility and set aside some money from their after-tax profit to convert the shanty houses and the old dormitories. Large as it may need to be, the investment to improve employee living standards and welfare must not be neglected. If necessary, the investment can come in instalments. This is a corporate social responsibility that must not be overlooked.

(3) Harmonious relationships between the enterprise and local residents

Every enterprise is located in a specific area and will come into contact with local residents. Whether or not the enterprise can maintain a harmonious relationship with them is vital to its production and the everyday life of its employees and their families.

The relationship between the enterprise and the local residents is multi-faceted. For example, it includes whether or not inconvenience or harm has been brought to local residents by the wastewater and air pollutants the enterprise disposes of, and by the solid waste formed in the production process and everyday life of the employees. It further includes whether or not the residents are disturbed by the noise of production and transportation vehicles. All of these may give rise to discontent. Moreover, when the enterprise needs temporary workers, can it set aside some positions for the local labour force? Can the enterprise provide help to the local residents with healthcare services, the education of the employees' children and other things such as culture, sports and entertainment? Sometimes these play a major role in improving the relationships with local residents.

State-owned enterprises, especially large ones, as opposed to private small and medium enterprises, tend to face these problems. Large state-owned enterprises often find themselves in situations where they need to carefully manage these relationships, prevent conflicts and resort to consultation to resolve disputes.

In general, problems like these can be divided into two categories: old problems formed over many years, and new problems that emerge during the development of the enterprise. These two should be treated separately.

Regarding old problems formed over the years, if they have indeed been caused by the production process, the enterprise should make plans to deal with them a few at a time. It should compensate local residents and make arrangements to remedy the situation. It is up to the enterprise to decide on the problem of investment. Because the profit of state-owned enterprises used to belong to the government, the government should assume some of the cost, while the rest can be paid from the after-tax profit of the enterprise, in instalments if needed.

Regarding new problems that emerge during its development, the enterprise is responsible for their solution. It can include this spending in its costs, or pay for it from its after-tax profit.

In order that the enterprise may have a harmonious relationship with the local residents, it should, within its capacity, engage in activities that promote the public interest and improve the lives of local residents. These activities are useful for cultivating harmony between the enterprise and the local residents. The enterprise should not regard such spending as an extra burden, but as a long-term investment that will increase its social capital.

(4) Aid from enterprises for major national disasters

When major national disasters occur, all enterprises should, like the people in the whole country, participate in disaster relief. Such incidents have happened in recent years – for example, during the major flooding of the Yangzi River in 1998 and the earthquake in *Wenchuan, Sichuan* Province, in 2008. Even profit-making enterprises took part in disaster relief, regardless of whether they were state-owned or privately owned enterprises, and regardless of their scale and the size of their profits. They all showed their charitable nature by treating this as their social responsibility.

On these occasions, the money and the supplies the enterprises have donated can be registered under special spending, or as part of their after-tax income.

Viewed in this way, corporate social responsibilities are rich in content and wide in range. Yet, there are two points that need explanation. First, the realisation of the above-mentioned social responsibilities should be voluntarily carried out. The obligatory cases are inherited problems and problems relating to environmental remediation and protection. In special circumstances, while the enterprise should fulfil its social responsibilities, it may need to perform them a few at a time. In some cases, the government should still shoulder part of the expense. Second, as profit-making organisations, enterprises should not forget that donations are limited by the interests of the investors because enterprises must continue to exist and develop in order to fulfil the greatest corporate social responsibility – providing more quality products and services to society and stimulating national economic growth. Too much donation that would endanger the continuous existence of enterprises is unsustainable.

2 Harmonising the profit goal and the social responsibilities of the enterprises

As mentioned above, an enterprise, as a profit-making organisation, has a profit goal to achieve. If it fails to achieve the long-term profit expected by the investors, it cannot continue to exist. However, an enterprise must also shoulder its social responsibilities. The harmonisation of its profit goal and its social responsibilities is a subject that attracts much theoretical interest. This field contains many questions worth discussing. In practice, the enterprise must pay due attention to both objectives and must not focus on one at the cost of the other.

Let us summarise the problems we have discussed. At least the following propositions can be established, or are not much in dispute.

First, the greatest corporate social responsibility is to provide more quality products and service. In this process, the enterprise can fulfil its profit goal and satisfy the investors.

Second, the enterprise must uphold values of honesty and reputation during production and sales. Reputation is the most important social capital. The enterprise must make every effort to maintain its reputation and brand and to adhere to the moral and legal bottom lines. This is the basic requirement of corporate social responsibility. The increase in social capital and improvement of reputation will ensure that the enterprise can meet its profit goal. In this way, the profit goal and social responsibilities of the enterprise are harmonised.

Third, during production and operation, the enterprise is responsible for environmental protection and remediation, which is a social responsibility it must fulfil. Although to do this, the enterprise needs to make investments, upgrade or purchase equipment, conserve energy and reduce the disposal of wastewater, air pollutants and solid waste. This investment is worthwhile for the sake of posterity and the condition of the surrounding areas. It will improve the product quality and the health of the employees, as well as the relationship with local residents, so that the profit goal and social responsibilities can be harmonised.

Fourth, the additional spending to fulfil social responsibilities can directly help achieve the profit goal. For example, spending on improvements in housing, living facilities and public service facilities will not only provide solutions to the employees' difficulties, thus repaying the debt owed to them over the years, but will also strengthen internal unity, improve the employees' identification with the enterprise and boost efficiency. Even though the government may not provide much help to improve the living conditions of the employees, as long as the enterprise takes such measures it can incentivise them. It should be admitted that, if the enterprise pays attention to this problem and invests in instalments, it can fulfil both its profit goal and its social responsibility.

Fifth, we can further discuss the harmonisation of the enterprise's profit goal and social responsibilities from the perspective of market competition. Enterprises compete with each other to acquire more market share, and the image of an enterprise becomes ever more important and reflects its rise and fall. If an enterprise does not reduce its energy consumption and waste disposal or protect the environment, or if it cheats customers with poor quality products, upon discovery the media and the department for environment may report publicly its failure to carry out its social responsibilities. Once this happens, no matter what its past achievements are, the enterprise will be condemned by the public and its reputation and future will be ruined. Therefore, market competition is a massive pressure that will eliminate enterprises that disregard their social responsibilities. This is an international trend that no one can alter.

From the above five points, we can see that the enterprise's profit goal and social responsibilities can, and must be harmonised according to the current trends. Otherwise, the enterprise will be eliminated by competition.

3 Understanding corporate social responsibility from the perspective of "Homo sociologicus"

In economics, human beings as market entities are given a two-fold definition: "*Homo economicus*" and "*Homo sociologicus*".

As *Homo economicus*, a person pursues maximum profit. All the economic activities that he engages in serve to maximise profit. Parallel to the maximisation of profit is the minimisation of cost. If a person can achieve maximum profit with minimum cost, he will be considered a successful example.

As *Homo sociologicus*, a person has diverse goals that are not limited to the maximum profit. He will consider the good of society in addition to economic gains. For example, there are two places, A and B, where one can invest to build a factory, and A can generate a higher profit at lower cost than B. As *Homo economicus*, he will definitely invest in A instead of B. However, as *Homo sociologicus*, he might choose B over A due to one of the following reasons:

(1) B is his hometown. While A may have more favourable conditions, because of his love for his hometown he wants to help with economic development there to mitigate unemployment and increase the income and skills of the residents.
(2) When he was young, he lived and studied in B. At that time people slighted him. Now that he has ventured outside and become wealthy, he decides to invest in B to build a factory to change people's view of him.
(3) When he lived in B, he did wrong by the local people and feels regret. After years of hard work elsewhere, he has become wealthy and, in repentance, builds a factory in B to help with local economic development.

Whatever his motive, his investment can only be explained from the perspective of *Homo sociologicus* rather than *Homo economicus*.

A person has the two-fold characteristics of *Homo economicus* and *Homo sociologicus*. It is the same with an enterprise.

As a profit-making organisation, an enterprise will consider corporate social responsibilities from the perspective of *Homo economicus* in the following three respects:

(1)   The enterprise's fulfilment of social responsibilities will maximise the investors' interests

This consideration is based on the balance of short-term and long-term goals. According to short-term considerations, any additional spending on social responsibilities, whether this is listed under production costs or post-tax profit, will diminish the income of investors. According to the long-term consideration, however, when the enterprise fulfils its social responsibilities, it improves its image, the internal relationship with its employees and its external relationships with local residents, all of which will add to the future income of the investors.

(2)   Understanding the maximisation of the investor's interest from the relationship between monetary and non-monetary income

Monetary income can be seen on the books while non-monetary income cannot. Donations for public welfare in the form of monetary spending are necessary for the fulfilment of corporate social responsibility. However, the non-monetary income that an enterprise gains by fulfilling its social responsibility is not reflected on the books. For example, the brand, the image of the enterprise and its reputation in the industry are all related to the maximisation of the investor's interest. This must not be overlooked.

(3)   Understanding the maximisation of the investor's interest from the relationship between material and immaterial capital

Apart from a shift in perspective, this is not much different from the former case. Material capital can be calculated. For example, all of the spending on fulfilling social responsibilities diminishes material capital, but increases in fame, reputation and brand value also increase immaterial wealth. This, too, will help achieve the maximum benefit for the investors.

As mentioned above, an enterprise is both *Homo economicus* and *Homo sociologicus*. We can gain a fresh understanding of the above problems if we consider them from this perspective.

As *Homo economicus*, an enterprise must always strive for the maximum profit for the investors. However, as *Homo sociologicus*, it must consider the good of society. An enterprise is different from an individual; it will not have many personal considerations when choosing where to invest. It will focus more on the relationship between the good of society and the maximum profit of the investors. How to properly balance the roles of an enterprise as *Homo economicus* and *Homo sociologicus* relies on sound corporate governance and the ability and wisdom of the enterprise leaders.

Treating the enterprise as *Homo sociologicus*, its leaders must understand that its mission is not restricted to providing quality products and service to the society, necessary though these activities are. Moreover, it should cultivate people and ideas, pass on thoughts, uphold ideals and train an outstanding team of staff. The investors in the enterprise, its managers and employees must all strive for this goal to fulfil their social responsibilities. The achievements of the enterprise manifest themselves in the fact that everyone in the enterprise, from top to bottom, follows the ideal of social responsibilities. This is another great contribution to society and reflects the social benefit from the enterprise.

As *Homo sociologicus*, the enterprise must further understand that it must contribute to the peace and happiness of local residents and posterity. For example, the enterprise must make every effort to create a good natural environment suitable for contemporary and future generations to live and work in, so that all can enjoy happiness and peace. With this understanding, the enterprise will be more motivated to protect and remediate the environment. This is both the enterprise's social responsibility and a benefit to society.

In addition, as *Homo sociologicus*, the enterprise must know that the happiness of one person depends on the happiness of the people around him. Who can say that he is happy when he is surrounded by unhappy people? His happiness will be unsustainable. Only when the people around him become happier can he feel sustainable happiness. In fact, this is the proper understanding of happiness. This will elevate and deepen the enterprise's understanding of its social responsibilities.

4 The extension of social capital

We have developed some preliminary understanding of social capital from the discussion in Section 1: it is an immaterial capital that exists in human relations. One increases his social capital by having better and more acquaintances. The most important social capital is reputation. A good reputation ensures that one can utilise his social capital. The collapse of reputation represents the bankruptcy of social capital.

Now that we have analysed corporate social responsibility, we can further discuss the concept of social capital. Both individuals and enterprises can possess and accumulate social capital. That its discovery and possession applies not only to individuals but also to enterprises is called the extension of social capital.

The social capital enterprises possess is also immaterial. It is reflected in human relations, the relationship between enterprises and between enterprises and the government. If all of these relations are harmonious, enterprises can enjoy smooth production and operation activities, and the timely resolution of disputes. When they encounter various difficulties, they will receive more help from other enterprises and individuals and meet with less resistance. This is the same as individuals: if a person has good relations with other people, they will help him when he is in trouble.

When individuals start their own business, material, human and social capital is indispensable. The same applies to enterprises, whether they are newly established or expanding. Both individuals and enterprises may receive help with material and human capital from their social capital. The enterprises' understanding of social capital is in no way inferior to that of individuals.

For example, in the 2008 financial crisis, enterprises in many Chinese coastal cities, especially small to medium privately owned ones, faced many difficulties. During that period, I was leading an investigation team of the Subcommittee of Economics of the CPPCC to conduct research in some coastal cities. I learned that a new phrase, "stick together", came into vogue in the local areas. Small and medium enterprises "stuck together for warmth", "stuck together to go through the winter" and "stuck together to venture abroad". This means that they should unite to look for ways to tackle challenges together, support each other when they lacked funds but could not find loans and avoid being cheated when they ventured into foreign markets. This showed that small and medium enterprises appreciated the importance of social capital in practice. Experience demonstrates that social capital supports the mutual trust between enterprises and promotes understanding and sincerity between their leaders. Enterprises must not slack off in this regard.

If enterprises make every effort to fulfil their social responsibilities, this will lead to improved mutual understanding and mutual trust. This also guarantees that social capital will extend to the enterprises. The enterprises will be more committed to their social responsibilities if they and their leaders understand that, by valuing trustworthiness and reputation and fulfilling social responsibilities, they will have more social capital and that the enterprises will run more smoothly.

Provisional summary: the Chinese path and new progress in development economy

Economists in some Western European countries started investigating development economics as early as the 19th century, among whom the most influential one was the German economist Liszt. Liszt elaborated when a country started industrialisation late, what kind of economics theories and policies it should adopt so as to catch up with a country with earlier industrialisation (e.g. Britain). His contributions to the economics history were his critiques of British classical political economics theories which then had a mainstream status in economics world. The classical economics theories, he claimed, were not applicable to Germany, a country which started industrialisation relatively late.

Despite all this, development economics thrived mostly at the end of World War II. At that time, researchers in this field explored such issues as: how could agricultural society be transformed into an industrial society? How could production components like capital, land, labour, technology, etc. be constructed and play their role? In particular, how could Asian and African countries which were to abolish their colonial and dependent status start their journey of industrialisation shortly? Mr *Zhang Peigang*, a Chinese scholar, made ground-breaking research in this field. His works written in the late 1940s attracted the attention of international economics academia and were widely recognised as the frontline research in development economics.

Since the late 1970s, the Chinese path, with China's Reform and Opening-up and the rise of the Chinese economy, has been increasingly known and valued by other countries. It is both a road of dual transformation, composed of developmental transformation, (transition from an agricultural society to an industrial economy) and institutional transformation, (transition from a planned economy to a market economy) and a road of sustainable socioeconomic development. China's practice has added a lot of new content to development economics research, opened up many new research areas and also provided experience and lessons referential to many other developing countries. In fact, the Chinese path of dual economic transformation has suggested that development economics has advanced greatly owing to the collective participation of Chinese economists. That makes them feel deeply proud, because in the past 30 years' debate and exploration, involvement and practice, Chinese economists have collectively published numerous papers, survey reports and policy recommendations in numerous domestic journals influential to the development of the Chinese economy. Only a small portion of the research was published in overseas journals. It is owing to the collective participation of Chinese economists that development economics research has made unprecedented progress and the vision of international researchers has been greatly broadened.

Next, I will explain the relationship between the Chinese path and development economics in three aspects.

1 Debate over the economic system as an inevitable part of development economics research

Developing countries, whether former colonies or dependent countries of Asia or Africa, were all hoping after their newly-gained independence to achieve the transition from an agricultural to an industrial society. Such transition involved the transition of the economic system and was solely transition from a traditional to a capitalist economic system. It differs from the transition from a planned to a market economic system in China, Russia, Eastern European countries, Mongolia, and Vietnam etc.

The transition from a planned to a market economic system is to be discussed in the next section, while transition from a traditional to a capitalist system, where most developing countries were involved, will be analysed from the following three perspectives.

First, the traditional economic system, mentioned here, mainly refers to the pre-capitalist economic system in these newly-independent Asian and African countries. It is most evidenced in their land systems, which usually involved three types. The first type was a system where land was shared by a clan, and a land portion was allotted to a farming household. In villages, elders or chiefs, still in power, exercised their power through elders' or chiefs' meetings. The second type is the land tenancy system where landlords took charge of the land. That is, the land was divided into plots and leased to farming tenants, who paid their rents in real products. The third type was the large estate system where a plantation system was implemented, and employees helped with production. As an exchange, employees were paid with wages, or given a small piece of land to provide sources of livelihood for their families. No matter what land types among the three the land system took, the vast majority of farmers were reduced to poverty. And they were firmly bound to land, whether it was commonly shared by the clan, or under the charge of a landlord in the tenancy system, or possessed by plantation owners. Farmers found it very difficult to break away from bondages.

Second, under the traditional economic system, especially under the pre-capitalist land system, it was very hard for newly-independent developing countries in Asia and Africa to start the industrialisation journey. This was because the majority of farmers were tied to the land, and also stuck in poverty. Therefore, preconditions for industrialisation, such as capital accumulation, an adequate supply of workforce, the establishment of the land trade market, the growth of entrepreneurs etc. did not exist, not to mention the springing-up of the technical personnel and the legalisation of property ownership protection. This means that if newly independent Asian and African developing countries did not reform their traditional economic system and change their socioeconomic situations deeply rooted in the system, they would be unable to carry out industrialisation smoothly.

Third, in the same vein, it cannot be ignored that what was underlying the traditional economic system was huge influences from traditional ideologies that match well with the traditional economic system. They involved fatalism, sense of hierarchy, conservative bent, nostalgia towards hometowns, submissive thinking to adversity and so on. They dominated thoughts and actions of various strata of society, making people commonly lack risk awareness, reluctant to make a living away from their home and set up businesses of their own. They thus make people caught in troubled inaction. Those are common faults of grassroots societies in the newly independent Asian and African developing countries.

Thereby, it was sufficiently evidential to overseas researchers in development economics that analyses should be made, from the beginning to the end, by linking newly independent countries' transition from an agricultural to an industrial society, to transition from a traditional to a capitalist economic system. That was their outstanding contribution. Indeed, getting away from the debates over systems was to break away from the feature analyses of the traditional economic system, particularly the study of obstacles caused by industrialisation by the traditional economic system, and made it very difficult for researchers to raise valuable points in national industrialisation research.

Nonetheless, research in this aspect has not been sufficient in explaining difficult issues that China came across in its transition from an agricultural to an industrial society. Those issues involved where those difficulties lay, how to overcome them and how to embark on a new path. They were different from issues that the newly independent Asian and African countries came across because institutional transformation in China after 1979 was not to throw off the shackle of a traditional economic system, i.e. pre-capitalist system, but remove the bondage of the planned economic system.

The Chinese Path is a dual transformation path where developmental transformation (transition from an agricultural to an industrial society) and institutional transformation (transition from a planned to a market economic system) overlap.

2 Transition from a planned to a market economic system as the essence of China's development economics

It should be borne in mind that implementing the planned economic system used to be thought as another path to industrialisation to differentiate it from the one achieved through marketisation and followed by some Western countries all the time. The Soviet Union in the 1930s used to be regarded as a successful example of the national industrialisation through implementing the planned economic system., After World War II, some eastern European countries, like the German Democratic Republic, the Czech Republic, Poland and other countries which had developed their industries to a certain extent based on marketisation, all moved to the planned economic system and continued to advance towards industrialisation. The People's Republic of China adopted the planned economic system after it was founded in 1949, and the adoption was not a contingency. First, with the Soviet Union as a precedent, it was held that it was feasible to develop industry under the planned economic system. It could not only mobilise human, financial and material resources to quickly establish large-scale industrial enterprises and realise the ideal of industrialisation but also enable agriculture to embark on the road of the collective economy under the planned economic system. Second, on the founding of the People's Republic of China, China was under the boycott and blockade of the major Western countries and only the Soviet Union, and Eastern European countries which had implemented the planned economy had some exchanges with China. Those were the prevailing circumstances right at that time, and China had no other choice apart from the planned economic system. Third, in the Kuomintang-controlled areas, railways, telecommunications and many important industrial and mining enterprises were owned and operated by the state. After the Liberation, they were all taken over, so it was logical to develop a planned economic system and a model with state-owned and state-operated large industrial and mining enterprises. It was in this context that the planned economy was established in China in the 1950s.

Nevertheless, years of practice tells us that it is not a success to build a prosperous and powerful industrialised country through a planned economic system patterned on a Soviet Union model. Limitations of the planned economic system became increasingly obvious: issues like low resource use rate, poor business efficiency and shortages remained unsolved; the collectivisation of agriculture reduced farmers to poverty, and the long-existing imbalance due to the opposing state between urban and rural areas was not eased. All limitations led to the Great Debate in 1978, entitled "Practice is the sole criterion for testing truth." The debate was a profound ideological liberation movement for China. It made ideological preparations for the 3rd Plenary Session of the 11th Central Committee of the CPC held in December 1978. From then on, China entered a new stage of Reform and Opening-up.

What is the Chinese path? It is a path of Reform and Opening-up with unique Chinese characteristics. To be more specific, it is a path of dual transformation. Developmental transformation is the transition from an agricultural to an industrial society, which has been discussed and concerned in development economics and the path of the institutional transformation, which has not been a research issue in development economics. The institutional transformation does not study how to break away from the traditional economic system (pre-capitalist system) or how to transit from a traditional to the capitalist system etc., but how a planned economy with Chinese characteristics is transformed into a market economic system. That is an issue to which development economics has not been able to give particular attention. The debate of Chinese economists in the dual transformation process has enabled them to make their contributions to the pioneering of research scope of development economics.

In short, the major reason for China's institutional transformation to possess unique characteristics does not entertain the idea that it needs to break away from the traditional economic system (pre-capitalist system). Rather, it is because China needs to get rid of the planned economic system. The orientation of the transformation is not to build a capitalist system but to adhere to the socialist system and establish the market economic system through institutional adjustment. In China, the traditional economic system (pre-capitalist system) was dissolved in the democratic and socialist revolution phases, and therefore, apart from those at the ideological level, influences of the traditional economic system no longer occupied mainstream economic status. While the influences of traditional clan society still exist in ethnic minority and remote mountainous regions, traditional forces and ideological influences have also been greatly reduced. China's institutional transformation lies mainly in the transition from a planned economic system to a market economic system.

How to get rid of shackles of a planned economic system and meanwhile, maintain the socialist system is the greatest contribution of the Chinese path to theories and practice in development economics. Recalling the tremendous social and economic changes in China since its Reform and Opening-up 30 plus years ago, we cannot but feel gratified for China's achievements, for we have not laboured in vain; rather, we have become rigorously confident.

The Chinese path will be continued, and there is still a long distance to go before the fulfilment of dual transformation. Given this perspective, it is still too early to draw a conclusion concerning China's dual transformation, and yet, we can at least make the following three preliminary statements:

First, as has been emphasised in this book, for a developing country like China, the overlapping of the institutional and developmental transformation is particularly important. That is because the planned economic system has a greater impact on the economy than the traditional one. In other words, once the planned economic system has been established, its control on the economy certainly unified politics and economy: the great majority of the rural areas, industry and commerce, would have to be transformed into the model of collective agricultural organisations, and state-owned and state-operated enterprises in accordance with strict government mandates and therefore became difficult for them to break away from the planned economic system. The traditional economic system (pre-capitalist system) did not have such a huge impact. Neither was it possible to have such controlling power over the countryside (let alone cities). Thus, it was somewhat easier for the newly-independent countries in Asia and Africa to develop into capitalist countries than for China to establish a market economic system. In China's dual transformation, if the institutional transformation were not prioritised, it would not be able to be truly accomplished. That is to say; it would be difficult for an agricultural society to be transformed into an industrial society.

Second, as clearly stated in Chapter 1, the reform of property ownership must be prioritised in developing countries, like China, which had established a planned economic system for the transition. It applied to both urban and rural areas. By contrast, the newly independent developing countries in Asia and Africa needed to achieve developmental transformation, i.e. transition from an agricultural to an industrial society. Unlike China, they did not need to reconstruct microeconomic foundations. In other words, they did not need to prioritise property ownership reform through defining and clarifying property ownership and turning microeconomic units (including enterprises and individuals) into real market entities. Those were primary issues that needed to be solved in the transition from a planned to a market economic system, while there was almost no market entity issue in developing countries which got rid of the traditional economic system (the precapitalist system) because market entities came into being naturally through the disintegration of the clan society.

Third, it was not easy to return to the traditional economic system (pre-capitalist system) after having walked out of it; instead, it was much easier to resume the planned economic system at the early stage of the Reform and Opening-up after a market economy was initiated. This was the major difference between China's institutional transformation and that (transition from a traditional to a capitalist system) of the newly independent Asian and African developing countries. Why was there such a big difference? It was related to significant differences between the traditional (pre-capitalist system) and the planned economic system.

Bear in mind that under the shackle of the traditional economic system, people were bound to a clan society; or subject to landlords' disposal as tenants, paying rents or restricted to the plantations as employed labourers. Once they broke away from the traditional economic system and participated in market activities, few of them were willing to go back to traditional means of production or the constrained or restricted life. They yearned for market outlooks and held their prospectus for engagement in marketing activities. It is different from cases in the planned economic system. Take China for example. Not only was the planned economic system established as a manifestation of the will of the government and implemented according to its original plans, but it was also a complete system, established over years and dominating the production and living of the urban and rural residents in political, economic, social and cultural aspects, and making people fall into "path dependence", the so-called "institutional inertia" formed under the planned economic system. Additionally, the planned economic system over the years also created habitual media environments, where only production and life implementing and following the planned economic system accorded with the norms; deviating from it equalled betrayal being guilty of heterodoxy and taking an evil way. At the early stage of the reform, whenever unemployment, inflation and economic disorder occurred, some people would say: "The planned economy is still better" or "The series of issues were incurred due to the deviation from the planned economic system". There occurred the voice of "going back to the planned economic system". This was very common in the 1980s. Should the top layers of the Central Committee have not made major principles and policies of insisting on the Reform and Opening-up, it had been impossible for China not to have returned to the planned economic system. Chinese economists all experienced this process, and the situation remained fresh in their memories.

Therefore, regarding shaking off shackles of the planned economic system and turning to the market economic system, China faced far more difficulties than those newly independent Asian and African developing countries when they tried to get rid of the traditional economic system (the pre-capitalist system).

3 Accomplishing dual transformation by continuously deepening the Reform and Opening-up to benefit the people as the most important experience of the Chinese path

The 1980s was an era of exploration. Chinese economists were collectively involved in the great debate and big exploration. This was something unprecedented in the history of development economics. Although before and after World War II there was much debate in academia on how to achieve industrialisation in developing countries, there was no specific discussion on how China could transit from a planned to a market economic system and meanwhile, from an agricultural to an industrial society. The reason might be that Chinese economists did not have an experience of living in the planned economic system; nor did they suffer from famine years, nor were they sent to the countryside to work with a production team, nor did they cultivate moors or farmland in reclamation areas; nor did they experience unforgettable grassroots' lives of China. In a word, they had no knowledge at all or a very shallow knowledge of China's social reality in the era of the planned economy. Thus, they were unable to propose their research scope and have first-hand experiences of profound meanings and twists and turns of Chinese dual transformation.

Chinese economists could not forget debate and exploration in the 1980s; nor could they forget the landmark Southern talk of Comrade *Deng Xiaoping* at the 1992 Spring Festival and the promotion of reforms in China, the expansion of opening-up and the rapid economic growth. The subsequent 10 years was the era of deepening reforms and the take-off of the economy. Since then, the market economic system has been gradually established, and the probability of retreating to the planned economic system has become smaller and smaller. It was no longer possible for those who wanted to reverse the progress of the Chinese economy to lift big storms. A younger generation of economists, who lived in transition from a planned to a market economic system, who entered universities after the re-opening of entrance examinations to colleges/universities, who worked in the political circle, research and development institutions or enterprises, who studied overseas, returned and were engaged in the teaching and research in China, or working in government sectors, were all involved in the great cause of China's dual transformation. There is also a generation of young people who transferred themselves from inside the system to outside the system, participated in the building up and development of the private enterprises and became experts who knew not only the current situation of China but also received systematic theoretical training and possessed practical economic working experiences. They joined the collective Chinese economists and became new-born forces in the Chinese economics circle. Meanwhile, economists and explorers much younger than the earlier-noted are eager to contribute their ingenuity and dedication to the cause of China's dual transformation.

The reason why the Chinese path has added new content to development economics and broadened the field of study is inseparably attributed to great efforts of three generations of economists, the senior, middle-aged and junior ones. Who has contributed to development economics with Chinese characteristics? It is right that the collective Chinese economists composed of three generations: the senior, middle-aged and junior generations. Their further exploration, debate, new proposals and participation made it impossible for China to return to the old road of the planned economy any more. Those were also their contributions.

The Reform and Opening-up have brought along substantial benefits to the general public. That is the strong evidence that the dual transformation has been upheld. To farmers, the promotion of the pre-contract agricultural system in the 1980s and the rise of the township enterprises enabled the great majority of farmers to benefit from stable and increased production, having enough to eat and entering township enterprises to work. Their income increased and they would never want to return to people's commune era. In the early 1990s, the Chinese economy after Comrade *Deng Xiaoping's* Southern Talk was switched to the fast lane, where migrant workers went to the East, the South of China or worked in cities. Though they felt tired and were having a hard life, they, through their experiences, felt that there was something to expect and they would never want to go back and be restricted to the narrow countryside, living a life without hope or expectations. It is the strongest support for the removal of the planned economic system. Therefore, an important conclusion can be drawn that: as soon as the clough was opened, farmers and people willing to establish enterprises rushed out, irresistibly like tides. That is the path of dual transformation and also the path of China.

Nevertheless, there is no endpoint in improving people's livelihoods, increasing their income and letting all citizens share fruits of economic development and reform. We can only move step by step towards established objectives, and cannot be too anxious in achieving the goals. On the journey, there are still many obstacles to be overcome. We cannot ignore the existence of "welfare rigidness". Surpassing our current developing stage or developing beyond our capabilities will only create difficulties for ourselves, or even let us fall into the "welfare trap", unable to extricate oneself from the plight and leading to endless troubles. Experience and lessons from some Western market economies are alerts to us.

Never should the spirit of pioneering enterprises with arduous efforts, the spirit of innovation, the spirit of sharing weal and woe and the spirit of prioritising integrity and credibility be abandoned, as they have always existed in Chinese history, and Chinese people have always been proud of them. When the *Hakka* people moved from the Central Plains to the south, they relied fully on those spirits and took root in the hot, humid and wild land in *Guangdong, Fujian* and *Jiangxi*, and migrated from those places to the world. At the end of the *Qing* Dynasty and the beginning of the Democratic Republic of China, migrants from *Shandong* and *Hebei* brought along their old and young to the East. Just within a few decades, the development of the northeast began to take shape. Was it owing to the same spirits that people in *Shanxi, Shaanxi and Gansu* "went west of the gate" (*zouxikou*) and developed the west part of the Inner Mongolia into places suitable for habitation within a short span of several decades? Didn't people in *Guangdong* and *Fujan* "go to Southeast Asia" (*xia nanyang*) and people in *Zhejiang* "venture to western Europe" (*chuang xi'ou*) rely on the earlier-noted spirits? Nowadays, the dual transformation continues, and China dream is being accomplished. A lack of pioneering spirit, the spirit of innovation, sharing and prioritising integrity and credibility can only make us stagnate on the road or even fall into the trap.

If it can be said that the practice of the Chinese path has enabled the Chinese people to add much new content and new experience to development economics research, it should never be forgotten that after the economy has entered a new phase, it should retain and carry forward such spirits as pioneering, innovation, solidarity, integrity and credibility. Similarly, they are the contents that cannot be ignored in the Chinese path.

Postscript to the Chinese edition

Chinese Economy in Dual Transition, now presented to readers, was brewed in my writing plan for a long time, and some chapters and sections were written intermittently. However, my resolution to complete the whole book was made around September 2002 and up to now (July 2013) it has taken about 10 months to complete the draft.

With regards to the book, I hold that following *Chinese Economy in Disequilibrium* (published by Economic Daily Press in early 1990), it is another of my representative works on Chinese economic reality. In line with the thread of thoughts in *Chinese Economy in Disequilibrium*, this book still takes property ownership system as the core topic, discussing land ownership approval; further reforms of state-owned enterprises, maintaining ownership of private enterprises, income distributional system reform, urbanisation, independent innovation, industrial upgrading, and the creation of social capital, etc. In *The Provisional Summary – The Chinese Path and New Progress in Development Economy*, I mentioned that the collective participation of Chinese economists which had broadened the research scope of development economics, added new content and elaborated that the essence of Chinese development economics was the development economics transiting from the planned to the market economic system. That is also Chinese economists' collective contributions to development economics.

In anticipation of the publication of the book, I extend my sincere thanks to the following students for their help: *Zhu Shanli, Lin Shuanglin, Liu Wei, Yu Hongjun, Cheng Zhiqiang, Jiang Cheng, Teng Fei, Liu Yuming, Huang Guohua, Zhang Wenbin, Zheng Shaowu, Zhao Jinyong, Fu Shuaixiong, Yin Jun and Wu Yuqin.*

I would like to give my heart-felt thanks to *He Yaomin*, chief editor of China *Renmin* University Press, *Liu Jing*, director of the Economics Branch, *Jin Mei*, senior editor, *Pan Weilin* and *Wang Hanxia*, executive editors and the like. It was owing to their efforts that the book was able to meet readers shortly after the submission of the script.

15 July 2013,
Guanghua School of Management,
Peking University

Index

For Product Safety Concerns and Information please contact our EU
representative GPSR@taylorandfrancis.com
Taylor & Francis Verlag GmbH, Kaufingerstraße 24, 80331 München, Germany